Cusac, Anne-Marie.
Cruel and unusual

CRUEL AND UNUSUAL

ANNE-MARIE CUSAC

Cruel and Unusual
The Culture of Punishment in America

YALE UNIVERSITY PRESS   NEW HAVEN & LONDON

Published with assistance from the Louis Stern Memorial Fund.

Portions of Chapters 9 through 12 first appeared in *The Progressive*.

Set in Scala and Scala Sans type by Keystone Typesetting, Inc. Printed in the United States of America.

Library of Congress Cataloging-in-Publication Data
Cusac, Anne-Marie.
Cruel and unusual : the culture of punishment in America / Anne-Marie Cusac.
p. cm.
Includes bibliographical references and index.
ISBN 978-0-300-11174-3 (cloth : alk paper)
1. Punishment—United States—History. 2. Prisons—United States—History.
3. Prison administration—United States—History. 4. Prisoners—United States—Social conditions. I. Title.
HV8693.C87 2009
364.60973—dc22   2008042943

A catalogue record for this book is available from the British Library.

This paper meets the requirements of ANSI/NISO Z39.48-1992 (Permanence of Paper). It contains 30 percent postconsumer waste (PCW) and is certified by the Forest Stewardship Council (FSC).

10 9 8 7 6 5 4 3 2 1

For Judith Strasser, journalist and poet. Without her support and perceptive criticism, I could not have written this book.

And for Morgan, with wishes for a happy life.

Excessive bail shall not be required, nor excessive fines imposed, nor cruel and unusual punishments inflicted.

—Eighth Amendment to the U.S. Constitution

CONTENTS

ACKNOWLEDGMENTS

During my first months with the *Progressive,* my editor Matthew Roth-schild asked me to report on a new prison technology called the stun belt. I did not want that assignment, but I accepted it because I loved my job. At the time, I, like many Americans, strongly disliked criminals. I thought the stun belt seemed to be a good idea. But the experience of reporting on the stun belt changed me into someone willing to question why our authorities punish the way they do. The story generated media attention and an Amnesty International campaign against the belt. Eventually, information from that story went to the United Nations Committee against Torture. The assignment I didn't want became the first of many articles I wrote about punishment. I thank Matthew—the driving, sharp-minded, kind editor behind ten years of my investigative journalism—from the depths of my heart.

Nor would I have managed to write this book without Judith Strasser, poet and journalist, formerly of the Wisconsin Public Radio magazine *To the Best of Our Knowledge.* Thank you, Judy, for the emotional courage, support, good humor, criticisms, and intelligence you gave.

To those strong and helpful minds, I need to add many other names. Meg Schoerke read this book in its first draft and helped me to improve my work. I am grateful to my parents for their sustaining talks. Enormous thanks go out to my brother, who advised me to write this book and who wouldn't let me off the hook when I, at first, demurred. To the others connected to me by blood and by marriage, in this country and in others, my thanks for your love, support, and interest. Special thanks go to the many who on hearing of my project said they thought it important. These include the staff of the *Progressive,* especially Ruth Conniff, Elizabeth Di-Novella, and Amitabh Pal, and my colleagues at Roosevelt University. Those who expressed belief in this endeavor also include peers, fellow writers and reporters, and friends, whose words I have not forgotten: Dean Bakopoulos, Paul Breslin, Barbara Briggs, Allison Chaim, Robin Chapman, Anne Clauser, John Conroy, W. S. Di Piero, Barbara Ehren-reich, Susan Elbe, Jill and Freddie Feldman, Reginald Gibbons, Catherine Jagoe, Jesse Lee Kercheval, Mary Kinzie, Jim Kirby, Fred McKissack, Erin Middlewood, John Nichols, Sara Parrell, Alan Shapiro, Alison Townsend, Ron Wallace, Anne Wilder, and many more Wisconsinites, Chicagoans, neighbors, friends, and colleagues. Finally, a thank you to John Watson, whose interest in the book, consideration, and understanding of the demands of this project provided critical support during my last months of work.

I am grateful to my literary agent, Scott Mendel, who approached me with the idea of doing a book on punishment. I also thank my editors at Yale University Press, Christopher Rogers, Laura Davulis, and Margaret Otzel, who led me through a rewarding process of critique and revision. To the two anonymous reviewers who wrote with care about the manuscript, my heartfelt gratitude. Your words benefited this book tremendously.

CRUEL AND UNUSUAL

Introduction

MY GRANDMOTHER AND I HAD SPENT HOURS sorting through family photographs when one—of a baby in a baptismal gown—silenced her. When she didn't speak, I searched for something to say and came up with the easy observation that the baby was cute. "He's a rapist," she answered. From the moment my grandmother pronounced him "rapist," I saw in the photo no tiny innocent in white lace but a guilty, frightening man. Accompanying my new vision was an odd flush of disproportion: we could look at an infant and perceive the child as evil.

This is a book about America. It is about sheriffs and television and God. It is about patriotism and national identity. It is about American culture, from television to religion to national politics. It is about the inspiration this country gives to many others. It is about how Americans punish.

Over the past thirty-five years, the form of punishment in the United States has changed enormously. Our laws are harsher now. Convicts serve longer sentences than they once did for identical offenses. As a result, our prison and jail facilities are more crowded than those in other Western democracies. The numbers can startle. The United States, with 5 percent of the Earth's population, is home to nearly a quarter of its prisoners. Since 1973 the nation's imprisonment rate has multiplied more than five times, leaving the United States with both the highest such rate in the world and the largest prison system. One percent of our population is now in prison. More than seven million Americans, or one in thirty-one adults, were either confined or on probation or parole in 2006, the last year for which statistics are available. More than two million inmates reside in our state and federal prisons and local jails; another five million are probates or parolees. This vast system is ours at an expense: $45 billion.[1]

The mounting prison population appears to have little connection to the decade-long drop in violent crime in this country. Nor are most U.S. prisoners guilty of violence. According to 2002 figures, 19 percent of state felony convictions were for violent crimes, 5 percent of these being murder convictions. Nonviolent crimes involving drug possession or trafficking made up 31 percent of total state felonies. Burglary, fraud, and other economic crimes amounted to another 32 percent.[2]

There are a few other complexities to consider about the differences between the typical American prisoner and the stereotypical one. Many U.S. inmates today are mentally ill. Others, even in our supermax facilities (designed to house the worst of the worst), have recently been children.[3]

As the prison population has leapt, physical treatment of the inhabitants has changed. Jails and prisons now make use of control devices that would probably have been outlawed as inhumane only decades ago, including the stun belt and the restraint chair. Some of these tools can cause significant pain.

The change in the physical treatment of our domestic prisoners translated to sometimes extreme corporal treatment of alleged terrorists overseas in the years following the attack on the World Trade Center. The Bush administration has tried to enshrine in law coercive interrogations that would violate traditional interpretations of the Geneva Conventions. "Abu Ghraib" is perhaps the most notorious proper noun of Operation Iraqi Freedom.[4]

But for all these transformations, and for all the popularity of "tough on crime" talk in the past decade, American punishment is still almost invisible, conducted in our government's private spaces rather than, as was once true, in the public square. That near-invisibility of our criminals and their treatment can make it easy for the rest of us to disregard prisons. This is a book about the hazards—to our communities, our families, our personal lives, and our democracy—of ignoring American convicts and the methods of punishment currently employed.

Many symptoms of the transformation of American punishment are not isolated in the prison cell but can be found in our daily lives. Some ingrained cultural habits are part of this metamorphosis; they both support the new punishment and cause it to proliferate in our homes, our streets, and even our habits of thought. I am including here the shows we watch on television, the way many of us treat children, and some influential religious practices. Punishment is omnipresent—and often explicitly linked to criminality—in each of these arenas to an extent that was unthinkable a few decades ago. But the metamorphosis, embedded in the details of busy lives, can be difficult to recognize.

During the 1990s and the first years of the new millennium, I wrote a series of investigative reports on new punishment and control methods. This work had an unpredictable effect on me. It made me wonder whether I was noticing just one manifestation of a more drastic cultural change and also whether ordinary Americans were transforming along with our punishment devices and procedures.

I noticed an increase in new weapons and machines for policing and prisons. The novel technologies, nearly all of them aggressive in purpose but coolly promising to "control" or "restrain," proliferated across the landscape of American justice, often with little regard for questions of whether or not such devices could kill those they were supposed to subdue. Advertising materials for many of these devices promoted the pain they would cause a disobedient or unruly inmate; one manufacturer described a new corrections tool as "devastating." I also observed a difference—and sometimes a tension—between corrections officers, who were often skeptical about the new devices, and the politicians and entrepreneurs who promoted them. There appeared to be a similar disparity between older and younger police and corrections officers, with the younger ones more accepting of devices and ideas that suggested criminals needed extreme control, even pain.[5]

As a reporter, I had ample opportunity to discuss my work with strangers, casual acquaintances, family members, and friends. The way people talked to me about prisoners contrasted with conversations I remember from the 1970s, a decade when many saw time in prison as a means of helping convicts. The idea of prisons as a place to serve and heal prisoners had pretty much disappeared by the mid-1990s. My discussions with those who asked me about my work—during which my explanations sometimes prompted anger or disapproval—made me suspect that many people wanted prisoners to feel hurt while in prison. The people I spoke with sometimes called the prisoners "bad guys" or "creeps" or "evil." While I sympathized with their angry responses to crime, I wondered whether the broader public was beginning to understand criminality as a permanent character trait.

It seemed I was witnessing an emerging sensibility that understood the criminal and the crime as inseparable. The crime was embedded in the criminal's identity, a fixed and inextricable aspect of self. And crime acts, in turn, were the logical outcome of something our society was coming to interpret as having been there all along—a presence with persistence in our convicts, what we might think of as the criminal personality. An illegal act was evidence of a deeper problem, an innate stain. Such an understanding of crime as enduring in certain personalities and people, I was to learn, echoed the permanent physical marks—brands, holes in nose cartilage, gaps left where ears were once attached—by which early American governments and their European predecessors could signal who among their citizens had committed heresy or adultery or theft.[6]

Others have also noticed a shift in the ways people think about, talk about, and treat criminals. Historian Philip Jenkins, sociologist David Garland, and law and social policy specialist Jonathan Simon all tie the prison boom to broad cultural changes. In his recent book *Decade of Nightmares,* Jenkins sees a rise in a rhetoric of evilness applied to, among others, criminals. This shift started in the mid-1970s, a date that others have associated with a sharp turn from rehabilitation to retribution in American corrections. Some historians and sociologists have remarked on a cultural shift, a reaction to the 1960s. Garland understands a constriction in the promise of plenty as linked to a steep decline in sympathy toward criminals and poor people. Like Jenkins, Garland notes the increased use of such words as "evil" and "wicked" to mean convicts. Simon sees an ever-expanding metaphor of crime that has drastically altered our government and allowed it to intrude upon daily lives.[7]

The philosophical ground to their arguments, and mine as well, is Michel Foucault's *Discipline and Punish,* which linked "the birth of the prison" to changes in labor, education, and literature, to name just a few. Foucault's work is a mighty horse; those of us who try to understand what punishment means must wrangle with his ideas. *Discipline and Punish* is troubling partly because of its breadth but also because Foucault got some facts wrong. For one thing, the prison was not "born" in the eighteenth century, as he claimed. Versions of our modern prison existed for centuries before then. *Discipline and Punish* is also a puzzle because its narrative is linear. Foucault did not anticipate retribution's return.[8]

Understandably, the resurgence of pain has implications for punishment methods. But it is not likely that such a radical thing as a shift in the popular understanding of selfhood would be isolated to criminals. If criminals are "evil," if they are permanent "bad guys," if, in a sense, they become their crimes once they commit them (or are wicked from infancy), then perhaps our society is starting to see all of us in a similar way—there is no self to separate from our actions and to improve or forgive, much less redeem.

HOW TORTURE CAME BACK AND NO ONE NOTICED

As a child in the 1970s, I was fascinated by the past, which I instinctively understood as disclosing revelations about the confusing present. Among the many novels, biographies, and histories I read were a few books that described or hinted at the brutal physical tortures of the past. I studied pictures of the wheel, the rack, hot irons, pincers, and the Iron Maiden. The books comforted. The torture described in them existed in the past and, for the most part, in other countries. I was imbibing one of the great American myths: the United States was more humane than other countries, and in its modern independence it had rejected the brutal past.

The 1970s are long gone and with them some American optimism. Nevertheless, recent books on torture oriented toward an audience of children continue to assume that painful physical punishments occurred long ago or in distant countries. Until recently, some adult academic books made similar claims. "Pain is no longer delivered in brutal, physical forms. Corporal punishment has virtually disappeared, to be replaced by more abstract forms of suffering, such as the deprivation of liberty or the removal of financial resources," wrote David Garland in 1990. By 2000, Garland had corrected this statement: corporal punishment had returned, he said.[9]

My interest here is not so much whether Garland and the other authors were correct or incorrect. Rather, I am fascinated by the power of a myth that during my growing-up years described the past as situated solidly, as if embedded in cement, as if it could never rear up and launch forward and grab hold of us.

I had just begun imagining this book when the Abu Ghraib scandal broke. During late spring of 2004, many Americans were feeling let down by the evidence that their country was not the force for humaneness it had claimed to be. But if one looks closely at some of the changes in American culture that began in the 1970s and that involved widespread preoccupations with evil and pain, one can see Abu Ghraib coming a full thirty years before it hit.

Put another way, in American culture we have a tradition of punishment that draws on religious, specifically Christian, assumptions, even when it seems secular in its workings. This tradition traveled to this country with the European colonists.[10] When the predominant religious impulses in our country understand evil as a force occupying specific people, we tend to punish those people. And because those people are supposedly evil, it comes to seem right to hurt them. In Puritan Massachusetts, anxiety about evil attached, among others, to so-called witches and heretics. Some were executed, mostly by hanging, others tortured to death. Beginning in the 1970s, as several scholars have argued, popular belief that the Devil was taking human form—specifically that of children, criminals, and Islamic terrorists—became prevalent in the United States. As I will show in this book, beliefs that pain was an appropriate method for dealing with these three groups also gained ground.[11]

Powerful ideas about punishment and torture were part of America's ideology almost from this country's inception. Beliefs that the United States would go about things in a new way, a more humane way, that this country would be different from others and from its own colonial past were not always accurate. But they applied psychic pressure that prompted the nation toward a course it might otherwise have evaded. At times, as this book shows in its first chapters, those beliefs brought about kinder treatment for inmates. By the 1970s, they led to a way of punishing that had the potential to change inmates for the better. And that was about the time the American public decided to stop believing in its own humaneness.

PUNITIVE INNOVATION AND THE NEW AMERICA

In America, punishment is populist. As Samuel Walker writes in his classic history *Popular Justice*, "The special character of American criminal justice lies in the high degree of direct and indirect popular influence over its administration."[12]

In the United States, many of us are inclined to think of popular influence as an inherent good. What is "popular" and what is "democratic" can seem synonymous. The magnetism of American popular culture—whether early rock 'n' roll, televised beauty and talent and sport competitions, or the most-trafficked blogs—depends partly on this dynamic. The run-up to any national election is a powerful example of the confluence of popularity and politics, and it is a mediated (with an intentional emphasis on *media*) mass experience.

It is not exactly democracy we enact in flipping the channel. But in the United States, determining the most popular television show, pop hit, new star, or candidate can take on an excited energy because such choosing is a kind of vote. *American Idol,* for instance, capitalizes on the American love of popularity voting.

What does all of this chatter about elections and *American Idol* have to do with punishment? Popular influence has an energetic, democratic side. It also has grim manifestations. "Popular influence . . . accounts for both *the best and the worst* in the history of American criminal justice," writes Walker. "Some of the worst injustices in our history . . . have occurred when the people took the law into their own hands."[13]

Vigilantism—late nineteenth- and early twentieth-century lynching, for instance—is notorious. But Walker's warning is broader. He sees in American criminal justice a frequent representative vigilantism. "Many of the worst abuses of official criminal-justice agencies represent a form of 'delegated vigilantism,' " Walker writes. "The public has tended to condone, if not encourage, police brutality directed against the outcasts of society or the mistreatment of inmates in penal institutions."[14]

If vigilantism can be delegated, then in a time of national punitiveness it behooves us to wonder just what the give-and-take is between the public and the public's criminal-justice representatives. How does the public condone mistreatment indirectly, as Walker argues it does? What are the cultural conduits? Politics and the news media would seem to be natural message-bearers, but so would popular culture.

If our nation's favorite television shows, video games, and news programs are any measure, many Americans think about punishment all the time. Shows about police have been popular since the days of radio drama.

But never before the early twenty-first century did they so saturate the airwaves.[15]

Police shows consistently appear among the top ten favorites. In 2004, *CSI* and *CSI Miami* were particularly popular. And crime and punishment television can be long-lived. *NYPD Blue* was more than ten years old by the time it went off the air. *COPS* and *America's Most Wanted* have been on television since the late 1980s and are among the top six longest-lived shows still airing. They have outdistanced *The Andy Griffith Show, I Love Lucy, M*A*S*H, Seinfeld, Friends, E.R., Everybody Loves Raymond,* and many other television classics.[16]

Crime and punishment shows so saturate our airwaves that it will be a rare American who is not aware of them. Why has this type of programming become dominant? It is not possible that the answer has to do with escapism, since crime and punishment television treats one of the central social concerns of our time, and one of our greatest public worries.

Any adequate answer is apt to be complex, involving such things as crime rates, political messages, and the low cost of producing police dramas and reality shows. I make no claims to being a television-genre expert. But a partial explanation may be that we are trying out a shift in the popular understanding of our "bad guys."

Portrayals of badness and goodness have undergone a profound change in movies and video games, as well as television, since the 1970s. But popular culture is hardly the only arena of American experience.

PAIN AND THE BAD GENERATION

Let's have a glance at American childhood, long thought a reserve of innocence.

In the 1970s, badness seemed to be winning in our prisons. In that decade, policymakers and researchers reacted against rehabilitation, declaring (on dubious evidence) that the method had failed and that prisoners were just as corrupt when they came out of prison as when they went in.

Newsweek featured the new theory of permanent criminality in a February 27, 1978, story with the headline "The Criminal Mind." But the "criminal mind" considered in the article was not that of an adult prisoner. It wasn't an adult mind at all. It was the mind of a child: "Some kids are just bad. They lie and cheat and skip school; they try to bully their parents, rejecting love if it is offered. When these children grow up, they rob, embezzle, rape and kill. Crime turns them on." According to a new theory, such children are not mentally ill, "they are simply wicked."[17]

The generation targeted as evil, Philip Jenkins notes, was Generation X.[18]

I am part of that demonized generation called X. As a child I owned a Ouija board. My parents, who considered it a toy, gave it to me for Christmas. My brother and I liked to pretend to contact Einstein and Mozart with it. We were that square.

In the summers, our neighbor's extended family would visit. Among them was my neighbor's brother, who was a preacher. I hadn't heard of his denomination. One afternoon he interrupted our play, asking whether we were using the Ouija board to contact evil spirits. After some minutes, our denials satisfied him. He let us go. My embarrassed neighbor apologized for her brother's behavior. It was all over, but I didn't play with my Ouija board much after that. Shame had distorted my parents' gift into an object I no longer felt good about touching.

I was a few years from adolescence when the preacher confronted us. I had grown up in a religious climate that the nineteenth- and early twentieth-century philosophy of childhood innocence had nourished.

In earlier decades of the twentieth century, that philosophy played an important role in parenting guides. For instance, in the 1927 advice book *Your Growing Child: A Book of Talks to Parents on Life's Needs,* author Henry Addington Bruce warns parents against exposing their children to religious horrors. "When in the course of instruction the parent or Sunday-school teacher says too much about such things as hell, the Devil, and the punishment of sin, much harm may be done," he cautions.[19]

My parents shared the prevalent faith. I had received, and adored, a social gospel that taught me to look for good in others and to make the difficulties of the world easier for those who suffered. I had almost never heard the words "Satan," "evil," or "Devil." I knew that I and other children could be unkind, but that was about all the bad I thought we could accomplish.

The preacher and his alien language of wickedness and spirits startled me into a theological truth-system that implied that all I had learned about Christianity was wrong. The preacher was not alone in his beliefs. Nationwide, against the prevalent idea that all children were innocent, mounted a competing and opposite belief—that some children were evil.

Secular equations of children and badness, or criminality, appear elsewhere as well. American schools have long had the tendency to discipline students in ways that echo the punishment of criminals, as chapter 7 shows. Perhaps this is because punishment philosophies are limited to their cultural and historical moments. That is, if one American institution subjects crooks to retribution, a second institution probably would not treat a student with a method, such as rehabilitation, considered outmoded for prisoners. In recent decades, students who break the rules have been subject to the enforcement of real police officers who patrol the halls of many U.S. schools.

If city police sometimes come under scrutiny, so too do school officers. In 2007, the *New York Times* published an editorial on the presence of police in New York City schools. The officers had brought order to the schools, observed the newspaper. But students had reportedly been "belittled, shouted at, abused, and inappropriately touched by police officers and the school security workers they supervise." The stories of mistreatment, which *Times* columnist Bob Herbert collected, were not isolated. The New York Civil Liberties Union "describes students being roughed up for minor infractions—like eating in the hallways or failing to have a hall pass—and even baited into fights by security personnel," reported the *Times* editorial. The New York City police denied the allegations.[20]

It was not the first time a major newspaper had complained about officer treatment of students. "Security guards at schools should not rough up kids as if they were hardened criminals," wrote columnist Robert L. Jamieson Jr. in the *Seattle Post-Intelligencer* in 2004. "Students, even unruly ones, shouldn't be shackled like dogs."[21]

Unlike a schoolteacher using a whipping post or solitary confinement on students, as happened in past centuries, the daily presence of real police officers in schools indicates that these public institutions now interpret all young people as potential criminals. When a real officer appears in a public school, the presence of law enforcement eases any potential transition between a student and the legal system. The two institutions, once separate, are linked.

Other U.S. institutions exhibit a similar preoccupation with child criminality. During the same decades police became common in schools, so did the practice of giving children adult sentences rather than sending them to juvenile justice facilities. In 2006, the American Civil Liberties

Union and the ACLU of Michigan filed a petition with the Inter-American Commission on Human Rights. The organizations asked the commission to rule that giving children prison sentences of mandatory life without parole was a breach of the Declaration of the Rights of Man. "Over two thousand children have been sentenced to spend life in prison without the possibility of parole," observed the petition.[22]

The idea that children possess innate purity is still part of our culture. It accompanies, like a photographic negative, the image of the bad child. The pure child lies behind some of the most famous of our recent laws, for instance those that seek to protect children from exploitation or sexual predators. It also plays a role in a question Peter Applebome, writing for the *New York Times,* asked in 2006. Why was it that during his Long Island childhood, he was able to ride his bike as far as he wanted and could play street football with his friends after school, "but children now live in permanent lockdown," with their lives and activities, often to the hour, carefully planned?

Applebome draws on the work of Steven Mintz in forming his explanation, citing the number one reason as having to do with "an explosion in parental anxiety over child abductions, sexual abuse, and crime, a panic almost entirely due to saturation news media coverage and not . . . to any glaring increase in whatever dangers lurk beyond your crabgrass."[23]

The hyperorganization of contemporary childhood draws motivation from a perception of children as potential victims and vulnerable innocents. Parents who do not attend at all times to their children, that fear implies, expose them to criminals. But highly managed childhood depends as well on a fear Applebome doesn't mention—that unwatched children may become criminals.

Applebome's homage to lost childhood freedoms is interesting in part for the metaphor he chooses to describe the childhood he sees today: "permanent lockdown." The American institution known for lockdowns is the prison.

THE SAVING POWER OF SPANKING

Punishment and, more specifically, punitive pain directed toward children are also evident in another influential segment of American life: religion. Some sectors of the American Christian Right express vocal fondness for tough-on-crime policies, and at the same time advocate corporal punishment of children. Children, they say, are born into the sin of Adam and inhabited by Satan. Since the 1970s, this version of child rearing has proved popular and has generated its own body of literature. For these Christians, physical punishment is an article of faith and even a form of worship. It is also preventative: it stunts juvenile delinquency, they argue.

As I was finishing edits on this book, I took a break to telephone a friend from my high school days. She asked me about my project. My friend, a pious Catholic, responded to my description of Christian spanking by recalling that a family member by marriage had recently chastised her for a supposedly lax discipline style. It was better to spank children, giving them affection afterwards, said the relative, adding that the instruction to do so was in the Bible.

The timing of the surge in interest in religious spanking, the 1970s, is critical because religious interest in punishment is not isolated from American society as a whole. Other American cultural institutions also began to turn to retribution during that decade.

Given the extensive religious history of punishment, it is perhaps not surprising that the return to hard justice coincided with a rise of punitive religious advocates. In the mid-1970s, at about the time that the American public was questioning whether prisoners could ever be rehabilitated, a little-known group of orthodox Presbyterians began writing and publishing. They called themselves Reconstructionists, Puritans, and Calvinists, and they advocated a return to biblical law, including extensive use of execution for such crimes as adultery, blasphemy, heresy, theft, and homosexuality. Some Reconstructionists advocate execution of disobedient and recalcitrant adolescent children by stoning.

The execution-by-stoning arguments of the Reconstructionists are more than brutal. They are spectacular, and in this they resemble the "chastisement" that happens in some modern-day churches, where disobedient children receive whippings in front of the congregation. Both stoning and public chastisement echo the corporal punishment methods imported from Europe to the American colonies. They are public displays of shame.[24]

The religious idea of evilness has entered the secular world of forensic science. In response to criminals who derive pleasure from violence or who commit offenses of extreme cruelty, "a few forensic scientists have taken to thinking of these people as not merely disturbed but evil," reported the *New York Times* in 2005. One forensic scientist argued that the term "evil" was useful in understanding criminals for a practical reason: "A consideration of evil may be a more clear-eyed appreciation of who should be removed from society and not allowed back."[25]

THE PROBLEM OF HIDDEN PAIN

My preoccupations in writing this book involve more than the recent American return to pain. I am concerned because the pain in our jails and prisons (and in Abu Ghraib) has mostly occurred in spaces that, in the last several decades, are increasingly isolated and more and more resistant to the eyes of journalists and reformers. Pain was not always so cosseted.

In this book I will have a great deal to say about pain, but first I want to address what public punishment in the American colonies may have meant. I am preceded in this effort by a long history of thinking about public executions; such ideas include theories that governments of the time displayed their power through spectacles of death and hurt. I am also aware, as Stuart Banner cautions in his excellent history of the death penalty, that pain in the public square became unfashionable partly in response to technological developments that made secure prisons possible rather than as a result of moral improvements in the people who did the punishing.[26]

Nonetheless, a community that uses public pain understands criminals as existing within that community. Though shamed, hurt, and perhaps shunned during the punishment, those criminals who are not hanged return to their families and friends once their pain ends. A community that hurts people in a central meeting place acknowledges the centrality of punishment to its makeup. Public crowds are witness both to the pain and to the fairness of its execution.

Nowadays, punitive pain tends to happen in spaces hidden from ordinary citizens. Pain has been professionalized and isolated. The combination makes it difficult for any of us to understand physical hurt when it touches our convicts. Because of this privatized pain, and its burial behind concrete walls, most of us neither recognize convicts as fully our own nor see the centrality of pain to our culture.

Among other things, this secluded practice exacerbates an impenetrability inherent in pain; those who experience it have difficulty communicating it, and those who hear about it have trouble imagining it. Elaine Scarry observes in *The Body in Pain,* her analysis of Amnesty International torture documents, that physical pain is characterized by "unsharability"; it "resist[s]" and "actively destroys" language. While the personal experience of pain can be so overwhelming as to wipe out access to the world, she writes, it is almost inarticulable, most often conveyed in moans and screams. The difficulty of understanding another's pain is complicated by the problem of communicating it. For unpopular populations such as prisoners, the difficulty of communicating that hurt may be as insurmountable as razor wire fences and thick walls.[27]

Most of us on the outside probably prefer it that way. If it is never easy to imagine another's pain, it is considerably more difficult to sympathize with the pain of someone who has violated the law and, in some cases, injured or killed another human being. Although pain is, in the early twenty-first century, an important part of American punishment, many of us do not let ourselves know that this is so.

PUNISHMENT AND DEMOCRACY

An understanding of the criminal personality as saturated with badness, so that petty behaviors signal other evils, appears to underlie the spying efforts of the George W. Bush administration. Under the Bush administration, which is strongly influenced by the Christian Right as well as by the appalling attacks of September 11, 2001, criminality is defined not simply through illegal actions. Rather, for that government criminality is an identity fixed in the personality, revealed and recognized by a whole host of signs. So library receipts can signal future terrorist acts.

It is important to note that this way of understanding the criminal did not originate with the Bush administration. It has been part of our culture since at least the 1974 Charles Bronson movie *Death Wish,* in which the main character punished muggings and attempted armed robbery with death. Only a few decades ago, Americans saw the essential nature of the criminal as separable from the criminal act. Now the crime is the essence of the criminal, and larger crimes can be predicted from the commission of smaller ones. This understanding of the criminal personality as irredeemable leads us to punish harder and punish longer. As my research indicates, use of punishment tools (like the ever-expanding spying system of the U.S. government) are seeping into segments of American life—elementary schools, hospitals—that we would not ordinarily think of as criminal turf.

Before the emergence of the criminal self in the 1970s, the United States was home to a different idea about identity, one that saw all of us, including criminals, as malleable. Personalities could be reformed and redeemed, an idea that had big implications for every citizen. It was connected to other American ideas, including the belief that people could better themselves through education and hard work, and that Americans should not be stuck with the lots their births dealt them. Our punishment practices cannot be separated, any more than can our literature or movies, from our identity as a people.

The large proportion of our population that has been in prison brings the prison experience closer to many lives. In addition, punishment laws have the potential to affect cherished American institutions. The organization Demos and such books as Jeff Manza and Christopher Uggen's *Locked Out* and Sasha Abramsky's *Conned* argue that the numbers of ex-con nonvoters are now so vast that they can tip national elections.[28] In recent years, the ways that we punish have crept into our lives in a wide assortment of ways. They have transformed our small towns, created expansive and well-lit zones of population concentration in our rural landscapes, and drastically altered the kinds of shows that appear on prime time television. They influence the news we get, the politicians we elect, the apartments we rent, and the houses we buy, as well as whether we lock our doors and windows or purchase expensive alarm systems or live in a gated community.[29] They even, because of the surge in prison labor, affect the price of the clothing and services we purchase, and the wages American workers earn. They influence how we raise and educate our children. They help form our sense of right and wrong and our understanding of what the government should and should not do. They help mold religious practices and how many people imagine God. But perhaps most profoundly, they help to determine how we think, particularly the ways we envision character—our own and everyone else's. And they are shaping our future.

The cultural shift described in this book departs from the tradition of punishment that characterized the United States of America from its inception. For two hundred years, that tradition was regarded as distinctly American, a break with the corrupt and cruel ways of the Old World, a democratic necessity, and a matter of national pride. The changes documented here are profound and far-reaching. We have yet to see where they will take us.

CHAPTER 1

When Punishment Is the Subject, Religion Is the Predicate

IN 1634, THOMAS HARTLEY, from Hungars Parish, Virginia, sent a letter to John Endicott, the former governor of Massachusetts. The letter contained an account of torture by ducking stool: "It is undeniable ye they endeavor to live amiably, keep ye peece in families and communities, and by divers means try to have harmony and good-will amongst themselves and with Strangers who may sojourn among them. For this they use a device which they learned in England, they say, to keep foul tongues that make noise and mischief, silent, and of which I must faine tell you."

The "device," explained Hartley, was especially for punishing women, being designed to deal with a particular area of crime associated with females. One might call it misdemeanor-by-mouth: "They have a Law which reads somewhat in this wise: 'Whereas it be a sinn and a shame for scolding an lying Tongues to be left to run loose as is too often the way amongst women, be it therefore enacted ye any woman who shall, after being warned three severall times by ye Church, persist in excessive scolding, or in backbiting her neighbors, shall be brought before ye Magistrate for examination, and if ye offence be fairly proved upon her, shee shall be taken by an Officer appointed for ye purpose, to ye nearest pond of deepe streame of water, and there, in ye presence of said Magistrate and of her accusers, be publickly ducked by said officer in ye waters of ye pond or streame until shee shall make a solemn promise ye shee'l never sin in like manner again.' "

The law wasn't just on the books. It was used.

> I saw this punishment given to one Betsey, wife of John Tucker, who, by ye violence of her tongue had made his house and ye neighborhood uncomfortable. She was taken to ye pond near where I am sojourning, by ye officer who was joyned by ye Magistrate and ye Minister, Mr. Cotton, who had frequently admonished her, and a large number of People. . . . At ye end of ye longer arm is fixed a stool upon which sd Betsey was fastened by cords, her gown tied fast around her feete. The Machine was then moved up to the edge of ye pond, ye Rope was slackened by ye officer, and ye woman was allowed to go down under ye water for the space of half a minute. Betsey had a stout stomach, and would not yield until she had allowed herself to be ducked 5 severall times. At length shee cried piteously, "Let mee go! let mee go! by God's help I'll sin no more." Then they drew back ye Machine, untied ye Ropes and let her walk home in her wetted clothes, a hopefully penitent woman.[1]

The colonial American ducking stool could cause physical shock and hurt. If misused, it could kill. In his letter, Hartley reveals both the public's engagement in the spectacle and the woman's terrified expectation of drowning as, again and again, the ducking stool arm forced her to remain under water for half a minute.

Betsey was a loudmouth and nasty. Such types are usually not popular in intimate social contexts, such as a contemporary office building or, in 1634, a small village. The selection of Betsey for several minutes of terror and struggle for air likely had some serious neighborhood, not to mention spousal, animosity behind it. In the American colonies, many punishment practices (most, like this one, imported from Europe to the New World) tended to be public performances, as Hartley's reference to "a large number of people" indicates. Betsey—vulnerable, captive, ridiculous, messy, sodden—makes a ghostly appearance in today's dunking booths, common at rural American fairs. Nowadays, such games are supposed to be all in fun, dumping Boy Scouts and local softball heroes into waters where they choke and struggle and gasp as members of the public try out their aim in a ritual that has no little hint of mock payback.

In colonial times, though, a dunking was a serious legal concern. Governmental representatives oversaw the application of hurt to the local nuisance. A less visible but more significant presence than the magistrate, officer, and crowds in the scene Hartley evokes is what Betsey appeals to as "God." The punishment Betsey fights and succumbs to is a religious ceremony.

As I will argue, American punishment has, with the possible exception of several decades in the twentieth century, been a religious and, more properly, a Christian activity. Religion provides some of the comfort and the pleasure the American public and politicians can derive from punishment. In other words, it is more satisfying to cause pain to another if you know you are right. And the easiest way to know you are right is to understand your actions as God's will. But as this history of American punishment unfolds, it will become clear that the God the punishers call upon commands different punishments at different historical moments.[2]

In Betsey's case, the God represented by the officer, the magistrate, and the minister has, via ostensibly divine—but locally administered—law, ordered the immersion of a loud woman. Hartley understands the punishment in religious terms. He writes that Betsey "would not yield until she had allowed herself to be ducked 5 several times." Yielding mimics religious conversion. After fighting her punishment for several minutes, the woman gives in to it and calls out, promising to turn to "God" for "help" and to "sin no more." A sharp tongue, which in today's world would be annoying behavior, is for Betsey and the people who witness her punishment an offense against both community and God.[3] Only after they see evidence that Betsey has undergone inspired change do the officials end the punishment.

Hartley's final words—that Betsey, walking home in her "wetted clothes," is "a hopefully penitent woman"—are revealing. "Penitent" is a religious term, meaning one who has done penance. According to the 1551 Council of Trent, which articulated Roman Catholic Church doctrine in response to the challenges of reformers like Martin Luther, "as a means of regaining grace and justice, penance was at all times necessary for those who had defiled their souls with any mortal sin" and was a process "for the reconciling of the faithful who have fallen after Baptism."[4] "Penance" and its associated meanings have been present in American punishment for centuries. One of the synonyms for prison is penitentiary, which derives from the Middle English *penitenciarie,* an "episcopal prison."[5]

THE SOURCES OF AMERICAN PUNISHMENT

In his recent history of the death penalty in America, Stuart Banner makes a point of discounting myths about execution scenes in the early United States. The philosopher Michel Foucault, one source of those myths, in *Discipline and Punish* described European execution scenes as something of a free-for-all, replete with pickpockets and raucous, sometimes rebellious crowds. In the new country, at least, writes Banner, such scenes, characterized by gravity and quiet, resembled church services.[6] Prominent ministers of the day presented well-attended gallows sermons and related moral tales about the life and downfall of those about to be executed. Printed broadsides of such texts sold so well that one scholar sees execution literature as the root of American popular culture.[7]

In addition to religiosity, pain, and its accompanying anticipatory terror, characterized these more serious punishments. Early American executions, both the colonial and the postrevolutionary variety, were for the most part accomplished through hanging. The goal of hanging was an efficient and less-than-painful death. In practice, however, those close enough to watch got an eyeful. In a history of the British death penalty, V. A. C. Gatrell describes deaths on the hanging scaffolds, also popular in the American colonies. "What they watched was horrific," writes Gatrell. "People did not die on it neatly. Watched by thousands, they urinated, defecated, screamed, kicked, fainted, and choked as they died." The choking, kicking migration to death often took minutes.[8]

Executions could follow a more painful course if the crime seemed heinous. Under early American laws, women who murdered their husbands and slaves who murdered their masters burned at the stake, a slow and excruciating execution method intended to punish "petit treason." These crimes were a small version of treason, or the act of overthrowing the state, because the law interpreted the home as mirroring governmental power relationships.[9]

Execution methods shared an emphasis on pain, but they had other commonalities as well. Shame was integral to American colonial punishment. Like pain, shame attached to particular bodies via public displays and in some cases through physical marks. The woman in the stocks, the man with his ears nailed to the pillory, the heretic with an *H* seared into her forehead, the drunkard standing in bilboes (a kind of leg iron) in the hot sun, the woman convicted of sodomy with a half-inch hole carved into the cartilage of her nose (a practice Thomas Jefferson recommended), and the loud woman wearing a gag or a cleft stick—all of these criminals endured great shame. The proximity of shame to pain is evident in this list. The physical marking of faces and forcing of bodies into uncomfortable postures both cause hurt and set the suffering body apart from others, so that onlookers will notice and disapprove.[10]

For the most part, the American colonies inherited their criminal codes from Europe. The predominant influence was Britain, although the legal system of the Netherlands influenced punishments in New York. As the preceding examples have suggested, many laws that the American colonies inherited had their roots in medieval Christian, specifically Roman Catholic, religious practices.[11]

The European rulers of the American colonies used painful physical punishments as a way of maintaining social order from overseas. The king had two bodies: his physical body housed in Europe and the spiritual body, which could inflict severe pain from thousands of miles away.[12]

Corporal punishment thus had a religious component even when the punisher was a monarchical government and not a church. The overseas royalty enjoyed their power through a godly endowment. But the religious aura translated nicely to governments that understood crimes as offenses against God. In a bow to Deuteronomy, the Massachusetts legal code of 1648 prescribed execution for children older than sixteen who "shall curse or smite their natural mother or father." The Massachusetts God was a jealous one. The prevailing Calvinist sensibility in that colony selected Quaker "heretics" for special treatment. The Massachusetts Colonial Records of 1657 list the punishment for Quakers who return to towns that had banished them: "A Quaker if male for the first offense shall have one of his eares cutt off; for the second offense have his other eare cutt off; a woman shalbe severly whipt; for the third offense they, he or she, shall have their tongues bored through with a hot iron."[13]

The nexus of punishment and religious belief is obvious in some colonial laws, such as those that insisted upon church attendance or rebuked blasphemy. But it is also present, for example, in laws regulating sexual activity. More expansive than our contemporary definition of sodomy as anal sex between two men, sodomy laws of the day included, for example, sex with animals.[14]

Sodomy laws began as church laws. In the sixteenth century, however, the English royal court usurped the right to punish sodomy crimes. The transfer of punitive power coincided with the decision of Henry VIII to leave the Catholic Church, which had refused to annul the king's marriage to Catherine of Aragón.[15] Under Henry VIII, church and royal law were no longer in tension. The king was aligned with God, and the king's wishes dressed in divine clothing. Sodomy laws, like other felonies, provided an opportunity for the king to wrest moral power from the church.

One of the sodomy laws of Henry VIII is important in American history because versions of it, derived from medieval church law, traveled into colonial jurisprudence. In 1533, the Act of 25 Henry VIII, chapter 6, determined that the "detestable and abominable vice of Buggery [sodomy] committed with mankind or beast" was a felony punishable by death.[16] Both Plymouth Colony and the Massachusetts Bay Colony maintained laws punishing sodomy with death, a law that continued when the two became a single colony.

Other colonies adopted the death penalty for sodomy. Some imitated the 1533 law. For instance, Rhode Island's first attempt to regulate sodomy was explicit about its lineage: "First of sodomy, which is forbidden by this present assembly throughout the whole colony, and by sundry statutes of England. 25 Henry 8, 6; 5 Eliz. 17. It is a vile affection. . . . The penalty concluded by that state whose authority we are is felony of death without remedy. See 5 Eliz. 17."[17] In this way, the colonies inherited the tradition of eliding civil and religious power and transferred the practice to colonial governance.

PUNISHMENT, COLONIAL STYLE

Between 1608, the date of the first execution in the colonies, and 1785, when Joseph Ross, one of the last executed for the crime of sodomy, was hanged in Pennsylvania, just over fifty people were executed in the American colonies for sex crimes including "sodomy," "bestiality," "buggery," rape, attempted rape, and adultery.[18] The heyday for sex-crime executions occurred during the first few decades of punishment in the American colonies. In the thirty-six years that followed the first execution in the new colonies, a full third of the twenty-four executed died for sex crimes. These included five sodomites and two adulterers. One was a convicted rapist.[19]

Although the southern and northern colonies alike followed the English law, "the New Englanders' reliance on the Old Testament caused them definitional difficulties," writes Mary Beth Norton. Sodomy law in those colonies had a definition that was both expansive and unstable.[20]

"Sodomy" was a flexible term. Under one set of legal codes, that of the Reverend John Cotton of Plymouth Plantation, the "unnatural filthiness" of sodomy that was to earn the punishment of death included "fellowship of man with man" and "of woman with woman" as well as "buggery, which is carnal fellowship of man or woman with beasts or fowles." A succeeding version of the law in the Massachusetts Bay Colony eliminated the prohibition against what we now call lesbian sex, and a later version also saved young boys and those who suffered homosexual rape from the death penalty. These last two groups, which our current society would consider victims rather than perpetrators, still suffered punishments but not execution.[21]

New Haven provides an example of how broad lawmaking in the colonies could get. The New Haven legal code of 1656 adopted the provisions against sodomy and bestiality that appeared in the Laws and Liberties of the Massachusetts Bay Colony, "but New Haven did not stop there," writes Norton. The New Haven legal code also considered sex between women, sex with immature girls, and masturbation in front of others to be potential capital crimes.[22]

In practice, sloppy application aroused public antagonism. Although capital convictions for sodomy generally required two witnesses, local governments did not always follow such rules. For instance, George Spencer came to the attention of authorities because "it was thought that a recently born deformed piglet resembled him."[23]

Death for sex crimes may have seemed unduly harsh to some colonists. "As was true in adultery cases, some colonists expressed their dissatisfaction with the application of the death penalty to those found guilty of sodomy and bestiality," writes Norton. As earnestly as the New Englanders appear to have believed in the importance of regulating sexual behaviors, vocal disagreement may have slowed down the rate of capital convictions. Moreover, some sex crimes received more frequent punishment than others, and sex regulation via execution happened relatively early in the life of most colonies. The colonies held only two executions for adultery. Both of these occurred in the Massachusetts Bay Colony in 1643. Likewise, the most concentrated executions for sodomy and bestiality occurred before 1644.[24]

DEVILISH CRIME WAVE

After the first surge of hangings for sex, such punishments lost popularity as the colonies turned to executions for piracy or witchcraft. The colony with the reputation for witchcraft executions is Puritan Massachusetts. It is important to note, however, that possessions and witch trials occurred in other colonies and countries and in the decades before 1692, the year of the Salem witchcraft trials. "Colonial courts tried more than eighty such cases from 1647 to 1691, resulting in twenty executions and many more fines, banishments, and whippings," writes historian Kenneth Silverman. "Dozens of other episodes circulated by conversation and gossip."[25]

The infatuation with execution for witchcraft lasted until the famous Salem trials, which produced nineteen hangings and one "pressing" under rocks. The pressing was an attempt to persuade Giles Corey to confess to being "a dreadfull wizard," as his accusers Ann Putnam and Mercy Lewis put it. Corey, who didn't utter a confession, died for his silence. Thereafter, the number of hanged witches dropped precipitously. From 1693 on, the colonies executed no witches.[26]

Witchery proved to be as slippery a category as sodomy. Determining what makes a witch a witch was a definitional puzzle that helped along the famous Salem bloodbath.

Like sex crimes, witchcraft was an offense against God; a witch worshipped outside of Christianity and was in league with Satan. The Devil seemed urgently present in the decades leading up to the Salem trials; possessions were more numerous. Beginning in 1647, the number of witchcraft executions increased, with eight accused witches getting the noose between 1647 and 1660. During that same period, just three died for sodomy and bestiality crimes.[27]

Kai Erikson, author of an influential sociological study of the Salem witch trials, perceives 1692 to be the year of a Puritan "crime wave."[28] His understanding of the witch trials as a crime wave is a link to contemporary society. In making his argument, Erikson draws on the writings of Emile

Durkheim in *The Division of Labor in Society*. Crime "may actually perform a needed service to society by drawing people together in a common posture of anger and indignation," writes Erikson, summarizing Durkheim.[29]

To argue in this vein is to claim that crime waves say more about societal needs than they do about crime rates. That is, the witch crimes achieved social prominence (and led to so many deaths) because the Puritans profoundly needed the kind of self-definition that denied membership to some formerly included in their community.[30]

The need arose not because the number of witches increased but because of other pressures. In the 1670s and 1680s, the Puritans faced the possible loss of their Massachusetts charter, Erikson notes. "The sense of impending doom reached its peak in 1686," he writes. "For a moment, it looked as if the holy experiment was over." Adding to these pressures were local battles. "In a colony that depended on a high degree of harmony and group feeling, the courts were picking their way through a maze of land disputes and personal feuds," notes Erikson.[31]

Lest his point get lost, Erikson notes that during crime waves communities begin to penalize behaviors they formerly tolerated. The number of crimes doesn't necessarily increase, but the punishments swell. In recent years, scholars of American imprisonment have begun using Durkheim to explain recent American crime waves. They argue that contemporary American crime waves gain energy in response to what Erikson (in writing of the Puritan "crime waves") describes as "a rash of publicity."[32]

Some of the Puritan crime publicity came from the prominent Boston minister Cotton Mather. In 1689, several years before the Salem executions, Mather, minister of Old North Church, published *Memorable Providences, Relating to Witchcraft and Possessions*. The book described the possession of the Godwin children, from "a pious Family in Boston," and the trial and execution of Goody Glover, a washerwoman.

Memorable Providences was the talk of Puritan communities throughout New England. About eighteen months after its publication, observers began to see the events of Mather's book echoed in the possessions that hit Salem Village. As the Reverend John Hale put it, the young women in Salem were "in all things afflicted as bad as John Goodwin's children at Boston, in the year 1689."[33] Samuel Parris, whose daughter and niece started the fits of possession that spread to other girls in Salem, used

Mather's methods in attempting to cure the girls of witchcraft. The methods failed.[34]

In *Memorable Providences* Mather promises to give proof of witches, writing that "New-Engl. has had Exemples of their Existence and Operation." Mather recounts the narrative of the eldest daughter of the afflicted family, who questioned Goody Glover about some missing laundry. Glover responded with the sort of loud-mouthing that condemned Betsey to the ducking stool. The result of the verbal nastiness was bad news for Glover. The girl acted as if possessed.[35] Odd behaviors spread through her siblings. The family consulted doctors, one of whom decided that the behaviors were so inexplicable that "nothing but an hellish Witchcraft could be the Original of these Maladies."[36]

During the daylight hours, reports Mather, the children made bizarre physical movements and complained of pains: "Sometimes they would be Deaf, sometimes Dumb, and sometimes Blind, and often, all this at once." The children exhibited strange physical behaviors. "One while their Tongues would be drawn down their Throats; another-while they would be pull'd out upon their Chins, to a prodigious length," he reports. "They would have their Mouths opened unto such a Wideness, that their Jaws went out of joint; and anon they would clap together again with a Force like that of a strong Spring-Lock." A similarly violent spring motion happened "to their Shoulder-Blades, and their Elbows, and Hand-wrists, and several of their joints."

The behaviors ended at the same time of day. "About Nine or Ten at Night they alwaies had a Release from their miseries, and ate and slept all night for the most part indifferently," he writes. The oddity of a demonic possession that allows children to eat when hungry and sleep when tired does not appear to have occurred to Mather.[37]

Mather took the oldest girl to live with him, where he plied her with tests. One of his frequent quizzes involved reading materials. Noting that the Bible caused the child "very terrible Agonies," Mather determined that she could read works that his Puritan sect considered heresies. "I brought her a Quakers Book; and That she could quietly read whole pages of; only the Name of God and Christ she still skip't over, being unable to pronounce it, except sometimes with stammering a minute or two or more upon it," writes Mather. "I entertained her with a Book that pretends to prove, That there are no Witches; and that she could read very well, only the Name Devils, and Witches, could not be uttered by her without extraordinary Difficulty." Books that conveyed beliefs Mather would have agreed with were unacceptable to the spirits. "I produced a Book to her that proves, That there are Witches, and that she had not power to read," he writes. Catholicism, on the other hand, appealed to the demon. "A popish Book also she could endure very well; but it would kill her to look into any Book, that (in my Opinion) it might have bin profitable and edifying for her to be reading of," writes Mather, who never seems to wonder that the spirits capture his prejudices like a photo negative.[38]

As with Goody Glover, the Salem accusations at first fell against townspeople who made others uncomfortable: a woman who neglected to attend church, a beggar who muttered phrases under her breath when townspeople refused to give her food, and a slave who had baked a "witch cake." As the circle widened, however, it enclosed what Salem considered upright citizens. Eventually, 160 people awaited trial.[39]

HOW MAMMON TURNED HOLY

The British bequest to the colonies included what was called "common law." The first appearance of British common law on the new continent was established in Virginia between 1609 and 1612. Capital offenses in this legal system included murder and manslaughter, rebellion, tumult, conspiracy, sedition, mutiny, rape, adultery, and incest.[40]

But Britain also allowed the early colonies some punitive independence. For instance, the 1609 Second Charter given to the Virginia Company stipulated that the colony could, within reason, establish its own legal code. In addition to the hanging crimes Britain bestowed, the new colony also executed people guilty of speech crimes, most of them religious in nature: blaspheming "Gods holy name," speaking "impiously or maliciously against the holy and blessed Trinitie, or any of the three persons," uttering "any word," or carrying out "any act, which may tend to the derision or despight of Gods holy word," or pronouncing "traitorous words against his Majesties Person, or royal authority." Virginia's laws also punished sodomy, sacrilege (theft from or trespass in a church), robbery and burglary, and making a false oath.[41]

In addition to the hanging crimes, Virginia colonial law specified corporal punishment for small-time religious offenses. A person who "unworthily" demeaned herself "unto any Preacher, or Minister" earned several whippings and had to plead forgiveness three times in a public place. Missing one of the twice-daily church services meant loss of pay for one day's work. As with other punishments, multiple infractions led to more severe treatment. A citizen inclined to avoid church would get a whipping for a second infraction and six months in the galleys doing hard labor for the third. Other Sabbath infringements were more serious. Those who worked or played on the holy day would lose a week's pay. On the second offense, such criminals got a whipping. The third transgression merited death. Sex with the wrong person led to public whippings, which increased to three per month for the third such violation. Uttering "disgracefull words" or committing "any act to the disgrace of any person in this Colonie" were punished in 1610 with what must have been an uncomfortable sleeping arrangement: "being tied head and feete together, upon the guard everie night for the space of one month," in addition to other penalties.[42]

Accompanying the crimes against God were crimes against money and property. "There were . . . several capital crimes dealing with the economic well-being of the colony," writes political historian Ronald J. Pestritto. These included: "stealing from a Native American coming to trade, trading with the Native Americans without authority, embezzling or defrauding the colony, embezzling or robbing a fort, selling overpriced goods, and destroying an animal without permission of the government. The colony later extended the death penalty to such crimes as taking a fruit or vegetable from a garden or vineyard. There were several capital crimes associated with exploration and shipping: deliberately failing to return from a scouting, fishing, hunting, or trading voyage; departing by ship without permission; and selling any commodity of the colony to a departing ship."[43]

Pestritto suggests that Virginia's expansive capital statutes may have had to do with anxiety about the success of the colony. "From the earliest criminal law in Virginia, it is apparent that strict discipline was a top concern," given the failures that had occurred at Jamestown, he writes. Virginia also maintained a number of corporal punishments designed to regulate the work and economic habits of its populace. Any first offender for the crime of leaving work early spent the night with head tied to feet. Second and third offenses for that crime earned a public whipping and a year in the galleys, respectively.[44]

Virginia's capital code may have been extensive, but the colony executed only ten people between 1609 and 1699. In numbers of hangings, it was outdone by Connecticut, which hanged a dozen malefactors during the same time period; Maryland, which executed fifteen; and Puritan Massachusetts, which topped all the colonies at ninety-nine hangings.[45]

During the eighteenth century, Virginia grew bloodier as the colony and, in the later years, the new state shifted the directives of the extensive code into physical reality. At 386 executions during that century, out of 1,391 in the colonies as a whole, Virginia saw more than a quarter of all capital killings, more than any other colony. Notable in this century were the many hangings for economic crimes, which had claimed only one life in the seventeenth century—that of Daniell Frank, hanged in 1622 for stealing a calf. Also notable is the lack of executions overall in the colony for traditional religious crimes.[46]

In its accelerated executions for and attention to property crimes during the eighteenth century, Virginia appears to have been a colonial shadow of Britain. During the eighteenth century, the mother country enforced bloody statutes protecting economic property as never before and developed new laws designed both to control the labor force and to confine wealth to those who already possessed it.

During the eighteenth century, "most of those hanged had offended against the laws of property," writes Peter Linebaugh of British executions in *The London Hanged*. Whereas punishments had once been attached to religious prescriptions, observe several historians, in Britain moral energy had begun to transfer to property and wealth. "Labour, the curse of fallen man, had become a religious duty, a means of glorifying God in our calling," writes Christopher Hill of eighteenth-century Britain in *Puritanism and Revolution*. "Poverty had ceased to be a holy state and had become presumptive evidence of wickedness."[47]

In these few sentences, Hill captures two peculiarities that also characterize American punishment. The first, rather obvious, is that moral, legal behavior changes over time. The second is that as those definitions change, they tend to draw with them a religiosity that endows the new rules with ancient authority. Thus, punishment for vastly different, even conflicting, offenses will often take power from religion, even when the punishing government is expressly secular.

In eighteenth-century Britain, the number of crimes meriting the death penalty grew from approximately fifty in 1680 to more than two hundred in 1820. The new laws, writes historian Douglas Hay, were often "related to specific, limited property interests," enacted as favors, "for the mere asking," and without debate.[48]

For the British king and the government, punishment, including the spectacular display of death-making on the gallows, served a critical social function. The eighteenth-century British rulers "cherished" capital punishment, writes Hay. They cherished it partly because of its capacity to inspire terror.[49]

In terror resided religious meanings—as in the awestruck contemplation of God—and political power. "In its ritual, its judgments and its channeling of emotion the criminal law echoed many of the most powerful psychic components of religion," writes Hay, who suggests that the religious meanings of the scaffold, because they had more "bite" in the eighteenth century, overshadowed those of the church.[50] In an age when God, via government, punished with pain and death, new property crimes became religious matters in Britain and perhaps in its shadow colony Virginia, which like other American colonies also accelerated executions for property crimes.[51]

CHAPTER 2

"A Heart Is Not Wholly Corrupted"

REVOLUTION, RELIGION, PUNISHMENT

BENJAMIN RUSH, REVOLUTIONARY, signer of the Declaration of Independence, early abolitionist, professor of chemistry, "father of American psychiatry," and foe of yellow fever was a passionately religious man. He craved symmetry between his personal and his political beliefs. Rush consistently extended his thoughts and his religious life to politics, and vice versa, and he placed himself in the thick of the day's political excitement. He exemplifies both the religious ferment and the punishment transformations that followed the Revolution.

As can be seen from his correspondence, Rush identified himself as a Presbyterian as late as 1784.[1] Then, in 1785, he experienced a religious conversion. In a letter dated October 15, he wrote of hearing Elhanan Winchester, a preacher who spoke of the doctrine of final restitution—the idea that all beings on Earth belong to the creator and will return to God.[2] This idea electrified Rush, who thought the belief appropriate to the new republic. "The spring which the human mind acquired by the Revolution has extended itself to religion," he wrote. Rush claimed that the major denominations were transforming in response, shifting away from such Calvinist ideas as predestination (the belief that all people, before birth, have a predetermined final destination—either heaven or hell—which they cannot alter during their lifetimes).[3]

Rush's was a Christian interpretation of Enlightenment thought characteristic of some of his fellow reformers. The new United States experienced a version of the Enlightenment that was "not about the effort to 'rationalize' things spiritual," writes Nina Reid-Maroney, "rather it [was] about the effort to sanctify things rational."[4] The Presbyterians did not transform quickly enough to suit Rush. When his wife was out of town, he wrote her a letter dated August 22, 1787, informing her that he had discharged his obligations to his former church and was no longer a member. Rush became a Universalist, a member of the denomination Winchester helped to found.[5]

In his letter to his wife, Rush writes at length about his encounter with a group of convicts, a subject that at first glance seems unrelated to his decision to leave Presbyterianism. He describes "an high scene before our doors" that occurred the previous day when he met a group of "wheelbarrow men," prisoners with shaved heads who did hard labor in the streets of Pennsylvania. "One of the wheelbarrow men (who were all at work in cleaning our street) asked me for a penny. I told him I had none but asked him if a draught of molasses beer would not be more acceptable to him. He answered in the affirmative." Rush ended up supplying the entire group with beer while a crowd "as usual gathered around them."[6]

Writing of the prisoners, Rush continued, "One of them struck me above the rest. . . . He took a large dog in his arms and played with him in the most affectionate manner. 'This dog,' said he 'came from England with me and has been my companion ever since.'" In the prisoner's love for his dog, Rush found both religious meaning and an idea he would come to advocate as public policy. "A heart is not wholly corrupted and offers at least one string by which it might be led back to virtue that is capable of so much steady affection even for a dog," he writes. "The conduct of the dog excited my admiration and conveyed a faint idea by his fidelity of that infinite love which follows the human species, however much reduced by distress, debased by crimes, or degraded by the punishments of a prison, of ignominy, or of pain."[7]

Rush's epiphany about those most "debased by crimes" did not occur in isolation. In that same year, the first prison-relief organization in Europe and North America, the Philadelphia Society for Alleviating the Miseries of Public Prisons, reinvented itself. (After a brief existence as the Philadelphia Society for Assisting Distressed Prisoners, in 1776, it was closed by the British.) Rush joined the founding meeting of the organization when it was reinstituted.[8] The year 1787 was significant for Philadelphia in yet another way: political leaders gathered in the city to create the new United States government. Concern about the well-being of prisoners was part of the postrevolutionary cultural climate.[9]

Rush thought that a shift in legal systems should bring about wholesale cultural change. "We have changed our forms of government, but it remains yet to effect a revolution in our principles, opinions, and manners," he wrote in 1786. It was an idea he repeated in his letters to influential men of politics. "I wish to see America acquire a national character and, instead of receiving, to impart manners and customs to the strangers of every description who reside among us," he wrote in a 1781 letter to John Adams.[10] Among the things Rush wished to see change were the systems of education (he advocated free schools, what is known today as public education), the instruction young women should receive (among other things, "astronomy, natural philosophy, and chemistry"), the disciplining of children, and the punishment of criminals.[11]

Rush's sense that the new republic's education of young women should encapsulate revolutionary cultural change is evident in "Thoughts upon Female Education, Accommodated to the Present State of Society, Manners, and Government, in the United States of America," an address he gave at the Young Ladies' Academy in Philadelphia in 1787 and later published as an essay. In the first paragraphs, Rush advocates a breach with his country's colonial past, writing, "The education of young ladies, in this country, should be conducted upon principles very different from what it is in Great Britain, and in some respects, different from what it was when we were part of a monarchical empire."[12]

"Thoughts upon Female Education" also concerns criminality and punishment, a juxtaposition characteristic of Rush, who understood punishment and education as entwined. After ridiculing traditions of dress that leave "our ladies panting in a heat of ninety degrees, under a hat and cushion, which were calculated for the temperature of a British summer," Rush goes on, tying his disapproval of British female costuming to colonial scaffold cruelties. "We behold our citizens condemned and punished by a criminal law, which was copied from a country, where maturity in corruption renders public executions a part of the amusements of the nation."[13]

The comparison between the encumbrances of women's clothing and fun on execution day is not so great a stretch as it might seem. Both are habits that, as Rush sees them, the new country "copied," rather than considered. Both lead to physical discomfort—with execution the more vicious of the two—that the new nation has not yet come to understand as unkind. The inability to recognize either the nastiness of requiring heavy clothing on a ninety-degree day or the brutality of amusements at an execution Rush credits to "maturity in corruption," a weakening of sympathetic understanding, and an unthinking acceptance of inherited, or imposed, tradition. Just as parents must put aside empathy in order to dress their daughters in a manner that will cause them to suffer, so too must the public displace its humane concern to enjoy scaffold entertainments.

Having drawn this parallel between "hats and cushions" and celebrations at hangings, Rush issues a call for the new nation to "awake from this servility" and to "adopt manners in every thing, that shall be accommodated to our state of society, and to the forms of our government." Fashions for young women and the behavior of people who gather at the foot of the scaffold must change if the young country is to replace the monarchical system with a democratic republic. In making this argument, Rush discloses his conviction that cultural trends determine political ones.[14]

Three years later, in "Thoughts upon the Amusements and Punishments Which Are Proper for Schools," Rush again draws a parallel between education methods and treatment of criminals. "In barbarous ages every thing partook of the complexion of the times," he begins. "With the progress of reason and Christianity, punishments of all kinds have become less severe. Solitude and labour are now substituted in many countries, with success, in the room of the whipping-post and the gallows."

He goes on to note that the treatment of schoolchildren does not follow the progress he praises. "The rod is yet the principle means of governing them, and a schoolmaster remains the only despot now known in free countries." In a young nation newly liberated from tyranny, the message that a whipping schoolmaster was no better than a "despot" would have caused a clang of recognition. In decrying the classroom despot, Rush draws on personal experience, both as a revolutionary and as a former student, writing, "I recollect, when a boy, to have lost a schoolmate, who was said to have died in consequence of a severe whipping he received in school."[15]

Rush presents a series of arguments against corporal punishment of schoolchildren. Whippings in front of classmates confound a developing conscience and can lead to crime, he argues. "Corporal punishments inflicted at school, have a tendency to destroy the sense of shame, and thereby to destroy all moral sensibility," he writes, tying the loss of these traits to future criminality: "The boy that has often been publicly whipped at school, is under great obligations to his maker, and his parents, if he afterwards escape the whipping-post or the gallows."[16]

In contrast to parents who today spank out of religious obligation, the eighteenth-century essayist Rush discusses the corporal punishment of children in religious terms, but to different ends. Instead of a vengeful God who demands physical hurt of those who disobey, Rush says painful punishment is devilish. "I have sometimes suspected that the Devil, who knows how great an enemy knowledge is to his kingdom, has had the address to make the world believe that *ferruling, pulling* and *boxing ears, codgelling, horfing,* &c. and, in boarding schools, a little starving, are all absolutely necessary for the government of young people, on purpose that he might make both schools and schoolmasters odious, and thereby keep our world in ignorance; for ignorance is the best means the Devil ever contrived to keep up the number of his subjects in our world." (What Rush calls "ferruling," a word derived from the fennel plant, is a beating with a flat wood instrument, such as a ruler. "Horsing" suggests a colonial punishment, also in use in the U.S. military at least through the Civil War, sometimes called a ride on the wood horse.)[17]

Alongside such religiously motivated arguments, Rush includes one his republican philosophy had inspired: "I conceive corporal punishments, inflicted in an arbitrary manner, to be contrary to the spirit of liberty, and that they should not be tolerated in a free government."[18]

A RELIGION TO FIT A REVOLUTION

Many revolutionaries, like Rush, sought a religion compatible with their political beliefs. For some patriots, liberal Christianity and republicanism were not just compatible, they were inseparable. "I have always considered Christianity as the *strong ground* of republicanism," Rush, in one of his many comparisons between the Gospel and republican thought, wrote to Thomas Jefferson.[19] Others left Christianity altogether, preferring a belief system along the lines of Deism. Jefferson avoided saying whether he followed a religious faith or not. What these revolutionaries had in common was their tendency to seek a belief structure that emphasized freedom of thought, consistent with their understanding of a democratic republic and in contrast to the monarchy and inherited religions they resisted.[20]

Republicanism was a powerful motivator for Rush. "Capital punishments are the natural offspring of monarchical governments," he writes in his 1792 essay entitled "Considerations on the Injustice and Impolicy of Punishing Murder by Death." "Kings believe that they possess their crowns by a *divine* right; no wonder, therefore, they assume the divine power of taking away human life. Kings consider their subjects as their property; no wonder, therefore, they shed their blood with as little emotion as men shed the blood of their sheep or cattle." The monarchical faith, Rush implies, was barbarous, leading some men to treat others as they would "property," or domestic animals. So too were the trappings of such a faith barbarous, including executions.[21]

At a political meeting "convened at the House of Benjamin Franklin, Esq." in Philadelphia 1787, Rush read from his essay "An Enquiry into the Effects of Public Punishments upon Criminals, and upon Society." Much of this essay concerns the influence of such punishments on the citizenry. "All *public* punishments tend to make bad men worse, and to increase crimes by their influence upon society," he writes. Rush goes on to claim that public punishments spike crimes because public physical cruelties harden people. In response to public punishments, "the principle of sympathy" will "cease to act altogether." He warns that widespread loss of feeling for other human beings harms all other forms of social cohesion, including familial love and respect for the poor and the weak. Likewise, convict labor on the streets "will render labour of every kind disreputable." Rush's understanding of public punishments suggests that their presence in a society will cause it to rot.[22]

In his dislike of public punishment, Rush anticipated the cross-national middle-class revulsion that, in the nineteenth century, led to moving executions indoors in both the United States and Britain.[23] But Rush's critique is large. He argues from practicality: execution "lessens the horror of taking away human life, and thereby tends to multiply murders." He argues from religious conviction: "The punishment of murder by death is contrary to *divine revelation*." Rush also claims that public physical punishments confuse the conscience of otherwise innocent onlookers: "Public punishments, so far from preventing crimes by the terror they excite in the minds of spectators, are directly calculated to produce them. . . . To see blows, or a halter, imposed in cold blood, upon a criminal, whose passive behaviour, operating with the ignorance of spectators, indicates innocence more than vice, cannot fail of removing the natural obstacles to violence and murder in the human mind."[24]

Rush prescribes a penitentiary, actually two penitentiaries—one calculated to "have a beneficial effect not only upon health but morals," the other calculated to terrify. In the better-known version of this essay, published in his *Essays, Literary, Moral, Philosophical*, which he collected in 1798, Rush emphasizes the religious meanings of his proposed punishment: "Let a large house be erected in a convenient part of the state," he writes. The design he suggests would promote contemplation and monastic privacy: "Let it be divided into a number of apartments, reserving one large room for public worship. Let cells be provided for the solitary confinement of such persons as are of a refractory temper." The prisoners, he says, would work throughout most of the day, in silence: "Let a garden adjoin this house, in which the culprits may occasionally work, and walk." Rush's conversion experience finds voice in his call for the penitentiary. "This spot will have a beneficial effect not only upon health but morals, for it will lead them to a familiarity with those pure and naturall objects which are calculated to renew the connection of fallen man with his creator."[25]

But in 1787, the year Rush converted, finding evidence of "infinite love" in a dog and a "string" that could lead a corrupted heart to goodness, the prison he advocated didn't communicate optimism. Any member of the public who ventured to find this "house" would get an eyeful and an earful. "Let the avenue to this house be rendered difficult and gloomy by mountains or morasses," Rush writes. "Let its doors be of iron; and let the grating, occasioned by opening and shutting them, be encreased by an echo from a neighboring mountain, that shall extend and continue a sound that shall deeply pierce the soul." Inside, all was to be gloomy. The "officers of the house," Rush admonishes, should "be strictly forbidden ever to discover any signs of mirth, or even levity, in the presence of the criminals." Its name should also "increase the horror of this abode of discipline and misery."

The light and dark prison images in Rush's versions of *An Enquiry into Public Punishments* capture a conflict inherent in American punish-ment—one contested throughout the nineteenth century and into the twentieth and twenty-first. Punishment was supposed to "terrify" yet it was also supposed to reform.

HOW CALVINISM CONTINUED IN A TIME OF REFORM

The "benevolent" version of the penitentiary advocated by Rush, with its emphasis on forgiveness and the salvation of all souls, was a marked contrast to the prevailing punishments of his day, many of which commu-nicated Calvinist meanings. Some historians have suggested that in the decades following the Revolution, the social power of the traditional clergy fell precipitously. The seeking after a more "republican" religion on the part of Rush and others inspired by the Revolution gives that impres-sion. But, if the ministry lost its authority on Sundays, on execution days Calvinism stood on the scaffold.[26]

On June 10, 1797, the Reverend Nathan Strong of the Presbyterian Church in Hartford, Connecticut, preached prior to the execution of Richard Doane, who was convicted of killing his friend during a drunken fight. Preachers often published expanded editions of their gallows ser-mons, containing, as Strong's does, a biography explaining the moral dissolution of the executed man and extra warnings for readers. This well-loved genre of the time, explains Daniel A. Cohen in *Pillars of Salt, Monu-ments of Grace: Literature and the Origins of American Popular Culture, 1674–1860*, started with Cotton Mather and amounts to the beginning of crime literature and also marks the origin of U.S. popular culture.[27]

In the postrevolutionary Republic, the Presbyterian and Congrega-tional churches were holdouts for Calvinist thought, and Nathan Strong's gallows sermon for Richard Doane is a classic bit of Calvinist preaching. It unites civil with divine law and declares both punitive, seeing the strong arm of God in the state noose. "The infinite goodness of God is an ac-knowledged truth; but this is no certain evidence you are going to happi-ness, for his goodness may require him to punish you in another world as he doth in this," Strong admonished Doane.[28] The contrast with Rush's curative God who saves all could not be greater.

But Calvinism isn't the only voice in this sermon. Strong launches into a tirade against drinking houses that would sound appropriate to a Progressive-era temperance supporter more than one hundred years later. "This prevailing vice, is greatly promoted by tipling houses and dram shops, where the incautious gradually acquire a habit which proves their ruin." Other parts of the sermon locate the source of the crime inside Doane, but this passage comes close to blaming crimes that follow from drunkenness on bars that sell liquor—a social argument that anticipates twentieth-century explanations of criminality. Strong's solution to the problem of alcohol is not the punitive gaze of God but government intervention in the selling of draughts.[29]

Nor does Strong appear to have been in full control of the religious meanings offered before the scaffold. Doane selected a verse from the Old Testament prophet Hosea. The scripture reading preceded Strong's sermon: "For I desire mercy and not sacrifice, and the knowledge of God more than burnt offering." The convict's craving for "mercy" rather than what is presumably his own "sacrifice" and "burnt offering" draws on a more merciful concept of God than Strong's absolute ruler whose "goodness may require him to punish you in another world as he doth in this."[30]

Doane's expression of his desire for "mercy and not sacrifice" seems to have made Strong nervous. In the printed version of his sermon, Strong included a footnote to Doane's selected scripture: "The preacher is sensible that many will suppose the text improper for the occasion. It was chosen by the prisoner, and he could not be so well pleased with another." Strong explains that Doane, "on reading this passage," experienced "what he supposed Divine light, an astonishing view of God's character." Strong's description of Doane's ecstatic recognition resembles the infinite love Rush identified in the dog companion to the wheelbarrow man; both reactions imply a discovery of benevolence.[31]

If, as Foucault suggested, governments tend to use spectacular and painful punishments to exhibit their power before a public, then the rhetorical struggling in Strong's gallows sermon may imply a broader tussle over meanings. Executions may have allowed the new government to demonstrate its power to quell internal disturbances and implicitly to control the public at large. But the new republic used the religious forms associated with colonial power in order to do so. Those religious forms increasingly seemed inadequate and inappropriate, at least to thinkers like Rush and criminals like Doane. The republican promises, the rising popularity of an all-forgiving Christian God, and the more Calvinistic threats vibrated in tension.[32]

PUNISHMENT AND SOCIAL CHANGE

In retrospect, we can understand Strong's sermon as well as Rush's pre-dictions of widespread changes in manners as anticipating cultural shifts that affected punishment, in addition to other social practices. It is my argument in this book that changes in American punishment occur alongside, and in relation to, other significant cultural changes. Rush's belief that education of young women, punishment of prisoners, treat-ment of school children, and religious practices would all change in re-sponse to the Revolution proved prophetic.

Before the American Revolution, religious beliefs influenced punish-ment methods in the colonies. As the eighteenth century closed and the nineteenth century opened, religion again proved a prime mover. But if in twelfth-century Britain a punitive Christian God demanded that govern-ments kill sodomites, in eighteenth-century America it was the benevolent God of Rush and of Doane's plea that determined the painful punishments of the past to be the work not of God but of mistaken mankind.

The attention of people of faith to punishment; their claim to author-ity on the subject; their struggles over the meanings of good, evil, forgive-ness, and pain; and their influence on the public debate set a pattern that would repeat throughout the nineteenth and twentieth centuries and seems to be continuing, in the works of Sister Helen Prejean and Chuck Colson, into the twenty-first. In this secular society, punishment has re-mained a peculiarly religious subject. It is also a public subject, with ordinary citizens, particularly those motivated by religious convictions, weighing in again and again.

Benjamin Rush's writings can still sound urgent and independent to a modern reader. But in regard to punishment, at least, he was more a popularizer of existing thought than an innovator. The religious roots of the execution laws meant that in times of competing religious values, communities would argue about how best to punish, with punishment philosophies sometimes taking on the energy of religious fervor. As the United States began to define itself, that's what happened. The Revolution was fertile ground for new Protestant movements, many of which would have been condemned as "antinomian heresies" in earlier decades. In New England, the early Universalists and Unitarians began defining themselves as distinct from the Calvinists both because they disagreed with the doctrine of the Trinity and because they did not believe that all human beings bore the sin of Adam. If God was good, their thinking went, how could God's creation be evil?[33]

In the eighteenth and nineteenth centuries, the battle against corporal and capital punishments divided along religious lines—between the inheritors of Calvinism and religious minorities, such as the Quakers (who had been among the punished in many colonial American communities because they were seen as heretical). The argument, ostensibly about corporal punishment, was also about the nature of the soul. Those who believed man was born into sin tended to believe that physical hurt was a necessary component to punishment. Those who believed that people were good or neutral from birth looked on corporal punishment with disfavor. This division over meanings also affected child-rearing concepts and beliefs about corporal punishment in the schools, and it continues today.[34]

THE QUAKERS AND THE NEW PUNISHMENT TECHNOLOGY

The history of punishment reform in America is rife with examples of those who suffered the cudgel of the state and found in that experience inspiration to issue a call for humane treatment. Among the Quakers, a minority group that often faced discrimination, was William Penn, who spent a term at Newgate, the legendary London prison, as punishment for his refusal to take an oath, an act forbidden by his Quaker faith. In 1682, Penn sailed up the Delaware River, under the sanction of Charles II, to found Pennsylvania and to set out a new legal code. Penn did something extraordinary for his time. With the exception of floggings, Penn ended most forms of public torture, retaining capital punishment only in cases of murder. It was the beginning of reform in America, with Penn making the nearly unprecedented argument that crime prevention, restitution to the victim, and reform of the prisoner should be the sole purposes of punishment.[35]

From 1676 until Penn's arrival, Pennsylvania had been governed under its first set of laws, known as the Hempstead laws. Like the laws of New Haven, which the colony of Pennsylvania drew on as a model, the Hempstead laws derived from English common law. Capital crimes included the act of denying "the true God and his attributes," kidnapping, sodomy, buggery, murder, false witness in a trial involving a capital crime, invading a town or a fort, and smiting one's parents. This last crime indicates that the Pennsylvania code allowed for the execution of children. As the statute made clear, a conviction of smiting depended solely on parental testimony. "At the complaint of the said Father and Mother, and not otherwise, they being sufficient witness thereof, that Child or those Children so offending shall be put to death."[36]

Like other European-influenced statutes, the Hempstead code of Pennsylvania included a healthy helping of corporal pain. For instance, thieves received a mark with a hot iron on the brow. If caught a second time for the same crime, the recalcitrant thief got a second brand plus a whipping. The third time captured, the thief was to be put to death. Forgers received three days in the pillory, in addition to financial and other penalties.[37]

When Penn changed the laws of Pennsylvania, he was not acting alone but with the support of his fellow Quakers, members of the Chester Assembly. As the Hempstead laws had the backing of God and king, so did Penn draw on the authority of religious men. Before the Chester Assembly of Quakers left for their lives in the New World, they approved the "Laws Agreed Upon in England," which Penn had composed.[38]

One of the benefits of corporal punishment rarely noted by its critics is its low cost. The versions in place in the American colonies were also simplistic, in comparison to the technology Penn was about to propose: prison. Penn required counties in Pennsylvania to "build a sufficient house, at least twenty feet square, for restraint, correction, labor, and punishment of all such persons as shall be thereunto committed by law." According to Penn's code of laws, "all prisons shall be workhouses for felons, vagrants, and loose and idle persons. . . . All prisons shall be free, as to fees, food, and lodging."[39]

Other of Penn's ideas approved by the Chester Assembly included the choice between a five-shilling fine or five days in prison on a diet of water and bread as a punishment for blasphemy. Those guilty of "defiling the marriage bed" merited a whipping in public and a year in prison. (Those caught falling into the wrong arms more than once—whether in a case of adultery, sodomy, or incest—got life in prison.) Many other crimes received combination punishments of fines plus prison terms. Instead of death for smiting a parent, convicted children "were to be put in prison at hard labor for as long as the parent desired."[40]

The hard labor, the stripped diet, and the public whippings in William Penn's Pennsylvania may today seem harsh or even cruel. But, in Penn's time, these were astonishing decreases in punitiveness, and they attracted notice from overseas. The British government relieved Penn of his duties as proprietor in 1692, not long after the ascension of King William. Some historians suggest that Penn lost his job because of royal dissatisfaction with the Pennsylvania criminal code. He returned to proprietorship in 1694 to develop a second version of the code, one that allowed for more corporal punishment but that was still much milder than those in other colonies.[41] But the British government remained uncomfortable with Penn's reforms. After 1718, England required all government representatives in the colonies to swear an oath, a rule that effectively removed all Quakers from public office as their faith forbids the swearing of oaths. Penn died in that same year.[42]

After Penn's death, Britain began enforcing a more execution-heavy punishment code on Pennsylvania: "twelve crimes punishable by death, five by branding, one with the loss of ears, eight by whipping, two by servitude, thirteen by forfeiture, twelve by imprisonment, and five by fines. These penalties remained essentially the same throughout the remainder of the colonial period."[43]

But Penn had left his mark. Prison optimism took hold in the new republic. This is not to say that the prison is a uniquely American institution. Historian Pieter Spierenburg has shown that correctional houses held criminals in sixteenth-century Britain and northern Europe. Prior to the Revolutionary War, governments maintained jails primarily for containing suspects prior to trial. Some of these jails were notoriously easy to escape from, as the exploits of Jack Sheppard, the famous thief and British escape artist, make clear.[44]

By the late eighteenth century, a broad social shift favored prisons in Europe and America and "transformed the meaning of incarceration," writes Edward L. Ayers in *Vengeance and Justice: Crime and Punishment in the Nineteenth-Century American South*. "Social tensions created a receptive audience for the growing number of religious and secular thinkers in Europe, England, and America who attacked the inefficient and inhumane dungeons and corporal punishments of the past." After the American Revolution, England could no longer transport its criminals to that large expanse of the New World, and so searched out other technologies. Faced with an apparent crime wave, Americans sought practical solutions that suited their revolutionary goals.[45]

The late eighteenth-century prisons are modern partly because for the first time a philosophy shored up the physical structures. They are American not because Americans invented the buildings but because America *wanted* prisons more avidly than any other nation. It is arguable that Americans wanted prisons because they believed in a country based on freedom, the prison antithesis. Americans built their penitentiaries eagerly and prolifically, fiddling again and again with prison philosophy and punishment styles. For two centuries, the country acted as though it thought punishment perfectible.[46]

Shortly after the new country won independence, the state of Pennsylvania transformed an old jail into the first modern prison, the Walnut Street prison in Philadelphia. In 1776, Pennsylvania established in its constitution that the legislature should "proceed as soon as might be, to the reform of the penal laws, and invest in punishments less sanguinary, and better proportioned to the various degrees of criminality." The Walnut Street prison was renovated in 1790 to create small cells, segregating the most dangerous inmates into solitary confinement where, as punishment, they were not permitted to work. The Walnut Street prison also separated the sexes and banned liquor sales inside, thus setting the precedent for incarceration practices across the new country.[47]

Also in 1776, a group of Quakers invented the "Philadelphia Society for Assisting Distressed Prisoners," the first such organization in either Europe or the New World. The organization's name signals a profound leap in the public's perception of prisoners. Instead of understanding criminality as an identity marked on the body through physical hurt, many Americans began to see the convict as a person to be looked upon with pity, someone in need of aid. And with the prison, that profound technological and philosophical development in the history of humankind, came new ideas about punishment and criminality, many of them similar to the ideas Rush expounds in his letters and essays.

The modern prison took on energy in the American colonies, where drunkards and loud women had long suffered bodily punishments imposed by far-off governments. The prison was one of the ways that the new republic began to establish its identity as distinct from that of Britain.

The spirit of rebellion that led to the Revolutionary War had gained nearly as much energy from public humiliations and physical injuries as it had from unfair taxes. A distant king, who allowed neither the taxed nor the punished a say in their welfare, imposed all of these obligations. The sense that the British sovereign was both unfair *and* cruel added to the emergent nation's fervor for rebellion. Banning most hurtful bodily punishments and restricting the death penalty came to be seen as patriotic acts in the new republic.[48]

The dread of hanging for treason, in addition to the reputed barbarity of the British troops and of the loyalists to the crown who remained in the American colonies, led American revolutionaries, including Rush, to think of crime and punishment when they strove to distinguish themselves from the British.[49]

THE ENLIGHTENMENT AND RATIONAL PUNISHMENT

Although the founders of the United States were certain that they were embarking on a new experiment in contrast to the old cruelties of England, the U.S. debate did not happen in isolation. The founders were participants in the Enlightenment, an eighteenth-century international philosophical movement that stressed reason, rejected traditional authority and nationalism, and saw human society as progressive. Voltaire, John Locke, and Cesare Bonesa, marquis of Beccaria, had all suggested prior to the American Revolution that punishment could serve a less religious and more rational purpose. Prussia and Russia had both curtailed capital punishment.[50]

The letters, autobiographies, and other papers of the founders of the United States suggest that many of them read the writings of Beccaria, author of a 1764 volume entitled *On Crimes and Punishments*.[51] For Beccaria, retributive punishment, exacting a physical toll of the convict's body in payment to the state, was not in the best service of governments, which, he argued, should seek to decrease crimes through tactics such as education and rewarding "virtue" rather than revenge. Punishments should be less severe but more consistent; torture and capital punishment should be done away with altogether. "Is it possible that torments and useless cruelty, the instrument of furious fanaticism or the impotency of tyrants, can be authorised by a political body, which, so far from being influenced by passion, should be the cool moderator of the passions of individuals?" he asks, presupposing a beneficial and rational government. Suggesting the uselessness of revenge punishment, he adds a second question: "Can the groans of a tortured wretch recall the time past, or reverse the crime he has committed?"

Many of these ideas, whether from Beccaria or simply a response to the revolutionary spirit of the time, entered the debate of the founders as they attempted to determine what the new United States would become. In his autobiography, Thomas Jefferson indicates that at the time Virginia and the other twelve colonies were debating their futures, "Beccaria and other writers on crimes and punishments had satisfied the reasonable world of the unrightfulness and inefficacy of the punishment of crimes by death; and hard labor on roads, canals and other public works, had been suggested as a proper substitute."[52]

But, as Rush's eager advocacy suggests, there was also something homegrown—and religious—about much New World thought on punishment. The thinkers who were deciding to punish in a new way were aware of the novelty of the American experiment.[53]

The subject of punishment made some prominent appearances in revolutionary America. It turns up in the Declaration of Independence. The Declaration expresses concern about instances of false justice, in which the British government protected its own soldiers "by a mock-trial from punishment for any murders which they should commit on the inhabitants of these states." In the same sentence, the Declaration accuses Britain of punishing the American colonists under false pretenses, "depriving us in many cases of the benefits of trial by jury [and] transporting us beyond seas to be tried for pretended offences."

Again and again in his autobiography, Jefferson links punishment to other topics he considers critical to the success of the new republic. For a government of the people, he implies, careful controls so as to guarantee fair trials and punishments are essential. In discussing the Constitutional Convention of 1787, for instance, Jefferson expresses discomfort. "The absence of express declarations ensuring freedom of religion, freedom of the press, freedom of the person under the uninterrupted protection of the Habeas corpus, & trial by jury in civil as well as in criminal cases excited my jealousy. . . . I expressed freely in letters to my friends, and most particularly to Mr. Madison & General Washington, my approbations and objections."[54] The list of Jefferson's republican necessities is striking. They include what have become our understood freedoms: freedom of religion, freedom of speech. Next to these, he emphasizes the rights of those brought to trial and punished.[55]

In 1796, the Virginia legislature turned to the subject of punishment reform. (It had previously broached the issue in 1776.) "They adopted solitary, instead of public labor, established a gradation in the duration of the confinement," writes Jefferson. He had drawn one of the early designs for a modern prison, a building that would help to bring about the ameliorations in punishment that he desired, basing his drawings on a French prison built for extensive solitary confinement of inmates. Jefferson's architectural contribution was not without political implications; he wished to influence the debate. He submitted the drawing "in the hope that it would suggest the idea of labor in solitary confinement instead of that on the public works, which we had adopted in our Revised Code."[56]

Jefferson's architectural blueprint proved influential. Not only did the legislature adopt extensive labor in solitary confinement as one of its guiding standards, it also drew on Jefferson's idea for the prison. "Its principle accordingly, but not its exact form, was adopted by Latrobe in carrying the plan into execution, by the erection of what is now called the Penitentiary, built under his direction," Jefferson writes.

Jefferson's observation that prisons were being called by a new name is, strictly speaking, inaccurate. A version of the word "penitentiary" was identified with prisonlike church confines in medieval England. But Jefferson's writing captures the moment that a religious term made its way into the lexicon of the new democratic republic.[57]

Both Rush and Jefferson talked about punishment at length and often with passion. For these visionaries and politicians, punishment was not a subject one could speak of in isolation. Rather, in punishment was contained the new nation. What American punishment was, so too would America become. In retrospect, that perspective has proven prescient. Where punishment has headed, the rest of the nation has followed.

ENLIGHTENMENT EPILOGUE:
RETRIBUTION AND REPETITION

Benjamin Rush was characteristic of Enlightenment writers in his rhetoric of eager passion for change. His essays and letters reveal a man persuaded of his own rightness and enthusiastic about the new United

States he advocates as a humane departure from the old ways. Rush was loved in his time, a factor in his influence on the direction of the new nation. ("I know of no character," wrote John Adams, "who has done more real good in America.") So it is worth noting that two of Rush's popular ideas had a sometimes uncomfortable effect on their supposed beneficiaries.[58]

As others have noted, Rush and his contemporaries sometimes substituted extreme control for the public pain they decried.[59] For the mentally ill, Rush, who believed madness to be an overexcitement of the blood, designed a "tranquilizing chair." "I have lately designed a chair and introduced it into our hospital to assist in curing madness," he wrote in a letter to James Rush in 1810. "It binds and confines every part of the body. By keeping the trunk erect, it lessens the impetus of blood toward the brain. By preventing the muscles from acting, it reduces the force and frequency of the pulse, and the position of the head and feet favors the easy application of cold water or ice to the former and warm water to the latter. Its effects have been truly delightful to me. It acts as a sedative to the tongue and temper as well as to the blood vessels. In 24, 12, six, and in some cases four hours, the most refractory patients have been composed. I have called it a traquilizer." The chair included straps to bind the torso to the frame, the arms to the armrests, and the shins to the chair legs. Rush enclosed the bound person's head in a box.[60] Rush also shared the Quaker belief in the benefits of solitary confinement. He believed the method would act as an agent of conversion for those thus secluded.

Both long-term solitary confinement and the tranquilizing chair entered nineteenth-century prisons. Both caused controversy during that century. These control methods gained reputations not of kindness but of cruelty. Extensive solitary confinement, said its detractors, drove prisoners mad. Investigations showed that guards abused inmates in the tranquilizing chair.[61]

In the 1990s, the United States returned both to long-term solitary confinement and to something called the restraint chair, a close replica of Rush's original design. (The current versions of the device differ in one significant detail from Rush's version: while binding the body, they allow the head to remain free.) Prisons and jails seized on these two solutions. The return to control had—given the historical evidence—predictable results.

The restraint chair and extensive solitary confinement were Enlightenment inventions, born at a time when men like Benjamin Rush believed every person, including every criminal, had a heart attached to "one string by which it might be led back to virtue." Such beliefs in the neutrality or goodness of human beings guided the U.S. criminal justice system for nearly two centuries. And when the methods Rush advocated were later exposed as ineffectual and hurtful, prisons turned away from them.[62]

But twenty-first-century Americans live in a different society. Today, when both extensive solitary confinement and the restraint chair have again become common in jails and prisons across the country, complaints that such methods lead to hurt are no longer as effective as they once were.

In 2000, the United Nations Committee against Torture demanded that the United States "abolish electroshock stun belts and restraint chairs as methods of restraining those in custody" because use of such devices "almost invariably leads to breaches" of the international treaty against torture. The United States has banned neither device, and the chastisement from the United Nations did not lead to much public discussion. This perceived need for control and restraint devices, despite strong international censure, is the result of a marked cultural change.[63] In general, American culture no longer understands a criminal's heart as "not wholly corrupted."

CHAPTER 3

Reforming the Reforms

ON A HILL THAT ONCE bore a cherry orchard at the northern edge of Philadelphia rose a massive symbol of the land of the free—the Eastern State Penitentiary of Pennsylvania. The Philadelphia Society for Alleviating the Miseries of Public Prisons had prodded the state legislature for decades to construct such a building, and the society rejoiced in the structure. A pamphlet published by the society in 1830, when the building was partly finished and already housing inmates, devotes sentences to the "large sums" spent on the prison. Total expense when the building is finished, as reported in "A View and Description of the Eastern Penitentiary of Pennsylvania," "will be four hundred and thirty-two thousand dollars." The building was one of the most costly of its time.[1]

The pamphlet praises the new prison's "solidity and durability," grandeur, and size. It is "the most extensive building in the United States," taking up ten acres. Having emphasized "large masses" of gray stone that form the structure, the pamphlet turns to the edifice's moral meaning: the Eastern Penitentiary was a substantial spectacle not for those inside, but for the public. "The effect which it produces on the imagination of every passing spectator, is peculiarly impressive, solemn, and instructive."[2] The hope that the penitentiary's "large masses" would weigh on people's minds suggests proximity to a time when punitive pain in town squares instilled shame in the punished and warned onlookers.

The Eastern State Penitentiary façade both echoes the colonial past and departs from it. It displays and encloses punishment, shutting off the convicts from the view of the citizenry. It also ensures that the message the public receives will come from the punishers and not the punished, who at least while suffering agonies in the colonial American square had opportunities to appeal to their audiences.

Inmates housed inside the Eastern State Penitentiary probably saw little of the building's impressive façade. Regulations required prisoners to wear hoods whenever they left their cells, so as to discourage them from learning escape routes, speaking to guards, or seeking distractions from the silence that was supposed to seal their lives.[3]

Almost as revealing as the description of the prison façade is the attention given to the surrounding landscape in the pamphlet: "The Eastern State Penitentiary is situated on one of the most elevated, airy, and healthy sites in the vicinity of Philadelphia." The pamphlet endows the landscape with moral messages. The site, like the building, would lend the prisoner an "elevated" and "healthy" life. The ambitions of the penitentiary promoters were as grand as their rhetoric; they believed the building could improve people. But again, the prisoners would have had a difficult time viewing the scenery. At the Eastern State Penitentiary, a fortress-style wall surrounded the cellblocks and most inmate windows faced onto yet another wing of the prison.[4]

The Eastern Penitentiary is also, according to the pamphlet, a symbol of the "liberal, humane, and enlightened character of our commonwealth." At the same time that the prison conveys Enlightenment values, it displays power. "The Penitentiary is the only edifice in this country which is calculated to convey to our citizens the external appearance of those magnificent and picturesque castles of the middle ages, which contribute so eminently to embellish the scenery of Europe."[5]

Only fifty-four years after the American Revolution, in a nation founded on such phrases as "Give me liberty or give me death" and "All men are created equal," a potent symbol of the new United States has been found—in a prison. In a nation of liberty, the penitentiary flamboyantly displayed confinement. In a nation founded on equality, the massive enclosure declared that all people were not the same. And in a nation of independence, the high walls proclaimed the virtues of dependent populations. In the American penitentiary, we can find the attractions of the monarchical past and the contradictions of the American project. The penitentiary could compete with the castles of Europe not simply because of its bulk, but because a massive prison, like the grand castles, allowed some men to rule others.

Within this symbol of governmental strength, the pamphlet authors assured, all was to be kindness, conducted on behalf of the improvement of the inmates. "Every means which have been devised by philanthropy and experience for effecting reformation will be zealously applied."

Yet, even as it celebrated its hulking achievement, the society was on the defense. Those who favored a less expensive prison model had already attacked extensive solitary confinement as cruel. The pamphlet authors, who saw isolation as fundamental to their redemptive project, offered the Eastern State Penitentiary as evidence and protested that those who accused the new institution of hardness just didn't understand. "From this outline of the system it is obvious that the charge of cruelty, which ignorance and misrepresentation have attempted to attach to it, is untenable," they wrote. "The humane and intelligent, who have sanctioned its adoption in our community almost unanimously, certainly require no defence of the purity of their motives."[6]

Purity of motive was on display down to the building's name. "Let the name of this house convey an idea of its benevolent and salutary design, but let it by no means be called a prison, or any other name that is associated with what is infamous in the opinion of mankind," Rush had proclaimed. Rush was a founding member of the Philadelphia Society for Alleviating the Miseries of Public Prisons—the group that so desired the prison it would call by a very different name. "Penitentiary," for the moment, fulfilled the longing. With the newly popular word came a powerful metaphor. The inmates were more than criminals; they were religious penitents seeking repentance, forgiveness, and religiously inspired transformation. That any repentance from the inhabitants emerged under duress did not seem to trouble the penitentiary fans.[7]

The Eastern State Penitentiary of Pennsylvania was a panopticon—the prison model the British inventor and statesman Jeremy Bentham propounded. The panopticon design resembled an octopus with a central body (which housed the warden and the guards) and eight surrounding legs (cell blocks). Bentham's design allowed the guards to observe the prisoners at all times without being seen. This architectural pattern, which became for philosopher Michel Foucault a metaphor for surveillance and power in his 1979 classic *Discipline and Punish,* characterized several early American prisons.[8]

INDOOR PAIN

Despite assurances of benevolence, in practice, prison policies and cultures retained codes requiring repetitive inmate pain. In some cases, the pain that communities had employed out-of-doors moved inside. This was true of whipping, a common punishment both before and after reformers invented the penitentiary.

But the nineteenth century also saw painful innovations. The new prisons, by nature, corralled hundreds who didn't want to be there. As Foucault noted, an ideology of control guided penitentiary construction.[9] Day-in, day-out solitary confinement did not free inmates from extra measures of control, or from punishments that emphasized denial of their bodily needs. Common punishments in the Pennsylvania system, noted an anonymous pamphlet from the Boston Prison Discipline Society, included "being deprived of meals, put into a dark cell, and a straight jacket."[10]

Five years after the Eastern State Penitentiary received its first inmate, a legislative investigation found severe ill treatment. "It was substantiated beyond a question of a doubt that iron gags, strait jackets, the practice of ducking, mad or tranquilizing chairs, severe deprivations of food and more minor punishments were made use of, in some cases with severe results," writes historian Negley Teeters. Rush's tranquilizing chair, intended as a kindness, appeared as a torture machine.[11]

Cruelty was not isolated to Philadelphia. At the penitentiary in Pittsburgh, notes the pamphlet published by the Boston Prison Discipline Society, guards put disobedient prisoners into a box. Such a container, described as "just large enough to hold one man," would have restricted movement. It also hurt. The box is "so fixed, that the inmate cannot lean one way or the other; while, to prevent kneeling down, there is a piece of hard wood or iron put through the box," says the pamphlet. A disobedient inmate would have had to stand bolt upright. Painless at first, the box would shortly cause fatigue and, after hours, exhaustion and physical distress.[12]

In 1839, the *North American Review* reported, "In one case a man had died under the infliction of the gag," at the Eastern Penitentiary. "Another had been seriously injured by the profuse dashing of water upon him in mid-winter. Other cases existed of the excessive use of the strait jacket, of bruising, and confining prisoners in dark cells with only eight ounces of bread daily." The article concluded with an understatement: "These are sufficient to show, that the solitary system is, by no means, of necessity merciful."[13]

Within fifteen years of the opening of the first penitentiary in the world, prisons sprang up in Connecticut, Massachusetts, New Jersey, New York, Pennsylvania, and Virginia. Each featured extensive isolation.[14] But there were problems with solitude. In 1821, not long after a serious riot at Newgate Prison in New York State, the state separated out eighty-three of the most serious offenders for isolation, where they were to remain silent. A year later, five of those men had died, and many had lost their minds. One convict "jumped to his death as soon as his door was opened," reported the brochure for a recent exhibit on the Auburn prison. The state, in a panicked response, pardoned those who were still living and adopted what became known as the "silent system," also called the "Auburn system," a prison style that most of the country quickly imitated. The Auburn system housed inmates in solitary cells by night but allowed them to gather during the day for such activities as work, meals, and worship. This "silent" system forbade talking at all times.[15]

Beliefs that crime was communicable posed a challenge. Auburn, and many of the prisons that imitated it, often maintained disciplined silence via liberal use of the lash.[16] Punishment for talking and other infractions was commonly a flogging. In colonial governments, whippings had been ritualistic, public affairs, generally preceded by trial and often recorded in official documents. Such formalism did not suit the silent system.

"At the Sing-Sing prison they punish with whips," records the pamphlet of the Boston Prison Discipline Society. "In the workshops, under the elevated seats where the keepers sit, may be seen these implements, which the keepers have power to use on the bare back, without reporting the case, and without a hearing for the prisoner." New York's Auburn prison was a bit less informal: "The officers use cowhides. They inflict punishments without consulting a higher officer, and report their doings about once a month."[17]

Our contemporary use of such words as "lash," "whip," or "flog" usually means a single-stranded or a three-stranded braided rope or piece of leather. But in the mid-nineteenth century, American prison inmates were thrashed with a tool that ensured multiple blows for every swing. A popular weapon capable of causing excruciating pain, the "cat" (or cat-o'-nine-tails) was often handmade and consisted of a handle fastened to either six or nine leather thongs, each tied around a bullet.[18]

In a July 17, 1844, letter that the legendary reformer Dorothea Dix claims she received "from the Warden at the state prison at Auburn," the warden describes the process he used to determine that the cat was more humane and effective than isolation. "Close confinement is injurious and uncertain in its effects. I should resort to it if reasonable flogging proved insufficient," he wrote. "After much anxious reflection I have come to the conclusion, that moderate punishment with the cat, producing temporary smart, without permanent injury, is the most consistent with true humanity." He recognized, however, that even the cat could have drawbacks. "Where this punishment has been carried to excess, as has been at times the case in former years, both mind and health were permanently injured."[19]

Dix's writings indicate that other colonial torments had made their way indoors. "The *gag* is another form of punishment, which seems to me shocking and extremely objectionable; yet it is sometimes employed," writes Dix, who notes that guards had twice gagged an "incorrigible prisoner" in Philadelphia's Eastern State Penitentiary.[20] If the gag was not "a usual means of discipline" at the Eastern State Penitentiary, it seems to have been common at Sing Sing. "Application of the gag" often affected female mouths, as Sing Sing had a rule against lashing women.[21]

Water punishments also soaked criminal bodies. Guards rebuked inmate infractions with "*douche* or bolt-bath" at both the Trenton and the Auburn prisons, Dix says, but both wardens had stopped using the punishment. As the Auburn warden explained his decision to cease discipline by *douche* in his July 17, 1844, letter to Dix, "Punishment with cold water has often been most effectual, in subduing the refractory, but I believe is often detrimental to health, and has therefore been discontinued at this prison."[22]

Two years later, an inmate died due to what a local coroner's jury called "severe flagellation." The government responded with a new law: "No keeper in any state prison shall inflict any blows whatever upon a convict, unless in self-defense or to suppress a revolt or insurrection."[23]

And so, cold water returned to Auburn. A brochure accompanying a 2003 exhibit at the Cayuga Museum in Auburn, New York, offers a description of what contemporaries called "the shower bath." This "true torture device . . . consisted of a barrel about 4 1/2 feet high with a discharge tube at the bottom. The prisoner was stripped naked, bound hand and foot, with a wooden collar around his neck to prevent his moving his head. The barrel, with the inmate inside, was placed directly under an outlet pipe, where water, sometimes iced, would pour down."[24] The Auburn shower bath suffered a fate similar to that of the cat. It "was discontinued at Auburn Prison in 1858, after the death of an inmate from this punishment."[25]

By 1869, *Western Monthly*, a Chicago magazine, was boasting of the accomplishments of "the prison reform organizations of New York, Boston, and Philadelphia," which it credited with doing away with "many of the evils" in prisons. The motivating energy in bringing about these changes, claimed the publication, was "the spirit of Christianity," which ensured that "the lash, the shower bath, and other tortures which ignorance and cruelty invented for the punishment of prisoners, have now almost entirely disappeared from the State Prisons and Penitentiaries."[26]

SQUEAMISH REFORMERS

In *Discipline and Punish*, Foucault noted that the movement of the times was toward shutting away those who violated the law, so that punishment became, in Foucault's term, something "hidden." Foucault associated this shift with a state that had begun to feel shame about the punishments it enacted. Others, particularly the historian V. A. C. Gatrell in writing about the movement of British executions indoors, have suggested a middle- and upper-class "squeamishness": "Aversion to the scaffold crowd was the chief reason for abolition, but the higher squeamishness played its part too. At executions 'a new sheriff occasionally almost faints,' it was reported in 1866."[27]

American reformers were also squeamish about public executions. Charles Spear targets visceral squeamishness—discomfort at seeing another in physical pain— in his much-read 1844 book, *Essays on the Punishment of Death*. He includes several stories designed to show just how ghastly hanging can be and to create a brew of emotions in the reader. Composed of anxiety, squeamishness, disgust, and (somewhere in there) sympathy, these emotions furnished Spear and his public with a belief in their own humanity. Such words as "feeling," "sympathy," and "humane" recur throughout Spear's writings and those of his fellow reformers. Against "feeling," Spear places the "unfeeling," those who carry out the punishments: "The law stands all ghastly and bloody! There is the judge ready to pronounce the sentence! There is the cold, unfeeling sheriff ready to do its bidding."[28]

But even as the reformers complimented themselves with the language of sensibility and insulted those who punished as "unfeeling," their movement backfired. Executions did not end. They, along with other physical punishments, moved indoors.[29]

But there is more to the story of American punishment. While public punishment worried the reformers, what was happening *inside* the prisons, away from public view, also troubled the Pennsylvania society and other reform organizations.

In 1787, the Philadelphia Society for Alleviating the Miseries of Public Prisons published its constitution. In the preamble, its members announced their project as religious. Because of the Christian necessity to treat those who commit crimes with kindness, they determined, the society would "extend our compassion to that part of mankind who are the subjects of those miseries" inside prisons.[30] The preamble suggests that the Philadelphia Society was from its beginning cognizant of the mistreatment that could hide away in prisons. "By the aid of humanity, their undue and illegal sufferings may be prevented."[31]

The society demanded changes. In fall 1788, a later article reports, "the following defects and abuses were indicated in the treatment of prisoners." The list includes "insufficient clothing for the untried" (the clothing the society was sending into the prison for poor inmates was "taken by force" and "exchanged for rum"); extreme lack of food for some prisoners ("the daily allowance to persons committed for trial was only a half of a four-penny loaf, while those detained as witnesses had no allowance at all"); lack of beds ("the inmates of the gaol lying indiscriminately upon the floor, unless supplied with something better by their friends"); "promiscuous association" of inmates of different sexes, who were "even locked up together in the rooms at night"; the "indiscriminate intermingling of criminals, untried prisoners and debtors," which, the society argued, "led, in many instances, to the conversion of debtors and innocent parties into criminals"; children of the prisoners housed in the jail and "exposed to all the corrupting influences of association with confirmed and reckless villains"; and idle prisoners.[32]

Fifty years later, the society was still investigating the prison. In April 1849, it uncovered racial disparities: "The attention of the Society was called to what was alleged to be a marked difference between the length of sentences passed on colored convicts compared with those passed on whites, and also the comparative mortality of the two classes."[33]

A process of experiment and critique continued into the late twentieth century. When the sick failed to heal and the penitent lost faith, prison reformers took note. Reformers both inside and outside the heavy walls managed to reinvent the prison and shield the prison from controversy, by critiquing it and changing it themselves.[34]

THE COUNTER-REFORMERS

Reform had more than one voice in nineteenth-century America. "We are told by a class of objectors to the death penalty that it is a relic of a barbarous age, and if once proper, is no longer so when society has made such advances as we now behold," writes the Reverend Timothy Alden Taylor in a book published in Massachusetts in 1850. "Our reply to this is, that capital punishment originated with the Most High; that it was enacted as a legal, civil statute on earth in the purest period of the world since sin entered the Garden of Eden."[35] Among Taylor's complaints is what he perceives as misplaced sympathy. "The victim of his appalling deed is immediately forgotten; the wife who has been made a widow, and the children who have been rendered fatherless in consequence of the assassin's blow are left to weep in unpitied solitude, while the wretch who has filled them with grief and covered them with mourning is embraced by numberless comforters."[36]

Southern prisons resembled the heavy structures of the northern cities, and the southern states constructed them at about the same rate.[37] But southern criticisms of incarceration were many.

Edward Ayers in *Vengeance and Justice: Crime and Punishment in the Nineteenth-Century American South* describes the northern states as invested in "dignity," or "the conviction that each individual at birth possessed an intrinsic value at least theoretically equal to that of every other person," however much society violated that principle in practice.[38] Dignity motivated its believers like a religion and contributed to the North's enthusiasm for penitentiaries. As the nineteenth and twentieth centuries progressed, reformers extended the mantle of dignity to more and more people—slaves, prisoners, workers, immigrants, children—who in an earlier century would not have sheltered beneath dignity's folds.[39] By contrast, the early American South celebrated "honor," which, writes Ayers, applied to "only adult white males."[40]

For those skeptical about dignity, government intervention in the lives of convicts seemed like serious overreaching. "To Southerners at the time and to many subsequent historians, the element of coercion that lay behind so many of these reforms seems to make a mockery of dignity," writes Ayers.[41]

"How is this pretended humanity to be exercised?" questioned Louis Reneau, a Tennessee state representative, in 1826. "It is by taking a man who by the present law can only be sentenced to have a few stripes, and a few weeks imprisonment, and shutting him up in the penitentiary, there to be kept at hard labour, and to be whipped and driven at the whim and pleasure of his master." The word "master" reveals a tactic disgruntled southerners employed—comparing the penitentiary to slavery.[42]

For some critics, the new prisons were "dangerously unrepublican" because they "hid the coercion of the state from its citizens," writes Ayers, who quotes a Georgia politician asking the perceptive question, "Which was the more barbarous, to whip at the whipping post, or to turn them over a barrel within the walls of the Penitentiary and paddle them?"[43]

If the debate over punishment never ended, the voices of Taylor and other southern critics were muted for about two hundred years. But when they gained power again in the late twentieth century, they did so with gusto.[44]

GOD'S CHILDREN OR GOD'S MADMEN?

Day-in, day-out solitary confinement was supposed to heal spirits. In a tiny cell, with the company of only the Bible, the guards, and spiritual advisers, former crooks were expected to become God seekers. Such metaphors as "child" and "religious penitent" implied the treatments prisoners were to receive. "It is with convicts as with children; unseasonable

indulgence indiscreetly granted, leads to mischiefs which we may deplore, but cannot repair," wrote the reformer Dix, implying a child/
prisoner-raising strategy of guarded rewards.[45]

But once "separate system" prisons were up and running, critics
began to say that years of loneliness could indeed change crooks. Change
them into madmen.

As the penitentiary model spread from Pennsylvania to other locations, some new prisons while incorporating solitude also deemphasized
it. This was true in places that followed what became known as the New
York, or Auburn, system, also called the silent system, which, in addition
to solitary cells, maintained open areas where inmates could congregate.
"The great difference of the two prisons is this: at Pittsburg, the prisoners
sleep in their cells; work in their cells; receive instruction in their cells;
worship in their cells, and (what shall I say?) have a soil-pan in their cells,"
notes the anonymous author of a nineteenth-century pamphlet. The author contrasts this thoroughly confined inmate life with a prison in Massachusetts: "At Charlestown, the prisoners sleep and eat in their cells;
work in the shops; worship in the chapel; receive instruction in the chapel,
in the shop, at the cell doors, or wherever the warden, chaplain, inspec-
tors, or other authorized persons, wish to communicate it." Pittsburgh,
the writer makes clear, is modeled on the Pennsylvania system advocated
by Rush. Charlestown is more akin to that featured in the Auburn, New
York, prison. Because of its ability to bring inmates together in groups for
such events as work duty or worship, the Auburn system proved less
expensive than the Pennsylvania model. The pamphlet makes this claim
often enough to suggest it is authored by someone who is as concerned
with finances as he is with the well-being of prisoners.[46]

But the writer of the pamphlet makes some troubling criticisms.
Quoting from prison documents, he traces several years in the life of the
Philadelphia and Charlestown prisons. On January 1, 1838, for instance,
the physician of the "New Penitentiary" in Philadelphia reported "fourteen cases of dementia," all of which the physician attributed to masturbation (also called "the solitary vice" and "onanism" in this pamphlet). The
Charlestown physician, by contrast, recorded no such cases. In January
1839, the medical reports showed a similar trend: eighteen in Philadelphia, one in Charlestown. And on January 1, 1840, Philadelphia recorded
twenty-six prisoners with symptoms of mental illness: "*White prisoners,*

thirteen; colored prisoners, thirteen; mania, one; monomania, one; hallu-
cination, seven; dementia, nine; other forms of diseased mind, eight;
caused by the solitary vice, fifteen; by intemperance, four; unknown,
seven."[47] In Charlestown, characterized by the silent system the author
prefers, things were different. "No case of insanity is mention by the
physician for the year ending September 30, 1839."[48]

The pamphlet also lists the death rate in the Pennsylvania-style prisons as much higher than that at Charlestown. "Dividing the number of
prisoners by the number of deaths, it gives one death in twenty-five prisoners at Pittsburg, Penn.," whereas the Charlestown prison reported a
single death among 171 prisoners.[49] The author does not make clear what
he believes caused the differences in death rates.

Among those the pamphlet quotes is a doctor at a New Jersey penitentiary modeled on the Pennsylvania version, who suggested that some of
the childlike qualities so idealized by reformers of the day might have
been symptoms not of redemption but of mental breakdown. "Among the
prisoners, there are many cases of insanity," reported the doctor in 1840.
Although some of the convicts had shown evidence of mental illness
when admitted, "there are many who exhibit a childlike simplicity, which
shows them to be less acute than when they entered." The childlike traits
appeared with time and affected all of the inmates "who have been more
than a year in the Prison." The doctor, who attributed insanity to "onanism," suggested that the development of mental "softening" was likely to
reduce crime. He thus advocated isolation as a way of encouraging a soft,
childlike mind. "Continue the confinement for a longer time, and give
them no other exercise of the mental faculties than this kind of imprisonment affords, and the most accomplished rogue will lose his capacity for
depredating with success upon the community."[50]

But, the physician suggested a more dire future for convicts who did
not receive the benefits of "kind usage, religious and moral instruction,"
that he witnessed at the New Jersey Penitentiary. "Were another course
pursued in this institution . . . in less than a year the New Jersey Penitentiary would be a Bedlam."[51] Instead of leading penitent criminals to conversion, critics maintained, solitary confinement destroyed their minds.

Many European countries adopted the Pennsylvania model, and
American advocates trumpeted this widespread affection as proof that the
separate system was beneficent. In an 1847 pamphlet about the prevalence

of the Pennsylvania system in France, a Mr. Sumner, a resident of Boston traveling in Europe, recounts the words of Count Dichatel, minister of the interior for France. Like his counterparts in America, the minister understood extreme captivity as permitting spiritual freedom. "The cell must be regarded as a means of living alone, and in a state of complete moral liberty," Dichatel tells Sumner. "The system of separate imprisonment is one of protection rather than of constraint. The cell of the prisoner is his house." Having removed criminals from their previous, presumably unfit, homes, the cells become enclosures of domestic tranquility.[52]

Sumner continues, demonstrating the French liking for convict solitude. "There are now twenty-three of these prisons occupied and many more in the course of construction. In all of them which I have visited,— what with their wooden floors and doors, their nicely painted walls, their fountains and garden walks,—there is a neatness and an air of comfort and cheerfulness, which would surprise those, who in America, have conjured up horrors at the idea of separation." The paint, "neatness," "garden walks," and "cheerfulness" all emphasize an idealized, large, well-kept home where a man, tired of public life, might make his retreat.[53] In European penitentiaries, argues Sumner, death and sickness among the inmates who live in solitude are rare. So is mental illness.[54]

Sumner, like other reformers of his day, uses the language of kindness and comfort in his discussion. The noun "abuse" also appears frequently, suggesting a struggle over its meaning. Sumner uses the word to condemn the city of Boston's plan to do away with solitary confinement, a rumor he heard from the French undersecretary of state for the interior. He warns that his hometown "will certainly enjoy an unenviable notoriety if it determine to defy public opinion, to reject the example of wise governments, and to maintain an abuse, which the voices of so many wise and good men have been raised to denounce." The abuse, for Sumner, is not years of isolation but the endangering of men's souls through exposure to other criminals.[55]

But while reformers praised the French penitentiaries and haggled over the meaning of "abuse," European prisoners in solitary were, like their American counterparts, losing their minds.

"The American penitentiary, and the Philadelphia System, became world-famous; no important visitor to the United States neglected to tour its penitentiaries and to bring back their principles for emulation in Europe," writes former Harvard Medical School psychiatrist Stuart Grassian. "The results of this national experiment with prolonged solitary confinement were catastrophic. The incidence of mental disturbances among prisoners so detained, and the severity of such disturbances, was so great that the system fell into disfavor and was ultimately abandoned."[56]

Scandinavian countries relished solitary confinement. The Danish Institute for Human Rights tells the story of a farmhand named Henrik Nielsen who in 1866, at eighteen years of age, was sentenced to imprisonment at Vridsløselille penitentiary. "Henrik was in good health when arriving, and the initial phase of his imprisonment seemed to go well," reports the human rights group. But, after a time, "It was recorded in the prison files that Henrik hallucinated; in particular, he started hearing things. He believed that someone bore him ill will, and that the warders wished to harm him. Henrik was generally very timid and anxious. After this the young man was assigned work in the open air, but upon his return to the cell he became completely deranged. Henrik Nielsen was then moved to a mental hospital in the province of Vordingborg."[57]

Nielsen was one among thousands. An 1890 ruling by the U.S. Supreme Court noted that as a result of solitary confinement, "[a] considerable number of the prisoners fell, after even a short confinement, into a semi-fatuous condition, from which it was next to impossible to arouse them, and others became violently insane; others still, committed suicide; while those who stood the ordeal better were not generally reformed, and in most cases did not recover sufficient mental activity to be of any subsequent service to the community." The Court suggested that in the mid-nineteenth century, "the whole subject attracted the general public attention, and its main feature of solitary confinement was found to be too severe."[58]

In Europe, popular opinion also turned against the punishment method that once seemed humane. Even Denmark ended the practice. "The Scandinavians were, rather interestingly, much more reluctant to leave behind large-scale isolation, but solitary confinement was abandoned in Vridsløselille during the 1930s."[59]

Use of solitary confinement declined over the course of most of the twentieth century. But in the 1980s and 1990s, despite the lessons of the nineteenth century, long-term isolation again seemed a good idea. When Grassian presented testimony in 2005 to the Commission on Safety and

Abuse in United States Prisons, an organization funded by the Vera Institute of Justice, he spoke of the past as a means of addressing contemporary concerns—the return of madness to isolated prisoners, now housed in the new supermax prisons.

THE STORY OF HARRIE

In 1871, a man who called himself "Harrie" published *An Illustrated History and Description of State Prison Life by One Who Has Been There. In Two Parts: One Showing the Cruelties and Horrors of the Old System; the Other, the Reformatory Advantages from the New. Together with a True and Detailed Account of the Maltreatment and Cruelties Formerly Practiced upon Prisoners; also, Shame-Faced Criminalities with Female Convicts, Mutinies, Murders, Starvings, Whippings, Hair-Breadth Escapes, Sketches and Incidents, Narratives and Pen-Pictures, Sunshine and Shade, Illustrative of Prison Life.* If that title is not enough to tickle curiosity, Harrie provides an affidavit of sorts: "WRITTEN BY A CONVICT IN A CONVICT'S CELL. THE AUTHENTICITY OF WHICH IS VOUCHED FOR BY THE HIGHEST OFFICIALS AND COMMITTEES."[60]

Harrie claims to be writing from the state prison in southern Indiana where he is serving a sentence for a crime he does not name. Halfway through his tale of penitentiary life, he offers a mini-history of U.S. punishment. Nineteenth-century reformist pamphlets often provided such histories, making the present look good by comparison with past cruelties. But though reform is Harrie's aim, he decries the end of corporal punishment. The exchange of "the gallows, the whipping post, and the pillory," for the penitentiary was a merciless one, he argues. "These modes of punishment . . . were really not more barbarous and degrading to humanity than the corporal punishment almost daily inflicted on convicts in the penitentiary, with that more modern and facile instrument known as the 'cat-o'-nine-tails.' "[61]

Not only were the punishments of the American colonies "civilized," Harrie insists they were downright mild. "Standing in the pillory a few hours on court-day, exposed to public gaze, or the application of a few stripes, generally laid on very lightly by the sheriff of the county, though humiliating, were by no means cruel or unreasonable penalties for grand larceny, arson, burglary, and other crimes of greater turpitude."[62]

Unlike the southern penitentiary critics motivated by a culture of honor, Harrie believed in the dignity of his fellow prisoners. He wrote for an audience of reformers, those who called for improvements in the treatment of inmates but who also tended to invest their faith in the potential of prisons to wreak powerful, conversion-style changes in their inhabitants. This audience would have found Harrie's declaration shocking.

In the context of the treatment Harrie claims he witnessed, his nostalgia for colonial punishments is more than reasonable. Shortly after he entered the prison, a guard gave him a list of rules to read. Several of them described the requirement of absolute quiet—a clue that the southern Indiana prison was an Auburn- or silent-style one. The list ended with these two sentences: "For all violation of the prison rules the laws of the State authorize the warden to inflict such punishment as he may deem necessary. This authority will be exercised in all cases when it is necessary to secure strict discipline and obedience to the prison rules and regulations." The warden of the Indiana prison served as the judge and jury for physical punishments, as did other wardens at the time.

The guard returned and asked Harrie whether he had read the list. When Harrie answered that he had, the guard emphasized the final, broad policy.

> "Did yer notice the last one?"
>
> "Yes, sir."
>
> "Well, sir! Do you know what we do with men here for punishment?"
>
> "No, sir."
>
> "We lick 'em! shirt 'em, and lick 'em! and, mind you now! if yer hit a lickin here yer'll carry it to yer grave; come on now!"[63]

By "carry it to yer grave," the guard meant that the whippings left scars.

Harrie invited his readers to peer at a scene reformers were unlikely to glimpse. "There, surrounded by half a dozen fiends in human shape; naked and upon his knees, is the poor fellow who just passed us on his way to the office," Harrie writes, his vision transforming the crowd of guards into agents of the underworld:

> A powerful brute stands over him, grinning like a fiend incarnate. In his brawny hand he holds that merciless instrument of torture, the cat-o'-nine-tails; rising upon his toes, he brings the

hard-twisted, bullet-tipped thongs *down* upon the poor victim's bare back, each blow counting nine lashes, eating into the tender flesh, and drawing forth the shrieks of pain we heard. Five blows are struck, counting forty-five lashes, when his torturer stops for breath.

"Talkin' in yer sleep, was yer?"

"Yes, sir!" sobs the victim, "If I talked at all, I talked in my sleep."

"Well, d——n yer! if yer can't sleep without talkin', yer had n't better sleep. Here, Jo! give him five more."[64]

For the Calvinists, crime was the work of the Devil and physical punishment the demand of God, but in this scene representatives of the underworld are not criminals but government agents. "Fiend," the word Harrie repeatedly associates with the guards, means "Devil," "demon" (both words associated with the Christian concept of Hell), and "an extremely cruel person," according to the *Merriam-Webster Dictionary.* Like Harrie's claim that public, corporal punishments are preferable to mistreatment inside prisons, this symbolic reversal was designed to shock his reform-minded readers, many of whom were liberal Christians who saw punishments as, at least in potential, godly pursuits. As if to skewer the conscience of his audience, Harrie comments, "Let us draw a veil over the scene; let us not listen to his groans, his prayers, or his curses. Think you *he* will reform?"[65]

The Southern Indiana State Penitentiary made private the once-public whippings, increased pain with the cat, and made arbitrary use of the lash. "This is not much of a document, but it is enough upon which to get you whipped," Harrie writes—"document" meaning the guard's claim against an inmate. The prisoners, whom Harrie calls "victims" (turning conventional crime-and-punishment vocabulary on its head), did not learn that they were up for punishment until they received the command to *"strip for the cats!"* Harrie reports that the inmates saw no one but the men who whipped them. A word with the warden was out of the question, as was an appeal. "Very often the men do not know for what they are punished," notes Harrie. "No questions are tolerated!"[66]

In one morning, as many as thirty inmates might be "catted," Harrie reports. A single cat involved nine lashes. "Twenty-seven lashes, or three 'cats' are the least ever given," Harrie writes. "Some will take ninety or a hundred without flinching or uttering a groan. But as they come out, the white lips and set teeth tell how they have suffered."[67]

In this depiction of prison life, the prisoners offer each other mercy and a gentle touch. Harrie writes of a man "who had received *two hundred and seventy* lashes." Harrie describes pulling the man's shirt, caked with blood, up from his skin. "I have loosed it, the bruised skin coming away in places with the coarse shirt, and covered the raw flesh with oil. As I did so, my heart has grown sick and my head dizzy."[68]

The act of touching the skin with oil is a New Testament reference; the disciples of Jesus anointed him. With this image, Harrie turns the "catted" prisoner into the opposite of the "fiends" who whipped him. He becomes holy in his physical pain and his anointment. It is no accident that Harrie next turns to a religion-tinged censure of the reformers: "Oh, ye prison philanthropists! Why do ye not, instead of surfeiting us with tracts, and words that can only produce contempt under this treatment, *remedy our wrongs?*"[69]

Harrie also has choice words for the misuse of punitive work. Punishment reformers of the eighteenth and nineteenth centuries placed a high value on labor, which the convicts were to perform whenever not engrossed in sleeping, eating, Bible study, or worship. As the author of *A View and Description of the Eastern Penitentiary of Pennsylvania* explains, "The labour in which the convict will be employed, is considered as an alleviation, not an aggravation of his sentence." Work will seem appealing "perhaps for the first time in his life, as a means of preventing uneasy feelings, of producing relief and pleasure." Guards sometimes punished disobedient inmates at the Eastern State Penitentiary by *prohibiting* them from work.[70]

Toil does not offer the inmates "relief"; rather, it helps to relieve several of them of their lives. Harrie tells the story of William Board, a big young man. "He was the largest man in the prison, and a noble-looking fellow." When Board took ill, he received a job assignment that guaranteed he would not recover easily. Board "was put at work upon the brickyard," a job change not so much for Board's benefit. "Men are not put at work here until they are weakened down by sickness, for fear, if they are well and strong, they will run off," comments Harrie.[71]

The brickyard was not a plum job: the yard "is situated outside the walls, is without shelter, and intolerably hot. The poor fellows who work here come dragging themselves in at night, so tired that it is with difficulty they gain their cells." Board was a dedicated laborer. He resisted the pleas of his fellow prisoners to seek a doctor, saying "that if he went to the hospital he would never come out alive." But "one day he had been pushed very hard; that night he was so ill that, time and again, he asked to be taken to the doctor." The guards did not respond to his requests. The next morning, "he was carried to the hospital, and in *five* hours this great strong man was a corpse—worked to death!"[72]

Work is a theme in the death of Patrick Maher, known to the inmates as "Crazy Pat." When Maher first arrived at the prison, Harrie says, he "was deranged." Even so, he "would still do what was told him, and work very well if let alone and not urged." But the work ethic didn't last. After committing what Harrie terms a "slight absent-mindedness," Maher endured a lashing. "He returned to the shop raving, and absolutely refused to work," according to Harrie. The guard sent Maher to the office, where he again endured another whipping "and a ball and chain ordered on him," in addition to a diet of bread and water. After several days, the guards again ordered Pat to work, but "he would only jabber Irish and grow wild."[73]

The guards placed shackles on Maher's hands and feet and let him sit near the shop door. Harrie reports that the guard in charge of the shop resented Pat's new privilege. " 'If he won't work, I'll make it hell for him any way,' said he, and taking Pat to the office, he got a straight-jacket added to the other irons."[74]

The straitjacket that Harrie describes bears little resemblance to the fabric styles that bound the arms to the back. It "consists of a bar of iron reaching from the top of the head to the small of the back," writes Harrie. "About six inches from the top is a clasp ring which passes around the neck, completely throttling its victim. At the shoulders there is a cross-bar with a ring on each end. Through these rings the arms are passed, and then the upper ring clasped around the throat." The position may sound uncomfortable, but it is relaxed in comparison with what comes next. "By means of a screw at the back, all of these are now tightened, drawing the shoulders back, the head up, and the victim straight as an arrow. It is impossible to move the shoulders or back, and if the head is moved, the iron collar around the neck strangles the victim."

According to Harrie, the guards would keep Maher in the straitjacket until the man began to faint. Then they would remove the device from his body, "and sometimes a bucketful of cold water thrown upon him to keep him from playing off, as they called it." Harrie blames the straitjacket for turning "poor, addled Pat" into "a raving maniac."[75]

Once the straitjacket came off, guards chained Maher during the day to a ball and at night to an anvil. When Maher grew agitated, the guards experimented. "I'll stop his running and jerking around," announced the warden in response to Maher's thrashing. The warden summoned a guard with a body-sized sack. "After a severe struggle," during which time Maher bit the warden's finger, "he was got into the sack, with his handcuffs still on, and it sewed close about his neck." The warden then began to tease Maher. "And taking a stout linen handkerchief from his pocket, he would whip it about Pat's face, until he would snap at it with his teeth; then, after letting him get a good hold, he would give it a sudden jerk." Meanwhile a guard who stood close to Patrick "would kick him in the breast and side."[76]

Later, guards removed Maher from the body sack. After that, "they never opened his cell-door again until they opened it to carry him to his grave." The prison staff rationed Patrick's food. "Sometimes for two days he would have nothing but water; then F——r would come down and throw him some bits of corn bread, as you would throw food to a caged animal," writes Harrie. Maher responded in kind. "And much like a famished beast would poor Pat grabble up the last fragments and eat them."

After about seven weeks of such treatment, Maher expired. Harrie uses the event to press his religious argument. "My reader, Patrick Maher was *starved to death!*" he writes. "He died alone, in his iron-bound cell, with no eye but God's upon him. The angel who recorded his death recorded its *manner,* and at the same time wrote that fearful indictment upon which his murderers must be tried *in the day of judgment.*"[77]

Not all is a hell of ill treatment in Harrie's 500-plus-page memoir of prison life. On page 221, scandal arrives at the Southern Indiana State Penitentiary, and by page 225, the investigating committee fires the warden. After that, things changed for the better.[78]

Harrie devotes the second half of his book to explaining the positive effects that could be realized if inmates were treated well. "Why, I have seen the hardened criminal, the brutal murderer, weep at the gambols of an innocent child," he writes. "Was not each tear a message from the heart that told of buds there, ready to burst into a new life?"[79]

Harrie's insistence on the humanity of those around him and on their goodness continues to the end. In the book's final pages, Harrie receives a pardon that will allow him to return to his wife and child. He begins "crying" and comments, "I tell you there are men within yonder walls whose friendship we value. Many poor fellows who, although they have been unfortunate, carry within their striped jackets honest hearts."[80]

Sentimentalized portrayals of captive groups characterized reformist writings throughout the nineteenth century. The rhetorical practice, which was broad enough to include women and children, captives of the home, implied the worth of the speaker or writer. Earlier, in the eighteenth century, what became known as "sensibility," or the capacity to feel deeply, became a moral marker.[81]

By the 1830s, a sympathetic understanding of physical pain became a critical emotive force in the antislavery movement. Although "slaves had suffered for many generations," writes historian Elizabeth B. Clark, "in the 1830s their stories became newly audible and visible in the North, where graphic portrayals of slaves' subjective experience of physical pain emerged as common antislavery fare." The genre of the slave narrative, argues Clark, "served as a vehicle for new arguments for a 'right' to bodily integrity." Clark argues that shifts in liberal and evangelical philosophy, a broad phenomenon that encompassed many different churches as the influence of Calvinism faded, led to a pervasive turn against both godly and human cruelty.[82] In addition to the physical hurts of slavery, reformers focused their sympathetic energies on other forms of suffering, including wife and child beatings, bodily hurt to animals, and corporal punishment in mental hospitals and prisons. The language of rights communicated in the Constitution began to extend to individuals the original document did not name.[83]

By the mid- to late nineteenth century, when Harrie wrote his book, these moral values were in full leaf. The burgeoning anticruelty movement is visible in the organizations devoted to animals that appeared in the United States in the decades after the Civil War. The first animal welfare organization in the United States opened in 1866. By 1870, there were similar societies in five states, writes Jennifer Mason, and by the

1890s, "Every major U.S. city and quite a few small towns had a society for the prevention of cruelty to animals."[84]

As Mason points out, the theme of animal cruelty appeared in American literature of the period, including works by Harriet Beecher Stowe and Nathaniel Hawthorne. Often, the invocation of cruelty against animals allowed writers to address other social issues. For instance, the African-American writer Charles Chesnutt repeatedly uses the figure of dog killings to address the charged subject of lynching.[85] Chesnutt could assume his contemporary readers would understand the implications of dog killing because the humane movement of the time was not isolated from other social movements, including abolition. In 1890, when the novel *Black Beauty* appeared, it bore on its title page the words, "The Uncle Tom's Cabin of the Horse."[86]

AFFECT AND THE PRISONER

In American literature about prisoners, emphasis on a convict's capacity to feel paralleled the rise of the reformers. In his anecdote about the beer-drinking wheelbarrow man who loved his dog, Rush emphasized the word "heart." That "heart" became evident because the criminal showed devotion to a dog.

But Harrie's use of "heart" has traveled a distance from Rush's. If Rush's analysis leaves room for a "heart" to be almost but not "wholly corrupted," Harrie's idealized prisoners have, despite their crimes, fully "honest hearts." Even if capable of murder, those hearts can "burst into a new life." Thus Harrie's emphasis, in his descriptions of his fellow convicts, on words like "hearts" and "weep" or "crying."

Sentimentality, particularly when applied to those under government control, was a potent thing, as both Harrie and the artist who illustrated his book seem to have realized. The book's first illustration shows Harrie arriving home after a government pardon. He has placed his hat on the ground and is kneeling, his wife's hand in his. In the pleasant room with the accoutrements of comfort and an impressive portrait on the wall, a child sleeps under a canopy. The prisoner is a gentleman.[87]

CHAPTER 4

Punishment Creep

SIMILARITIES CAN BE FOUND among nineteenth-century punishments in closed societies, locations—such as schools, ships, and plantations—without extensive public oversight and where one group of people
controls another. Partly because of the lack of outside regulation, partly
because of the intensive day-in and day-out nature of relationships in
closed environments, punishment there can acquire an extreme cast.

Perhaps the easiest way to convey this understanding of punishment
history is to compare corporal punishments in the public square—a fixed
number of lashings, a letter branded on the forehead, a tongue bored
through with a hot iron, a lopped-off ear—with the migration of similar
hurts into Harrie's penitentiary. Although the public square mutilations
were agonizing for the punished, the convict often went free afterward. In
the Southern Indiana State Penitentiary, the suffering happened over and
again, without judge or jury, the extent of the hurt determined not by the
law but by those who guarded, cared for, supposedly sought the reform of,
and presumably feared and felt aggravated by their charges. In some
cases, drawn-out tortures meant death, although the victim was serving a
prison—not a capital—sentence.

Punishment wanders in many directions, and its vectors are often unclear. We can trace a few of them, however. Physical punishments of the sort
that involve intentional pain tend to have religious sources. Just as corporal

punishment of prisoners derived from medieval church law,[1] nineteenth-century corporal punishment of children and of slaves has religious roots. Corporal punishment of military rule breakers follows the pattern of prisoner corporal punishment, with the one who has wounded the community —in this case the military community—feeling retributive hurt.

Punishments that focus on individual liberty (or lack of it) and internal transformation, in contrast, have their source in the Enlightenment thought and liberal religious philosophy that enthralled Benjamin Rush. Confinement and liberty are aspects of individuality; without freedom, one cannot define and determine oneself.

Sometimes, though, punishment appears to wander from one societal group to another. Lancastrian schools, with their emphasis on extreme restraint, showed up in this country in the 1790s, the same decade that the penitentiary, with its accent on severe confinement, became popular. Harrie reports that his prison ended physical cruelties in the 1860s, the same decade the Emancipation Proclamation freed the slaves and the Humane Society of the United States was formed. In the late twentieth century, treatments used first on criminals and suspects—police officers but also devices such as tasers—entered public schools.

In American history, punishment methods have never stayed put in the places where we tend to think of them—in cells with crooks. Especially when they appear innovative, punishments tend to enter, among other places, schools. It is important to look at American prisons partly because they often indicate what happens elsewhere.

Punishment and control methods can travel through time as well as space. Thus we find Benjamin Rush's tranquilizing chair resurfacing as a control device in late twentieth-century jails and prisons. Repetitions of public punishments from the past reappear these days in some churches and families (see chapter 7).

The eighteenth- and nineteenth-century reminiscences of American schoolchildren, members of the military, and slaves still speak of suffering, to those who seek their words. Each of these closed worlds contained men, and sometimes women, who functioned as guards, though they bore other titles: schoolmaster, captain, overseer. And because schools had doors, plantations had property lines, and ships found isolation on the seas, methods that communities had come to regard as inappropriate for convicts often lingered on in the privacies these locations afforded. Both the Reverend Warren Burton and the American antiquarian Alice Morse Earle, writing in the late nineteenth century, note that some schoolteachers made use of "a chip perpendicularly between the teeth" or cleft sticks pinched onto vocal children's tongues, sometimes with the leaves still attached. This punishment echoed the gags and sticks applied in colonial times to scolding or gossipy females and to male liars and blasphemers.[2]

The warning the history of punishment creep provides rings loudly in this chapter. Whatever horror and harm criminals inflict on our society, Americans need to care about the treatment they receive. We cannot afford to avoid such concern. Narrow arguments about the hardening of prisoners and the danger that released convicts may rob or attack again are important, but the public should attend to pain in prisons and jails for a much broader reason: because punishment creeps. We cannot confine our punishments to our convicts; the historical and modern-day record shows that we have failed in this. If a style of punishment—for example, electrical shock or whipping—seems useful behind bars, society accepts it elsewhere. Outside the confines of the prison or jail, the pain method tends to be more spontaneous, less subject to restraint, and, because culturally embedded, resistant to change. In one recent example, American punishment toured overseas to a famous jail in Iraq: Abu Ghraib (see chapter 12).

Whether the punishment be rehabilitory or corporal, a nation's attitudes toward the methods it adopts have a tendency to pervade its culture. They move into and through society, affecting (and shaped by) sometimes surprising things—our jokes, popular culture, political attitudes, and influential religious practices. As we punish, so we are.

PUNISHMENT CREEP AND SLAVERY

Perhaps the most disturbing and familiar area of punishment creep in American history is the use of pain to control people according to race. In the colonies, those whom the local community perceived as outsiders or different tended to receive punishment more often and, in some cases, more severely than those the town saw as its own. Such discrepancies applied to religious minorities, and they also affected strangers, foreigners, and people of different races.[3] Slavery, which placed controls on large groups of people, exaggerated the racist punitive impulse. It is almost impossible to miss, in the lists of executed, the many who died for the crime of "slave revolt."[4] But large numbers of black people died for other crimes as well. The Maryland Act of February 22, 1824, for instance, punished with the penalty of death any slave who intentionally struck members of his or her master's family so as to bruise or draw blood.[5]

Even as penitentiaries—filled with a nearly all-white population[6]—rose in the South, the southern states maintained legal systems that inflicted corporal pain on slaves for behaviors that were not crimes when committed by white people. Guilty white people tended to go to prison. Slaves, who had no freedom to lose, got the lash both on the plantations where they lived and again in the town square for the same behavior. A Mississippi law listed a punishment of thirty-nine lashes for any black person, whether slave or free, who dared to act as a minister of the gospel. Thirty-nine lashes was likewise, according to a Mississippi Act of June 18, 1822, the punishment for slaves who spoke in a manner considered inappropriate to a white person or who hit a white. In Georgia, any slave who might "presume to strike any white person" was to suffer death on a second offense. In South Carolina, a slave who made the mistake of setting boats off their moorings received thirty-nine lashes and also lost an ear. Gatherings of black people, including for religious worship, garnered whippings. In some states the law gave the power to punish to any white person who might come upon a group of seven or more black men. This transferal of punitive authority over black people from the state to the entire white populace was, to say the least, a dangerous instance of punishment creep.[7]

Thus, in the South, punishment facilitated racial control. And racial control depended on pain.

The Reverend Josiah Henson, Harriet Beecher Stowe's model for the Uncle Tom of her influential novel, wrote two autobiographies during his lifetime. He began each with the same formative story, which illustrates the collusion of Maryland law with the ravages of the plantation. In *The Life of Josiah Henson, Formerly a Slave*, he writes, "The only incident I can remember, which occurred while my mother continued on N.'s farm, was the appearance of my father one day, with his head bloody and his back lacerated. He was in a state of great excitement, and though it was all a mystery to me at the age of three or four years, it was explained at a later period, and I understood that he had been suffering the cruel penalty of the Maryland law for beating a white man. His right ear had been cut off close to his head, and he had received a hundred lashes on his back. He had beaten the overseer for a brutal assault on my mother, and this was his punishment."[8]

Widespread acceptance of such physical hurts depended on the religious beliefs that undergirded American slavery. As was true of many who exercised corporal punishments in other places and times, those who beat slaves justified the pain by quoting the Bible, in some cases citing the same passages that others used to defend the corporal punishment of convicts and children.

Frederick Douglass wrote of his master's religious experiences, "In August, 1832, my master attended a Methodist camp-meeting held in the Bay-side, Talbot county, and there experienced religion." Conversion seems to have changed the master's behavior in many respects. "His house was the house of prayer. He prayed morning, noon, and night. He very soon distinguished himself among his brethren, and was soon made a class-leader and exhorter. His activity in revivals was great, and he proved himself an instrument in the hands of the church in converting many souls. His house was the preachers' home."[9]

Douglass thought that conversion might cause his master to treat his slaves as people. "I indulged a faint hope that his conversion would lead him to emancipate his slaves, and that, if he did not do this, it would, at any rate, make him more kind and humane. I was disappointed in both these respects." Religion failed to inspire his master to free his slaves: "If it had any effect on his character, it made him more cruel and hateful in all his ways; for I believe him to have been a much worse man after his conversion than before."[10]

Getting religion seemed to give Douglass's master more reason to punish. "I have seen him tie up a lame young woman, and whip her with a heavy cowskin upon her naked shoulders, causing the warm red blood to drip; and, in justification of the bloody deed, he would quote this passage of Scripture—'He that knoweth his master's will, and doeth it not, shall be beaten with many stripes.'" Douglass's understanding that Christianity should inspire kindness and enable people to see each other as human beings is an interpretation similar to Benjamin Rush's ecstatic insight into the wheelbarrow man's heart. His more orthodox master uses Christianity to bolster his authority, to put down evidence of independent thought, or "will," and to justify pain.[11]

An overseer named Mr. Hopkins, who appears in Douglass's narrative, also used religious rationales for his punishment protocol. Under the Hopkins system, speaking loudly in response to the master's address, forgetting to remove one's hat in the presence of a white person, responding to accusations with attempts at self-vindication, suggesting changes in work practices, and accidentally breaking hoes or plows all got the whip. While some of these "violations" are simple accidents, others suggest self-awareness and self-respect. In orthodox Christian terms, however, they are evidence of "will," or Adam's sin. Parents and schoolteachers often perceived willful behaviors in children as deserving the lash, and Douglass's narrative shows that some nineteenth-century slave owners saw black people in the same light. Even a gaze could suggest evidence of will. "Does a slave look dissatisfied?" writes Douglass, summarizing the habits of Mr. Hopkins. "It is said, he has the Devil in him, and it must be whipped out."[12]

THE SCHOOLHOUSE WHIPPING POST

New ideas about curtailing pain as a treatment of both convicts and students gained momentum in the years that followed the American Revolution. But these new ideas did not at first mean a widespread change in schoolroom discipline styles. Even as orthodoxy splintered and innovative ideas about physical pain, religion, the state of the human soul, and penitentiaries gained popularity, punishments in American schools retained their painful purpose.

In the late eighteenth century, schools practiced formalized whippings. For example, about eight years after the Revolution ended, the town of Sunderland, Massachusetts, constructed a schoolhouse. Built into the floor was a whipping post. Years later, in 1897, the whipping post was donated to the Memorial Hall Museum in Deerfield, Massachusetts. According to Susan Flynt, museum curator, it came with this note: "Whipping Post—used in a School house in Sunderland built in 1791. Scholars were tied to it and whipped in the presence of the school." The note suggests the reasoning for placing a whipping post in the school floor: to be effective, the punishment had to be a public warning—in this case to fellow students.

The Sunderland whipping post is no exception. Schoolhouses sometimes raised posts in the street or yard outside the classroom door.[13]

Teachers varied their whipping strategies with homemade lashes. Historian Herbert Small writes of a Master Thurston who taught in 1797 in Boscawen, New Hampshire. Thurston's "ferule" was two pieces of sole leather stitched together with a sheet of lead in-between. Alice Morse Earle describes a device designed to create blisters on the skin of the schoolchildren. The "flapper," she writes, "was a heavy piece of leather six inches in diameter, with a hole in the middle. This was fastened by an edge to a pliable handle. Every stroke on the flesh raised a blister the size of the hole in the leather."[14]

Histories of American education mention numerous devices for beating students, including the "ferule" or paddle, rattan, cowhide, a five-foot sapling called "the heavy gad," and even the cat-o'-nine-tails. One school master called his cat-o'-nine-tails a "tattling stick." "The whipping with this tattling stick was ordered to be done upon 'a peaked block,'" Earle writes.[15]

Convicts were still whipped in eighteenth-century towns, but such punishments had pretty much died out in favor of prisons (and indoor lashings) by the mid-nineteenth century. Not so school whippings, which seem to have occurred both frequently and in view of other students.[16]

In 1848, a school in Stokes County, North Carolina, maintained a list of misbehaviors and the number of lashings each act of disobedience would receive. One of the top lash-getters, "bandy," was a game of ball toss. Some of these forty-seven lash-earning deeds would be considered discipline problems today, but the list also includes activities twenty-first-century Americans regard as natural to children:

Rules of School

NO.	LASHES
1 Boys & Girls Playing Together	4
2 Quareling	4
3 Fighting	5
4 Fighting at School	5
5 Quareling at School	3
6 Gambleing or Beting at School	4
7 Playing at Cards at School	10
8 Climbing for Every foot Over three feet up a tree	1

Rules of School (*continued*)

NO.	LASHES
9 Telling Lyes	7
10 Telling Tales Out of School	8
11 Nick Naming Each Other	4
12 Giving Each Other Ill Names	3
13 Fighting Each Other in Time of Books	2
14 Swaring at School	8
15 Blackgarding Each Other	6
16 For Misbehaving to Girls	10
17 For Leaving School without Leave of the Teacher	4
18 Going Home with each other without Leave of the Teacher	4
19 For Drinking Spirituous Liquors at School	8
20 Making Swings and Swinging on Them	7
21 For Misbehaving when a stranger is in the House	6
22 For waring Long Finger Nailes	2
23 For Not Making a bow when a Stranger Comes in or goes out	3
24 Misbehaving to Persons on the Road	4
25 For Not Making a bow when you Meet a Person	4
26 For Going to Girls Play Places	3
27 Girles Going to Boys Play Places	2
28 Coming to School with Dirty face and Hands	2
29 For Caling Each Other Liars	4
30 For Playing Bandy	10
31 For Bloting Your Copy Book	2
32 For Not making a bow when you go home or when you come away	4
33 Wrestling at School	4
34 Scuffling at School	4
36 For Not Making a bow when going out to go home	2
37 For Weting Each other Washing at Play time	2
38 Girls Going to Boys Play Places	2
39 For Hollowing and Hooping Going Home	3
40 For Delaying Time Going Home or Coming to School	4
41 For Not Mak.g a bow when you Come in or go Out	2
42 For Throwing Any Thing Harder than your trab ball	4
43 For Every word you miss In your Hart Leson without Good Excuse	1
44 For Not Saying yes Sir & no Sir or yes marm or no marm	2

Rules of School (*continued*)

NO.	LASHES
45 For Troubleing Each others Writing affares	2
46 for Not washing at playtime when going to Books	4
46 For Going & Play.g about the Mill or Creek	6
47 For going about the Barn or doing Any Mischief about the place	7
November 10th, 1848	Wm. A. Chaffin.[17]

For a teacher assiduous enough to follow rules to the letter, the list implies significant work duties. In his history of American schooling, the Reverend Warren Burton comments, "Half the time was spent in calling up scholars for little misdemeanors, trying to make them confess their faults and promise stricter obedience, or in devising punishments and inflicting them."[18]

Burton's book, originally published in 1838, recalls punishments of his childhood. In addition to the common use of ferules on hands, hickory sticks on feet, and rods against backs, Burton describes classroom punishments that resemble the stocks and pillories. Other punishments, while not versions of colonial penalties, echoed them in their tendency to place the students' bodies in poses that would prove painful. "Some were compelled to hold out, at arm's length the largest book which could be found, or a great leaden inkstand, till muscle and nerve, bone and marrow, were tortured with the continual exertion. If the arm bent or inclined from the horizontal level, it was forced back again by a knock of the ruler on the elbow. I well recollect that one poor fellow forgot his suffering by fainting quite away."[19]

In similar uses of the body as a tool of torment, teachers would ask their students to sit on nothing or to bend over and grasp a nail in the floorboards. In this last exercise, evidence that the student was attempting to relieve pressure by bending the knees would lead to a whack on the behind.[20]

By 1847, whippings were entrenched, shored up with scores of traditions, in numerous sectors of American society.[21] One of those groups is the military.

A SOLDIER'S PAIN

In colonial times, preferred punishments for soldiers had been, like those afforded convicts, creative and painful. Examples include shackling soldiers to wood logs, tying soldiers "neck and heels" together for long periods of time, and "picketing," by which the culprit, with one arm strung outstretched above his head, had to balance on a sharpened stake on his opposite shoeless foot. "The agony caused by this punishment was great. . . . It so frequently disabled soldiers for marching that it was finally abandoned as 'inexpedient.' "[22] A nausea-inducing punishment was the whirligig, a cage enclosing a soldier "made to revolve at great speed." Earle writes, "In the American army it is said lunacy and imbecility often followed excessive punishment in the whirligig."[23] These punishments occurred alongside bloody scourges with the cat-o'-nine-tails. In the military, punishment by cat sometimes took place during a game called "running the gauntlet" (whereby the offender dashed between members of his regiment, who would slash at the runner with whips).[24]

In cases of excessive inebriation or riotous behavior, a ride on the wooden horse, or "timber mare," was popular in both the British and the Dutch colonial forces. "This horse consisted of two or more planks about eight feet long, fixed together so as to form a sharp ridge or angle, which answered to the body of the horse," wrote Francis Grose. The angular structure of the body of this device, with its acute top edge corresponding to the horse's spine, was designed to hurt. "On this sharp ridge delinquents were mounted. . . . In this situation they were sometimes condemned to sit an hour or two; but at length it having been found to injure the soldiers materially, and sometimes to rupture them, it was left off about the time of the accession of King George I." Grose notes, however, "A wooden horse was standing in the parade at Portsmouth as late as the year 1750."[25]

The horse makes an appearance in Revolutionary War documents. In 1776, "Preseding Officer" Thomas Cleverly, soldier, was convicted of playing cards. "The Court are of the Oppinion that Thomas Cleverly ride the Wooden Horse for a Quarter of an hower with a muskett on each foot." The court martial bears the signature "Paul Revere Presdt." The muskets added weight to the soldier's legs, increasing the pain.[26] In the Revolution, under Generals Washington and Charles Lee, "Lessons of respect were enforced upon the men by fines, the pillory, the wooden horse, thirty to thirty-nine lashes, and drumming out of camp," reports Louis Clinton Hatch.[27]

Given the tendencies of punishments to travel, it is less than surprising to find a wooden horse making a civilian appearance in 1787 when the city of New Haven punished James Brown, a stranger convicted of horse-stealing. Brown's punishment was to be "confined to the Goal in this County 8 weeks, to be whipped the first Day 15 stripes on the naked Body, and set an hour on the wooden horse, and on the first Monday each following Month be whipped ten stripes and set one hour each time on the wooden horse."[28]

By the 1860s, public pain applied to convicts was pretty much out of the question. But in the military, intentional hurts lingered. In the closed societies of Yankee prisons, the wooden horse offered an excruciating ride to Confederate soldiers in full view of the camp. In one Civil War narrative, the wooden horse corralled in the military prison at Camp Douglas, just outside Chicago, bears the name "Morgan's Mule."[29] In addition to its "razor back," this sixteen-foot-tall and thirty-foot-long machine had numerous "ribs," ensuring that multiple military prisoners could receive simultaneous punishment. The punishers increased the physical distress by tying ballast weighing "from twenty to one hundred pounds" which "generally consisted of bags of sand" to the prisoners' ankles. "The cords which held these weights often cut through the skin of the ankle," writes John Copley, a Confederate prisoner at the camp.[30]

The Camp Douglas prison also made use of techniques that appeared in nineteenth-century classrooms. Much as some teachers required their students to grasp a nail in the floor, the military men who ruled Camp Douglas used a technique called "reaching for corn," or "reaching for grub." During this pain game, armed soldiers would tell their charges that under the snow lay corn grains, which the prisoners should gather to eat. "The guards would point their pistols, cocked, at the heads of the prisoners, make them bend their bodies over in a stooping posture, until the tips of their fingers would touch the ground under the snow and ice, the knees having to remain perfectly stiff and straight and not bend in any manner," writes Copley. The Confederate prisoners would remain bent over for as long as four hours. "Often these men would stand in that position until the blood would run from the nose and mouth; the guard would stand by and laugh at it," writes Copley.[31] At a time when, according to Harrie, cell life had changed for the better in Indiana, the situation was different for the Civil War prisoners just north of Chicago. Harrie published his account in 1871. In the cold winter of 1864–65, Yankee soldiers ridiculed the physical harm they caused their Confederate charges.

Punishment methods are not static or restrained within the context of the criminal justice system. In the military, strategies of pain—corporal punishment methods that we might associate with torture of criminals— were employed for other uses.

REFORM CREEP

Philosophies of punishment—some would call them ideologies—seem oddly catchable, like viruses. This is true whether the philosophies are rehabilitory or retributionist. Periodic punishment crazes (whether they wound or avoid bodily pain) happen because ideas about what humans are—whether good or evil or in between, whether best left free or best restricted in their movements—entwine with punishment practices.

By the nineteenth century, activists exposed the punishments hidden in schools, prisons, insane asylums, and the military, and on plantations. Punishments that controlled and directed through hurt came under attack in pamphlets and in autobiographical narratives (see chapter 3). Change was afoot. It would, among other things, have a strong effect on the treatment of students and animals. It would also affect behavior toward child laborers, slaves, the mentally ill, prisoners, and members of the military.[32]

By the nineteenth century, even as closed societies continued to lay on the lash, activists and writers expressed a loud discomfort with corporal punishment, insisting on the humanity and the goodness of those subjected to it. Narratives of punishment from the nineteenth century are common. They include Harrie's and other stories of prison life, many school stories, accounts of life at sea and in the military, and slave narratives. These autobiographical narratives tend to incorporate detailed descriptions of punishment and suffering. In them the language of pain carries political purpose: their authors and their distributors wanted to change the country.

A struggle over religious meanings preceded the end of American slavery. Despite the Christian beliefs that propped up the institution, competing philosophies were afoot in the South as they were in the North. Douglass's hope that conversion would cause his master to change his punishments suggests as much. So does the following passage from him, which associates physical cruelty with the sin of blasphemy and with devilishness. In it Douglass uses the word "fiendish," the adjective form of "fiend," the word Harrie used to describe brutal guards.

"Mr. Severe was rightly named: he was a cruel man. . . . He seemed to take pleasure in manifesting his fiendish barbarity. Added to his cruelty, he was a profane swearer. It was enough to chill the blood and stiffen the hair of an ordinary man to hear him talk. Scarce a sentence escaped him but that was commenced or concluded by some horrid oath. The field was the place to witness his cruelty and profanity. His presence made it both the field of blood and of blasphemy." Here Douglass associates slave whippings, which owners sometimes understood as biblically ordained, with the Mosaic sin of blasphemy—a colonial capital offense. Like other writers of his time, Douglass is attempting to alter the meaning of Christian sin.[33]

RESTRAINT AND SOLITARY CONFINEMENT IN THE CLASSROOM

A social shift is one thing. Social improvement is quite another.

The rise of the Lancastrian schools, precursors to the modern U.S. public school system, parallels the emergence of the American penitentiary. Joseph Lancaster established the system that bears his name in Britain in 1798. The first American Lancastrian school, offering instruction to large numbers of working-class and poor children, was started in New York City in 1806. It was the city's first public school.

Soon American newspapers trumpeted the spread of the popular schools. On April 1, 1814, an editorial in the *Raleigh Register* extended congratulations to "our fellow citizens on the prospect of establishing in the Preparatory School of our Academy, the highly approved mode of teaching children the first rudiments of Learning, invented by the celebrated Joseph Lancaster of London."[34]

Lancaster was an educational reformer with much in common with the prison activists of his day. A Quaker, Lancaster abhorred corporal punishment, and this dislike led him to innovate. In his system of schools, he followed the example of prisons in maintaining strict discipline systems based in physical restraint.[35] The Lancastrian schoolroom discipline plan correlated not only with the Quaker demand for prison solitary cells but also with many of the punishments inside penitentiaries that restricted bodily movements—think of the bag that enclosed all but the head, the metal straitjacket, and the boxlike enclosures for disobedient inmates described in chapter 3.

Absence of cudgels notwithstanding, some of Lancaster's recommendations would have caused young students discomfort. The 1805 edition of his book *Improvements in Education* includes a section on "Offences and Punishments." Lancaster reserves "severity," by which he means lashings, for "vice and immorality."[36] A boy who misbehaves "has liberty to put a wooden log round his neck, which serves him as a pillory, and with this he is sent to his seat. This machine may weigh from four to six pounds." The log was a mild punishment.[37] If the log doesn't work, Lancaster suggests that teachers "fasten the legs of offenders together with wooden shackles: one or more, according to the offence." Lancaster specified that his shackle was a single wood piece between six and twelve inches long, with each end "tied to each leg." It was designed to slow and tire the child.[38]

As the student reoffends, the restraints turn more encumbering. If the leg shackles fail, Lancaster recommends "wooden shackles fastened from elbow to elbow, behind the back," tying the legs together, or suspending boys "in a sack, or in a basket" from the school roof.[39] For unreformed recidivists Lancaster suggests yoking together in groups as many as six boys and forcing them to walk backwards. He points out that a misstep can "cause the yoke to hurt their necks" or pull the group to the ground.[40]

But the punishments Lancaster considers most "effectual" involve close bodily restraint in combination with isolation. He advocates "confinement after school hours" and suggests that schoolmasters avoid the "inconvenience" of having to remain in the schoolhouse after closing "by tying [children] to the desks, in such a manner that they cannot untie themselves." An "incorrigible" truant might be "tied up in a blanket, and left to sleep at night on the floor, in the school-house."[41]

Lancastrian confinement echoes the essays of Benjamin Rush and other advocates of isolation. The punishment was supposed to change the guilty student "by placing him in confinement of one kind or another, till he is humbled, and likely to remove the cause by better behaviour in future."[42]

Travelers in the early 1800s reported Lancastrian schools up and down the Eastern Seaboard and as far south as New Orleans. Among the public institutions in New Orleans, noted a *Commercial Directory* of large American cities from 1823, are "*two medical societies, a charity hospital, the New Orleans Library Society, 4 Lancastrian Schools,* and many other institutions literary and benevolent." The schools' popularity—like the rise of penitentiaries that favored restraint over pain—was a sign of the time.[43]

By the late eighteenth century, as prison advocates praised the virtue of extensive solitary confinement, schoolmasters and mistresses included the method in their panoply of punishment. Given Pennsylvania's fondness for the penitentiary, it is not surprising to find a Reading school that contained, according to a 1785 description, a "dark hole against the chimney to put bad boys in." Another room against a schoolhouse chimney "used as a dungeon for punishment" appeared in Peterborough, New Hampshire.[44]

The Massachusetts Education Commission, writing on punishment in the schools in 1868, described schoolmasters who took solitary confinement to an extreme at Girard College, a boarding school for disadvantaged children. The report describes "boys incarcerated under lock and key, for weeks upon weeks, in mid-winter, in the topmost rooms of the college building, where no heat was allowed them, no light permitted when evening came, no books given them to read; stripped of their clothes, in some instances partially, and in others almost entirely; obliged to answer all the calls of nature in these rooms, and fed upon bread and water."[45]

THE RISE OF THE PURE CHILD

Though challenged by thinkers such as Rush, the tendency to associate children with sin continued into nineteenth-century America. In sin, people saw not only the work of the Devil but also the nurture of criminals. In the 1840s, according to Bernard Wishy, articles in *The Mother's Assistant* and *Parents Magazine* praised maternal organizations that sought to spare young children from criminality by coaxing them to "public profession of their faith in Christ." The articles described the mothers groups as saving children otherwise destined for prison. "Stories were printed about a poor convict, fated for prison since youth because his mother had not had the help of a maternal association." In such groups we can see, dispersed into a public and popular form, the idea that some children belong to the Devil at birth and need to be redeemed.[46]

But new ideas about children emerged. The popular belief that they were evil began to shift to its near opposite, characterized by what Wishy describes as "assumptions of their essential innocence, or at least moral flexibility." Corporal punishment lost ground to directives guiding parents to nurture innocence into adulthood.[47] In this understanding of human potential, the pure child changed into a criminal only because of the corrupting influence of the world. The enthusiastic hope of Benjamin Rush, that the convicts drinking beer in his yard might enjoy a purity of heart that could lead them back to goodness, took on the energy of a popular movement centered around children. The reversal was gradual, and competing understandings of both children and criminals co-existed for much of the century.

By the 1830s, more and more writers advised parents to avoid hurting their children in response to bad behavior. One of these advocated "shouting hours," when parents would permit their children to make a ruckus. Others suggested that children misbehaved because they were mistaken or immature. Child play and noise, those "natural" behaviors that had troubled the Puritans, became evidence of "Christian liberty."[48] By 1844, Horace Mann proposed that Massachusetts schools restrict whippings. In the southern states, Braxton Cramers made similar recommendations.[49]

The popular literature of the time grappled with the new child-raising. In 1835, Catharine Maria Sedgwick published a best-selling novel with the resonant title *Home.* Early in the story, Haddy, a young daughter of the Barclay family, takes "a new, unfinished, and very precious kite belonging to her brother Wallace," cuts a hole in its center, and thrusts "into it the head of her pet Maltese kitten."[50]

Wallace comes upon the scene, grabs hold of the kitten, and throws "it into the tub of scalding water." The kitten dies. Mr. Barclay commands Wallace to go to his room, where he will spend the next several weeks alone—a home version of solitary confinement. "You have forfeited your right to a place among us," Mr. Barclay tells his son. "Creatures who are the slaves of their passions, are, like beasts of prey, fit only for solitude."[51]

Over the next few weeks, "Wallace went to school as usual, and returned to his solitude, without speaking or being spoken to. His meals were sent to his room."[52] In his contemplative seclusion, Wallace changes —as would the ideal prisoner in a solitary cell. Tempted to fight with a friend who teases him, Wallace resists his urge to hit. As Wallace explains to his father, the act of self-governance was difficult: "I had to bite my lips though so that the blood ran."[53]

"God bless you, my son," responds the father to his boy who has chosen obedience. As the two head to dinner, Wallace reveals that the extensive isolation pressed him to find help in God.[54]

As Wallace and Mr. Barclay's invocation of God suggests, the new nurturers were developing a child-centered religious style. This new way of thinking about religion had a powerful effect on popular American philosophies of punishment, both of children, as the Barclay home suggests, and of prisoners.[55]

Sedgwick's interest in punishment and religion went beyond the world of her novel. A Unitarian raised in a Calvinist church, Sedgwick in later years became the first person to head the Women's Prison Association.[56]

In 1847, Lyman Cobb published the popular and influential *The Evil Tendencies of Corporal Punishment as a Means of Moral Discipline in Families and Schools*. "Perhaps there is no question which has agitated the public mind, during the last eight or ten years, more than the subject of corporal Punishment in Families and Schools," he writes.[57]

Cobb says he writes from "a sense of religious duty." His repeated references to criminality show how nineteenth-century Americans saw child rearing, treatment of criminals, and religion as entwined. In criminal punishments, Cobb finds a parallel to child discipline. Identifying "the gallows and the prison" as "the *ultimate resorts* to restrain or cut short the perpetration of crime—not the *means* of moral discipline," Cobb asserts that if nations find hangings less useful, so should parents and teachers understand that lashings will not lead to better children.[58]

Throughout his book, Cobb echoes nineteenth-century complaints about public corporal punishments and executions—that they will "harden" and corrupt those who view them—and he extends these arguments to child rearing. His strategy depends on a shared understanding with his readers that public physical punishments are outmoded. "Suppose the Common Council of the city of New York, should erect a *public* whipping-post in the Park, in front of the City Hall," he hypothesizes. "How long would it be permitted to stand there? *Not one single day.*" Although cities had eradicated whippings in public squares, discipline-by-lash had found a home in schoolhouses. For Cobb, the contradiction is a source of righteous anger. "Let it be remembered now and for ever, that *whipping* in the school-room IN THE PRESENCE OF THE SCHOOL is the *same,* in its *demoralizing* and *hardening* influence on the pupils who witness it, as the PUBLIC WHIPPING IN THE PARK, except and ONLY that in the schoolroom, it is in MINIATURE!!!!!" (emphasis Cobb's).[59]

Cobb not only equates beatings of children with those of convicts, he also echoes Rush, arguing that lashings can create devious and revengeful children and, eventually, criminals.[60] Cobb's belief opposes his orthodox competitors, who thought floggings were an indispensable tool to *save* children from sin.

Other members of the movement toward pain-free child rearing took inspiration from prison innovations. In 1871, Jacob Abbott recommended a mini-penitentiary: a mother who noticed her child misbehaving would call out the word "prison," whereupon the child would retreat to an isolated corner of the house to reflect on her misbehavior. In this early precursor of the "time out," the parent would call out again after a few minutes—this time the word: "free."[61]

The steep shift in prevalent religious belief did not go unnoticed. "By 1900, the notion of infant depravity had been almost completely abandoned in theological debates about a child's 'essence,'" writes Wishy. "God was no longer conceived as an absolute being or power with little feeling or reason nor as an irate judge. He had become the rational and loving Father, in the world and caring for it. The older antagonism between the little viper and the stern God with his earthly surrogates, the parents, had disappeared."[62]

By the first years of the twentieth century, even Presbyterianism, that direct heir of Calvinist orthodoxy, had revised its doctrine of infant damnation to one of infant salvation.[63] Such widespread beliefs affected understandings of criminality: criminals were made, not born.

GOD IN THE FLOGGED SAILOR

Aboard ship, torture could take on a bizarre quality perhaps exacerbated by boredom. Two examples, known as "ducking att the yarde arm" and "keel-hauling," as described by a chaplain on a seventeenth-century British royal vessel, will suffice:

The ducking att the yarde arme is, when a malefactor by havinge a rope fastened under his armes and about his middle, and under his breech, is thus hoysed up to the end of the yarde; from whence hee is againe violentlie let fall into the sea, sometimes twise, sometimes three severall tymes one after another; and if the offence be very fowle, he is also drawne under the very keele of the shippe, the which is termed keel-rakinge; and whilst hee is thus under water, a great gunn is given fire righte over his head; the which is done to astonish him the more with the thunder thereof, which much troubles him, as to give warning untoe all others to looke out, and to beware by his harms.[64]

Geoffrey Abbott, the author of *Execution,* comments on this passage:

It should be remembered that the height of the old sailing-ships was considerable, the fall in itself resulting in possible injury being sustained on hitting the surface of the sea; and then to be dragged, half-drowned, across the hull, which was invariably encrusted with limpets, mollusks and other marine creatures, their shells rasping flesh and muscle off one's bones, must have been an ordeal in itself. The very width of the ship meant that the miscreant would not rapidly surface on the other side. . . . Even if not actually condemned to death by these means, as many were, it is hard to see how a man, no matter how hardened to the stringent conditions of nautical life, could survive such an ordeal, especially when the sentence decreed that it should be repeated two or more times.[65]

Floggings were also common on board ship, on both British and American vessels. But, during the nineteenth century, revisions in the religious meaning of punishment also reached the armed forces. In his book against corporal punishment of children, Lyman Cobb included several passages devoted to whippings in the British and American navies. A Boston paper quoted by Cobb, for instance, editorializes about navy floggings, "The idea of *cutting a man's flesh off his bones,* seems to us to be worthy only of a country inhabited by *savages* or *demons.*" The reference to "demons," that is, evil spirits, echoes Harrie's use of the word "fiends" to describe the guards at the Southern Indiana State Penitentiary and Douglass's use of "fiendish" to describe the whipping, blaspheming overseer. The equation that once linked the punishers to God and the punished to sin has reversed.[66]

The Boston paper was not the only publication to derive the new equation. One popular and much-reprinted 1840 memoir of life at sea, *Two Years Before the Mast,* recounts a lashing of two seamen. Richard Henry Dana's writing carries the religious and reform temper of his time: "A man—a human being, made in God's likeness—fastened up and flogged like a beast!"[67] For Dana, the idea of a beaten man is abhorrent because humans reflect God. The emphasis on the flogged man as akin to God echoes contemporary arguments about the innocence and godliness of children and prisoners. Parents and officials were once stand-ins for God, inheriting holy authority and expressing it in whippings that would drive evil from the bodies of children and criminals. Dana's memoir turns on its head the argument that for centuries buttressed whippings.

Nine years later, and just months before the U.S. Congress outlawed navy floggings, Herman Melville published *White Jacket,* his novel of life at sea on a navy vessel. In his tale of life aboard the *Neversink,* Melville, like Dana, makes a moral case against whippings. "Join hands with me, then; and, in the name of that Being in whose image the flogged sailor is made, let us demand of legislators, by what right they dare profane what God himself accounts sacred." Further, endowing higher officers with the power to punish at will is undemocratic. A captain, who can whip as he wishes, "is an absolute ruler, making and unmaking law as he pleases," writes Melville. "Irrespective of incidental considerations, we assert that flogging in the Navy is opposed to the essential dignity of man, which no legislator has a right to violate; that it is oppressive and glaringly unequal in its operations; that it is utterly repugnant to the spirit of our democratic institutions; indeed, that it involves a lingering trait of the worst times of a barbarous feudal aristocracy; in a word, we denounce it as religiously, morally, and immutably *wrong.*"[68]

Like Rush and his contemporary revolutionaries, Melville understands corporal punishment as befitting absolute monarchy, not democracy. The religious reversal he presses in describing the punishers as profaning God and the punished as "sacred" is also democratic in its implications, valuing as it does the individual over the official who exploits a dubious inherited power.

The nineteenth century was a moment when pain spoke to the populace. Reformers felt for those who suffered and, in turn, influenced the general public and those who made policies. A voice that claimed physical hurt had authority. It was worth reading. It motivated its readers. It conveyed energy that engendered societal transformation.

But influential old ideas, including the once-standard belief that children were the issue of the Devil, don't disappear, even when they seem to evaporate. Repressed, subject to popular dislike and disapproval, they fester and sometimes go into hiding, only to make a public appearance when the social climate warms.

CHAPTER 5

Vigilantism and Progressivism

THE WORDS "VIGILANTISM" and "Progressivism" do not often appear in the same sentence. Yet at their height in the early twentieth century, the two trends shared a cultural moment and a preoccupation with punishment. Both are responses to the liberationist movements of the nineteenth century. Progressivism in the northern United States took on a reformist role that resembled the purpose of its predecessors but, critically, transferred the motivating energy from religion to science. Southern Progressivism, vivid in the notorious chain gangs that rebuilt the South—and cost many prisoners their lives—was like its northern counterpart a modernizing attempt to replace the brutal corporal punishment many slaves had previously suffered. Vigilante lynchings of black Americans harked back to the power many southern states gave their white residents to punish offending slaves. Vigilante crowds often removed the rumored offender from the oversight of the criminal justice system, frequently with the complicity of the local sheriff. Some black people were lynched for behaving as free men. With its emphasis on public killings before large, often celebratory crowds, lynching also discarded the nineteenth-century reforms that had moved executions indoors.[1]

MADNESS WITH A METHOD

If history is a contest of ideas, the concept of retributive killing never really lost. Official hangings declined considerably in the early twentieth century as more so-called humane execution methods, such as the electric chair, came into practice.[2] When governments did erect scaffolds, they tended to do so indoors, away from crowds.

But professionalized punishment had an unprofessional shadow. As the number of official hangings dropped, lynchings reached their height. These public killings flourished, flamboyant in their rejection of the legal system, the penitentiary, and all the restraints these institutions implied. Corporal pain in many lynchings was overt. Crowds gathered to watch.

Before the removal of scaffolds from the public square, the public sometimes took the convict's side against the more impersonal government and its representative, the hangman. The opinions of a population that seemed pro-punishment might swing the other way, depending on what the government let people see. One example of this is the hanging of John McCaffrey, who in 1850 drowned his wife, Bridget, in Kenosha, Wisconsin. His hanging, the first in the new state, drew a gathering of between two and three thousand.

McCaffrey struggled in the noose for five minutes. He took eighteen minutes to die. Citizens expressed their disgust. Newspapermen wrote that McCaffrey's execution was a blotch of shame on the new state. Wisconsin dropped capital punishment like a hot fork.[3]

Other states suffered public crises of conscience. In Minnesota in 1906, William Williams was hanged for the murder of a boy who had been his lover. The rope selected for his hanging was too long by a half foot. After Williams dropped to the floor, guards rehanged him, a process that lasted fourteen minutes. Local newspapers described the bungled execution. "Would the man never die?" asked the *St. Paul Dispatch*. Politicians reacted by silencing the papers. The public turned against both the news gag and the botched hanging; Williams was the last person executed in Minnesota.[4]

But the crowds that condoned lynchings were anything but compassionate. The discrepancy between official government hangings of convicted criminals and lynchings of reputed, mostly black criminals reveals that "reform creep" (see chapter 4) was slow and incomplete. Crowds still could experience public pleasure in humiliating and torturing a man, especially if he was black. The account of a lynching contained in an April 1924 article about the Ku Klux Klan is an almost uncanny repetition (with the exception of the final bullets) of torture and execution methods that were once common. The victim, Tom Price, was a porter at the local hotel whose wife, a laundress, "was fired by one of her male employers because she insisted on remaining faithful to her legal spouse." In response, "Price, in a moment of angry bravado, threatened the white man." He was lynched two days later:

> The first step in the execution was the whipping which raised crimson gorged weals on the negro's naked body. Then a match was set to the straw and sticks—but not too many of these: the flame was not intended to kill. As the flames reached his flesh the negro writhed and screeched in agony, but only now did the real torture commence. So tightly was Price wired to the post that his tense body could not shrink when one of the white men advanced with a brace and bit. Into the muscles of the groin cut the biting tool. Time after time he fainted to be revived again as the torture was stayed. From the crowd came again and again that animal growl—lustful and cruel. The game was nearly over. A slash of knives and another form of medieval torture had been revived. The fire was now kicked out and the unconscious, but the still living, negro was dragged to a tree at the side of the square. As his limbs jerked and danced at the end of a rope, his body was riddled with bullets.[5]

The cruelty of these events is enormous. The mob drills into the man's groin and burns him at the stake—enough to cause him extraordinary pain but not enough to kill him. This torture resembles early punishments when those condemned to death by drowning were half-drowned first, so the suffering would last as long as possible. Death or half-death by fire was a common medieval church punishment in Europe. Historian Harry Elmer Barnes, commenting on Price's lynching, notes that during the Middle Ages, "it was not uncommon for the victim to be snatched from the flames after being thoroughly seared, left to suffer with his burns and then be returned to the flames at a later period. Burning might also be preceded by or combined with other forms of punishment, usually divers types of mutilation." In the description quoted above, a white population imposes the lynching, intent on exhibiting its power by destroying a man's body, much as royal rulers sought to keep the lower classes in line through torture and execution spectacles. Like those spectacles, the lynching occurs outdoors and in public view, with the aim of inflicting humiliation.[6]

The U.S. historical record shows lynchings in twenty-six states. Although it occurred in northern states, including Illinois, North Dakota, and Minnesota, the practice, like the exploitation of black labor on chain gangs, was most popular in the South. Most lynching took place in the sixty years following the Emancipation Proclamation of 1862. Many lynchings punished black people for behaving like the free people they now were, for doing such things as not stepping to the side to let a white person pass or for disagreeing with a white person in a business transaction. Anthony Crawford, for instance, dared to haggle over cotton prices. A crowd of approximately four hundred lynched Crawford, hanging him and pitting his body with two hundred gunshot wounds. These punishments perpetuated Christian slavery-era ideas that saw pain as a critical response to evidence of "will." As noted earlier, the notion that "will" was an expression of evil when exhibited by children or slaves was a strongly held belief. As the lynchings indicate, the implication of this once-popular religious idea is that "will" sometimes merits death. The history of the religious philosophy we might call "beating the Devil out of them" is littered with the bodies of convicts, children, and slaves, but its murderous implications are most evident in American lynchings.[7]

Post–Civil War lynchings were a vigilante response to crime anxiety. The perception of a rise in crime related to the end of slavery appears, for instance, in the autobiography of southern slavery advocate Bill Arp. "Alas for the negro! Before the war there was not an outrage committed by them from the Potomac to the Rio Grande. There was not a chain gang nor a convict camp in all the South. Now, there are five thousand in the chain gangs of Georgia and fifteen thousand more in the Southern States. Here would be fifty thousand if the laws were enforced for minor offences, but we overlook them out of pity."[8]

Perceptions depended on perspective. W. E. B. Du Bois understood the South as forcing black people into crime: "If my own city of Atlanta had offered it to-day the choice between 500 Negro college graduates— forceful, busy, ambitious men of property and self-respect, and 500 black cringing vagrants and criminals, the popular vote in favor of the criminals would be simply overwhelming. Why? because they want Negro crime? No, not that they fear Negro crime less, but that they fear Negro ambition and success more. They can deal with crime by chain-gang and lynch law, or at least they think they can, but the South can conceive neither machinery nor place for the educated, self-reliant, self-assertive black man."[9]

In 2000, sixty postcard photos of lynchings from 1883 to 1960 went on exhibit at the Ruth Horowitz Gallery in New York City. James Allen, an Atlanta antiques dealer, had collected the images. Often sent through the mail, either as warnings or as boasts, the postcards carried messages like: "This is the barbecue we had last night. My picture is to the left with a cross over it, your sone [sic] Joe." Although the postcards showed scene after scene of charred bodies hoisted in the air and black people hung from trees and telephone posts, "what takes the breath away is the sight of all the white people, maskless, milling about, looking straight at the camera as if they had nothing to be ashamed of, often smiling," observed *New York Times* critic Roberta Smith. "Sometimes they line up in an orderly fashion, as if they were at a class reunion or church picnic. Sometimes they cluster around the victim, hoisting children on their shoulders so that they can see, too."[10] A lynching was, for many white Americans, a crowd-attraction.

Although formal hangings of criminals had lost official sanction, in many cases police and politicians knew of lynchings and failed to act or even joined in. On October 10, 1911, State Legislator Joshua Ashley and the editor of the local paper, the *Intelligencer,* led a mob in Anderson County, South Carolina, to Willis Jackson, accused of attacking a white child. The mob hung Jackson upside down in a tree, shooting him. After the lynching, the *Intelligencer* published an article acknowledging that a staff member—whom it did not identify as the editor—had attended Jackson's lynching. He "went out to see the fun with not the least objection to being a party to help lynch the brute," noted the paper.[11]

Between 1880 and 1893, lynchings took the lives of nearly seven hundred people in the United States.[12] From 1880 to 1905, not a single person was convicted in connection to a lynching. Despite condemnations from presidents, local justice protected the perpetrators.

Lynchings were public in their force, in their spectacle, in their proclamation of guilt without trial. The fear that propelled them was also communal. A strong and pervasive fear that black men were raping white women
suddenly appeared among southerners at the end of the 1880s, writes
Edward L. Ayers in *Vengeance and Justice: Crime and Punishment in the
Nineteenth-Century American South*. The abrupt emergence of the "crime,"
unconnected to any actual increase in black-white rape, is part of what links
lynchings to two other punitive phenomena discussed earlier—the Salem
witchcraft trials and the rise of a belief in literal evil that the rhetoric of the
1970s tied to criminals, particularly juvenile delinquents. In these three
instances, the fear response to questionable evidence of "crime" and "evil"
spread energetically and led to extreme shifts in punishment.[13]

"To deny either the irrationality or rationality of lynching . . . is to miss
its essence," writes Ayers. "Lynching was madness, but with a method."
Like the witch trials, in the lynching scare, "people thought they knew
what they were doing: combating an elusive but terrible foe. . . . Defenders
of justice in both cases had always to be vigilant for signs of the impending visitation—which had a way of appearing just when people were looking for it."[14]

Histories of the Salem witchcraft trials point out that fear of strangers
may have fed the fervor. Ayers makes a similar suggestion. He points out
that lynchings surged well after the Civil War, at a time when southerners
younger than thirty would be unable to remember slavery. What they
would remember instead, he notes, is "racial distrust, conflict, and blood-
shed." The tendency of violent criminals to be young suggests that most
lynchers and their victims emerged from this group. "These men, white
and black, feared each other with the fear of ignorance. . . . They saw each
other dimly, at a distance."[15]

That dim vision, combined with efficient publicizing of rape rumors
and lynching news, fed anxiety from county to county, largely because
lynchings—unlike other crimes—received fervent attention in the printed
press.[16] Historians of the Salem witchcraft trials have also argued that the
surge in accusations stemmed, in part, from disruptive social changes,
with the village transforming from a protective communal society to one
based on early capitalism.[17] Ayers spots a similar phenomenon in lynching and the nearly simultaneous vigilante outbreaks in the Georgia
mountains known as whitecapping.[18]

A SCIENCE OF PUNISHMENT

In the prisons, at the turn of the nineteenth century, a revolution based on science was under way. The Progressive reformers were in many ways a continuation of the nineteenth-century activists who entered the prisons and criticized the cat-o'-nine-tails, the cold water treatments, the tranquilizing chairs, the gags, and extensive solitary confinement. The Progressives believed, as had Benjamin Rush and the Quakers, that criminals could change for the better and that prisons could help achieve such transformations.

The Progressives found severe physical mistreatment in the prisons they entered, including such devices as a pulley system that stretched convicts' bodies. What historian David Rothman calls "perhaps the most incredible torture instrument of the period" was a "water crib," six feet long and three feet deep. Guards positioned the inmate face down in the trough, hands restrained in handcuffs. They then poured water into the device. "The effect was of slow drowning," writes Rothman. A guard at the Kansas prison that used the water crib boasted to investigators of the crib's efficiency and (by comparison to the deranging effects of solitary confinement) humaneness. "You take a man and put him in there and turn the water on him and that wilts him at once. He wilts and says he will be good. It might take days in a blind cell [solitary confinement] until his system was all deranged."[19]

Unlike their predecessors, many Progressives found guidance not in religion or morality but in science. The Progressives sought to quantify and measure American criminality and punishment, which for so long had been the realm of religious impulses. An irrational system was about to succumb to rationality.[20]

The Progressive vision was an optimistic one, and it quickly brought about major social changes. The turn to government and to the promises of science had its source in an American life that was increasingly urban. "America's cities were afflicted with poverty, disease, overcrowded slums, and crime, and the developing biological and social sciences provided a fresh interpretation of crime's causes," write Thomas G. Blomberg and Karol Lucken.[21]

But as with the nineteenth-century penitentiary reform frenzy that preceded them, the Progressive reformers cannot be congratulated for unadulterated "purity of motive." Some Progressive penal reforms were "designed to address the problems and new political strength of the increasingly organized and assertive industrial working class," comments Jonathan Simon.[22]

The Progressive era is generally thought to encompass the years 1890 through 1913, but its influences were long-lasting. For Progressives, punishment was to be highly individualized. "Rehabilitation," a key Progressive word, meant adjusting punishment to the needs of each offender. The term also understood crime as no longer a moral trouble but a solvable scientific problem.[23]

The Progressives looked for the sources of crime in the environment (for instance in poverty), in the offender's psychology, and, infamously, sometimes in the convict's genetic makeup.[24] The Progressives also favored adjusting punishment according to how rehabilitated they believed the offenders to be; those who showed progress were to serve shorter sentences. The Progressives are the inventors of systems—including probation, parole, and the indeterminate sentence—designed to ensure that the officials managing the prisons had the discretion to determine when inmates would be released. The new policies rewarded evidence of positive change in the convict with movement toward freedom. Under such a system, a thief who refused to change could serve a longer sentence than a murderer who claimed personal transformation.[25]

Progressivism trickled into cultural depictions of punishment, including children's books. In 1913, L. Frank Baum published *The Patchwork Girl of Oz*. The book, number seven in the fourteen sequels to *The Wonderful Wizard of Oz*, endows the magical Land of Oz with a Progressive-style prison. When a boy named Ojo is arrested for picking a plant that can be used for negative magic, Baum expounds a theory of criminality. Much as the Progressive prison reformers would have argued, the reason for the crime is Ojo's background; he is desperate and wants to help a family member: "Ojo was by nature gentle and affectionate and if he had disobeyed the Law of Oz it was to restore his dear Unc Nunkie to life. His fault was more thoughtless than wicked, but that did not alter the fact that he had committed a fault."[26]

A soldier with green whiskers leads Ojo to prison. They stop at what Baum describes as "a pretty house" just inside the city "in a quiet, retired place." Inside, Ojo looks about "in amazement, for never had he dreamed of such a magnificent apartment as this in which he stood. The roof of the dome was of colored glass, worked into beautiful designs. The walls were paneled with plates of gold decorated with gems of great size and many colors, and upon the tiled floor were soft rags delightful to walk upon. The furniture was framed in gold and upholstered in satin brocade and it consisted of easy chairs, divans and stools in great variety. Also there were several tables with mirror tops and cabinets filled with rare and curious things. In one place a case filled with books stood against the wall, and elsewhere Ojo saw a cupboard containing all sorts of games."[27]

The accoutrements of luxury, leisure, child-play, and intellectual reward dazzle Ojo. He begs to remain in the dream home "a little while before I go to prison."[28]

"Why, this is your prison," answers a woman named Tollygiggle, who turns out to be his jailer. She commands the soldier to remove the boy's handcuffs, and Ojo looks at a picture book, eats supper, listens to Tollygiggle read him a story, and, incredulous, asks, "Why is the prison so fine, and why are you so kind to me?"[29]

Tollygiggle answers with the Oz punishment philosophy. "We consider a prisoner unfortunate," Tollygiggle tells Ojo. "He is unfortunate in two ways—because he has done something wrong and because he is deprived of his liberty. Therefore we should treat him kindly, because of his misfortune, for otherwise he would become hard and bitter and would not be sorry he had done wrong." Tollygiggle explains that Ozma, the ruler of Oz, "thinks that one who has committed a fault did so because he was not strong and brave; therefore she puts him in prison to make him strong and brave. When that is accomplished he is no longer a prisoner, but a good and loyal citizen and everyone is glad that he is now strong enough to resist doing wrong. You see, it is kindness that makes one strong and brave; and so we are kind to our prisoners."[30]

Ojo thinks over Tollygiggle's words, then offers up a competing philosophy: "I had an idea," he says, "that prisoners were always treated harshly, to punish them."[31]

Tollygiggle is horrified. "That would be dreadful!" she says. "Isn't one punished enough in knowing he has done wrong? Don't you wish, Ojo, with all your heart, that you had not been disobedient and broken a Law of Oz?"[32]

Ojo's response suggests that the house of kindness has already begun to rehabilitate him. "I—I hate to be different from other people," he admits.[33]

The Progressives invented the idea of separating juvenile offenders from adult populations and treating them differently.[34] In Oz, Ojo receives a mother figure for a jailer because he is a child. His jail is homelike and filled with the toys and books and hot food a child needs to learn and grow. Imprisonment in Oz takes the idea of individualized treatment to its logical extreme. Ojo is alone with his nurturing guard.

In 1999, the U.S. government shuttered a Progressive-era prison in Lorton, Virginia. Like Ojo's prison in Oz, the Occoquan Workhouse had no locks or bars and no surrounding walls when first built in 1909. (Officials installed them in the 1940s.) Prisoners lived in dorms rather than cells.[35]

The Occoquan Workhouse was started in response to a local scandal that received national attention. In 1908, a penal commission under the direction of President Theodore Roosevelt uncovered what Roosevelt called "really outrageous conditions in the workhouse and jail" in the capital city, Washington, D.C. The commission advised a wholesale shift in the punishment of the D.C. inmates. With an act of Congress and the condemnation and purchase of nearly 1,200 acres, a prison farm was born.[36]

"The theory was that if people were put in a wholesome environment, they would thrive and improve morally," explained an Associated Press reporter as the farm was closing. "Wholesome," to Progressives concerned about poor immigrants and slums, meant country living. Hard work, much of it in the out-of-doors, was also part of the formula. Prisoners at the Lorton facility made bricks and built the prison hospital, dorms, ice plant, laundry facility, and bakery. The farm included a dairy and a beef herd as well as hogs. Prisoners ran the dairy and the slaughterhouse, a sawmill, a blacksmith shop, in addition to working the fields and a large orchard. Though not self-supporting, the prisoners could and did feed themselves.[37]

The emphasis on sunshine, fresh air, and tilling the soil suggests that the Progressives were overidealizing country life. Training in rural work did not prepare urban convicts to return home.

Even if easily criticized, the prison farm, like other Progressive-era punishment inventions, was a far cry from its predecessors. This is because, unlike punishment in previous centuries, it was not religious in its aims. It was scientific. While demanding reforms, the Progressives asserted the benefits of a new approach to punishment: data collection.

Influenced by the new social sciences they had studied in universities, the Progressives believed that "to understand and solve a social problem," they needed to "gather all the 'facts' of the case. Armed with the data, they would then be able to analyze the issue in 'scientific' fashion and discover the right antidote," writes Rothman.[38]

The Progressive emphasis on science meant that its punishment programs should have been vulnerable to claims that they were ineffective, but for a long time, although many people knew of high recidivism rates, the Progressive prison system seemed invulnerable to critique. Once institutionalized, the radical shakeup hardened into institutional programs. In the decades that followed, facilities and programs were so often overcrowded, their individualized treatment so expensive, and thus underfunded, that rehabilitation was often superficial in practice. Historians suggest that "the very existence of the rhetoric of reform and the reality of a few limited successes in particular institutions may well have provided an excuse to avoid wider and more fundamental changes."[39]

Even so, the inheritors of Progressive prison farms, reformatories, and juvenile halls also provided decades of data that showed something amazing: the right kind of punishment can change convicts. Carefully administered rehabilitation does stop some ex-cons from returning to crime. That message all but disappeared when retribution roared to life.[40]

PUNISHMENT DISPARITIES, OR HOW PAIN KEPT GOING

Pain in prisons did not end with the advent of Progressivism. In 1927, Leon D. Whipple's *Story of Civil Liberty in the United States* included a passage from San Quentin prisoner Jacob Oppenheimer about his time in a canvas straitjacket. The prison staff forced Oppenheimer to endure "4 days and 14 hours incessantly" in the garment. "I slept neither night nor day," notes Oppenheimer in his account. "The bodily excretions over which I had no control in the canvas vice, ate into my bruised limbs adding pain to pain. My fingers, hands and arms finally became numb and a paralyzing shock stunned my brain." Once free of the straitjacket, "I managed to drag off my saturated clothes. . . . What a sight I beheld. My hands, arms, and thighs were frightfully bruised and had all the colors of the rainbow. My body was shriveled like that of an old man and a horrible stench arose from it."[41]

In 1947, a researcher named Mabel Elliott noted widespread harsh physical punishments for small infractions in the nation's prisons. "Insolence, complaining about the food, failure to work diligently, lack of neatness in the appearance of one's clothing or one's cell can scarcely be considered criminal conduct, however distasteful such behavior may be," she writes. "Yet for just such offenses within the walls, prisoners may be locked in the 'hot box' with the heat turned on and suffer all manner of torture. Some men have even died in such metal cages."[42]

Other writers of the period described hot boxes, also called "dog houses" and "sweat boxes." "The sweat boxes are small coffin-like cells just large enough to suspend a man in an upright position," writes Walter Wilson. "A small hole the size of a silver dollar lets in the only air. The cell is placed in the hot tropic sun, or sometimes a metal plate underneath is heated with fire."[43]

This extreme version of solitary confinement caused some well-publicized deaths. "In 1932 the papers were full of the details of how Arthur Maillefert, a young New Jersey boy on a Florida chain gang, was whipped unmercifully and then placed in a sweat box with a chain around his neck until he died," reports Wilson. "Willie Bellamy, a frail Negro boy still in his teens, was whipped into unconsciousness and then placed in a sweat-box, where he died."[44]

Elliott's 1947 report cites an *Attorney General's Survey of Release Procedures*, which found "corporal punishment was in practice in at least twenty-six prisons in 1939, and whipping with a strap was allowed in the following states: Alabama, Arkansas, California, Colorado, Delaware, Indiana, Kentucky, Louisiana, Mississippi, Missouri, Tennessee, Texas, Virginia. The number of strokes permitted varied from one to twenty-five. Colorado also permitted ball and chain and cold baths."[45] Although northern prisons still used pain for convict control, the prevalence of southern states on the list suggests a punishment disparity between the South and the North.

The popular autobiography *I Am a Fugitive from the Georgia Chain Gang!* by Robert E. Burns eventually became a movie, winning a huge audience. Burns's disclosures, often conveyed with a tone of revelation and horror, target a northern audience. "The purpose of *I Am a Fugitive*, like most muckraking accounts of Southern prisons, was to suggest how out of step with modern life Dixie remained in the 1930s," writes Alex Lichtenstein.[46]

Lichtenstein's purpose is not to undercut the horrors of the southern lease system, but to show that it is not a throwback to a past better left behind but "decidedly modern" and Progressive. "The chain gangs which built the roads of the twentieth-century South became an enduring symbol of Southern backwardness, brutality, and racism; in fact, they were the embodiment of the Progressive ideals of southern modernization, penal reform, and racial moderation," Lichtenstein writes. The brutality of convict leasing, he argues, had to do with "the process of modernization itself."[47]

Both northern and southern states worked convicts hard in the late nineteenth and early twentieth centuries. "The state with the greatest value of prison goods produced in 1923 was Alabama with close to $7,500,000," writes Walter Wilson. "Next came Kentucky with over $7,000,000. Georgia was third with over $5,000,000. Other leading prison-labor states, each producing over $2,000,000 worth of goods in 1923, follow in the order of their importance: Michigan, Maryland, West Virginia, Minnesota, Wisconsin, Connecticut, Tennessee, and Oklahoma."[48] This 1933 accounting from a left-wing author concerned with the effect of prison labor on unions shows the financial center of U.S. prison labor to be the southern states, though the Midwest is also prominent.

Northern prison work systems generally brought contract labor inside penitentiary walls, where government employees supervised the work. The South took punishment outside, turning responsibility for the convicts over to contractors. Prisoners were cheap labor. States that contracted out their convicts could provide fewer cells and guards, and less food, bedding, and clothing. The physical well-being and the security of the prison laborers became the contractors' responsibility. The states could also make money with lease fees.[49]

In the years following the Civil War, the state of Georgia, like the other southern states, turned against the penitentiaries "in favor of penal labor that appeared more appropriate to Reconstruction Georgia's economic needs as well as the sudden preponderance of black convicts," writes Lichtenstein. Whereas pre–Civil War penitentiaries had housed mainly white convicts, "the state's capacity to punish now focused on ex-slaves who fell afoul of the law."[50]

The focus of contract labor was moneymaking rather than punishment. One penitentiary warden "noted that the contractors had a habit of overworking the convicts to the point of exhaustion or disease, returning the sick convicts to the penitentiary, and then demanding fresh, healthy replacements to fill their quota of leased laborers," writes Lichtenstein. "Sixteen of the 211 convicts working on this railroad died between May and December 1868."[51]

Contractors administered whippings and other physical punishments in an effort to extract more and more work. On railroad gangs, many convicts reported that overseers beat convicts in order to pick up the work pace. "Many deaths by whipping did in fact occur when convicts claimed to be unable to continue work, often due to sickness and fatigue, and the overseer would administer some 'medicine' with the lash," writes Lichtenstein. "One overseer 'wanted to kill [a sick convict],' since he was 'no account and Grant, Alexander & Co. could not afford to feed him for nothing.'" The system of contract labor was characterized by "the desire to drive convicts to the limit, and yet care for them under less than sanitary conditions," notes Lichtenstein.[52]

The prison camps bore evidence of the contractors' overwhelming emphasis on making money. "Housing conditions in the chain gang camps are the worst imaginable," writes Wilson. "One form of house for the prisoners is a cage-like cell, mounted on wheels, so that it can be moved from place to place as the camp follows the jobs. The cage is about 13 feet long, 8 feet high, 7 feet wide, and looks more like a cage for ferocious animals than anything else in the world, except that the convict-animal cage is not gilded as are those of the animals in a circus. Such a cage is a 'home' for about 20 men." Accounts of the time suggest that the contractors did not launder convict bedding. "When night comes the tired workers come from work to find a piece of coarse, dirty cloth stretched over lumpy straw, usually alive with bugs," writes Wilson. "This is their bed."[53]

The convicts also bedded down on iron. Less secure than a cell, the rolling cages demanded encumbering restraints, with each man locked to every other body in his row. "All the men are forced to lie down on their bunks in rows. A long chain is then run through the short leg chains which are riveted to the legs of the men. Thus every man is securely fastened to every other man, and can't get out of the chain even to go to the toilet—a hole in the floor of the cage—without waking all the men on the chain. In case of fire the men are held together until unlocked from the long chain." Wilson reports that the mesh of metal chaining prevented escape at some critical moments. "In several cases fires, under such circumstances, have resulted in loss of life," he writes.[54]

"Above all," writes Lichtenstein, "corporal punishment and outright torture—casual blows from rifle butts or clubs, whipping with a leather strap, confinement in a 'sweat-box' under the southern sun, and hanging from stocks or bars"—happened daily for "the most insignificant transgressions." The black prisoners bore that pain most often.[55]

Perhaps nothing is as revealing as the strategies some convicts used to avoid corporal punishment. "To escape the inhuman punishment meted out for inability to do the required quota of work, men frequently mutilate their bodies," writes Wilson. "Workers in Alabama mines, up until 1928, frequently put dynamite caps in their boots and blasted off toes or feet, or attached the caps to fingers and then smashed them with a rock. When the officials found too many such cases, they discouraged it by giving the men severe lashings as soon as they were partially recovered from their injuries." One Tennessee convict, Wilson reports, described a friend of his who could not stand "the toil and monotony of the treadmill labor in the shirt factory." In desperation, the friend, in his own words, "borrowed a hatchet, laid my hand on the block and off came John Thumb —it didn't hurt much. Anyway, it was worth it." Another convict, this one a foundry worker, "poured molten lead into his shoe and had to keep his leg in plaster of Paris for several weeks and ended up a cripple."[56]

Among the best-known accounts of chain gang work in the South is that of muckraking journalist John Spivak. As his narratives make clear, the technologies of pain, restraint, and encumbrance could be inventive. He recounts the story of a convict on the chain gang punished by having cuffs studded with long spikes bolted to his ankles. "David sat on the ground and held first one foot and then the other on a block of wood while the spikes were being riveted. The eye between the two steel prongs fitted closely around the ankle, with just enough space for pants to be pulled through when changing clothes. The weight on his feet was heavy when he rose. With his first step the projections clashed noisily against each other." The blacksmith notices and warns David, "Spread yo' laigs."

Spivak makes plain the implications of David's new spikes: "These twenty-pound weights permanently riveted around the legs are a drawn-out torture leading to exhaustion. During the day they rub against the legs, creating sores which often become infected. Such infections are known as 'shackle poison.' At night the convict's rest is repeatedly broken by the need of raising his legs whenever he turns in his bunk."[57]

David witnesses another convict "lying near the stocks in the blaze of sun, trussed up like a pig ready for slaughter," writes Spivak. "His legs and arms, tied with ropes, pointed to the sky, the whole body kept motionless by a pick thrust between the tied limbs. His mouth was open. The veins in his temples and arms stood out, swollen, and swarming over the face and arms and neck were myriads of tiny red ants."[58]

A third prisoner's body bent forward at a right angle, torso and arms extended parallel to the ground, writes Spivak. Ropes secured his hips and legs to one post, his wrists to another.

> The unresisting Negro, with his back to the post, was laced to it from ankles to hips with a rope and the one tied to the cuffs slipped about the second post. . . . The guard pulled sharply. The convict's torso jerked forward, bending at right angles, his arms outstretched. His head drooped between his arms. The sweat on his back and arms glistened in the light.
>
> "Stretch!" the warden ordered harshly.
>
> The guard pulled until the rope was as taut as a tuned violin string.
>
> "Oh Jesus!" the Negro screamed. "Yo' pullin my arms out!"
>
> The rope was wound around the post and tied, leaving the convict stretched so the slightest movement threatened to wrench his shoulders from their sockets.[59]

The corporal punishments were many, common, deliberate variations on a theme. They must have seemed entrenched. But in the decades that followed the stories recorded by Spivak and others, in a legacy of Progressivism, American punishment slowly left most intentional physical pain behind.

CHAPTER 6

The Devilish Generation

NEAR THE END OF *The Exorcist,* William Blatty's 1971 novel, the mother of a young girl who has just survived a horrific possession tells a priest why she has a stronger faith in the Devil than in God. "The Devil keeps advertising, Father," she says. "The Devil does lots of commercials."[1]

The novel makes explicit a few of these "commercials." The book's opening page contains four epigraphs. The first tells the story of Jesus commanding the demon that calls itself Legion to leave a man. The second is a segment from an FBI wiretap of three gangsters who hung their victim on a meat hook for "three days before he croaked." One gangster giggles at the memory of the man "floppin' around" in response to electric shock from a cattle prod. The third epigraph describes Communist tortures of praying Christian children. The fourth lists three nouns that should have made inhabitants of the late twentieth century shiver: Dachau, Auschwitz, Buchenwald.[2] An epigraph later in the book implies that the Devil is in the U.S. Army.[3]

If Satan lives on in the Mafia, Soviet Communism, Nazism, and the U.S. military, as the epigraphs insinuate, it seems hardly surprising that the king of Hell would send a demon to a rental home in Georgetown, near the seat of American power.

In his provocative recent history of the United States, *Decade of Nightmares: The End of the Sixties and the Making of Eighties America,* Philip

Jenkins argues that the 1970s—not the 1960s and the 1980s, as is commonly held—was the important, transformative decade of the late twentieth century.[4] In the mid-1970s, according to Jenkins, American culture jolted through change. Among other things, the upheaval generated widespread belief in evil. The popular conviction posited inherent wickedness not in actions or temptations but in specific people.[5]

Beginning just after 1975, that is, soon after the United States withdrew from Vietnam, Jenkins argues, an "anti-sixties" reaction set in. This backlash led to a "dramatic . . . break in American history and culture." A popular "pessimism" combined with rejection of rational thinking. "At home and abroad, the post-1975 public was less willing to see social dangers in terms of historical forces, instead preferring a strict moralistic division: problems were a matter of evil, not dysfunction." The new rhetoric of evilness affected discussions of war, American foreign policy, domestic poverty, terrorism, drug use, and crime. It also attached to children.[6] According to the view of human nature implied by this "strict moralistic vision," evil people are static things. Neither wicked nor holy people can change.

Many traditional American democratic ideals conflict with interpretations of human beings as wholly evil or wholly good. Common American ideas and sayings seem preoccupied with encouraging personal transformations. The American Dream, for instance, whether it applies to new immigrants, entrepreneurs, or children, concerns change. Immigrants gain a new nationality and the opportunity for a new life. Entrepreneurs can alter their material circumstances and through their ideas and hard work create a new business. Children given access to American public education can remake themselves and move beyond their parents' circumstances. In 2003, President George W. Bush signed into law the American Dream Downpayment initiative, which offers financial assistance to low-income citizens for a first home; the name of the law implies transformation via home ownership. An almost identical set of meanings accompanies the Declaration of Independence's invocation of the inalienable rights of "Life, Liberty and the pursuit of Happiness." "Pulling oneself up by one's bootstraps" implies a class shift.

An understanding of evil as rooted inside some human beings does not easily accompany a set of ideals based on the capacity of people to transform. As suggested in earlier chapters, the belief that human beings could reform underlay the philosophy of prisons and penitentiaries, dating from the revolutionary exuberance of Benjamin Rush. As American culture increasingly connected evil with individual human beings, it abandoned hope of rehabilitating them.

National anxieties had attached to earlier generations. The June 7, 1968, cover story in *Time* magazine described that year's graduating class as "the troubled and troublesome Class of 1968." The article listed social difficulties of the time—the assassinations of John F. Kennedy and Martin Luther King Jr., the Vietnam War—and offered this analysis: "Such pressures, direct and indirect, have a profound impact on the 630,000 seniors who will pick up diplomas this spring. . . . Those who are in the really new mold sometimes show it by defiance in dress: beards beneath the mortarboards, microskirts or faded Levis under the academic gowns. More often, and far more significantly, it emerges in a growing skepticism and concern about the accepted values and traditions of American society. Many smoke pot. Fewer than ever remain virginal. Yet it is also true that the cutting edge of this class includes the most conscience-stricken, moralistic, and, perhaps, the most promising graduates in U.S. academic history."[7]

Despite the suggestion that baby boomers had turned against American traditions, the article offered a nuanced analysis. This is not the case with *Time*'s 1977 description of the juvenile delinquents of Generation X. For instance, "The Youth Crime Plague," the cover article for the week of July 11, seems to abandon any attempt to understand the young criminals: "How can such sadistic acts—expressions of what moral philosophers would call sheer evil—be explained satisfactorily by poverty and deprivation? What is it in our society that produces mindless rage? Or has the whole connection between crime and society been exaggerated? Some of the usual explanations seem pretty limp." The first sentence offers a key to the punitive rationale of the time: if children are evil, rather than victims of their circumstances, there is no longer any need to help them.[8]

Newsweek featured the Generation X delinquent in its February 27, 1978, story headlined "The Criminal Mind": "Some kids are just bad. They lie and cheat and skip school; they try to bully their parents, rejecting love if it is offered. When these children grow up, they rob, embezzle, rape and kill. Crime turns them on." According to a new theory, such children are not mentally ill, "they are simply wicked."[9]

As Jenkins comments in *Decade of Nightmares*, "Generation X children, born in the mid-1960s, entered their teens and were regularly depicted by the media as dangerous and uncontrollable." Popular media portrayed the adolescents as young criminals. "In 1977–1978, it was children of thirteen and fourteen who were at the center of the new anti-drug panic, presumed to be the targets of underage vice rackets; the pressing criminal danger was believed to be remorseless violent offenders of fifteen or sixteen."[10]

SATAN WAS A POP STAR

In the pop culture sphere, anxiety about the young surged in the popular preoccupation with diabolical magic. Observers of the 1970s noted a widespread fascination with the occult. "The evil entities of the past have descended to us," writes social critic Nicholas Cavendish in *The Powers of Evil*. "In the last few years there have been so many cases of people convinced that they are possessed by evil spirits that professional exorcists have not been able to cope with all of them, and in Britain and America the revival of interest in magic, witchcraft, Ouija boards and the occult in general has brought numerous reports of people badly scared by what they believe to be evil forces." To support his argument, he cites "Hello! Is Anybody There?" a pamphlet issued by the Evangelical Tract Society, that "maintains that the spirits who communicate through mediums or Ouija boards are not the souls of the dead but 'demon spirits—the spirits of Devils that impersonate the dead and possess the bodies of those who indulge in these practices. . . . They are evil spirits without a body, so they will try to take over yours if they can.' "[11]

At the time, the country was experiencing a tilt toward fundamentalist Christianity. According to Jenkins, the pronounced change was a response to profound social anxieties: "In a time when all human institutions and orthodoxies were crumbling and the world might be facing terminal crisis, people naturally sought firm teachings and definitive answers." Along with the popular Christian movement came an apocalyptic philosophy that included a belief in a living embodiment of evil: the Antichrist, also known as the child of the Devil. What had seemed an implausible argument only a decade earlier—the existence of a Devil in people you could point to on the street—by the mid-1970s had started to seem natural.[12]

In the late 1960s and 1970s, depictions of the Devil popped up in areas often considered secular—for instance, at the movies. Satan was a pop star. Historians have argued that movies preoccupied with children who carry the Devil inside, such as *The Exorcist* and *The Omen,* indicate late 1960s and 1970s American sensibilities. In these movies, anxiety attaches not to children generally but to children of the age group soon to be labeled and worried about and demonized and castigated as Generation X.[13]

Many horror films of the time endowed serial killers with supernatural powers—they sometimes rise from the dead or seem unhurt by wounds that would kill a mortal, writes Jenkins.[14] The association of diabolical magic with murder indicates that pop culture was giving similar treatment to children and criminals, much as the broader culture had in past centuries, when child discipline in the classroom paralleled convict punishment.

In the 1968 film *Rosemary's Baby,* a young couple moves into an old and beautiful apartment building called the Bramford. They receive warnings from friends, who advise them that the place has a bad reputation—allegations of child murders and devil-raising within the walls. But Rosemary and her husband, a modern, secular couple, don't heed the warnings.

The Bramford does indeed house devilish neighbors. Within a short time, Rosemary's husband, Guy, a struggling actor, has traded his soul, not to mention his wife's body, for a successful career. One night, the neighborly coven appears naked in Rosemary's bedroom, and a leathery creature with yellow slits for irises rapes her while she is half-conscious. Impregnated with the Devil's son, Rosemary believes she is carrying a baby she and Guy have conceived.

Rosemary's Baby focuses on the baby boomer parents, who are associated with 1960s social disruption in the film. The argument is a simplistic and powerful one: that the sins of what was known as the "disobedient generation" are to blame for wicked babies. The themes of social disturbance, crime, and drug use crop up in the first minutes of the film, implying that Rosemary and her husband are members of the generation that came of age in the 1960s. As Rosemary and her husband examine the apartment they will soon rent, her husband jokes, "No marijuana?" as Rosemary lists herbs the deceased former tenant grew in her kitchen.

Such topics also occupy the best-selling novel on which the film is based. In one chapter, Rosemary meets a young woman in the basement laundry room of the Bramford. Mistaking her for a famous actress, Rosemary begins a conversation. As it turns out, her new acquaintance, Terry, is a former dope fiend and prostitute. She has been rescued, or so she thinks, by the Castavets, an intrusive elderly Satanist couple. "I was starving and on dope and doing a lot of other things that I'm so ashamed of I could throw up just thinking about them," says Terry. "And Mr. and Mrs. Castavet completely rehabilitated me."[15]

"Rehabilitated" is a word that by the late twentieth century had a strong association with criminality. The prison system "rehabilitated" its inhabitants. But if the prisoners in penitentiaries were once expected to turn their thoughts to God, the Castavets expect an opposite transformation of Terry. They are priming the young addict with "health food and vitamins" and "check-ups" because they expect her to become Satan's lover. The issue of Terry's rehabilitation is to be a bouncing baby Devil.

But the young woman sees only salvation from a criminal life. "I would be dead now if it wasn't for them. That's an absolute fact. Dead or in jail," she tells Rosemary.[16] Fifteen pages later, Terry falls out of an apartment window and dies, either by suicide or by murder, after learning that the coven expects her to bear Satan's child.

When the Castavets invite Rosemary and Guy for dinner, Minnie and Roman engage their new neighbors in a probing conversation, during which they seem to seek evidence of a break from tradition that will link the young couple to the 1960s disobedient generation. Asked about her beliefs, Rosemary confides that she was once religious, "but now I'm an agnostic." She also admits, while washing dishes, to estrangement from her family, "because Guy isn't Catholic, and we didn't have a church wedding." Rosemary's admission that she has followed her own generation rather than the traditions of her midwestern family makes her as ready for impregnation-via-Satan as did Terry's criminal behavior. Criminality and other forms of social disobedience are, in this film, yoked together and tied to evil.[17]

In the final scene of both the book and the movie, Rosemary stands above her baby's bassinet with a butcher knife in her hand. Having realized that her child is the Antichrist, she is thinking of killing him. Instead, this baby boomer decides to nurture and raise the child, who is both Satan and Rosemary's baby boy. Social upheaval has birthed a Devil—a member of Generation X.[18]

Like Rosemary, Chris, the mother in *The Exorcist*, is not religious. A divorcee raising a daughter, Chris is the star of a film about a professor who sympathizes with and joins a student insurrection reminiscent of the Vietnam War–era teach-ins: in her beliefs, her marital status, and her career, Chris is entangled with the disobedient generation. Her household proves as vulnerable as Rosemary's.

Consistent with the temper of the time, the novel distances itself from its Enlightenment inheritance and implies supernatural, rather than scientific, explanations for both a demon-child and criminality. After Chris's daughter Regan contacts someone named "Mr. Howdy" with her Ouija board, urinates on the carpet, tells a family friend he is going to die, and behaves as though frozen to her shuddering bed, Chris takes her to doctors who use advanced medical machines and theories on Regan. In explaining the child's behavior, one doctor implies a faith in reason the novel does not share. "It isn't rare to find destructive and even criminal behavior" caused by a brain disorder, the doctor says. "There's such a big change [in behavior], in fact, that two or three hundred years ago people with temporal lobe disorders were often considered to be possessed by a Devil."[19]

Similarly, when Chris asks a priest how to get an exorcism, the priest rebuffs her with science. But no scientific or rational theory works because, as the novel's readers well know, Regan has the Devil inside her.[20]

Whatever dream worlds books and movies might offer, we can't fully separate them from lived existence. *The Exorcist* proves this point; it created a widely reported social phenomenon. The novel was a best seller, the film a blockbuster. The lines for tickets wrapped entire city blocks. But the oral and journalistic histories of *The Exorcist* moment suggest much more. A *Rolling Stone* review of the film observed that the audience for the film was anxious, having heard "tales of grown men retching on their way to the rest rooms and fainting in the aisles."[21]

The lay Catholic magazine *Commonweal* also recounted the stories of vomiting and fainting in the theaters, as well as news that "priests from Denver to New Jersey report being sought out by those the film has deranged." The *Commonweal* reviewer, Colin L. Westerbeck Jr., suggested that there might be something diabolical in the film itself. "It all makes me wonder whether I ought to review *The Exorcist* or try to exorcise it," he wrote.[22]

As William Friedkin, *The Exorcist*'s director, noted, belief in a living Devil was evident among those who saw his movie. "Newsreel units" asked people waiting in line for tickets to *The Exorcist* whether they believed in the Devil, "and one after another, they said, 'Yes! Yes! Yes!'" recalled Friedkin in an interview. "I didn't realize how many people were prepared to accept a personified Devil."[23]

In the 1974 best-selling novel *Carrie* and its 1976 film version, anxiety about evil children offers a veiled commentary on the 1960s sexual revolution. The title character is a berated, awkward, terrified, and shy high school girl who wears homemade sack dresses.

Carrie also has the ability to move things with her mind—psychokinesis. She can slam windows and crack mirrors. Her psychic power increases along with her sexuality. One preoccupation of the novel is the source of her psychic ability—divine or diabolical. Carrie decides that she has ESP, but her mother has a different interpretation. She thinks her daughter is evil. Even Carrie entertains that possibility:

> She did not know if her gift had come from the lord of light
> or of darkness, and now, finally finding that she did not care
> which, she was overcome with an almost indescribable relief, as
> if a huge weight, long carried, had slipped from her shoulders.
>
> Upstairs, Momma continued to whisper. It was not the Lord's
> Prayer. It was the Prayer of Exorcism from Deuteronomy.[24]

Like Rosemary and Chris, Margaret White, Carrie's mother, reflects the liberal sexual attitudes of the 1960s. Despite her conservative Christianity, she had sex before marriage and, more important, *enjoyed* it. Because she experienced sexual pleasure in conceiving Carrie, Margaret believes her daughter is a Devil's child. Carrie was born in 1963, often described as the first year of Generation X.[25]

Shadows of criminality and punishment also stalk this novel, just as they do *Rosemary's Baby* and *The Exorcist*. In one scene, the adolescent girl has just gotten her period. Margaret responds with a homemade penitentiary. She locks Carrie in a closet with religious icons.[26] Carrie's solitary cell, a place of supposed penitence, is in this novel of the 1970s a cruel absurdity. Prayer in this penitentiary is sterile; Carrie will not be able to change herself back into an immature girl no matter how devout her request. What's more, as the novel progresses, the makeshift solitary cell is not strong enough to contain a Generation X adolescent whose extraordinary destructive powers may emanate from the underworld. Stephen King's brief meditation on punishment in *Carrie* echoes the critiques of rehabilitation among social theorists and the public at large, as well as the growing association of criminality with evil.

Carrie appears at first to be an innocent, abused by her worldly (and sexually active) high school peers. When the handsomest boy at school takes her to the prom and she begins to welcome her own beauty along with his attentions, the triumphant date seems like the ultimate in ugly duckling clichés. But as anyone who has seen the film knows, the swan doesn't linger long. At the moment when she acts like a normal teen on a date, she is about to prove herself capable of slaughter.

After a schoolmate attempts to shame Carrie by dousing the girl's head with pig blood, the metal bucket carrying the blood tumbles from the gymnasium ceiling, striking and killing Carrie's dream date. Carrie transforms into a possessed mass murderer. Her eyes, locked in a stare, transmit an unearthly power. She sets off the fire system, spraying liquid across the gymnasium and electrocuting anyone near the electrical apparatus set up for the dance band. She forces the gymnasium doors shut, trapping most of the students inside. She sets the place on fire, then heads home, where her mother, believing she is the Devil, stabs her.

Carrie is set in the future and is the story of the death and chaos that could result from a girl with malevolent powers. Given her birth date in the novel, Carrie would have been eleven on the date of its actual publication and the prom she devastates a high school event set in the future. The anxiety about evil children concerns the future, not the present. The story also concerns not just Chamberlain, Maine, but the entire society. "What happens if there are others like her?" asks one witness. "What happens to the world?"[27]

SYMPATHY FOR THE DEVIL

American books and films were not alone in seeing an up-tick of interest in Devils. Commentators began to argue that Devil worshippers were proliferating.

The murderous Manson family, responsible for the 1969 deaths of actress Sharon Tate and her friends, was often described as a satanic cult, a media epithet that increased public anxiety about Devil worshippers.

"Most self-respecting Satanists would consider the type of violence apparent in the Tate carnage to be utterly senseless and much too crude for their
taste," writes social critic Arthur Lyons in *The Second Coming*. But even the
careful Lyons saw Satanists all over America. "There do exist several inter-
state religious organizations devoted to devil-worship which have eccle-
siastical hierarchies and central headquarters acting as overseers of dispersed local covens," he reports, specifying training organizations in "New
York, Philadelphia, Chicago, and Los Angeles."[28] As for membership, "I
have been given estimates that run as high as 100,000, but that figure is
probably on the high side," he writes. "The important fact to note, however,
is not the present number of practicing Satanists in the United States but
rather the number of *potential* Satanists, which is undoubtedly impressive,
taking into consideration the phenomenal growth of these groups in the
last few years." "Potential Satanists" were almost certainly young people,
the same group that the films of the 1970s interpret as vulnerable to evil
and dangerous.[29]

Lyons's book does more than document anxiety. It reveals that the
popular worry about the Devil was starting to affect how people treated
each other in contexts formerly governed by laws and conventions. Oddly,
satanic fear extended to union organizing. In May 1968, Lyons wrote,
"The General Cigar Company asked the NLRB [National Labor Relations
Board] to void a collective bargaining election won by the International
Association of Machinists and Aerospace Workers on the grounds that
the union supporters in the Puerto Rico plant had practiced witchcraft on
employees to influence the election."[30]

Major religious figures also discussed evil as if it could walk and talk.
"What are the Church's greatest needs at the present time?" asked Pope
Paul VI in his November 15, 1972, address entitled "Confronting the Devil's Power." Seemingly aware that his answer might confound his modern
audience, the pope warned, "Don't be surprised at Our answer and don't
write it off as simplistic or even superstitious: one of the Church's greatest needs is to be defended against the evil we call the Devil."[31]

The pope went on to define evil. In doing so, he assumed that his audience would hold a rational belief system, defining evil as material lack—
hunger, for instance, or poverty. That was not what the pope had in mind.
"Evil is not merely an absence of something but an active force, a living,

spiritual being that is perverted and that perverts others." He urged a return to study of "this matter of the Devil and of the influence he can exert on individuals as well as on communities, entire societies or events."[32]

Three years later, Billy Graham published *Angels: God's Secret Agents,* which became a best seller.[33] Although its topic is angels, Graham's book contains a hearty discussion of the Devil. Graham points out that the ways his contemporaries talk about the supernatural seems to have altered radically in a short time. "Just a few years ago such ideas would have been scorned by most educated people," he writes in a section entitled "The Current Cult of the Demonic." "Science was king, and science was tuned in to believe only what could be seen or measured. The idea of supernatural beings was thought to be nonsense, the ravings of the lunatic fringe. All this has changed."[34]

As evidence, Graham tells his readers to visit bookstores, airport news kiosks, and university libraries. "You will be confronted by shelves and tables packed with books about the Devil, Satan worship and demon possession." He also cites film and television treatments of evil and "as many as one in four hard rock pop songs," including "Sympathy for the Devil" by the Rolling Stones. "Some polls indicate that 70 percent of Americans believe in a personal Devil," Graham writes.[35]

Graham gives *The Exorcist* special mention, suggesting that fear of personified evil had reached the eminent political minds of Washington, D.C. "Recently I had dinner with several senators and congressmen in a dining room in the Capitol building," writes Graham. "We began discussing the rising interest in the occult with special reference to *The Exorcist.* One of the senators, who had recently passed through a deep religious experience, said that due to his past experience with the occult, whenever he knew of a theater that was showing *The Exorcist* he would drive a block around it. He was afraid even to go near it. He said, 'I know that both angels and demons are for real.' "[36]

This story of a senator telling Graham he believes in a real Devil raises a question: did senators who held these kinds of beliefs enshrine them in legislation? Is it possible that the popular obsession with the Devil had an effect on our federal laws? As I will show in chapter 8, the answer seems to be yes. That effect is most visible in the ways that our nation began to see, and then treat, its criminals.[37]

THE DEVIL IS A POLITICAL BEAST

If 1970s Devil fascination arose at least in part because of an antisixties reaction,[38] that rejoinder to the previous decade was not always the emotive and unacknowledged one the devilish pop culture trends suggest. Some of the backlash was organized.

The planning and preparing for a "conservative revival" in American politics began with the mid-1960s work of "suburban warriors," writes Lisa McGirr.[39] Originating as a response to the Goldwater campaign and to fears about the spread of communism, the suburban revolution paralleled the other revolutions of the 1960s. It became an electoral force by responding to 1960s social trends. "These concerns now took on new dimensions, in large part in reaction to changes in family life, sexual liberation, a growing youth culture, and liberal Supreme Court decisions that expanded the scope of personal freedoms. As a result, various forms of 'domestic corruption'—obscenity, sex education, abortion, and, by the late 1970s, an ever more assertive gay liberation movement—became new targets of attack," writes McGirr.[40]

The forceful and assured presence of second-wave feminism, gay liberation, and black power, among other movements of the early 1970s, caused cultural conservatives to grow "increasingly anxious," writes McGirr. When economic trouble hit in the 1970s, the earlier worries "fused with a growing economic preservationism, the combination with which the Right would move into national political power in 1980."[41]

In this manner, the 1970s, the decade Jenkins sees as transformative, the decade during which the Devil walked the land, proved key to the Reagan revolution. Along with Devil fascination arrived an enormous popular religious awakening, often called "the rise of the Christian Right." McGirr understands the conversion explosion as a "cultural backlash" to the spread of liberal liberation movements, "social changes of the 1960s," and the resulting sense of personal threat among social conservatives.[42]

One of the great actors in the evangelical revival was the Reverend Chuck Smith, who chose to work among the disaffected 1960s youth and middle-class residents of California's Orange County. Smith founded Calvary Chapel, which acquired 25,000 members by 1978 and continues today as "one of the largest single churches in the country." A popular evangelical prophet, Smith warned of end times and threats to family structure and to the nation. In 1973, he prophesied, "The decline of the economy and government of the United States will open the doors to the rise of the anti-Christ to world power as head of the [European] common market countries."[43]

Smith's version of the Antichrist matches that of the 1970s horror films fascinated with the births of evil children and the meaning of their power. For instance, the 1976 film *The Omen* includes only one major deviation from Smith's story—in the movie the diminutive Antichrist ends up living with his adoptive family in the White House.

As McGirr notes, the literalization of evilness on the lawns and in the houses of America was part of the power of conservative Christianity and contributed to its political rise. "The emphasis on patriarchal family values, concern with 'evil'—crime, abortion, pornography—and the critique of 'centralized power' all went along with conservative ideas." As McGirr puts it, the automatic definition of social ills as "evil" made conservative Christianity attractive. Such thinking "provided comfort in a harsh world without challenging the underpinnings" of people's middle-class lives. "They won adherents exactly because they failed to account for the material causes for the social breakdown of families, for drugs, and for social violence, namely, the free market and the deep class divisions it generated."[44]

"FURTHER FROM GOD THAN I AM FROM THE DEVIL"

In 1980, Norman Mailer won a Pulitzer Prize for *The Executioner's Song*, his narrative of the life and death of Gary Gilmore, the first man executed when the United States reinstituted capital punishment in 1976 after a ten-year legal hiatus. Gilmore murdered two men he did not know in 1974. *The Executioner's Song*, a tour de force drawn from hundreds of hours of interviews with Gilmore's family and friends, court documents, and personal letters, offers a complicated portrait of an intelligent murderer, alternately regretful and thoughtless about his crimes.

Gilmore was a lifetime crook. From late childhood on, he spent most of his time in juvenile facilities, reform schools, and prison. As *The Executioner's Song* opens, Gilmore heads back to small-town Utah after serving a term for armed robbery. Mailer makes clear Gilmore's discomfort with life on the outside and his tendency to turn to small crimes—such as stealing six-packs—as a release from stress and sometimes as a whim. But *The Executioner's Song* also offers another, less rational explanation for the Gilmore murders: evil.

In one scene before Gilmore commits his murders, he calls out to his lover, Nicole. She runs too quickly to him, bumps into Gilmore, and hurts herself. Gilmore lifts her up, and she encircles him with her legs. "With her eyes closed, she had the odd feeling of an evil presence near her that came from Gary," writes Mailer. But rather than frightening her, "She found it kind of half agreeable. Said to herself, Well, if he is the Devil, maybe I want to get closer."

Nicole then asks her boyfriend. "Are you the Devil?"

Gilmore takes Nicole's question seriously. "At that point, Gary set her down and didn't say anything," writes Mailer. "It really got cold around them. He told Nicole he had a friend named Ward White who once asked him the same question."[45]

Later in the book, Gilmore refers back to this scene in one of his letters to her. "*Once you asked me if I was the Devil, remember? . . . I'm not. The Devil would be far more clever than I, would operate on a much larger scale and of course would feel no remorse. So I'm not Beelzebub. And I know the Devil can't feel love.*" Having distanced himself from the Devil, Gilmore suggests that, nonetheless, he is an evil creature. "*But I might be further from God than I am from the Devil. Which is not a good thing. It seems that I know evil more intimately than I know goodness and that's not a good thing either. I want to get even, to be made even, whole, my debts paid (whatever it may take!).*"[46]

In another letter to Nicole, Gilmore recounts a conversation with his mother. He told Bessie Gilmore that he desired execution because he had become "*somewhat evil. . . . I don't like being evil and that I desire not to be evil anymore.*"[47]

It is not only Gilmore and his intimate acquaintances who find him diabolical. Toward the middle of the book, when Gilmore is imprisoned, he and Nicole decide to commit suicide at the same moment. Both take pills, and both survive. The nurses who treat Gilmore as he awakens see him as different from most would-be suicides. "He was coming on exceptionally strong. It was dangerous to get within reach. 'He looks,' said one of the nurses, 'like the demon that got into Linda Blair in *The Exorcist.*' "[48]

Gilmore's mother, Bessie Gilmore, claims to remember him as an evil child. When her son was a three-year-old, "she knew he was going to be executed" because "that was when he began to show a side she could not go near." But Bessie Gilmore recollects as criminal behavior what, to many other parents, would seem childish disobedience. When she tells Gary to avoid a mud puddle, he sits in it. As she remembers it, her emotional response is extreme: "It put a fear through her. Would he always be so defiant?"[49]

Gilmore interprets himself as a creature resistant to change, and particularly to the kind of reform for the better that was supposed to happen in prisons. Speaking to the prosecutor during a break in his trial, Gilmore says "that the prison system was not doing what it was designed to achieve, that is, rehabilitate. In his opinion, it was a complete failure."

The prosecutor picks up the theme. "Rehabilitation was hopeless," he tells himself in deciding to seek the death penalty.[50]

As powerful a read as *The Executioner's Song* remains today, Gary Gilmore, the prosecutor, Bessie Gilmore, Nicole, and Mailer are all creatures of their time. All saw Gilmore as evil and irredeemable. Evilness and its connection to both childhood and criminality was part of the cultural moment. So was the tendency to say that rehabilitation had failed. And, in a phenomenon linked to all of these trends, so was the tendency to understand bad behaviors, in their minor and major forms, as intertwined. The defiance of three-year-old Gary Gilmore was enough, by the 1970s, to be remembered as predicting his eventual execution for murder. This is to say that all of these people understood Gilmore as evil and rehabilitation as having failed *because* those were the ways people talked about criminals and prisons in the mid to late 1970s.

A moral argument about the nature of criminality resides in Mailer's and other books and films of the time. No longer is the criminal redeemable. Rather, criminality is intrinsic, evidence of the Devil inside.

"THE UNREACHABLES"

Criminality was not the only quality that came to seem intrinsic in the 1970s. "Behind [the ghetto's] crumbling walls," reported *Time* magazine in "The American Underclass," a 1977 article, "lives a large group of people who are more intractable, more socially alien and more hostile than almost anyone had imagined. They are the unreachables: the American underclass. . . . Their bleak environment nurtures values that are often at radical odds with those of the majority—even the majority of the poor. Thus the underclass minority produces a highly disproportionate number of the nation's juvenile delinquents, school dropouts, drug addicts and welfare mothers, and much of the adult crime, family disruption, urban decay and demand for social expenditures."[51]

The article's language reveals at every turn. The prose pays lip service to a harsh "environment" that "nurtures values" contradicting those of the rest of the country. But other word choices contradict the hint of environmental influence. The ghetto inhabitants are "intractable," that is, ungovernable and rigid. But "intractable" can also mean incurable, and a lack of a cure for an inhabitant means the inhabitant carries a disease. The word locates ghetto trouble *inside* people.

The intractables are characterized by a lack of social skills and a persistent negative emotional state. They are "socially alien" and "hostile," to the extent that most people can't imagine. The unimaginability of the hostile, alien ghetto inhabitants sets them even further apart from the rest of the country. They are "unreachables." The surface meaning of this noun seems to be that government intervention can't transform the lives of ghetto people, but "unreachable" has an extreme cast. It suggests lostness, as though no other human can locate or communicate with those who live there. The implication that the ghetto poor live in a remote, strange society and bear no qualities that can lead to human understanding is blatant.

Following the linguistic setup is a litany of offenses, some criminal, others irresponsible. The unreachables commit crimes: juvenile delinquency, drug dealing, drug taking. They leave school, live on welfare, cause the city to "decay," break down the traditional family, and demand money from the government.

The article also repeats the noun "underclass," a word that implies absolute bottomness: whatever class you might have thought was at the bottom, the underclass is under it. The underclass appears in this article as a personality type, complete with its own set of emotional tendencies, social traits, and criminal habits, even though in the article it is used to identify a large group of people.

Less than two months earlier, *Time* had placed "The Youth Crime Plague" on its cover. The accompanying article presented such questions as, "How can such sadistic acts—expressions of what moral philosophers would call sheer evil—be explained satisfactorily by poverty and deprivation? What is it in our society that produces mindless rage? . . . Or has the whole connection between crime and society been exaggerated? Some of the usual explanations seem pretty limp."[52]

Like the passage from "The American Underclass," this quotation mentions environmental arguments for behavior—"poverty and deprivation"—while at the same time rejecting them and adopting a countertheory: that the sources of bad behavior live inside individuals. Juvenile criminality, mentioned in "The Youth Crime Plague," appears also in the article about the underclass. The emotional state of "mindless rage" is no great distance from "hostile." The setting of "poverty and deprivation" resembles the "bleak environment" the underclass article associates with the ghetto. The two articles seem to describe the same people: urban ghetto poor. Although neither article states its racial assumptions outright, "underclass" is a noun that usually identifies minorities.

Why would *Time* magazine publish two articles in the short space of a summer, both positing a group of people living in a circumscribed location whose bad behavior, or "sheer evil," was not the fault of social conditions but instead resulted from "intractable," "unreachable," and permanent personality traits? The American cultural fascination with the Devil can't fully explain what seems a concerted effort in these passages to shift the meanings of "sheer evil," poverty, crime, society, environment, and personality. One explanation can be summed up in the phrase "demand for social expenditures," found in the article on the underclass.

THE UNDERCLASS AND THE LOSS OF
THE INDUSTRIAL ECONOMY

The word "underclass" originated in the early twentieth century, but it gained new energy in the hands of 1970s neoconservatives. They argued that poor, black urbanites were behaving in new, socially destructive ways. As one sociologist has noted, this argument amounted to a "resurgence of old images of the undeserving poor."[53]

Liberal scholar and social critic William Julius Wilson accepts the term "underclass," as well as the assumption of radical new behavior patterns among inner-city poor people. In *The Declining Significance of Race* and *The Truly Disadvantaged*, Wilson argues that racial attacks and racialized barriers to success are declining. For the first time since the antebellum years, black Americans have little to fear from overt racism, he writes. But that didn't mean the economic situation had improved drastically for African Americans. Even as expressed racism declined, new barriers sprang up. The new obstacles were economic and difficult to overcome. They "indicate an important and emerging form of class subordination," writes Wilson. These blocks to success did not target the black poor, but they disproportionately affected their lives and livelihoods.[54]

The key was unemployment. In the decades before 1950, "Blacks actually fared better in relation to white unemployment." After 1950, however, black unemployment figures soared. By the 1970s, what Wilson calls "structural changes in the economy" made jobs scarce "for unskilled Negroes in and out of the labor force." Black teenagers had it especially hard. "Each year since 1966 a greater than two-to-one black-white teenage unemployment ratio has been officially recorded," writes Wilson. "From 1970 to 1974, black teenagers' unemployment has averaged 32 percent, and the 1974 rate of 32.9 percent was close to two and a half times greater than the recorded white teenagers' unemployment."[55]

While the number of jobs for black teens went down, the number of black teens went up, increasing "almost 75 percent in less than a decade (1960 to 1969)." (The increase in white teens was 14 percent, observes Wilson.) Young black adults ages twenty to twenty-four showed a population growth almost as large. This "unprecedented increase" in the young black population, argues Wilson, accounted partly for the "delinquency, crime, and unrest in the ghettos."[56]

Not only did the young black population surge, so too did the "poverty population" in the largest U.S. cities. "Although the total population in these five largest cities decreased by 9 percent between 1970 and 1980, the poverty population increased by 22 percent," writes Wilson. And the proportion living "in poverty areas" also swelled—"by 40 percent overall, by 69 percent in high-poverty areas (i.e., areas with a poverty rate of at least 30 percent), and by a staggering 161 percent in extreme poverty areas (i.e., areas with a poverty rate of at least 40 percent)." Wilson notes that "these incredible changes" happened in a single decade.[57] The economy, veering its productive energies away from poor urban areas at the same time as young people entered their working years, created the underclass derided as morally bankrupt.

Other writers on poverty and social policy see a similar economic shift disproportionately affecting African Americans. As Thomas Sugrue notes,

"Detroit's postwar urban crisis emerged as the consequence of two of the most important, interrelated, and unresolved problems in American history: that capitalism generates economic inequality and that African Americans have disproportionately borne the impact of that inequality."[58] For Sugrue, housing segregation, despite decades of legal and personal battles against it, exacerbated the economic difficulties of Detroit's inner-city poor. "The combination of deindustrialization, white flight, and hardening ghettoization proved devastating," writes Sugrue.[59]

In Detroit, as in the cities Wilson studies, black teens and young adults "were increasingly alienated" and "most severely affected" by the disappearance of jobs from the city, writes Sugrue. An early 1960s governmental study of more than three hundred young residents of a depressed Detroit neighborhood indicates how some African-American youth were thinking about job opportunities even before the steep poverty of the 1970s arrived. "Not a single respondent" spoke of a possible career in "skilled trades, office, clerical, or technical occupations," notes Sugrue, quoting from the study. According to that report, "replacing the whole middle range of occupations" in the young people's expectations were a "range of deviant occupations—prostitution, numbers, malicing, corn whiskey, theft, etc." The report theorized that the youth saw their futures as criminal ones because "under conditions where a gap in legitimate opportunity exists in the world, such deviant occupations grow up to fill the void. The motif is one of survival; it is not based on thrill seeking."[60]

If that is the perspective on crime and employment in the 1960s American city, the imprisonment boom of the four decades since has altered the equation. On March 29, 2006, *The NewsHour with Jim Lehrer* featured a discussion about "the plight of black men." One guest was Harry Holzer, an economics and public policy professor at Georgetown University and a visiting fellow at the Urban Institute. "The data from the 1990s for many of us were really shocking and very discouraging," said Holzer. "The 1990s was the best economic decade in thirty years: booming labor markets, very tight labor shortages in some places." During that decade, "low income women, especially African-American women, were pouring into the labor market for a variety of reasons." Nothing of the kind happened to low-income and impoverished black men, however. "Black men were falling further behind, in terms of employment." Scholars, like Holzer, interested in what causes poverty and economic inequality, started trying to figure out the reasons for the widening disparity. "What really jumped out at a lot of us is the high rates of incarceration for a lot of these young men," Holzer told the audience.[61]

In *Punishment and Inequality in America,* Bruce Western writes that the recent positive spin on U.S. domestic economic policies depends on the sequestering of a large number of young black men away from the job market. If we were to factor those men into labor statistics, he notes, it's evident "that young black men have experienced virtually no real economic gains on young whites." Western's numbers also indicate that the actual black unemployment rate is 20 percent higher than the official one.[62]

This broad urban story acquires depth if we consider the suburban one. "In 1950, a quarter of all Americans lived in the suburbs; in 1960, a full third; and by 1990, a solid majority," write historians Thomas Sugrue and Kevin Kruse in *The New Suburban History.* Because of this enormous tipping of Americans into the suburbs, "the transformation of the United States into a suburban nation has had significant consequences for every aspect of American life." The suburbs have had a disproportionate effect on the national political agenda, squeezing government attention to the cities.[63]

The suburban triumph has caused profound economic and social changes, Kruse and Sugrue suggest. "Postwar suburbanization has fundamentally intertwined with the processes that reshaped postwar urban America, including capital flight, the concentration of African Americans in central cities, the hardening of racial divisions in housing markets, and the large-scale shift of governmental resources away from urban centers."[64]

The massive influence of the suburbs on so much in the last fifty years did not happen in isolation from federal policies, as numerous social historians have pointed out. David Freund, for instance, finds a governmental gift to suburbanites: "a unique postwar political narrative that obscured the origins of race and class inequality in the modern metropolis." The state "insisted that 'free market' forces, alone, were responsible for the gulf—economic and, increasingly, spatial—that separated the nation's haves from its have-nots." White people in the suburbs found the story an appealing one and "embraced" it "to justify racial exclusion."[65]

If the suburbs have much to tell us about how racialized poverty became entrenched in American cities, they also can shed light on the stark late-century shift in popular understanding of criminality. Given the enormous economic changes sweeping the urban poor in the 1960s and 1970s, why did *Time* magazine deal so lightly with environmental and social arguments, instead turning to talk about intractability and the religiously charged phrase "sheer evil"? The newsmagazine was participating in a time-honored practice. The separation of poor people from the rest of the populace according to "categories of merit" has a long tradition, as historian Michael B. Katz notes.[66]

The confluence of an economically buffeted population and the word "evil" has happened before. In a chapter headed "The Morphology of Evil" in his book *Poverty and Policy in American History*, Katz cites the 1880 census. "In 1880 seven special schedules of the federal census enumerated the 'dependent, defective, and delinquent' population of the United States. These were the blind, insane, prisoners, deaf-mutes, idiots, paupers, and homeless children," writes Katz. "Frederic Howard Wines, who supervised the enumeration, used two major arguments to defend treating the seven classes in one inquiry. The first was their essential similarity." Katz quotes Wines discussing the links between the different attributes. Crime flowed from other "dependent, defective, and delinquent" characteristics, according to Wines. "The physical and moral causes which are the occasion of insanity in one man excite another to crime. The connection between crime and pauperism is exceedingly close; so is that between crime and imbecility."[67]

Wines had a theory about his list of "defective" attributes. He thought them heritable. How did crime flow from insanity, pauperism, and imbecility, and vice versa? "There is a morphology of evil which requires to be studied," wrote Wines.[68]

Katz provides an analysis of why Wines lumped together blindness and criminality—traits that today seem utterly unlike each other. The combination of pauperism, imbecility, blindness, and criminality made sense in terms of government support. "Because they were dependent, they consumed resources; they had no productive role; they not only remained outside the universal market but drained it as well. . . . Wines's amalgamation of the seven classes of 'dependent, defective, and delinquent' people into one metaclass of 'defective types of humanity' did more than reflect the values of the universal market. It also served an important role in the formulation of public policy, for it justified the cheap and custodial quality of institutional care by defining dependence as the manifestation of an inferior and hopeless condition."[69]

As Katz's work makes clear, lexicons of "evil" can support governmental policies. This is particularly true when the language emanates from political officials.

The 1880 "morphology of evil" served a political purpose. So too did a version of that morphology that wafted up from hell in the 1970s. Because of its religious heritage the word "evil" allowed for public policy decisions that would neglect or punish those who suffered in the declining industrial economy of the 1970s and 1980s. "Evil" made it easier to reject social and environmental explanations for criminal behavior. "Evil" also aimed for those people who, because of their youth, their urban neighborhoods, and their dependence on a disappearing economic system, were beginning to need financial help.

THE "FIEND" GOES TO JAIL

Money earmarked for the underclass did arrive. It paid for cells. Between 1987 and 1995, "state government expenditures on prisons increased by 30 percent while spending on higher education decreased by 18 percent," according to a report from the Justice Policy Institute.[70]

Philip Jenkins, who noticed a rise in the language of "evilness" in the 1970s, makes an argument similar to the "morphology of evil" that Katz saw in the 1880s census documents. Jenkins claims the linguistic shift led to much tougher 1980s crime policies.[71]

Even in the late 1960s, public officials talked openly of hellish creatures. One study of the drug war describes a monstrous image the Nixon administration adopted in 1968 to raise concern about the spread of marijuana. With the image of "the drug user as Vampire," writes Mike Gray in *Drug Crazy*, the Nixon administration caught hold of public worries and directed them against "junkies and dope smokers in a way that made perfect sense to an America whipsawed by war, riots, and an incomprehensible younger generation." The Nixonian strategy took energy from widespread misgivings about LSD and pot, which, the public guessed, "were at the root of the youth rebellion," and it responded to newspaper journalism that suggested "heroin was driving inner-city blacks to rape and pillage."

"On the nightly news," Gray writes, "these two images began fusing together as heroin and marijuana merged into a single dreadful scourge in the public mind."[72]

Nixon proved skilled at transforming public anxiety into public policy. "The problem has assumed the dimensions of a national emergency," said Nixon. "I intend to take every step necessary." To achieve those steps, writes Gray, "he would need emergency powers—preventive detention, unorthodox strike forces, more freedom to search, wiretap, and arrest. The Democrats in Congress, impressed with the whip-crack political power of Nixon's law-and-order message, backed him to the hilt."[73]

The idea of the drug addict as a vampire did not originate with Nixon. "Back in 1900, the country had looked upon addicts as unfortunate citizens with a medical problem," Gray writes. "By 1920, they had become 'drug fiends,' twisted, immoral, untrustworthy. Like vampires, they infected everything they touched. . . . The image—the Drug User as Vampire —was to become a driving force in the public mind."[74]

Gray traces the origin of this important public symbol to a man named Richmond Pearson Hobson, an energetic orator on behalf of temperance. His speeches included detailed explications of what he meant by the drug-fiend vampire. Hobson argued that heroin changes ordinary people into vampires who attack and transform others. "The addict has an insane desire to make addicts of others," wrote Hobson. "One addict will recruit seven others in his lifetime."[75]

Hobson made his speeches at a critical moment in the development of the nation's communication systems, the birth of commercial radio. "NBC, one of the new national networks, gave him uninterrupted free time on four hundred stations—an unprecedented audience," writes Gray. Hobson built his extended metaphor on the air. His linguistic strategy had enormous public effect. "By 1919 public attitudes about narcotics had shifted so radically that even government documents were referring to addicts as 'dope fiends,'" writes Gray, who credits Hobson's campaign with helping along the passage of prohibition.[76]

"Fiend," like other words that imply evil, is an elastic term. It elides with whatever it pairs with, altering that object or human being from a neutral creature to a negative one often understood as supernatural. As we have seen, the nineteenth-century prisoner Harrie spoke of his guards as "fiends." His use of the metaphor happened at a moment of a crackdown, within his own prison as in others of the time, on physical abuse of inmates. Like the guard-as-fiend language, "dope fiend" connects with external policies.

During the first Bush administration, the metaphor shifted to a "war on drugs," a phrase that implied an enemy deserving of annihilation. The moral sensibility of the metaphor inherited energy from Nixon's "drug fiend" as well as from the Johnson administration's War on Poverty; what's good and what's evil is implicit in all three. President George H. W. Bush was explicit about the policies he wanted for the enemy, saying in 1989 that he wanted to ensure "that when a drug dealer is convicted there's a cell waiting for him. And he should not go free because prisons are too full."[77]

In September 2007, Marc Mauer and Ryan S. King of the prison advocacy group the Sentencing Project published "A Twenty-five-Year Quagmire: The War on Drugs and Its Impact on American Society." Among the report's findings were these revealing statistics:

- Drug offenders in prisons and jails have increased 1100 percent since 1980.
- Nearly six in ten persons in state prison for a drug offense have no history of violence or high-level drug-selling activity.

This report also shows what other studies have demonstrated: that punishment for drug crimes in the United States is highly racialized, with African Americans comprising 37 percent of arrestees for drug crimes although they make up only 14 percent of all users.[78]

"Fiend" is, as previously noted, often has a religious connotation. When a government uses such language, it appropriates a religious idea in the service of policy; fiends, being hell creatures, deserve the punishments of that realm.

In *The Protestant Ethic and the Spirit of Capitalism,* his classic essay in social science, Max Weber understood American capitalism as religious, specifically Protestant. Those who succeeded, he argued, could see themselves (and be seen by others) as blessed by God. But Weber also perceived capitalism's punitive side, which he associated with religion. Those who failed in the marketplace failed morally.[79] Weber's thesis has been contro-

versial from the day he published it.[80] Yet his perceptive linking of capitalism, Protestantism, reward, and punishment provides an interesting
commentary on the last half-century of American social policy. It is a
relationship that recurs symbolically in that strange, enticing dream
world: American popular culture.

CHAPTER 7

Flogging for Jesus

PUNISHMENT, EDUCATION, AND THE DAMNED TOT

IN ONE OF HIS SERMONS, the Puritan minister Jonathan Edwards portrays parents in paradise gazing upon their dead children, who are suffering in hell. The parents, writes Edwards, look down, "with holy joy upon their countenances" as they perceive evidence of divine justice.[1]

But why are the tots in hell? For Edwards and many others of his era, all children are born damned.

Another passage from Edwards sums up his view of the state of the souls of children who have not yet turned away from their natural condition: "All are by nature the children of wrath, and heirs of hell. . . . As innocent as children seem to be to us, yet, if they are out of Christ, they are not so in God's sight, but young vipers, and infinitely more hateful than vipers."[2]

Historians have argued that American public education arose out of a concern with saving depraved children from Satan. In 1647, the General Court of Massachusetts established an obligatory system of schooling, the predecessor to our public schools.[3] The 1647 law, which acquired the nickname the Old Deluder Satan Act, makes explicit the religious purpose of educating the children of the colony. Ignorance was the Devil's provenance. Knowledge, specifically knowledge of the Bible, was holy: "It being one chiefe project of that ould deluder, Satan, to keepe men from the knowledge of ye Scriptures," wrote the founders of American schooling. "It is therefore ordered, that every towneship in this jurisdiction, after ye Lord hath increased them to the number of fifty householders, shall then forthwith appoint one within their towne to teach all such children as shall resort to him to write and reade."[4]

If children inherited Adam's sin and belonged to Satan, the act of teaching meant adults must destroy the part of the child's personality that was "natural" or present from birth, what the Puritans often described as "will." "Naturalness" for this community was a negative trait, associated with the "deluder Satan." "Surely there is in all children (tho not alike) a stubbernes and stoutness of minde arising from naturall pride which must in the first place be broken and beaten down that so the foundation of their education being layd in humilitie and tractableness other virtues may in their time be built thereon," writes the Puritan preacher John Robinson.[5]

"Broken and beaten down" is not a metaphor. But for Edwards and others of his moment, life was cruel. Children often died suddenly. Parental anxiety must have been excruciating, and it was only compounded by the worry that an infant could easily die years before its "naturall pride" ever gave way to godly salvation. George Marsden captures the pervasive fragility of life in his biography of Edwards: "Much of Puritan upbringing was designed to teach children to recognize how insecure their lives were. Every child knew of brothers, sisters, cousins, or friends who had suddenly died. Cotton Mather, under whose preaching Timothy [Edwards, Jonathan's father] had once sat, eventually lost thirteen of his fifteen children. Parents nightly reminded their children that sleep was a type of death and taught them such prayers as 'This day is past; but tell me who shall say / That I shall surely live another day.'"[6]

Marsden discusses Edwards in terms that can also apply to other writers of the time: "If there is an emphasis that appears difficult, or harsh, or overstated in Edwards, often the reader can better appreciate his perspective by asking the question: 'How would this issue look if it really were the case that bliss or punishment for literal *eternity* was at stake?'"[7]

Such an understanding imbues a phrase like "broken and beaten down" with parental concern and affection. As Marsden notes, "Likely the elder Edwardses subscribed to the principle of suppressing any signs of willfulness, although Puritan practices of child rearing varied and often included more displays of warm affection than is sometimes depicted. For those whose first concern was to prepare their children for salvation, the most loving thing a parent could do was to teach children the disciplines that would open them to receive a truly submissive spirit." Parents beat their children to save them from eternal damnation because it was possible an infant "viper" would not live till baptism.[8]

Some accounts of family life of the time imply that childish naturalness received dutiful domestic attention. Jonathan Edwards's grandson Sereno Edwards Dwight remembered his grandmother Sarah's method: "Her system of discipline, was begun at a very early age, and it was her rule, to resist the first, as well as every subsequent exhibition of temper or disobedience in the child, however young, until its will was brought into submission to the will of its parents wisely reflecting, that until a child will obey his parents, he can never be brought to obey God."[9]

Philip Greven, author of *Spare the Child: The Religious Roots of Punishment and the Psychological Impact of Abuse,* places the above passage next to a letter written by Jonathan and Sarah Edwards's daughter Esther Edwards Burr about her attempts to break the will of her firstborn child, Sally. "The methods of discipline implied in this grandson's account are detailed explicitly" in the letter, notes Greven. Burr writes: "I had almost forgot to tell you that I have begun to gouvern Sally. She has been Whip'd once on *Old Adams* account, and she knows the difference between a smile and a frown as well as I do. When she has done any thing that she Suspects is wrong, will look with concern to see what Mama says, and if I only knit my brow she will cry till I smile, and altho she is not quite Ten months old, yet when she knows so much, I think tis time she should be taught."[10] As Greven notes, "In the Edwards and Burr families, corporal punishments began in infancy, and thus pain was encountered before conscious memory began. . . . Infancy was the beginning but rarely the end of such punishments."[11]

Educational practices of the time suggest that many colonists, like Burr, understood learning and physical hurt as entwined. "And because the Rodd of Correction is an ordinance of God necessary sometimes to bee dispenced unto Children," begin the 1645 rules governing the Free Town School of Dorchester (today part of the city of Boston), "it is therefore ordered and agreed that the schoolmaster for the tyme beeing shall haue full power to minister correction to all or any of his schollers without respect of p'sons according as the nature and qualitie of the offence shall require whereto, all his schollers must bee duley subject and no parent or other of the Inhabitants shall hinder or goe about to hinder the master therein." The rules endow the schoolmaster with the power to subdue schoolchildren physically without oversight, no matter the hurt the young scholars might endure.[12]

Colonial school children were not alone in feeling the lash. Harvard College once flogged its disobedient students. Like the system of community schools, Harvard College had its origin in Puritan religious motives; the college was established to educate a ministry.[13] Among the punishments for rule violations at Harvard College in 1660 is this: "It is hereby ordered that the president and fellows of Harvard College have the power to punish all misdeeds of the young men in their college. They are to use their best judgment, and punish by fines or whipping in the hall publicly, as the nature of the offense shall call for."[14]

The public nature of the whipping echoes the "well laid on" lashes performed in colonial town squares. Accounts of the early years of Harvard College record punishments for such offenses as "speaking blasphemous words concerning the Holy Ghost," recorded in Samuel Sewall's diary. Governor John Winthrop notes in a 1644 entry, "Two of our ministers' sons, being students in the college, robbed two dwelling houses in the night." The students were caught and "ordered by the governors of the college to be there whipped, which was performed by the president himself."[15]

At least one Harvard College official abused corporal punishment. "Nathaniel Eaton, the first person placed at its head, was soon deposed, having been convicted of ill-treating the students by giving them twenty or thirty stripes at a time and keeping them on scanty and unwholesome food; of beating his subordinate, Nathaniel Briscoe, in an inhuman manner; and of other misdemeanors," reports John Gorham Palfrey in his *History of New England*.[16]

If religion bound education with whippings, early children's literature was similarly pious, instructive, and punitive. A high infant mortality rate contributed to the prevalence of ditties designed to convey to tots their damned state and to arouse fear that would bring about their subsequent redemption: "My days will quickly pass and I must be / Broyling in flames to all eternity."[17]

Cotton Mather had a hand in children's book publishing. In 1700, the pastor of the Old North Church in Boston added his own writings to a popular volume of children's ditties by the British author James Janeway. Published in an American edition titled *A Token for Children: Being an Exact Account of the Conversion, Holy and Exemplary Lives, and Joyful Deaths of Several Young Children*, it includes this cautionary burst: infants are "not too little to die . . . not too little to go to hell."[18]

THE GHOST OF "OLD ADAM" IN TODAY'S CHILDREN

In a resurgence of the idea that children are born sinful, the Janeway-Mather book is back in print and sold with other Puritan classics on some Christian Web sites.[19] Religion-inflected corporal punishment of children, once popular in an early American society that understood youngsters as evil, has also reappeared in homes, schools, and churches. In July 1998, Faith Temple Pentecostal Church on North Street in Milwaukee, Wisconsin, disciplined one of its members. A twelve-year-old girl who had paid too much attention to boys and had disobeyed her teacher was, according to press reports at the time, "told to sit in front of the congregation in what is called 'a heathen chair.'" Her parents then used what the mother described as "a little stick, a little bow and arrow, of fiberglass and plastic" to beat her.[20]

The girl's mother, who had four other children and was employed as a childcare worker, did not call the event a whipping. She gave it the name "chastisement" and said she was willing to go to jail for it. "It's something I believe in and I will continue to do," she is quoted as saying in the *Milwaukee Journal-Sentinel*. The church's pastor, David Hemphill, said that public whippings of children, which he termed "shamings," had occurred during previous services, but not for several months. The girl told the paper that lashings during worship were common at her church. In his comments to the press, the pastor quoted the book of Proverbs. "Foolishness is bound in the heart of a child," said Hemphill. "But the rod of correction will drive it far from him."[21]

Were it not for a tip left on a child abuse and neglect hotline at the Milwaukee Child Welfare Office, the chastisement at Faith Pentecostal Church might have remained a congregational secret. The event offers a glimpse of a faith practice important to some sectors of contemporary American Christianity. Similar punishment rituals, rooted in what their practitioners consider biblical duties, are repeated in homes, religious schools, and congregations across the country.

In its spectacular quality, the "chastisement" that happened in Milwaukee resembles the punishment methods imported from Europe and performed before the close-knit communities of the early American colonies—particularly the whippings, duckings, and other techniques intended to cause physical suffering. Modern-day religious chastisement is similarly painful, and in instances like the one in Milwaukee, it is a public display of shame.

THE BIRTH OF THE CHRISTIAN SPANKING MANUAL

Physical punishment in Protestant households is nothing new. In *Spare the Child*, a study of centuries of religious writings about physical punishment of children, including the 1970s and 1980s spanking guides, historian Phillip Greven notes that for centuries Christian parents of all persuasions have quoted the Bible, most frequently the book of Proverbs, to justify beatings. But before the 1970s, how-to books on godly spanking were all but nonexistent. In his foreword to the 1978 *Withhold Not Correction*, by Bruce A. Ray, Jay E. Adams expresses dismay at the absence of books that advised parents to correct their children in a "Christian" way. "But where can detailed instruction of this nature be found?" he asks. "Sometimes there is a chapter on discipline tucked away deep in the recesses of some monumental work on the Christian home or family, but at most there are only a few pages devoted to the actual application of correction and at best only a few obvious principles are considered." The Christian spanking guides share a lexicon of pain. The words "correction" and "discipline" in these sentences signify corporal punishment.[22]

The situation Adams bemoaned in 1978 no longer applies. Never before has spanking been such a money-making enterprise, with a thriving publishing industry and Web and magazine ads for wood and plastic "rods," complete with consolations that parents who spank are doing the right thing by their children and their society. Such Christian advocates of corporal punishment as James Dobson, Michael and Debi Pearl, and J. Richard Fugate have published best-selling child-rearing guides. Many of the 1970s books on religiously motivated spanking are available in new editions. Authors like Lisa Whelchel, best known for playing Blair on the 1980s sitcom *The Facts of Life*, are still emerging. According to a 2003 study by evangelical pollster George Barna, approximately half of the American public reads Christian books and one-third buys them. Parenting is a consistent subgenre of Christian publishing, making up 6 percent of sales. Not all Christian parenting guides advocate physical punishment, but a steady number do. Such advice books sometimes have folksy and humorous titles, for example *God, the Rod, and Your Child's Bod.*[23]

Christian spankers are related to today's punishment trends. The decades that saw a resurgence of the philosophy that claims Christians are under a godly obligation to punish children with a "rod" also saw dramatic changes in how society punishes criminals and in the ways popular culture treats the subjects of crime and punishment. In later chapters I will consider the return of retribution and technologies of control and pain to the penal system; tough-on-crime politics; and popular representations of crime and punishment in books, magazines, movies, and television shows (see chapters 8, 9, 10, and 11). For now, though, it is important to note that these transformations in distinct but influential parts of American society occurred together. The coincidence is not accidental. The disparate but nearly simultaneous changes signal a profound, extensive, and punitive cultural shift.

The 1970s, a decade that saw the return of retribution in American movies, such as the influential *Death Wish,* and a declaration among prison scholars and advocates that rehabilitation had failed the American prison system was the decade when Christian spankers started to organize and proselytize. Like early colonists, some contemporary evangelical and fundamentalist groups understand their religion as immersed in soul-saving physical punishments. Today it is not heretics and loud women who suffer God's violent concern. It's children.

Beginning in 1946 with the publication of Dr. Benjamin Spock's *Baby and Child Care,* a child-centered approach came to govern mainstream American thought about child rearing. In a shift researchers have linked to broader cultural changes associated with a postindustrial society, spanking approval declined from its height of 94 percent in 1968 to about 65 percent, a rate that has held level since 1990. Americans still approve of spanking in the home by a margin of two-to-one. Approval of in-school spankings is quite another matter, and many schools have ended or curtailed the practice, partly because of lawsuit fears.[24]

Spock markedly revised his own opinion on spanking from 1946, with the first edition of *Baby and Childcare*, where he remarks: "If an angry parent keeps himself from spanking, he may show his irritation in other ways, for instance, by nagging the child for half the day, or trying to make him feel deeply guilty. I'm not advocating spanking, but I think it is less poisonous than lengthy disapproval, because it clears the air for parent and child. You sometimes hear it recommended that you never spank a child in anger but wait until you have cooled off. That seems unnatural. It takes a pretty grim parent to whip a child when the anger is gone."[25]

In the 1985 edition, Spock writes, "Some spanked children feel quite justified in beating up on smaller ones. The American tradition of spanking may be one cause of the fact that there is *much* more violence in our country than in any other comparable nation." He adds, "In the olden days, most children were spanked, on the assumption that this was necessary to make them behave. In the 20th century, as parents and professionals have studied children here and in other countries, they have come to realize that children can be well behaved, cooperative and polite without ever having been punished physically or in any other way."[26]

It's hard to overestimate Spock's influence. Upon his death in 1998, the PBS show *The NewsHour with Jim Lehrer* remarked, "Dr. Benjamin Spock, who died yesterday at age 94, wrote the world's best-selling nonfiction book after the Bible. His *Baby and Child Care* influenced several generations of American parents and children in the post–World War II era."[27]

An important subgroup of Americans, however, endorses spanking. The pro-spanking Christians are a counter to Spock. Some of their books express dismay at Spock's influence on parents and children. One declares children of the 1970s to be "Spock-marked."[28]

For many of these writers, and for the parents who take their words to heart, spanking is the key to a peaceful home. It is a religious obligation, a method of driving out evil. It is essential to parents who want to go to heaven. It is a crucial weapon in the war against Satan. It returns an upended household to its natural order. The parents see God as commanding them to carry out the punishment and so believe themselves to be obeying a law superior to the laws of the United States. The beating is an act of faith.

Three decades since they first began writing in force, the Christian spankers have built a thriving publishing industry. Churches teach their discipline styles in sermons and in parenting courses. Evidence of an extensive Christian spanking subculture appears in the many advice books published and purchased on the subject and in press and lawsuit revelations of "Christian discipline" gone too far. The size of the spanking subculture, however, is hard to determine for several reasons. The guides that advise parents to use the rod also caution parents against confiding their discipline practices to others who might see the lashings as child abuse. Some Christian schools and churches paddle and whip their disobedient students, sometimes in public shaming rituals, such as the "chastisement" before the Milwaukee congregation. Over the last three decades, conservative Christian schools and churches have proliferated. These private religious institutions, however, are under no obligation to reveal their discipline practices. The same fears that may cause parents to hide their use of switches and sticks probably affect schools and churches as well.

SPANKING AND CRIME CONTROL:
A COHERENT SOCIAL PHILOSOPHY

In its late twentieth- and early twenty-first-century manifestations, American Protestant spanking plays a central role in an overarching theory about American society, its direction, its dangers, and its faults. For Americans who adhere to this philosophy, spanking is essential to the survival of the nation. American society is at risk, say spanking advocates, in large part because parents are too easy on their children. The absence of corporal punishment in many households, they argue, nurtures criminals.

Dr. James Dobson, the founder and chairman of Focus on the Family, is often considered the most influential evangelical leader in the country. His clout is cultural as well as political. He earned his popularity through his radio empire and his popular books. Dobson, with his silver hair and kindly voice, is a radio personality. His weekly radio show, on air since 1977, appears on approximately three thousand radio stations; audiences for his commentaries number about 220 million.[29]

Apart from his widespread influence on his listeners, Dobson is perhaps best known for his parenting advice, one tenet of which is the importance of spanking according to God's word. One of the more conservative of the spanking advocates, Dobson says the punishment should be prompt, consistent, delivered with a switch, and that parents should never paddle their children in anger. He sets age limits for physical discipline, suggesting that parents not begin spanking until the child is eighteen months of age and that they end most corporal punishment by age five, though the spankings can continue until about age twelve.[30]

There is a great deal of disagreement among authors of Christian parenting books as to the specifics of how to spank, but the texts tend to be consistent on the less technical details of corporal discipline. Among these authors, spanking is the weapon of choice against "the will" or "willfulness," that is, indications that the child is intent on following his or her own desires. For some of these authors, "will" can encompass ordinary responses to hunger, thirst, irritation, or even pain. The point, they agree, is to use corporal punishment to persuade children to follow the direction of their parents (who are stand-ins for other authorities, including God) rather than their own inclinations.

"Many of today's 'experts' argue that discipline is controlling and that it prevents kids from fully expressing themselves as individuals," writes Lisa Whelchel. "To that I say, 'Let's hear a hallelujah!' I've seen my child fully expressing himself, and it's not a pretty sight." Whelchel is the author of *Creative Correction: Extraordinary Ideas for Everyday Discipline,* a book published in 2000 and promoted by Dobson's Focus on the Family.[31]

For Whelchel, disobedience smacks of humankind's original transgression in the garden. "Tucker, like all of us, is a son of Adam, the first child on earth—so he comes by his sin naturally," she writes of her son. "In fact, the roots of misbehavior can be traced all the way back to Adam."[32]

And in Adam's past lie future dangers. "There are things within the heart of the sweetest little baby that, allowed to blossom and grow to fruition, will bring about eventual destruction," writes Ted Tripp, pastor of the Philadelphia Grace Fellowship Church, in *Shepherding a Child's Heart,* published in 1995. The danger is evident in behaviors that might seem innocent to the uninformed. "Watch a baby struggle against wearing a hat in the winter," he writes. "Even this baby who cannot articulate or even conceptualize what he is doing shows a determination not to be ruled from without."[33]

Those who see evidence of Adam in young babies can be less than sanguine about infant rebellion. Observing that "the years of real hope (Prov. 19:18) are actually much fewer than many of us realize," Bruce Ray advises parents, "That's why it is especially important to begin disciplining children scripturally right away, as soon as they are born." The words "disciplining children scripturally" mean spanking, usually with a "rod" or stick.[34]

Some spanking writings suggest there should be no upper age limit. Philip Lancaster, the editor of *Patriarch* magazine and its Web site (www .patriarch.com), is also the author of numerous articles that advocate holy hitting. In an endorsement of age-indifferent physical punishment so broad that it appears to include adults, Lancaster writes in "The Loving Art of Spanking," "The fool of any age deserves stripes on his back for his willful disobedience."[35]

The idea is to cause the disobedient ones enough pain that their wills break. "How hard and how long do you spank?" asks Lancaster. "Your aim should be to spank until you elicit a cry of repentance from the child. Some children will begin crying before the rod even makes contact with their backsides but, [sic] it is not mere tears that you are after. Other children will respond to the blows with the rod by crying out in protest or anger but, [sic] this is definitely not what you are after. This response must be distinguished from a cry that signals the child is yielding his will and yielding to the discipline. Call it tough love." What a cry of repentance sounds like, and how to distinguish it from other emotional responses to a painful blow, is unclear in these writings.[36]

Some writers advise parents to spank crying children until the cries stop. In their 1999 book *No Greater Joy*, authors Michael and Debi Pearl describe a family that "requested that we stay with them the entire week and critique their child training." During a car ride, the couple's "youngest boy, age two or three," wants to sit with his mother and begins to whine, then sob. In response to advice from the Pearls, the father pulls to the side of the road, spanks his son, puts him back in the child seat, and starts off again. When the child resumes crying, the entire process repeats. "There are those of you who will think that the twenty miles of spanking was cruel," write the authors. "Remember, this was not a daily event; it was a 'war to end all wars.' "[37] For his part, Tripp suggests a parent may be spanking much of the time the child is awake. "There may be days in which nothing much gets done because of the demands of consistent discipline," he writes.[38]

Many of these books acknowledge that the rod can leave marks. In *What the Bible Says about Child Training*, published in 1980, J. Richard Fugate describes an "exceptionally willful" child, who "will require more frequent and more intense whippings," probably "enough strokes to receive stripes or even welts." These are not signs of serious physical damage, he says. "Parents should not be overly concerned if such minor injuries do result from their chastisement as it is perfectly normal (2 Samuel 7:14; Psalms 89:32; Proverbs 20:30)."[39]

Home School Digest, a magazine that frequently includes articles advocating spanking, recently published "Chastening Children," by Jonathan Lindvall, who writes, "It should never be an intentional result, but if you chasten your children correctly, you will occasionally leave what the Bible here calls 'stripes' on their bodies." Lindvall dismisses the idea that such "stripes" could be signs of serious physical hurt. "A rod will leave very temporary reddened lines. Frankly, that is another good reason for modestly covering up this portion of the body."[40]

Many pro-spanking books exhort uses of the rod that go beyond Dobson's call for suppression of "willful defiance." One common concern of these books is negative emotions, which the authors often call "attitude." Roy Lessin, author of *Spanking: A Loving Discipline* as well as several Christian novels, advocates spankings for what he calls "wrongful attitudes," writing, "Cheerful obedience to parents is how a child pleases God." Lancaster advises, "To fail to discipline for inward, as well as for outward, rebellion is to assure that the heart will remain unyielding." Lancaster does not explain how to discover whether a child who behaves with seeming obedience is internally rebellious.[41]

Although some authors confine their chastising instruments to the rod, others are more creative. Quoting Proverbs 10:31 ("The mouth of the righteous brings forth wisdom, but a perverse tongue will be cut out"), Whelchel advises pinching a child's tongue with a clothespin to "discourage foul language." Whelchel's gag echoes colonial methods for punishing wrong speech. In a similar vein, Michael Pearl describes the day he hog-tied a boy named Asher for neglecting to pull up his pants, which were drooping. "I weigh 230 pounds and I am six feet, four inches tall," writes Pearl. "He is about four feet tall and weighs about fifty pounds. He put everything into his resistance." In order to tie the boy up, Pearl says, "I had to sit on his head and shoulders."[42]

Dobson's best-selling book entitled *The Strong-Willed Child* contains a scene from the home front involving the family dachshund, Siggie—named after Sigmund Freud—that sheds light on his view of child rearing. "Please don't misunderstand me. Siggie is a member of our family and we love him dearly," begins Dobson. "And despite his anarchistic nature, I have finally taught him to obey a few simple commands. However, we had some classic battles before he reluctantly yielded to my authority." One of the biggest battles occurred when Dobson returned home from a three-day conference. Siggie, relates Dobson, "had become boss of the house while I was gone."

"I had seen this defiant mood before, and knew there was only one way to deal with it," writes Dobson, who "fought him up one wall and down the other, with both of us scratching and clawing and growling and swinging the belt." The only reason, according to Dobson, that he managed to put Siggie to bed that night was that Dobson "outweighed him 200 to 12!"

What Dobson calls "the most vicious fight ever staged between man and beast" is a fable. "There is an important moral to my story that is highly relevant to the world of children," he writes. "*Just as surely as a dog will occasionally challenge the authority of his leaders, so will a little child—only more so*" (emphasis in original).[43]

STORY: THE ROD ONLINE

Although the rod described in the Old Testament book of Proverbs was a stick, some spanking advocates make use of other implements. Dobson describes his mother whipping him with a corset, an action he insists was both loving and in his best interest.[44] There are today a number of rods available on the Web, advertised in some Christian publications, and for sale in some Christian book and toy stores.

For $2, I was able to buy a "Speak Softly Spanking Stick" from the Web site of Kingdom Identity Ministries of Harrison, Arkansas. Of the devices I researched, the Speak Softly Spanking Stick, manufactured by Bible Star, a Fort Worth, Texas, company, seems most akin to the Old Testament rod. A little longer and thicker than a ruler, it elicited a respectable smack and a red mark when I tried it out on my thigh.

My next rod came from Child Training Resources, a home-schooling, family-run supplier of books on child discipline. This "chastening instrument," as it is advertised, a 9-inch-long, 1.5-inch-wide, and 3/16-inch-thick strip of polyurethane, bit more sharply than the Speak Softly Spanking Stick, probably because the polyurethane has a whip effect. "OUR CHASTENING INSTRUMENT," boasts the company, is:

- Flexible—produces the right amount of sting without injury!
- Unbreakable—will last a lifetime!
- Convenient—fits easily into purse or diaper bag!
- Affordable—buy one for kitchen, bedroom, car—wherever!
- Guaranteed—satisfaction or money back.

Another selling point is this rod's modern construction. It is a product of twentieth-century chemistry rather than wood: "Fulfilling the purpose and function of the Biblical rod, yet designed with today's parents in mind, our chastening instrument is perfectly suited for the loving correction of your little ones." The Web site offers "a free chastening instrument to leaders of child training classes with 15 or more people."

My chastening instrument arrived in a plain envelope along with a sales slip that read "God bless your parenting!" and listed a Bible verse, Ephesians 6:4. "And, ye fathers, provoke not your children to wrath: but bring them up in the nurture and admonition of the Lord," which I interpreted as a warning against hitting too hard. Also in the envelope was a set of "Basic Tips on Chastisement," among them:

Don't allow squirming or screaming during chastisement;
Give enough strokes to obtain obedience and a submitted will;
Lots of love and affection afterwards.

A "note" follows this list of tips. It reads, "Child Training Resources is not responsible for misuse of its chastening instrument." Versions of the same statement appear on the Web site and on the chastening instrument itself.

Advertisements for another spanking tool, called "The Rod," describe a nylon stick with a "cushioned vinyl grip" and a "safety tip" used for "chastening to promote godliness." "Why a Rod for Training?" asks the brochure, which offers the mini whip for $6.50 from Slide's Manufacturing of Oklahoma. It answers its own question: "The Means Prescribed by God." The advertising flyer claims that the rod benefits children in these ways:

- Promotes a loving atmosphere in the home
- Teaches responsible behavior

- Removes guilt and foolishness from their hearts
- Develops self-control
- Better atmosphere for learning
- Helps children to receive wisdom

The rod is "inexpensive," notes the advertisement, is "an excellent gift idea," and "allows for better parent/child relationship."

But when I sent for my own rod, I found I had missed out. The company returned my money with a letter informing me that Slide's had gone out of business. The letter did, however, offer advice on child rearing. "In this age, there are so many people who do not fully understand God's perfect plan for raising children (Proverbs 10:13) and often view biblical discipline as 'evil' or 'abusive.'" The letter continued, voicing concern about mistreatment with the rod. "So, we want to encourage you to discipline with much caution and with a great amount of love." Slide's exhorted me to "chasten" my children only for their benefit and not for my "own convenience."

This was no call to stop spanking. "God has given you the blessing of a very important job; training up arrows for His kingdom," concluded the letter. "Don't be dismayed by those who might disagree with you or come against you. We know that their battle is not with you or with us, but it is with the Lord (2 Chronicles 20:15)." The owners of Slide's Manufacturing explained they were pursuing other ministries, assured me that they would be praying for me, and asked for my prayers in return.

A CARPENTER WITH A MISSION

Joey Salvati does not read books about spanking, nor does he attend church or read the Bible. But "about three years ago" he got a message from God. "I do my prayers in the shower," says the New Kensington, Pennsylvania, carpenter, whom I speak to by phone in 2006. Over the course of several such shower prayer sessions, says Salvati, "It came to me four times: 'Make paddles. Give them away.' I just blew it off. The fourth time it hit me like a brick upside the head." Salvati rushed from the shower, grabbed a pencil and paper, and drew a basic wood board with a narrowing for the handle. On that handle, he drew a heart. Inside the heart he wrote the words, "Love, Joey."[45]

In three years, Salvati estimates he has given away between 600 and

700 of the white pine paddles. But even as he believes he is following the Lord, Salvati knows the paddles he is making to bring children to godly obedience could have other uses. On the opposite side of the handle from the words "Love, Joey" is another message: "Joey is not responsible for misuse of this product." An image of a stop sign with the words "Never in Anger" appears on both sides of the paddle. Why? "Because I know one day a nut's going to get one," says Salvati.[46]

On his Web site spare-rod.com, Salvati provides rules for punishment that he says came to him from God. The rules tell parents to spank while the child is clothed, to support the torso to prevent spinal injury, to communicate the infraction four times, and to hug and comfort the child afterwards. "If you do it this way, you're not going to beat the hell out of the kid," he says.[47]

According to Salvati's divinely inspired punishment continuum, children who are disrespectful get one swat. "Disrespect, that was number 1," says Salvati. "That one's there because, if you fix that, right off the bat you're fixing a lot of stuff." Children who do drugs get five hits. Parents are supposed to wait one minute between each swat. That way, the child has time to consider the misbehavior. Salvati suggests I try spanking my own leg with this method and see how long a minute is. I follow his instructions and find that if I hit my leg hard, I spend the next sixty seconds anticipating the coming blow. It is not a pleasant use of time.[48]

Salvati thinks children are more disrespectful now than in the past. "I think it has to do with both parents working and TV and music." According to Salvati, the increased disobedience he sees also has to do with prophecies about the end of the world: "Kids are supposed to be unruly toward the end, and I believe that the end's coming."[49]

THE ROD GOES WILD

Joey Salvati, who admits to spanking his son, who was at the time fifteen, and the rest of the Christian spankers don't apply the rod in a vacuum. Punishments are often in contention, and theirs are no exception. Countering strong beliefs in the saving power of spanking are people like Sue Lawrence, who runs the anti-spanking Web sites http://stoptherod.net and http://parentinginjesusfootsteps.org. The home page of parent ingin jesusfootsteps.org carries the bold notice: "ALERT! BABYWHIPPING BUSINESS—TAKE ACTION—CLICK HERE" Lawrence organizes an online activist group of 160 people, who, she says, are "working on this problem." Lawrence and her cohorts claim to have had rods and whips taken off the market, and they have repeatedly targeted Christian stores and online sellers of the devices.[50]

Some spanking critics, notably Greven, have expressed concern that even the more careful of the Christian discipline guides, such as Dobson's, may lead to abuse by communicating that physical pain is a legitimate means of controlling children.[51] Such arguments have been controversial because although some studies indicate that moderate spanking may harm kids in the long run, others suggest it is an effective and harmless discipline method.

But it is clear that some schools, churches, and parents who defend their actions as "biblical" are not confining their "chastisement" practices to a slap with a rod across the buttocks. Many guides advise parents to hide their discipline practices, but sometimes the pain methods go awry and as a result come to public notice. The stories of deaths and severe hurts suggest that punitive pain, though often hidden, may be widespread.

On March 16, 2006, the *Charlotte News Observer* reported that Lynn Paddock, a woman "accused of murdering" her adopted boy Sean, had found through the Internet "literature by an evangelical minister and his wife who recommended using plumbing supply lines to spank misbehaving children." After buying the books by Michael and Debi Pearl, Paddock "started spanking her adopted children as suggested." Sean did not die of these beatings but rather from what the local sheriff described as "being wrapped so tightly in blankets he suffocated." When authorities interviewed Paddock's other children, one of them told the officers about the pipe-beatings.

Paddock and the members of her church had discussed the child-rearing methods recommended by the Pearls, her lawyer told the newspaper, adding, "I think she was trying to do the right thing by her children." Michael and Debi Pearl declined the paper's request for an interview.

Dot Ehlers, the director of a North Carolina organization that guides parents in child rearing, told the newspaper that she had noticed the effect of Christian parenting guides on the parents sent to her office by the Johnston County Department of Social Services. "She said about a quarter of the 60 parents she instructs each week say their faith defends and encourages corporal punishment."[52]

In Austin, Texas, an instance of mischief prompted an extreme case of physical discipline at the Capital City Baptist Church. During a summer bible school program called "Olympic Summer," children were supposed to respond to questions from their teacher by searching for a Bible verse. But on July 3, 2002, Louie Guerrero wasn't playing by the rules: he pretended to have the answer even though he hadn't bothered to look for the passage, his teacher claimed.[53]

So Louie was sent to his pastor, Joshua Thompson, who ran the Spanish-speaking arm of Capital City Baptist Church. Joshua's father, Hank Thompson, who ran the main church, had adopted a no-spanking policy in 1990.[54] But Joshua had other ideas about discipline. Louie's mother, Norma Arellano, a church member, claims that Joshua Thompson "would preach that you can hit your child for four hours on the back, and that nothing will happen to him."[55]

Later that morning, Louie's mother and stepfather, Genovevo Arellano Sanchez, were running errands when Joshua Thompson called Sanchez's cell phone and told him that he had a "problem" with Louie he could not solve. The parents agreed to meet Thompson at their home. In the driveway, Thompson told Sanchez "they had a 'big problem'" that "revolved around Louie being a liar," according to the Austin Police Department's Affidavit for Warrant of Arrest and Detention in the case. "Joshua told Genovevo that he had tried to 'break' Louie but had not succeeded." "Break," Louie's stepfather explained to the police, "meant that the child in question repented the specific wrongdoing. This was normally achieved through physical discipline. . . . The solution that Joshua prescribed to Genovevo was for Genovevo to 'beat' Louie for '2 more hours.' "[56]

Sanchez did not continue the beating. He took his son to the hospital. At the children's hospital of Austin's University Medical Center at Brackenridge, the police noted that the boy's back was "covered in severe lacerations, bruising, welts, and bloodied broken skin which looked dark red in color." They found "bruising to both arms, legs, and buttocks," as well as to the right side of the boy's head. Because "the massive bruising had created waste from broken blood vessels, which had 'overtaxed' the ability of Louie's kidneys to clear his system," continued the affidavit, the boy went into kidney failure, spent time in intensive care, and received a blood transfusion.[57]

How had a paddling led to such physical danger? According to a summary of the witness statements of the paramedics who attended to Louie, the boy told them "he had been hit with a rod, a stick." A doctor testified that Louie had been beaten hundreds of times.[58] On the witness stand, Louie explained his understanding of why Joshua had beaten him while Joshua's brother Caleb held his arms: Joshua "said I had the Devil in me."[59]

Joshua Thompson's statements before the court suggest that he believed that he was helping the child by hitting him. His testimony indicates that he so strongly believed the punishment harmless that he did not realize he'd hurt the boy until much later.[60]

In December 2004, Joshua and Caleb Thompson were convicted of injury to a child and aggravated assault. Both were sentenced to long prison terms.[61] Five months later, the Thompson brothers settled a civil lawsuit filed by Louie Guerrero's family. According to the terms of the suit, the Thompsons promised to pay the child and his family $1.5 million.[62] The Thompson brothers are appealing the criminal sentence.

Like the Thompson brothers, the Reverend Arthur Allen, an ordained Baptist minister, lived a life of service. A pastor for more than thirty-five years at the nondenominational House of Prayer in Atlanta, Allen worked painting houses and landscaping while ministering to his 130-member congregation, some of whom credited Allen with helping them to turn their lives around after years of trouble, including homelessness, drug addiction, and crime. Some said he had saved their marriages and bought them houses. "When I come into the church, I was a whorehead," one worshipper told *Dateline NBC*. "I learned how to take care of my family the way that the Lord wanted me to take care of my family."[63]

The church was a close one, often meeting more than once a week and known for "marathon" services that began in the morning and lasted until late evening. Allen's devotion to his flock coexisted with a fidelity to punishment.[64] Allen told his congregation to hoist children in the air so they could receive whippings during services.

One Monday, a boy named Ricky Wilson, who attended a public school in Atlanta, stayed after class to talk with his teacher. He lifted his shirt. The teacher reacted with horror at the bruises and abrasions covering Ricky's stomach and chest. "I got a whipping at my church," the boy told her. "And David, my cousin David Duncan Jr., he got a whipping, too."[65]

A doctor at the Hughes Spalding Children's Hospital examined the boys. "His examination revealed that Ricky in his opinion had been hit on multiple occasions; that he believed his injuries to be severe," said the prosecution in its opening statement in the court case that followed. "And in his opinion, it took a lot of force for Ricky Wilson, Jr., to get these types of injuries." The doctor also expressed concern about the parts of Ricky's body that took the blows because "they were in his stomach cavity area and on his back" and because "they house his major organs," continued the prosecution.[66]

On January 18, 2002, the state of Georgia indicted Reverend Allen and several members of his congregation for assault and cruelty to children. Under the guidance of Allen, the group, according to the indictment, had held seven-year-old Ricky Wilson and ten-year-old David Duncan "suspended in the air" while they struck the boys.[67] Police reports and testimony in the case indicate that the congregants used a whip and a belt. Five, in addition to Allen, were found guilty.[68]

In the wake of revelations about Ricky Wilson and David Duncan, other former church members came forward to report that they, too, were beaten before worshippers at the House of Prayer. "You think those whippings are sanctioned in the Bible?" *Dateline* asked the Reverend Allen. "I know they're sanctioned in the Bible," he answered. Allen also told the jury at the Fulton County Superior Court that pain could prevent children from turning into criminals. "That's my child mugging you if I don't discipline him," said Allen.[69]

In Kansas City, a unique use of physical discipline at the home of Neil and Christy Edgar, pastor and "prophet" of the Pentecostal God's Creation Church, took the life of their adopted son. On the morning of December 29, 2002, Brian's adoptive father rushed the boy to the University of Kansas Hospital emergency room. But Brian had been dead for hours.[70]

Alan Hancock, the Wyandotte County coroner, described the boy's death for local newspapers. He said that someone had crammed an object like a sock into the boy's mouth and then taped over it. He also said that Brian appeared to have thrown up and that a belt had been tied around his chest. Brian had suffocated to death. The coroner had also found marks on Brian's body that suggested he had been trussed up many times before.[71]

On the night he died, tape bound not just Brian's mouth but also his entire body except for his nose. The Edgars and their babysitter, Chastity Boyd, used so much tape to secure the child that the parents went out to the grocery store to buy a new roll.[72]

Brian had been disobedient. A note police found in Christy Edgar's SUV read, "Brian has not had enough. He stole a piece of your candy." The note, which also said that Brian had told a lie, carried the fingerprints of the Edgars' babysitter and was directed to "Evangelist," a name for Christy Edgar. Brian's sister said he had been in trouble for taking cookies.[73]

The Edgars and a member of their congregation who had provided childcare were charged with identical crimes: the murder of Brian and two counts of child abuse in connection with two other Edgar children. The state's theory was "that all three defendants engaged, either as principals or aiders and abettors, in a continuing course of conduct wherein all three Edgar children were regularly tied up and bound with duct tape and various ligatures." The children were also frequently gagged.[74]

Neil Edgar and Chastity Boyd were both convicted of murder, a conviction they planned to appeal. Christy Edgar pleaded guilty and received a life sentence.[75] Five other church members pleaded no contest to child abuse charges and received probation sentences.

Witnesses testified that Christy Edgar was the church's prophet, and that among her prophecies was a revelation from God that church members should use binding of children as a means of discipline.[76] The prosecutor claimed Brian Edgar was once tied to a bed with his arms outstretched and his legs dangling, in imitation of the crucifixion.[77]

These individual cases are extreme and unusual. Most Christians who follow the religious discipline guides do not injure or kill their children. The point of such anecdotes is that they suggest a large, active body of Christians who use pain as a disciplinary method and who account for their practices by citing an old idea—that children are born evil. That idea connects to a widespread cultural emphasis on evil children as potential criminals, an emphasis present in horror movies, magazine articles, and the words of penologists, in addition to the Christian spanking subculture.

SPARE THE ROD AND RAISE A JUVENILE DELINQUENT

Some social scientists believe that the pro-spanking arguments that led to these extreme incidents might affect justifications for pain in other social circumstances—torture of detainees and harsh treatment of prisoners.

Prominent child punishment researcher Murray Straus defines this process, what he calls "cultural spillover," in *Beating the Devil Out of Them: Corporal Punishment in American Families,* "The concept behind the cultural spillover theory is that the more a society uses force for socially legitimate ends (using corporal punishment to correct misbehavior or to maintain order in schools, capital punishment to deter criminals, or wars to defend against foreign enemies), the greater the tendency for those engaged in illegitimate behavior to also use force for their own purposes."[78]

Rather than seeing in corporal punishment a spread of pain through society, however, most of the discipline manual writers see effective spanking of children as decreasing "willful disobedience" in society as a whole; they argue that enough good spankings will lower the crime rate. In the worldview of the Christian spanking books, authority is at risk. Not only does a disobedient child threaten his parents' authority, he is flouting God's will. Whereas a parent of a more secular sensibility might understand childhood disobedience as disruptive to the home, the spanking Christians tend to see it as linked to crime.

Dobson is explicit about the broad social aims of his corporal punishment theory. "By learning to yield to the loving authority . . . of his parents, a child learns to submit to other forms of authority which will confront him later in his life—his teachers, school principal, police, neighbors and employers."[79] In Dobson's writings, a parent who fails to "win decisively" risks a dangerous usurpation of natural authority. In *The New Dare to Discipline,* the demanding infant becomes "a tyrant" and "a tiny dictator."[80]

Like governments, authorities within the home maintain a threat of force against the incipient criminals in their midst. "Governments must use force to protect their citizens from both internal rebellion and external threat," writes J. Richard Fugate in *What the Bible Says about Child Rearing.* "Parents must also use force in the proper exercise of their authority." Fugate advises, "At whatever point a child chooses to rebel, his parents must utilize sufficient force to put down the revolt immediately."[81]

When spanking advocates start talking about submission to government authorities, it becomes evident that they want to do more than help parents to rear nice kids. Theirs is an argument about how to create a particular sort of citizenry—one that obeys.

Bruce A. Ray, author of the 1978 *Withhold Not Correction,* draws a direct link between the prevalent idea that children are innocent from birth and some of the most horrifying of the 1960s murders. "Thus when the President of the United States, John F. Kennedy, was gunned down in the streets of Dallas, it was not the man who fired from a nearby building who was to blame. It was society. When Martin Luther King was shot while standing on a balcony in Memphis, it was not the sniper who was at fault. Radio, television, and the press all led us into a period of national agony. What kind of society, they wailed, could create an environment where such things can happen?" Ray writes, going on to list the Robert Kennedy assassination and the shooting of George Wallace. "After all, the gunmen in all of these instances were once little babies bouncing on somebody's knee. They were innocent children born with blank tablets. It was society that shaped them, and it must be society that will hang. The individual cannot be held responsible." The remainder of his book advocates a return to spanking as insurance against such extreme crimes as assassinations. Children are anything but "blank slates" for Ray. They are budding murderers.[82]

Beverly LaHaye, better known as the founder and chair of Concerned Women for America and wife of Tim LaHaye, who is the author of the bestselling *Left Behind* series, is also the author of child-rearing guides, including *How to Develop Your Child's Temperament* (1977). In that book, LaHaye writes, "Every child has the potential of becoming a delinquent and a criminal when he is left to his own ways without instruction and correction."[83]

Fugate goes so far as to suggest the rod as a predictor of future criminality. "If a strong-willed child can seemingly withstand the rod with a grin on his face, he poses a dangerous problem," he writes. "His resistance to authority and strong will suggest that he could be a potential criminal."[84]

Some spanking advocates even suggest that in difficult cases, the rod should be set aside in favor of another Old Testament treatment for serious child rebellion—execution. "A rebellious child was put to death in Israel; there was no juvenile delinquency problem," writes Adams in the foreword to Ray's book. He is referring to ancient Israel.[85]

SPANKING AND AMERICAN POLITICS

The rise of the spanking advocates has coincided with the emergence of the Christian Right as a cultural and political force. Contemporary conservative Christianity in the United States can be understood both as an intellectual tradition and as a response to numerous societal changes, including the legalization of abortion, the end of prayer in the schools, the assimilation of gays and lesbians, the various spikes in the crime rate, and the challenges (such as child-centered parenting guides and revelations of child abuse) to American spanking.

Each of these issues made a cameo in the 1984 *Presidential Biblical Scorecard* published by the Biblical News Service, with editorial assistance from prominent Christian Right leaders Lou Sheldon, Tim LaHaye, and Gary Jarmin. The pamphlet includes such questions as, "Where do the presidential candidates stand on the biblical issues?" with the corresponding scorecard listing a pro-death-penalty statement from incumbent Republican presidential candidate Ronald Reagan, quotes from Democrat Walter Mondale suggesting his support for abolition of the death penalty, and verses from the Bible, all of which imply that capital punishment is the obligation of a Christian society. For instance, the list contains this tidbit from Leviticus 24:17: "And he that killeth any man shall surely be put to death."[86]

On the issue of "Parental Rights/Child Rights," the pamphlet includes numerous Scripture underlining the importance of spanking and poses these questions:

Do you believe children should
- Have the right to divorce their parents and receive "alimony"?
- Be eligible for minimum wage if they do household chores?
- Be able to charge their parents with child abuse if they use biblical disciplinary measures?
- Have the right to sue their parents for being "forced" to attend church or to avoid going places with them?
- Decide whether to have an abortion, quit school, or hire their own attorney?

The *Biblical Scorecard* then quotes Ronald Reagan as saying, "Parental authority is not a right conveyed by the state." The revealing quote from Mondale in this section of the scorecard comes from an interview with his wife in the May 26, 1983, issue of *Rolling Stone:* "Oh, no, he'd never spank the children. That's an admission of defeat and a loss of control."[87]

That a brief pamphlet should include as issues critical to the presidential election both the ultimate punishment for the ultimate crime and the whack on the buttocks for childhood disobedience is no accident. The authors of the 1984 *Biblical Scorecard* understood their constituency. For their voters, spanking and execution are two points on a continuum of appropriate physical penalties for human depravity. Crime prevention, for such believers, begins with a swat on a toddler's rear.

Sociological research shows that Christians who believe in the literal truth of the Bible, particularly Baptists and Pentecostals, are the most frequent users of corporal punishment in the home. A belief in the literal truth of the Bible also correlates with support for the death penalty. Such surveys suggest support for spanking and harsh punishment of prisoners is partly a result of the cultural spread of religious beliefs and not a phenomenon likely to respond to rational argument.[88]

GOD GETS TOUGH ON CRIME

In the final decades of the twentieth century, leaders of the Christian Right advocated the need for retributive justice, and they weren't talking about spankings. They were putting forth new ideas for handling drug dealers and crooks. In this behavior, they were in line with secular America.

Like other secular Americans, and like the popular culture they often deplored, Christian Right leaders spoke often of the problems of crime and drug addiction. In his book *Listen America!* (1981), Jerry Falwell lists the troubles he believes are afflicting America: "Divorce, broken homes, abortion, juvenile delinquency, and drug addiction." Falwell repeated similar lists throughout the 1980s and 1990s, often positing fundamentalism as a solution ("the church must return to the infallible Bible"), as he did in his November 17, 1996, sermon "Where the Battle Rages."[89]

But Falwell from the late 1970s on was much more than just a minister serving a congregation. A political leader, Falwell was part of a force energizing conservative Christian America. When he traveled, Falwell sometimes led "rallies," rather than services. One such rally was advertised with this sign:

Rally with Falwell:
God and Decency Rally
with Dr. Jerry Falwell
Thursday May 3, 7:30 PM
Citizens of Oklahoma *ARE YOU TIRED OF?*

. . . . Of paying traffic tickets when dope peddlers,
armed robbers, murderers and the like get off scot free?
If you are tired of these things, then attend this rally!
7:30 PM—Thurs. Night
Sponsored By
Concerned Citizens for Community Standards

Falwell did not just deplore crime; he invented punishments. In a 1986 sermon entitled "The Spiritual Renaissance in America," he selected drug dealers for punishment, proposing "that we immediately confiscate all their earthly possessions, take everything away from them personally, so that no matter how much money they are making, they lose it all with every infraction and have to start all over again."[90]

Falwell's idea is not corporal punishment per se, but it depends on a belief in the power of material pain. Material denial can have a corporal effect. The loss of "all their earthly possessions" might sound like an emulation of Christ's simplicity, but it would be a cruel punishment. It could mean homelessness, lack of adequate clothing, lack of adequate medical attention, hunger, and early death.

Falwell also wrote a blurb praising Fugate's book, which, according to Falwell, offered "excellent insights on the development of spiritually strong children and a Godly family by providing Biblical solutions." In Falwell's dual statements about child discipline and criminal punishments, we can discern an easy-to-mark continuum between spanking naughty kids and causing pain to prisoners. Both derive from a worldview that understands humanity as wicked, bodies as the source of corrupting desires, and hurt as purifying.[91]

It follows that Falwell's God would exact a physical toll on a murderer. In praising Virginia's then-governor Charles Robb for allowing an execution, Falwell brings home the point. "Capital punishment is biblical, of course. Genesis 9:6 commands it for murder, long before the law of Moses. The Law in Exodus 21:12–17 and in other places confirms capital punishment."[92]

In his November 24, 1996, sermon, "The Battle for the Bible," Falwell suggested that the current list of capital crimes in America is too limited. Citing the case of Brian Peterson and Amy Grossberg, the eighteen-year-olds who murdered their baby in a Newark, Delaware, motel, he comments, "If Brian had managed to kill the child by whatever means just moments before the baby's head emerged from the birth canal, he might have been charged with no more than practicing 'medicine' without a license, which certainly is not punishable by execution." Falwell's is not an argument for letting the eighteen-year-olds off but for extending the reach of the death penalty to include abortion.[93]

Falwell is not the only Christian Right leader who has suggested new uses for capital punishment. Pat Robertson, founder of the Christian Coalition, has spoken in favor of a painful execution method for anyone who believes in UFOs. On a July 8, 1997, broadcast of the 700 Club reported in Freedom Writer magazine, Robertson advocated stoning people who believe in UFOs, quoting Deuteronomy 17:2–5. If a belief in UFOs leads "somebody away from the true God, or away from Jesus Christ," that person is "in rebellion against God" and "refuses to take God's Law," said Robertson. In such cases, said Robertson, claiming to translate for God, "I want you to take him out and dispose of him."[94]

In the mid-1980s, the Trumpet, a newsletter published by the American Coalition of Unregistered Churches, featured a large ad describing "a book that will make your adrenaline flow, your brain hum and your blood boil!" The book was Is God a Right-winger? The ad posed a series of questions, for example, "Should all convicted killers on death rows be executed the same day?" "Should criminals be flogged and worked at hard labor?"[95]

Anyone who reads Is God a Right-winger? will learn that the answer to these questions as well as to the question of the title is yes. "I suggest that each state execute all convicted killers on the same day," writes Don Boys, a former Indiana state representative, president of Associated Christian Schools Curriculum, and the former administrator of a Baptist school in Indianapolis. "That will tend to make believers out of the killers and potential killers who are still walking the streets. They will then understand that we are serious about violent crime."[96]

For men who commit rape or incest that results in an abortion, Boys offers capital punishment. "Let's give the father the death penalty and the baby life!" he writes. "If I couldn't get the death penalty for rapists, I would demand they be castrated." Drug dealers would also earn the death penalty.[97] "Child-porn producers" get off a trifle easier. They "should be executed after a second conviction," writes Boys.[98]

Boys would return the American justice system to its colonial methods not just in widespread executions but in whippings of convicts, a practice he ties to spankings of disobedient children. "Most sensible people believe that there are times when a spanking is necessary for our children, so why can't we flog felons without hating them?" he asks. "And if a spanking, wisely administered, can be helpful to a child, why can't a flogging be helpful to a felon?" Muggers, child predators and abusers, those accused of porn crimes, "trouble makers," and those who participate in riots would receive whippings. "The flogging should be within reason, just as a child's spanking should be within reason," writes Boys.[99] Boys may, on the surface, seem like just an oddball. But he had influence and political ambitions. He served in the Indiana state legislature, where he introduced tough-on-crime legislation, some of which passed.[100]

THE OBEDIENT ADULT

Children do grow up. It is worth asking what will happen to the superobedient children the Christian spanking manuals seek to create when they become adults. The psychologist Alice Miller explores this question in her powerful study of the German population, *For Your Own Good.* "What becomes of all those people who are the successful products of a strict upbringing?" asks Miller. "It is inconceivable that they were able to express and develop their true feelings as children, for anger and helpless rage, which they were forbidden to display, would have been among these feelings— particularly if these children were beaten, humiliated, lied to, deceived. What becomes of this forbidden and therefore unexpressed anger?"[101]

Miller's conclusion is a dire one. She blames the manipulative, harsh, and physically cruel child rearing designed to create obedient children for the ordinary German citizens who did not rebel against the Nazi government. She ties the emotional response of many of Hitler's followers— adulation mingled with dread—to the same phenomenon.[102]

Numerous other studies show a complex correlation between home punishment and punitive social policies. In *The Politics of Denial* (1996), Michael A. Milburn and Sheree D. Conrad show a "direct link between childhood punishment and adult political attitudes." Among men who had been punished severely, those attitudes are punitive. Women, in contrast, tend to be somewhat more liberal if they had a childhood of harsh punishment.[103]

In regard to the death penalty, the pair suggests that the public supports capital punishment despite reasonable evidence that it does not deter crime. They tie this irrational support to childhood physical pain: "Despite the large body of evidence that it is not effectual, many people support the death penalty for a simple reason: a desire for retribution that is, in part, the result of rage they carry from childhood and of the need to take revenge for their childhood pain," they write.[104] Milburn and Conrad find support for their conclusions in other data. For instance, in analyzing a Harris poll of 1968, the two discovered, "even after removing the effects of education and income on political attitudes, the more an individual reported having been spanked, the more punitive were his or her political attitudes."[105]

Harold Grasmick, a researcher into corporal punishment and religious beliefs at the University of Oklahoma, has identified the prevalence of support for school physical punishments of children among Christian parents who believe in the literal truth of the Bible. In summing up the discovery, Grasmick noted that support for corporal punishment in the schools might be linked to other tough-on-crime phenomena. "Our findings raise the possibility that religious beliefs are at the root of a wide range of calls for harshness toward those who would break the rules," he writes.[106]

When Grasmick and a second group of researchers studied Protestant fundamentalism in relation to changes in public policy toward criminals, they found a correlation. "We found that religious affiliation is a significant predictor of retributiveness, and that, to a great extent, the effect occurs because fundamentalist Protestants are more inclined to interpret the Bible literally," wrote Grasmick and his fellow researchers. Grasmick and his colleagues predicted that recent shifts toward retributive punishment would be difficult to reverse because of their rooting in religious beliefs.[107]

PURITAN STORM ON THE HORIZON

In 1973, a little-known Presbyterian minister and former missionary named Rousas John Rushdoony published a volume entitled *The Institutes of Biblical Law*. Rushdoony's book received scant notice at the time, but it was part of the American preoccupation with punishment. The Rushdoony volume advocated some new (and very old) uses for execution.

Institutes, a book of more than eight hundred pages, is considered Rushdoony's most important work. It contains five years of his sermons, delivered between 1968 and 1972, and advocates applying what it calls "biblical law" to modern life. At his death in 2001 at the age of eighty-four, this theologian, who devoted his life to the furthering of theocracy, received obituaries in *Christianity Today,* the *Los Angeles Times,* and the prominent conservative magazine the *Weekly Standard,* which observed that Rushdoony, despite his physical and intellectual isolation from even conservative Christians, was an important theologian. Rushdoony's publications, noted the magazine, "played a major role in two of the most important developments in the past half-century of American religious life: the spread of Christian education in private and home schools, and the rise of the Christian Right."[108]

As Gary North, a Rushdoony follower as well as his son-in-law, explained in his eulogy, "The *Institutes* launched the Christian Reconstruction movement."[109] Tiny but prolific in its literary output, Christian Reconstructionism is notable less for its size than for its influential ideas, many of which are punitive.

Ideas about punishment and punishment practices are not static things. Not only do they evolve, they also move laterally through society, affecting our popular culture and American homes, religious institutions, and schools. That is why it is worth taking a look at this small group of Calvinist Christians.

Rousas John Rushdoony admired two past civilizations: the Puritan colonies and ancient Israel as governed by Old Testament law. Colonial New England's "adoption of Biblical law," wrote Rushdoony, "was a resolute return to the fundamentals of Christendom. Thus, the New Haven Colony records show that the law of God, without any sense of innovation, was made the law in the Colony."[110] Rushdoony called for a return to the biblical law that, he argued, had guided the Puritans. Even today, wrote Rushdoony, "Man is summoned to create the society God requires."[111]

One Reconstructionist idea popular with Christian conservatives is Dominion Theory, the philosophy that true believers should use democracy to establish control over the government. Although some members of the Christian Right, for example, Ralph Reed and Pat Robertson, have said that they simply want a seat at the table, the idea of a Christian takeover of the government is immensely popular among the grass roots of the movement. In "Puritan Storm Rising," an article published in the electronic Reconstructionist newsletter *Puritan Storm*, editor and author Jeff Ziegler writes that Christian dominion will enable a return to Puritanism. "Given time this will shake the very social foundations of The United States," he writes.[112]

The Christian Reconstructionists are explicit about what should happen next. The new government would establish a theocracy, outlawing all other religions. Women would become the property of their husbands. Society would run according to Old Testament law, which the Reconstructionists often call "case law."

Many Reconstructionists warn their followers against a violent overthrow of the current system. They talk, rather, of a national conversion. Widespread belief in "the judicially binding case laws of the Old Testament" is essential, writes Rushdoony's follower North, "before we attempt to tear down judicial institutions that still rely on natural law or public virtue. (I have in mind the US Constitution.)"[113]

Our system of punishment would be transformed. The reformers would abolish the prison system. It would no longer be necessary since most criminal offenses, including blasphemy, idolatry, heresy, prostitution, abortion, witchcraft, theft, and homosexuality, would earn the death penalty.

In defending the use of capital punishment for "idolaters," otherwise known as non-Christians, George Grant, a prolific author of Reconstructionist books and director of the King's Meadow Study Center, stepped up to the task. When asked, "But wouldn't a Christian Republic run according to God's Law become oppressive to non-Christians?" Grant responded, "When we start to pick and choose which Old Testament laws we will adhere to and which ones we won't, we ultimately set ourselves up as judges over God and over all of history."[114]

Reconstructionists differ, however, on whether the guilty should be stoned or burned alive, as the Bible proposes both forms of execution. North is adamant that stoning is preferable. Why? "There are many reasons. First, the implements of execution are available to everyone at virtually no cost." Part of the appeal of stonings has to do with their public and participatory qualities. Everyone, North suggests, can join in. "Executions are community projects—not with spectators who watch a professional executioner do 'his' duty, but rather with actual participants."[115]

The debate on the Christian Right about the appropriateness of stoning indicates the intensity of this group's beliefs. One of the more controversial passages from the Old Testament regarding punishment appears in Deuteronomy 21:18–21: "If a man have a stubborn and rebellious son, which will not obey the voice of his father, or the voice of his mother, . . . all the men of the city shall stone him with stones, that he die." An article in the *Christian Statesman*, the flagship publication of the Christian Reconstructionists, goes to great lengths to defend this passage, which, it claims, "is not about stoning disobedient children." A Bible verse that does refer to children, the article notes, is Proverbs 29:15, which tells parents to use "the rod and reproof." According to the *Christian Statesman*, stoning by the community applies only to "a grown son (and by extension to a daughter as well) who, for whatever reason, has rebelled against the authority of his parents and will not profit from any of their discipline nor obey their voice in any thing." Such young adults hold parental authority in contempt and "lash out" against their parents in word and action, argues the article. "It is a case where the evil character of the son is apparently set." Such a life is death. Thus, "Christians must not be embarrassed by the law of Deuteronomy 21:18–21, nor should they be chagrined when others try to use it to discredit the case laws of the Old Testament. Properly understood, it displays the wisdom and mercy of God in restraining wickedness so that the righteous might flourish in peace."[116]

Like their theological forebears, the New England Puritans, the Reconstructionists seem preoccupied with sex crimes. During a radio appearance on Atlanta superstation WSB, prominent Reconstructionist Gary DeMar talked about a few of the sex crimes that Reconstructionists believe merit the death penalty. "The Bible doesn't say that homosexuals should be executed," DeMar began. "What it says is this: if two men lie together like a man and a woman lie together, they are to be put to death."

The difference between executing someone because of identity and executing because of an act that, in twenty-first-century America, we often tie to identity is critical to DeMar. "If a guy comes up to me and he says, 'I'm a homosexual,' that doesn't mean that he's to be executed," he said. "If you understand Scriptures, it says very clearly, if a man comes up to you and says, 'I've murdered somebody,' that doesn't mean that person ought to be put to death."

Death comes not with hidden sodomy but with what DeMar defines as a "public" act, a term that has little to do with the open air or crowds. "Public," in DeMar's use of the term, means a return to the colonial idea that punishment for sex acts must have two witnesses. "You're going to have at least two witnesses who would come forth and testify against two people who engaged in sodomy," said DeMar, suggesting that would be a rare occurrence. "But, if it did happen, the severest punishment that could come upon somebody would be capital punishment." In the rest of the interview DeMar described how execution would also apply to women who have abortions, their doctors, and people who commit adultery. He suggested that laws would be preventative: "Most of the laws in the Bible were designed not so much to be implemented, but to keep people from practicing that particular behavior."[117]

Rushdoony, the founder of Reconstruction, has also writen about "theft," which he deems a capital offense. For Rushdoony, the term "theft" is expansive. In his writings, it includes such variations as extortion, fraud (including the selling of fraudulent goods), failure to tithe, failure to collect tithes, failure to pay workers on time, failure to leave the remains of the harvest in the field to feed the poor who are doing the work, extensive debt or mortgage (which is a version of robbing God, since man should not place his life in the ownership of anyone else). Unionism, kidnapping ("robbing a man of his freedom"), seduction ("robbing a girl of her virginity"), and patent infringement also make an appearance in his essay on theft. Bystanders are also "liable to the penalty for the crime."[118]

Witchcraft is a capital offense according to biblical "case law," argue the Reconstructionists in a direct echo of their Puritan forebears. Greg Bahnsen, like Rushdoony an influential philosopher of Reconstructionism, makes the case against witches. "Exodus 22:18 says, 'You shall not permit a witch to live.' What is forbidden here is not only witchcraft, but also that a witch should be permitted to live," writes Bahnsen in *By This Standard: The Authority of God's Law Today*.[119]

Frederick Clarkson, a scholar of the Christian Right, observes, "Reconstructionists insist that the death penalty is the maximum, not necessarily the mandatory policy. However, such judgments may depend less on Biblical Principles than on which faction gains power in the theocratic republic. The potential for bloodthirsty episodes on the order of the Salem witchcraft trials or the Spanish Inquisition is inadvertently revealed by Reconstructionist theologian Rev. Ray Sutton, who claims that the Reconstructionist Biblical theocracies would be 'happy' places, to which people would flock because 'capital punishment is one of the best evangelistic tools of a society.' "[120]

As much as this religious movement hearkens to its Puritan ancestors, it has its eyes on the future, a time when, in the words of prominent Reconstructionist Andrew Sandlin, the movement will attain "godly decentralized theocracy, the rule of the law of God."[121]

Whether the Reconstructionists ever manage to establish their version of the kingdom of God on Earth, their ideas already have had an effect. For instance, events over the past twenty years show that the punitive thought characteristic of the Reconstructionists holds inspirational power for the militant wing of the antiabortion movement. As mentioned above, under a Reconstructionist-style theocracy, both women who have abortions and the doctors who perform them would get the death penalty. That legalistic advocacy found resonance with antiabortion advocate Randall Terry.

From the mid-1980s through the early 1990s, the unofficial slogan of Operation Rescue, Terry's antiabortion organization, was, "If you believe abortion is murder, then act like it is."[122] Acting as though "abortion is murder" represented different things to different people. For many members of Operation Rescue, it meant loud protests at clinic entrances, chaining themselves to railings, and putting their livelihoods on the line, much in the way of the Vietnam War protesters of the 1960s. But the slogan had a punitive undercurrent: If abortion is murder, and if, under our legal system, murder is punishable with death, then abortionists deserve execution.

The slogan is also close to Reconstructionist statements on the subject. For instance, in *Ruler of the Nations: Biblical Blueprints for Government* (1987), Gary DeMar writes, "The long-term goal should be the execution of abortionists and parents who hire them. If we argue that abortion is murder, then we must call for the death penalty. If abortionists are not supposed to be executed, then they are not murderers, and if they are not murderers, why do we want to abolish abortion?"[123]

By the late 1980s, following the assassinations of several abortion doctors and clinic workers, Operation Rescue and Randall Terry came under scrutiny because of the slogan and because several accused of the murders claimed associations with the organization. Both Terry and Operation Rescue denied endorsing or advocating the murder of abortion providers.[124]

In a 1994 investigative report, *U.S. News and World Report* traced the genealogy of the militant wing of the pro-life movement, beginning with Michael Bray, a convicted clinic bomber. Bray's wife, Jayne, "was once a board member of Randall Terry's Operation Rescue," noted the magazine, which quoted Bray's credo: "I defend the termination by private citizens of practicing abortionists to defend innocent children." Another activist, named Joseph Foreman, was "a former member of Operation Rescue." Foreman, according to *U.S. News,* "recently formed the American Coalition of Life Activists with other antiabortion activists who defend the use of violence."[125]

"This was the logical extension of the kind of language and tactics they have used for years," Ann Baker, president of the National Center for the Pro-Choice Majority, told the *Cleveland Plain Dealer* in response to the 1993 killing of Dr. David Gunn by Michael Griffin. "You have people like Randy Terry saying if you believe abortion is murder, then act like it. Well, this guy did." Griffin was an activist with Rescue America, a splinter group of Operation Rescue. The group was protesting Gunn's clinic when Griffin killed the doctor.[126]

In 2001, the *New York Times* reported that one of Terry's "most avid followers in Binghamton was James E. Kopp, now charged in the 1998 murder of a doctor who performed abortions in Buffalo." The newspaper quoted Terry as saying, "I haven't spoken to Jim Kopp in twelve years," and "I hope he didn't do it."[127]

Paul Hill, who killed Dr. John Britton and James Barrett outside a Pensacola, Florida, clinic in 1994, claimed an allegiance to Christian Reconstruction. Hill, who studied under Bahnsen and who quoted Rushdoony, wrote to Gary North more than once, sending the Reconstructionist leader his position papers, including one entitled, "Was the Killing of Dr. Gunn Just? A Call to Defensive Action." A few months after the Hill shootings, North felt compelled to respond. In "A Letter to Paul J. Hill," dated September 29, 1994, North writes to Hill that he is headed to hell both because his church has excommunicated him and because "your act was, biblically speaking, an act of murder rather than the God-authorized defense of a just cause." Murder, in North's terms, "is the slaying of a human being by someone who has not been authorized to do so as a covenantal agent." This is the long way of saying that although abortion providers deserve to die, only the state should kill them. Charles Bronson–style vigilantism is out of the question for the Reconstructionists, who seek instead to overhaul the U.S. government.[128]

Some Reconstructionist-style rhetoric has entered mainstream politics. In the 2004 elections, Oklahomans elected Republican Tom Coburn to the U.S. Senate. In some of the more controversial moments of his campaign, Coburn, a member of a Southern Baptist congregation, echoed Reconstructionist sentiments, calling the race a contest between "good and evil" and telling a reporter from the Associated Press that he supported capital punishment for "abortionists and other people who take life."[129]

As much as its followers want to believe that their movement gets its cues from the Bible and the Puritans, Reconstructionism is entrenched in the American present. The Reconstructionist preoccupation with punishment, particularly punishment with a physical component, marks it as a late twentieth- and early twenty-first-century movement. It, along with the pro-spanking movement, is a religious manifestation of the punitive urges behind some of the popular tough-on-crime laws, control technologies, and police shows and horror movies, as I will explore in the next chapters.

CHAPTER 8

Pain Becomes Valuable Again

IN 1974, THE YEAR Gary Gilmore committed his murders, the first film of the Charles Bronson *Death Wish* series drew crowds to American movie houses. The crime rate was on the rise, and *Death Wish* offered an answer to crime fear. Featuring a citizen assassin and a host of ineffectual police officers, *Death Wish* is a propaganda film for vigilante justice. After the wife and daughter of a New York City architect are murdered, Charles Bronson, playing the role of their vengeful husband and father, walks the dark streets, hoping to attract muggers so he can shoot them. A central message of this film is that muggers will kill and thus deserve to die. In the film, mugging and murder are indistinguishable, one crook as worthy of ultimate punishment as another. Audiences cheered at the sight of Bronson punishing muggers with death, a revenge-lust that alarmed media outlets at the time.[1]

A little more than four decades earlier, audiences flocked to a different Hollywood treatment of crime and punishment. In the 1932 film *I Am a Fugitive from a Chain Gang,* Paul Muni, playing the convict James Allen, makes his getaway by stealing a truck and lobbing dynamite behind him so that the bridge, according to the screenplay, "crumples and collapses" just as the car carrying the pursuing guards starts across it. Crowds watching the scene roared approval.[2] The movie tells the story of a man who ended up on a Georgia chain gang after a wrongful conviction for robbery. There he encountered guards who worked men to death, whipped anyone who spoke out, and manipulated sentences so that they could keep the strongest workers long past their original release dates.[3]

Death Wish was connected to the social reality of the 1970s through its characters: in the first scenes, the main character, an architect and soon-to-be-vigilante, returns from vacation to hear about the rising crime statistics in New York City. *I Am a Fugitive from a Chain Gang* had a more specific connection to its historical moment. It drew on an autobiographical narrative by Robert E. Burns, who landed on a Georgia chain gang after he and two others robbed a man of $5.80.

On the Fulton County chain gang in 1922, each sixteen-hour workday "was an exact duplicate of the one preceding it. Only some nights more of us or fewer 'got the leather,' as it was called," writes Burns in his autobiography. After claiming that "the dirty filthy 'stripes' would stick to the wounds on the buttocks and cause inflammation and torture," Burns states that "torture" is "what a chain gang is for."[4]

The response to the film version of Burns's story was social transformation. "The reform of the southern chain gang system can be attributed to the public outrage generated by this movie," notes John O'Connor in the introduction to a 1981 edition of the screenplay.[5]

About four decades separates *I Am a Fugitive from a Chain Gang* from *Death Wish*. The two films convey similar messages: government officials in charge of punishment betray the public. But the films diverge in their reasoning. In *I Am a Fugitive*, official cruelties cause the moral dissolution of an otherwise ethical man. In *Death Wish*, the crooks are so dissolute they will commit murder as easily as theft, officials don't punish with enough efficiency or cruelty, and citizens must carry out their own revenge. In these two films one can see, over time, the failure in the popular imagination of the American prison system and the rise of belief in "evil" criminals who will not reform.

REHABILITATION AND ITS DISCONTENTS

Among those who paid attention to American prisons, rehabilitation became suspect in the early 1970s. The criticism started among the people who invented prisoner reform—the inheritors of Progressivism and the Quakers.[6]

Like the emergence of the devil-criminal and the devil-child, the attack on prisons was not well reasoned but was emotional and with political overtones.[7] In retrospect, one natural question is: what did these activists hope to achieve? According to a 1971 report published in book form by the American Friends Service Committee—that is, the twentieth-century Quakers—the reformers saw their project as part of a societal "revolution," wholesale social change. Inmates in Florida, Indiana, New York, California, and Washington D.C., had gone on strike and had "even maimed themselves to call attention to their plight," according to the report. "These upheavals warn the public that prisoners will no longer submit to whatever is done to them in the name of 'treatment' or 'rehabilitation.' " The minorities, women, and young people in the nation's jails and penitentiaries were "all seeking access to the nation's abundance and a reordering of its priorities." The revolution that began with an attack on the prisons was to lead to a substantial redistribution of material wealth and racial equality.[8]

The 1971 publication bore the title *Struggle for Justice: A Report on Crime and Punishment in America.* Its authors, members of the American Friends Service Committee, former prisoners and death row inmates, and family members of prisoners, censured the Quaker predecessors. "It would be naïve not to acknowledge the blunders that an uncritical faith can produce. The horror that is the American prison system grew out of an eighteenth-century reform by Pennsylvania Quakers and others against the cruelty and futility of capital and corporal punishment." The writers then announced, "This two-hundred-year-old experiment has failed."[9]

The writers of the pamphlet even question whether the decline in corporal punishment is a "humanitarian" development. Like Michel Foucault in *Discipline and Punish,* the Quaker authors suggest that efforts to rehabilitate inmates were less than kind. "These attitudes were considered humanitarian because they viewed some criminals as redeemable," they write. "It did not disturb reformers pursuing the rehabilitative ideal that the person who was identified as sick or abnormal was forced into a treatment routine and that he might experience this not as help but as punishment."[10]

The Quaker document contains a resounding, and for today's reader, dissonant call to smash prison walls. "If the choice were between prisons as they are now and no prisons at all, we would promptly choose the latter. We are convinced that it would be far better to tear down all jails now than to perpetuate the inhumanity and horror being carried on in society's name behind prison walls."[11]

The Quakers were dreaming. But they were not the only left-wingers who wanted to shatter those rehabilitative walls. In 1973, investigative reporter Jessica Mitford published *Kind and Unusual Punishment,* a cutting analysis of rehabilitation. "When is conduct a crime, and when is a crime not a crime? When Somebody Up There—a monarch, a dictator, a pope, a legislature—so decrees," writes Mitford in an echo of the Quaker skepticism. Toward the end of her book, Mitford reveals that she agrees with the authors of *Struggle for Justice,* which she terms a "thoughtful" publication.[12]

In the scholarly world, an attack on the prison system was also under way. In 1974, Robert Martinson published a review of 231 studies of prison treatment and recidivism rates in the liberal journal *Public Interest.* Entitled "What Works—Questions and Answers about Prison Reform," the article gave rise to the popular cliché about prison rehabilitation attempts, "nothing works." According to Martinson, "It is possible to give a rather bald summary of our findings: *With few and isolated exceptions, the rehabilitative efforts that have been reported so far have had no appreciable effect on recidivism.* Studies that have been done since our survey was completed do not present any major grounds for altering that original conclusion."[13]

Martinson, like the American Friends Service Committee writers, believed that his critique would lead to fewer prisons and many fewer prisoners, but that was hardly what happened. The cliché "nothing works" is an idea that Gary Gilmore echoed in his quest for execution.

In 1979, Martinson retracted his earlier claims, writing, "Contrary to my previous position, some treatment programs do have an appreciable effect on recidivism. Some programs are indeed beneficial. . . . New evidence from our current study leads me to reject my original conclusion . . . I have hesitated up to now, but the evidence in our survey is simply too overwhelming to ignore."[14] His retraction came too late. America had turned away from rehabilitation. A harsher law stalked the land.

MORE PRISONS FOR THE "WICKED"

To put the changes in simple terms, more Americans went to prison. Prisons still seemed helpful, though now as buildings used to segregate bad guys from good ones. Our nation began to take cultural ideas equating criminals with evil seriously enough to base policy on them.

Liberal and academic critics may have sympathized extravagantly with prisoners, but their attack on the prisons made the words of a group of tough-on-crime critics newly audible. "Wicked people exist. Nothing avails except to set them apart from innocent people," wrote political scientist James Q. Wilson in 1975. Because "we have trifled with the wicked, made sport of the innocent, and encouraged the calculators, . . . justice suffers, and so do we all."[15]

If criminals are indeed "wicked," as Wilson and so many other late twentieth-century commentators suggested, then attempting to *change* our thieves and drug dealers and murderers through work experience, drug and alcohol treatment, education and job training, and counseling, in the ways of the rehabilitators, will not work. Wickedness is not a character trait that is healable or educable or trainable.

The rhetoric of criminal wickedness continued through the 1980s and 1990s. President Ronald Reagan described a "stark, staring face—a face that belongs to a frightening reality of our time: the face of a human predator . . . nothing in nature is more cruel or more dangerous."[16] Wilson echoed Reagan's "stark, staring" when he wrote, "We are terrified by the prospect of innocent people being gunned down at random, without warning, and almost without motive, by youngsters who afterwards show us the blank, unremorseful face of a feral, pre-social being."[17]

Adjectives like Wilson's "blank, unremorseful" and Reagan's "stark, staring" imply absence of emotion or moral recognition. The descriptions are not of human beings but of embodied evil most akin, in American culture, to horror movie images. As Carrie destroys her classmates, Sissy Spacek, the star of the film version of the Stephen King novel, wears a face that is unemotive, stark, blank, unremorseful, and staring.

Young criminals, in particular, provoked sound bites designed to horrify and frighten. After Princeton Professor John Dilulio warned of a "rising wave of superpredators," the term caught the media's ear. It reappeared again and again in the mid-1990s. So did the words of James Allen Fox, a Northeastern University professor who in 1996 described a "teenage time bomb" that would detonate a "blood bath of teenage violence."

In 1996, *Time*, echoing Fox, published an article with the headline "Now for the Bad News: A Teenage Timebomb."[18] In the same month, a *Newsweek* headline announced, "'Superpredators' Arrive." The article's author asked, "Should we cage the new breed of vicious kids?" The question about caging kids was a serious one. In response to a terrible Chicago crime in which two boys, ages eleven and twelve, dropped five-year-old Eric Morse from a fourteenth-floor apartment, there was "a revolutionary change in how 'predator' juveniles are housed in Illinois," reported *Newsweek*. "A new law permits children as young as ten to be sent to juvenile prison."[19]

In 1996, the Berkeley Media Studies Group reported that more than half of all local news stories about young people concerned violence. The group also found that more than two-thirds of the news reports about violence centered on young people. The emphasis on young, violent criminals contradicted statistics showing that 57 percent of violent crime was carried out by adults over the age of twenty-five and 80 percent of violent crime by people older than eighteen.[20]

In 1997, the U.S. Justice Department released data showing that youth crime was dropping. In response to these statistics, Fox said that he never meant to imply that there would be a "blood bath," that in his writing "some of it was part of getting people's attention."[21]

Garland, who finds coded racism in Reagan's "stark, staring face," Dilulio's "superpredators," and similar language, writes, "In this inflammatory rhetoric, and in the real policies that flow from it, offenders are treated as a different species of threatening, violent individuals for whom we can have no sympathy and for whom there is no effective help. . . . The public knows, without having to be told, that these 'superpredators' and high-rate offenders are young minority males, caught up in the underclass world of crime, drugs, broken families, and welfare dependency. The only practical and rational response to such types, as soon as they offend if not before, is to have them 'taken out of circulation' for the protection of the public. Many of the most politicized penalties of recent years—mandatory sentences, incapacitation, the revived death penalty—are designed to do precisely this and little else."[22]

That Wilson's advice to separate the "wicked" resonated with the U.S. public is evident today. Sentence lengths are longer. The numbers of people living in the nation's prisons have soared since the mid-1970s, when Wilson wrote. Whether or not all of our criminals are wicked, our culture has striven since 1975 to "set them apart."

But there is more to the popular adoption of wickedness as a punishable trait. Our culture has a long history of understanding punishment in religious terms. "Wicked" has religious connotations. With the exception of those few decades when Progressivism attempted to harness science in the service of prisoner reform, American culture has understood crime punishments in religious terms. When people have defined criminals as evil, historically they have also understood them as deserving physical hurt. And as we turned criminality back into an affair with the Devil, our country again found pain to be useful.

PUNISHMENT AND CULTURAL CHANGE: WHERE, WHAT, HOW

A much-remarked phenomenon over the past two decades has been the growth in numbers of people incarcerated or under the supervision of the U.S. justice system. On August 9, 1995, the Bureau of Justice Statistics, part of the Department of Justice, announced that 1994 had seen the "second largest annual increase in history" in prison inmates. "The total number of men and women in prison last December 31 was 1,053,738—a new record."[23] By June 30, 2005, according to the bureau's Web page, "2,186,230 prisoners were held in Federal or State prisons or in local jails." In 2005, there were an estimated 488 prison inmates per 100,000 U.S. residents. The U.S. imprisonment rate is the highest among Western countries. It is also, reports penologist Michael Tonry, "seven to twelve times higher than most."[24]

It wasn't always so. During the 1930s, the United States had similar or lower incarceration rates than much of Europe. Rates continued at low levels through the early 1970s.[25] Tonry has taken a hard look at this phenomenon; he argues the numbers are mounting because our society has expanded its definition of what behaviors deserve harsh punishment. "Ordinary Americans made these things happen. Elected politicians proposed policies and enacted laws, but they would not have done it if they believed American voters would disapprove. . . . The public could not have been led someplace it was unwilling to go."[26]

How did the public go there? Tonry blames what he calls "moral panics." "For two decades, Americans thought they wanted single-minded toughness and they got it. The question is why they thought they wanted it," he writes. " 'Moral panics' are part of the answer. They typically occur when horrifying or notorious events galvanize public emotion, and produce concern, sympathy, emotion, and overreaction. Examples in recent years include the kidnapping of Polly Klaas in California and the crack-overdose death of Len Bias in Maryland." Tonry points out that the moral panics in response to these two events led directly to innovative and harsh penalties. "Results included, respectively, California's three-strikes law and the federal 100-to-1 crack cocaine sentencing law." Moral panics have also had a much broader effect on American punishment: "In recent decades, moral panics have magnified the effects of longer term changes in values and attitudes."[27]

The most obvious and commonly discussed attitude changes have been toward drug crimes. The number of people incarcerated for drug crimes in the United States "rose fifteen-fold between 1980 and 2000," reports a study on the economics of imprisoning drug offenders. New York's Rockefeller drug laws, some of the earliest of the punitive onslaught, provide a potent example. Under the Rockefeller drug laws, a person caught possessing four ounces or selling two ounces of some drugs earns a mandatory penalty of at least fifteen years and up to life in prison. The drug penalties under the Rockefeller laws are comparable to those that punish such brutal crimes as kidnapping, arson, or murder. They are more severe than many punishments for rape or robbery.[28]

In 1973, the year the Rockefeller drug laws were passed, the state of New York also passed Second Felony Offender laws, which drastically lengthened the sentences for those who commit second felonies. Together, the two sets of laws greatly expanded the New York state prison population. Over the next three decades, as other states passed repeat offender laws or laws that harshly punished drug crimes, the prison populations multiplied.

But moral panics have a past. "Americans have a long history of periodic intense anxiety about crime and disorder," writes political scientist Marie Gottschalk. Such anxious leaps in public attitudes have not historically led to corresponding jumps in prison populations. There has been a recent "dramatic and unprecedented transformation of penal policies in a more punitive direction."[29]

As Gottschalk points out, decades before American incarceration figures began to surge, an extensive institutional and ideological apparatus already existed. "With each campaign for law and order and against certain crimes and vices in earlier eras, state capacity accrued, as evidenced, for example, by the growth of the Federal Bureau of Investigation (FBI) and the federal prison system, and by the militarization of crime control." Even when public worry died down, the justice system did not shrink. Instead, "the institutional capacity of the government expanded over time."[30]

But something did change in the 1970s. A new array of groups "began to mobilize around criminal justice issues." In addition to the frequently cited role of conservative political groups, "what has been overlooked is the role of other groups, some of them identified with progressive and liberal causes," that helped create what Gottschalk calls a "carceral state."[31]

The victims' rights movement is particularly illustrative. "Being for victims and against offenders became a simple equation that helped knit together politically disparate groups ranging from the more traditional, conservative, law-and-order constituencies mobilized around punitive policies like 'three-strikes-and-you're-out,' to women's groups organized against rape and domestic violence, to gay and lesbian groups advocating for hate crimes legislation, to the Million Moms pushing for gun control," writes Gottschalk.[32]

Feminists concerned about rape and wife abuse called attention to their cause by emphasizing violence and criminality. Gottschalk argues feminists ended up co-opted. "By framing the rape issue around 'horror stories,' they fed into the victims' movement's compelling image of a society held hostage to a growing number of depraved, marauding criminals."[33] One of the big feminist projects was the 1994 Violence against Women Act. As Gottschalk points out, the act was part of the 1994 omnibus anticrime bill, which "allocated nearly $10 billion for new prison construction, expanded the death penalty to cover more than fifty federal crimes, and added a 'three strikes and you're out' provision mandating life imprisonment for federal offenders convicted of three violent offenses."[34]

Gottschalk argues that many liberal politicians, particularly Bill Clinton, also played a significant role in the war on crime, the drug war, and as a supporter for the victims' rights movement. Clinton is famous for interrupting his 1992 campaign to sign the warrant for the execution of Ricky Ray Rector, a mentally disabled Arkansas prisoner.

A perceptive critique in the liberal weekly the *Nation* broadens Gottschalk's thesis. "As much damage as radical feminists may have done in undermining due process, they seem less important than certain antidrug activists—in particular, certain black Democratic antidrug activists—whose efforts ran on parallel tracks," remarked reviewer Daniel Lazare.

Lazare's examples include Jesse Jackson, known for supporting the vig-ilantism of Nation of Islam adherents who conducted "vigilante-style drug patrols." Representative Charles Rangel, head of the House Select Com-mittee on Narcotics Abuse during the Reagan administration, accused that president of neglecting the drug war. "I haven't seen a national drug policy since Nixon was in office," Lazare quotes Rangel as saying. "So far, the Ad-ministration hasn't given it any priority." Antidrug activism may have been more effective at filling the prisons than were the feminist campaigns, Lazare argues. "U.S. prisons are not bulging with rapists and wife beaters, but they are filled with drug offenders, some 458,000 as of 2000."[35]

Sociologist David Garland has proposed that behind such political changes moved a cultural shift.[36] For Garland, prisons that emphasized offender reform occupied a particular cultural moment that has since vanished. In the context of the mid-century economy, when employment was easy to find and equality was increasing, "crime and delinquency could be viewed not as a threat to social order but as lingering relic of previous deprivations."[37]

In the 1980s, the economic climate changed. A long recession hurt workers. Companies began to renege on their promises to their employ-ees, women entered the workforce, families had two incomes, households shrank, divorces became common, unions lost power, and a relativist sensibility increasingly challenged Enlightenment principles. When the crime rate shot up, he writes, crime and criminals came to serve a sym-bolic function. They helped the government to excuse the shrinking of social programs that once benefited poor and otherwise vulnerable people and to build up the prison and policing systems.[38]

And this is where the new claims about the "underclass" made possi-ble a tactical rewriting of governmental policy, Garland argues. "Crime—together with associated 'underclass' behaviours such as drug abuse, teenage pregnancy, single parenthood, and welfare dependency—came to function as a rhetorical legitimation for social and economic policies that effectively punished the poor and as a justification for the development of strong disciplinary state."[39] Social program constriction thus parallels prison expansion.

Garland is not the only scholar to claim that Americans are punishing themselves into a radically different nation. Jonathan Simon, a specialist in law and social policy, argues that in recent decades, U.S. politicians from the local to the national have been "governing through crime." In so doing, they have crafted a "civil order built around crime," an order that, among other things, has drastically lengthened prison sentences, multiplied the numbers of criminal laws, and caused "the portion of the population held in custody for crimes" to grow "well beyond historic norms." They have done so because "governing through crime" is a political tactic that works—it draws votes.[40]

Simon uses a stretching metaphor in writing of crime. The metaphor allows government intervention in areas of American life that once seemed to have nothing to do with criminality. "It is not a great jump to go from (a) concerns about juvenile crime through (b) measures in schools that treat students primarily as potential criminals or victims, and (c) later still, to attacks on academic failure as a kind of crime *someone* must be held accountable for."[41] Simon notes that American schools once shared the rehabilitative aims of the prison system. The punishment shift, in turn, reconfigured American education. Crime concerns have led to an institutional overhaul, he argues, with such features as in-school detention and police in the hallways.[42]

Daily middle-class American lives have changed as well. Anxiety disproportionate to actual threat leads to such choices as gated communities; and protected home, work, and school locations. The ever-stretching crime metaphor enwraps the American family. "The family is treated as a locus of suspicions about crime that requires surveillance and intervention by criminal law institutions," writes Simon. "Parents are drafted as an extension of law enforcement."[43] Crime worry also encircles the workplace. "There is a new emphasis on screening potential employees for illegal behavior of almost any sort," writes Simon.[44]

Finally, "governing through crime" has caused a "vast reorienting of fiscal and administrative resources toward the criminal justice system." The result, argues Simon, "has not been less government, but a more authoritarian executive, a more passive legislature, and a more defensive judiciary."[45]

"Governing through crime" threatens to undermine democracy, financial responsibility, American ingenuity, and racial equality, writes Simon. Ultimately, he offers a pessimistic assessment. "Crime has become so central to the exercise of authority in America, by everyone from the president of the United States to the classroom teacher," he argues, "it will take a concerted effort by Americans themselves to dislodge it."[46]

"PUNISHMENT MUST, ABOVE ALL ELSE, BE PAINFUL"

Graeme Newman is a well-known penologist whose career has encompassed both defenses of rehabilitation and calls for pain. In 1981, he wrote against the widespread critiques of rehabilitation: "It is only a couple of hundred years since we gave up mutilating, disemboweling, and chopping up criminals, and we still cannot make up our minds whether to stop killing them. It would seem to me, therefore, that while the medical [rehabilitative] model has its own drawbacks, it has brought along with it a useful baggage of humane values that might never have entered the darkness of criminal justice otherwise."[47]

By 1985, in *Just and Painful*, Newman had swerved. "We have forgotten how to punish—although we are perhaps more fortunate in that our amnesia is only a couple of hundred years old," he wrote before calling for a return to corporal punishment: "We must take seriously what the advocates of retribution have been saying for a long time, but not truly understanding: Punishment must, above all else, be painful." In his book, Newman advocates electric shock and suggests that other forms of pain may prove just as useful. "We must reconsider the infliction of all punishments regardless of the kind of pain, whether mental or physical, that they produce."[48]

With a few exceptions, the return to retribution lacked something the Puritans understood as central to punishment: forgiveness. If the Puritans punished with physical hurt in the stocks and the ducking stool, after such punishments the convict returned to the community. Sin is something that, in the Puritan understanding of the term, all community members share.[49] Our contemporary understanding of wickedness is not so pervasive. Punishment of the "wicked," in our day, is isolating, as Wilson's demand that they be "set aside" implies.

No longer a public or spectacular art, the use of pain on our criminals and on those suspected of being so is rarely visible. Much of it goes on behind prison and jail walls. The new ways of making pain—among them devices such as the restraint chair and the stun belt—are acceptable partly because we don't see them and also because the manufacturers and users of such devices promise that they are humane. They are "control" technologies. Evil criminals, like the demon that entered Linda Blair in the film version of *The Exorcist,* are easily understood as out of control.

What were the neoconservative critics of rehabilitation attacking? Science. A punitive version of Christianity—once culturally repressed from the mainstream though never really gone—returned in secular clothing. When we understand criminals (and children) as evil, we are thinking in religious, and irrational, terms. In the last few decades, much of our country has, for the most part without acknowledging or admitting it, undergone something we might understand as a religiously influenced punishment conversion. That conversion affects prisoners in profound and sometimes damaging ways. In the American lexicon of punishment, when the Devil gets his due, it hurts.

CHAPTER 9

Pop Culture and the Criminal Element

PUNISHMENT AND THE BIRTH OF POPULAR CULTURE

COTTON MATHER, THE PROMINENT Puritan preacher, was also a runaway success as a crime-and-punishment author. One day he delivered an execution sermon about a woman condemned to the gallows for killing her child. Mather prayed that the death sentence of the "miserable Malefactor" "might bee so ordered in His providence, as to give *mee* a special Opportunity of glorifying my Lord Jesus Christ, on that Occasion." The woman's hanging was originally scheduled for a week when another preacher would deliver the execution sermon. But the judges in the case delayed the event and "allow'd her Execution to fall on the Day of *my Lecture*." Mather's response was ecstatic: "Now I feel that there is a *God*, and there is a *Christ*, and there is an *Holy Spirit*, and there are glorious *Angels*, and I am a Servant of the Lord, and a Fellow-servant with His *Angels!*"[1]

Expecting numerous onlookers to attend the sermon and hanging, the General Court "ordered the Lecture to bee held in a larger and a stronger House, than that *old* one, where tis usually kept," reports Mather in his diary. The spectators gathered by the thousands. "The greatest Assembly, ever in this Countrey preach'd unto, was now come together; It may bee four or five thousand Souls," writes Mather. "I could not gett unto the *Pulpit*, but by climbing over *Pues and Heads*." Mather understood himself as having additional access to godly speech on that day. "I preached with a more than ordinary Assistance, and enlarged, and uttered the most awakening Things, for near two hours together."[2]

In 1927, the historian Vernon L. Parrington, writing in *Main Currents in American Thought, 1620–1800*, expressed discomfort with Mather's enthusiasm. Having suggested that the minister's account threw an unattractive "light" on both Mather and his listeners, Parrington writes, "No sooner was the girl hanged—for whose safekeeping no good angel seems to have been available after the minister had bespoken his—than he hastened to the printer to arrange for printing the sermon."[3]

Mather "annexed" to his published sermon a history of convicts hanged "in this Land," a record of their gallows speeches and his pre-execution interviews with some of them "in their last Hours." He entitled the book *Pillars of Salt* after the story of the destruction of Sodom and Gomorrah from the Old Testament book of Genesis.[4]

In 1993, another book used the title *Pillars of Salt* to make a different point. The author, Daniel A. Cohen, found in Mather's published sermon —and the excitement it generated—evidence of the birth of American popular culture.[5] "Crime and punishment were sources of endless fascination for the readers of colonial and early national New England," writes Cohen. "Between 1674 and 1860, printers of the region issued hundreds of books, pamphlets, and broadsides relating to the lives and deaths of criminals. The literature consisted of a wide variety of genres, including execution sermons, conversion narratives, dying verses, last speeches, trial reports, crime novels, romantic biographies, and newspaper stories." As "clergymen lost their cultural monopoly, and criminals gained a literary voice" during the eighteenth century, the literature changed. By the early nineteenth century, "the print culture of crime evolved into a competitive industry, dominated by lawyers, journalists, professional authors, and cheap publishers, that saturated a mass consumer market with narratives of sex and violence."[6]

Observing that "perhaps more than ever before, the subjects of crime and punishment dominate American popular culture," Cohen sees in today's television, newspapers, magazines, and books a preoccupation with crime and punishment characterized by consistent money-making potential, a large quantity of material, low cost, reportorial style, and a balance of "didacticism and sensationalism"—all qualities, he points out, that are present in Mather's execution sermons and other publications of Mather's printer, Richard Pierce. Despite television's secular appearance, a religious heritage still colors crime and punishment shows. "Some modern television writers may be less conscientious than Puritan ministers in fitting morals to their stories, but most still at least go through the motions," writes Cohen.[7]

Cohen's thesis posits punishment as a cultural force, interwoven within the American fabric. If punishment binds us together, if it is the source of our popular culture, if its ritualized themes structure national community via mass media, then our society is likely to change when punishment tightens, loosens, or unravels.

The persistence of a ritual of punishing in American popular culture over the course of more than three centuries is a remarkable inheritance—a transferal and perpetuation of cultural meanings from one century to the next. Punishment leapt with ease from published sermons and broadsides to nineteenth-century novels to twentieth- and twenty-first-century radio, film, arcades, video games, and television. The theme dominates late prime time viewing and has leaked into the hours once reserved for family shows—as in the 8:00 p.m. slot occupied by *Cold Case* and the Saturday evening crime-and-punishment reality blitz on Fox. Anyone trying to understand what is happening in contemporary society and to the people we punish would do well to take a close look at crime television, though movies, true crime books, and video games also provide examples of the three-centuries-long American punishment fascination.

POP CULTURE PUNISHMENT

In *Discipline and Punish*, Foucault uses the phrase "spectacle of the scaffold" to suggest how eighteenth-century public executions augmented governmental power. Through physical pain and deaths performed before crowds, rulers displayed their strength. What Foucault saw as the movement of executions from outdoor public events to indoor, mostly private ones mirrored what he understood as a modification in the way rulers and governments manipulated authority. "The disappearance of public executions marks therefore the decline of the spectacle," observes Foucault. Once death by hanging moved indoors, he argues, governments ceased to emphasize their authority in a public and physical manner, instead turning to surveillance strategies. Foucault understands surveillance as symbolized through panopticon prison design, which rendered prisoner privacy impossible while the guards themselves remained hidden.[8]

In its emphasis on spectacle, however, contemporary American entertainment resembles the scaffold more than it does the panopticon. Spectacles flash, explode, vibrate, provoke, and dazzle throughout American popular culture. This trait is nothing new; it formed an integral part of American vaudeville.[9] Spectacles also characterize circuses (tightwire walkers, trapeze artists, lion tamers, acrobatic dogs). They populate the stages of the more eccentric rock artists, such as Ozzy Osbourne. Spectacles attract. They draw crowds. They sell tickets and ads.

Given contemporary home media, today's spectacles often don't take place outside in the presence of crowds. Astounding and provocative displays happen inside the American home, via television. In this spectacularity, contemporary police dramas and their cousins the true-crime reality programs enact some of the performances of the scaffold. They display the guilty (whether real or fictional) before a crowd, one that numbers in the millions.

During the week of July 16, 2007, six shows featuring crime and punishment made the list of the ten top-rated television programs. (The list included twelve shows because of several ties, meaning that half of the top-rated broadcast programs were cop shows.) The ratings were: *Law and Order: SVU* with an audience of 9.4 million, *CSI* with an audience of 8.9 million, *CSI: NY* with an audience of 8.7 million, *Criminal Minds* with an audience of 7.6 million, *CSI: Miami* with an audience of 8 million, and *NCIS* with an audience of 7.2 million.[10]

Like the scaffolds of old, contemporary crime shows emphasize corporal pain, but the repetitive pain belongs to the (often murdered) victims rather than to the guilty. The shows sometimes include explicit enactments—dazzling in their displays of lighting, music, gun blasts, screams, wounds, and dying spasms—of victim hurt.

Long ago, punishments entertained, warned, and horrified crowds. To witness punishment was to share in public emotion. Private though the experience of witnessing televised crime may be, it is also a communal act. A common emotional experience characterizes popular culture. "I start from the assumption that the emotions generated by popular culture are never personal; rather, to be popular, the text has to evoke broadly shared feelings," writes Henry Jenkins in *The Wow Climax: Tracing the Emotional Impact of Popular Culture*. "The most emotional moments are often the ones that hit on conflicts, anxieties, fantasies, and fears that are central to the culture."[11]

Ever since the advent of radio and television stories, "emotional moments" have characterized cop shows. In the late twentieth century and the early twenty-first, these popular televised cultural myths have acquired a punitive cast—violent crimes and implicitly violent punishments. Such television programming draws much of its power from shared emotions, such as those Jenkins describes. The "conflicts, anxieties, fantasies, and fears" that form audience response to police dramas have corollaries in lived social reality. The cop show fictions refer, usually obliquely, to the charged public reality of crime, criminals, and policing. Some shows offer details of specific police cases. For instance, in 2007, after astronaut Lisa Nowak was charged with attempting to murder a love rival, *Law and Order* featured a character that wore diapers to commit a crime. This odd detail was one of the peculiarities of the Nowak case. Assertions that Nowak had clothed herself in diapers in order to make her alleged 950-mile odyssey of revenge were the stuff of late-night talk shows in the weeks after the original news story. Months later, her lawyer disputed the diaper claim.[12]

The Soviet film director Sergei Eisenstein argued that performed spectacles excite and delight because of their relation to lived reality. In his essay "Montage of Attractions," Eisenstein advocates that film and theater adopt "attractions," defining these as "any aggressive moment in the theater, i.e., any element of it that subjects the audience to emotional or psychological influences verified by experience and mathematically calculated to produce specific shocks in the spectator in their proper order within the whole."

One "attraction" Eisenstein describes appeared in the Grand Guignol, a Parisian puppet theater, "where eyes are gouged out or arms and legs amputated on stage." Henry Jenkins calls attention to the discomfort of Eisenstein's "attractions." "Eisenstein doesn't simply want to make us laugh; he wants to make us squirm," writes Jenkins.[13] Eisenstein's "attractions" are provocative and violent. These adjectives also characterize crime and punishment, particularly murder and its implied punishment—execution—which, in late twentieth-century and early twenty-first-century America, preoccupied both the late evening cop shows and the evening news.

Writing about the true crime books and television shows, Mark Selt-zer calls attention to the collective function of the genre. "True crime is thus part of our contemporary wound culture, a culture—or at the least, cult—of commiseration," Seltzer writes, underlining the suspect commu-nalism of true crime. "If we cannot gather in the face of anything other than crime, violence, terror, trauma, and the wound, we can at least com-miserate."[14] In that commiseration, each audience member sees his or her "media doubling" in the crime victim. For Seltzer, "these small and intense melodramas of the wound acclimatize readers and viewers to take social conditions personally. These social conditions then, in turn, take on the form of a pathological public sphere."[15]

Unlike the scaffold Foucault described, televised crime and punish-ment is not top-down punitive authority. The action of choosing a police drama, accessible to any American in a household with a television, suits a public where popular fear drives not only the explosion of crime televi-sion shows but also prison-system expansion. It is democratic fear.

BIRTH OF THE COP SHOW

The strong ties between crime-and-punishment reality and American popular culture have been with us since Cotton Mather published his execution sermons.[16] Twentieth-century crime-and-punishment radio shows often drew on real police files. From its beginning, television has used the same techniques. In the early 1950s, the first two police shows debuted on black-and-white television sets. CBS's *Crime Syndicated*, a police drama, lasted until 1953. But NBC's *Dragnet*, a show about a dark-suited cop named Joe Friday, ran from 1951 until 1959, reappeared from 1967 to 1970, inspired a film parody in 1987, and came back in an unsuc-cessful third remake in 1989. (The show had also been a radio program.) The *Dragnet* mode, a stylized realism that drew on actual cases from the Los Angeles Police Department, paved the way for television realism in shows as different as *S.W.A.T., CSI, Hill Street Blues,* and *Cops.*[17]

Joe Friday didn't have many great lines. Most were phrases like, "Go on, Ma'am," designed to elicit stories of swindles, thefts, and murders. But the show captured the national imagination and changed American television. From its first year, *Dragnet* ranked among the top ten most popular shows on television. Its theme song made the hit parade twice. The opening voiceover ("Ladies and Gentlemen, the story you are about to see is true. The names have been changed to protect the innocent") and Friday's sentences at the beginning of each segment ("This is the city, Los Angeles, California. I work here. I'm a cop. . . . My name's Friday") became cultural touchstones. The show portrayed Friday as perpetually on the job—so much so that in the episode "The Big Break," the revelation of leisure time is startling when Friday, in describing Long Beach, tells the viewers, "Like you, when I get a day off, I go here, too. I'm a cop." In depicting the crime stoppers and solvers as almost never at rest, *Dragnet* stood at the front of a long line of reassuring images of police diligence and disturbing portrayals of officers whose occupations devour their private lives.[18]

Joe Friday rarely resorted to personal heroics. In some episodes, Friday talks about weeks and months that pass as he waits for a crook to make a misstep. His way of doing his job is sometimes so passive as to seem alarming compared with more recent police dramas. In some episodes, for instance "The Big Break" and "The Big Betty," Friday and his partner Smith camp out in the thief's residence only to get a call from headquarters saying that other officers have arrested the crook. The show expressed faith in the institution of policing as a whole rather than in an individual hero.

With *Dragnet*, the all-American cop show was born. The news media of the day recognized a cultural transformation. "The flood of *Dragnet* fan mail suggests that the U.S. completely forgets that it is a nation of incipient cop haters when its eyes are glued on Webb's show," noted a 1954 cover story on the series published in *Time*. The United States, according to the newsweekly, "has gained a new appreciation of the underpaid, long-suffering, ordinary policeman," as well as "its first rudimentary understanding of real-life law enforcement."[19] Indeed, many predecessors to *Dragnet* portrayed the police as inept. These included *The Green Hornet* and *The Shadow*. In both of those popular radio broadcasts, which appeared in the 1930s and 1940s, the police treated the hero as a criminal, thus often missing the real crooks. Britt Reid, lead character of *The Green Hornet*, was the wealthy publisher of the *Daily Sentinel*. Only his assistant knew of his more complicated identity as a crime fighter equipped with the most advanced technologies. Lamont Cranston, the alias adopted by the hero of *The Shadow*, could make himself invisible to both the police and his criminal nemeses. The outsider status of these heroes suggested a populist solution to crime. They didn't offer a complimentary portrayal of official American crime fighters.

The outsider theme has continued to have cultural resonance in vigilante movies, such as *Death Wish;* in films and television about renegade heroic officers, such as *Dirty Harry, Lethal Weapon,* and *Starsky and Hutch;* and in television shows featuring private eyes, such as *Charlie's Angels* and the 2005 *Eyes.* And ever since *Dragnet,* the renegade has had companions —official police officers caught in the daily grind. Together, these crime-and-punishment shows have created a central genre of American television. In *Glued to the Set,* Steven D. Stark observes that since 1951 television has shared *Dragnet* star and director Jack Webb's "utter obsession with crime."[20]

When Congress chastised the television networks for violent crime shows, such as *The Untouchables,* action television lost ground to the consoling, quietly heroic portrait of the comedic crime fighter. *The Andy Griffith Show,* a comedy centered on a southern, small town sheriff, aired throughout the 1960s, following a long period of low crime rates.[21]

The television series, featuring small-town sheriff Andy Taylor, quickly rose in popularity. For its eight years of production, the show appeared among the top ten favorites, and in the 1967–68 season it reached number one. Andy Taylor, the paternalistic, gentle, reasonable sheriff, runs a jail of mostly empty cells. He has little work. He goes fishing in his sheriff's uniform and guides his son, Opie, with the same gentle authority that he uses on the lawbreakers. Whole episodes of the show occur in which the only person breaking the rules is Opie. These portrayals of childhood disobedience have as much dramatic weight as the search for a killer does in some police shows today. Often, Andy's disapproval is enough to motivate changes in his son. The message is clear: the police officer is a father figure possessed of such authority that his stern look can avert or reverse criminal activity.

The show sets Andy's relaxed approach to crime up against the law-and-order preoccupations of his comic companion, Deputy Barney Fife. Fife is so keen on being hard on criminals, and so bumbling in his efforts to do so, that Andy forces him to keep a single bullet in his shirt pocket rather than in his gun where it might prove dangerous.

Barney Miller was the popular 1970s continuation of the Andy Griffith type. His precinct, however, is not in bucolic and thoroughly white

Mayberry but New York City, and the multiethnic department gets its share of drug users, prostitutes, and petty thieves. *Barney Miller*, like *The Andy Griffith Show*, exhibits a faith in the power of the paternalistic police officer to transform lives. But the show's primary interest is the cops and their days at the precinct, with an emphasis on humor and human foibles (such as the character Fish's continual need to use the bathroom). The cops share flaws with the criminals, but the flaws in the officers are not dangerous, and even the criminals rarely present a grave threat.

The 1970s was also a period of rising crime rates, and *Barney Miller* had company on the airwaves. Numerous crime action shows appeared in the 1970s: *Police Woman, S.W.A.T., Starsky and Hutch, Charlie's Angels*, to name just a few. These shows tend to feature active pursuits of the "bad guys," with car chases, disguising costumes, and shootouts. Serious danger to the police officer is the rule—a departure from *Dragnet*, which scarcely hinted that Joe Friday might end up dead, though it did sometimes mention the deaths of other officers. The pilot episode for *Starsky and Hutch* shows two hit men blasting the windshield of a red car with a white swoosh that matches Starsky's. The hit men kill the couple in the car, who happen not to be Starsky and his girlfriend.

Similarly, the first episodes of *Police Woman* and *S.W.A.T.* both feature the deaths of cops. After a young officer dies in Pepper Anderson's arms in *Police Woman*, she returns to the precinct office, downs a shot from a bottle she takes from a file cabinet, cries, asks the young man's age, learns he has two little children, and requests the day off. Pepper's boss grants her request with a guilt-inducing speech that suggests officers (much in the manner of Friday) would do well never to leave work. The crooks aren't going on vacation, he tells Pepper. "They'll be out there doing business as usual."

But overall, the seventies action dramas are optimistic. The goal of the police officer is to intercept criminals and prevent them from committing crimes. The officers in such shows often anticipate the next crime and set a trap to ensnare the bad guys. Like Friday, the heroes in these shows tend to get their men—and women.

The 1960s and the 1970s also featured television dramas, like *The Mod Squad* and *The Rookies*, that emphasized innovative policing methods and rehabilitation. In one early episode of *The Rookies*, a young police officer manages to talk a gang from a poor neighborhood out of a street battle.

Instead, the group directs its anger in a protest of their lousy garbage service by dumping their trash in front of the mayor's country club.

Those liberal policing methods, presented as new and associated with the younger generation of officers in *The Rookies*, were, by the time the pilot for *Hill Street Blues* aired in 1981, the predominant strategy in the New York City police department of Captain Frank Furillo. But *Hill Street*'s understanding of crime as an outgrowth of difficult social circumstances is embattled. The streets are not the only things that are rough in *Hill Street Blues*. So is the station house. Brawls erupt in the hallways and waiting rooms of what, in many other police shows, is a safe place for police officers, comparable to a home. Plenty of voices in the show argue that police should get tougher. In the pilot episode, when Furillo brings in gang members to help negotiate a hostage situation, another officer chastises him. "You're so damned intimidated by these minority action groups and these cowards," says Howard, who adds, "it's no wonder" the country is rotting. The pilot set the tone for *Hill Street*, which repeatedly suggested the liberal police had lost control, and that crime was winning.[22]

A significant change has marked crime television since: from the first episode of *Homicide: Life on the Street*, in 1993, the main subject of television crime has been murder. This is a contrast to the past. In 1970s and 1980s crime shows, murder was one of a host of crime possibilities, including jewelry heists (*Charlie's Angels*), soon-to-explode protest bombs set by resentful senior citizens (*Starsky and Hutch*), and a would-be suicide who attempts to burn down his own factory and stands inside shooting at—and missing—the fire fighters (*S.W.A.T.*). Ironically, the shift coincided with a drop in violent crimes, including murder. The drop began in 1993, the year *Homicide* premiered, and continued for more than ten years, as have shows that emphasize murder.

Perhaps the shows emphasized the most frightening of crimes because—despite the drop in the crime rate—public fear was rising. A 1994 *Los Angeles Times* poll was typical of national statistics at the time. It showed that the residents of Orange County ranked crime as their number one concern, a phenomenon that cut across class and racial lines. The poll showed more anxiety about crime than had appeared in either of the two previous years. Area crime rates had been dropping for a decade, observed the paper. And the sense that crime was out of control seemed to conflict with people's belief in their own personal safety; the great majority of those who responded to the poll felt safe in their communities and inside their homes.[23]

What many critics consider the height of the crime show occurred at a curious time: 2005, the year of unprecedented numbers of such shows and sky-high popularity, also saw the lowest national crime rates in thirty-one years. The television crime proliferation had more in common with the imprisonment rate—which also experienced unprecedented highs, mostly due to nonviolent drug crimes—than with the crime rate.

Crime television has so proliferated that the chairman and CEO of CBS, Lester Moonves, calls this period "the golden age" of crime drama.[24] The dominance of the crime genre seems likely to continue; in recent years, the proportion of crime-and-punishment-related pilots to other types of television drama has often been 50 percent or higher.

A quick glance at 2004 programming on the three major networks is instructive. On Sunday nights at 8:00 p.m. Eastern Time, *Cold Case* aired on CBS. In *Cold Case*, committed officers select old, mostly murder, cases relegated to the "cold" file and revive them. The show uses frequent flashbacks to the decade of the crime, to the dead victims (whom the show resurrects in order to develop personality, background, and emotional depth before killing them off again), and to the criminal. A central message of the show is that both victimhood and criminality persist even when the crime is decades old. At 9:00 p.m., also on Sunday evenings in 2004, audiences could choose between: *Law and Order: Criminal Intent* on NBC, in which the star police officer attempts to understand the criminal mind; *Crossing Jordan* on CBS, one of the many forensics shows on television in the early twenty-first century, this one set in a morgue; or *Alias*, a CIA show, on ABC. The crime-and-punishment pick for Monday night was CBS's *CSI: Miami* at 10:00 p.m. *CSI: Miami* is part of the expansive and popular *CSI (Crime Scene Investigation)* series, each set in a different city (Miami, Las Vegas, and New York City). Like *Cold Case* and *Crossing Jordan* the *CSI* shows emphasize murders over other crimes. In a typical episode of *CSI* or its spin-offs, the camera begins by showing a public place: a golf course, a hip-hop club, or a restaurant. It is an ordinary day or night. People are out having fun. Then something changes: lights go out, shots sound, people panic. A body turns up where the happy crowd once played.

Saturday evening also featured the popular *24*, an innovative drama about terrorism with traditional cop show features. On Tuesday, on NBC at 10:00 p.m., another member of the *Law and Order* franchise aired, *Law and Order: Special Victims Unit Choice*. (The *Law and Order* shows all follow police through a—usually violent—crime for a half hour, followed by a half hour tracing the resulting case through the courts.) *Law and Order: Special Victims Unit Choice* competed with *NYPD Blue*, a long-running show featuring a homicide squad, on ABC. On Wednesday, NBC aired two hours of policing with *Law and Order Blaze* at 9:00 p.m. and *Law and Order Embedded* at 10:00 p.m. On Thursday night at 9:00, CBS ran *CSI*. That same evening, CBS aired *Without a Trace*, which the network describes as "a riveting procedural drama about the New York Missing Persons Squad of the FBI." The team "details every minute of the 24 hours prior to the disappearance and digs into every facet of the victim's life, following one simple rule: learn who the victim is in order to learn where the victim is." On Saturday, Fox featured two hours of crime and punishment with the reality show *COPS*, which showcases police from various American towns and cities on the job, followed by a reality manhunt with *America's Most Wanted* at 9:00. Then, at 10:00 p.m. on NBC, prime time returned to fictional crime and punishment with *Law and Order: Special Victims Unit Coerced*.

The 2005 season, which witnessed the end of the critically acclaimed *NYPD Blue*, saw the addition of several new crime-and-punishment shows, including *CSI: NY, Numb3rs* (in which a mathematician enabled his FBI-employed brother to solve crimes by doing math problems), *Medium* (featuring a psychic housewife employed by the Phoenix district attorney's office), and *Blind Justice* (which starred a blind officer on a homicide squad), all of which more than made up for the loss of *NYPD Blue* in quantity, if not in quality. *Blind Justice* quickly left the airwaves. The 2007–8 season, newly advertised as I write, promises to continue the crime-and-punishment trend.

THE NEW COP SHOW:
FROM AVERT DISASTER TO LOCATE THE GUILTY

Crime-and-punishment shows have changed since the 1960s and 1970s. The old shows often portrayed officers determined to stop a crime in progress. For instance, in one classic *Starsky and Hutch* stomach-clencher, Starsky drives a car with a locked trunk full of TNT over a hill and leaps to safety as it explodes, averting an urban disaster. Most of today's shows have a different preoccupation. In them, police officers, often members of homicide squads or forensics teams, determine who is guilty after a crime has been committed and capture the crook. In the *CSI* and *Law and Order* shows, a gruesome murder or sexual crime tends to occur as the episode opens, catalyzing the hunt for the guilty. For instance, a young girl out past her curfew hurries home to find her parents dead, their heads severed. The job of the officers is to discover the perpetrator; the television focus is on guilt rather than attempted crime and on punishment rather than prevention. The assumption behind such a theme is that crime cannot be averted; what remains is to deliver the guilty to retribution.

The extreme efforts to thwart crime that characterized 1970s shows like *Starsky and Hutch* have passed to the characters who fight mass crimes, such as the terrorism fighters Jack of *24* and Sydney of *Alias*. Our domestic television cops have all but given up trying to stop television criminals, who, cruelly assured, often go about their crimes without hindrance. In abandoning the crime fight, our television police have morphed into the arbiters of good and evil; they tell their audiences who among the assortment of suspects deserves punishment.

Medium, while not centering on a homicide squad or a forensics officer, is as preoccupied as its contemporaries with uncovering guilt. Unlike other crime fighters, who can see only the physical traces of violence, Allison DuBois, the show's psychic main character, enables viewers to penetrate surface realities. (The character of DuBois repeats the realist tradition of cop shows by drawing on the autobiography of a real-life psychic crime fighter.) In her dreams and sometimes in her daytime intuitions Allison can perceive good or evil inside people. Her psychic abilities at times confound traditional definitions of criminality. In one episode, Allison decides that a do-gooder and a volunteer is, despite outward appearances, guilty—not because he has committed a crime but because she foresees that he will commit one in a decade. Allison accuses him of being "evil." The future criminal walks free, leaving Allison—and probably her audience—frustrated: the man is already guilty of murdering a young woman, although he hasn't committed the crime just yet. The idea of an impending death is more frightening than the completed murders of most contemporary cop shows, which tend to reward their audiences with communal catharsis when the police catch the crooks.

Criminality is, in *Medium* and in other areas of our culture, a permanent trait, something like personality, present long before a criminal commits the crime and long after the convict does time. But Allison's dreams sometimes deliver faulty information, leading her to go after the wrong guy. In other episodes, the dreams raise questions. If she helps imprison a pilot for the murder of his wife, her dreams inform her, a plane will crash, killing more than two hundred. The uncertainty about what it means to put someone away and the recognition that crooks have lives beyond their crimes and that those lives can benefit others suggest a wrangling with the meaning of punishment far beyond that of the standard crime show. That DuBois sometimes mistakes a "good" guy for a "bad" one is a complication that perhaps signals cultural anxiety about punishing the wrong people.

Medium is one in a group of shows that, like *CSI* and the *Numb3rs*, explore the religious roots of punishment and of crime shows by suggesting that in order to determine who dunnit, one must have access to information not available to ordinary people. In *CSI*, it's ritualized science; in *Numb3rs*, genius-level mathematics; and in *Medium*, ESP.

Access to such higher information suggests that crime fighters are members of a select group. The fancy science of *CSI*, the advanced mathematics of *Numb3rs*, ESP, or the old-fashioned police hunch that operates in more traditional crime shows are all forms of entrée to omnipotent knowledge the uninitiated cannot reach. This knowledge enables crime fighters to distinguish the wicked from the good.

In shows that emphasize harsh punishments like executions, this ultra-knowledge is comforting. It offers assurances that the law enforcers in the shows are selecting the correct people for death. The assurances offered by these shows, however, bear little relation to reality, where science and numbers and hunches can be tainted by human failing and where the wrong people do sometimes end up on death row.

Punishment is a little-remarked-on subject in police shows and movies. Television theorists have described cop shows as representing the search for truth, the conservative enforcement of societal strictures, or the purification of a polluted society. Although punishment is implicit in these last two themes, critics rarely address it explicitly. Punishment sets cop dramas apart from most other genres, with the possible exception of gangster flicks and Westerns. It is the backdrop and the goal of many police shows, whether of the career cop, the maverick hero, or the socially aware officer variety. Punishment in police dramas is always implied and sometimes mentioned, but it is almost never shown. Yet punishment is the end toward which the plot of a cop show careens. Once the officers spot and remove the source of trouble in the community, the crooks go somewhere. The television shows often record only their disappearance. But that disappearance carries a significance that can be signaled without explicit mention because its cultural meaning is strong. Unlike the cop shows, which on American television last either thirty or, more commonly now, sixty minutes, the implied punishment keeps going . . . past the end credits, past the final commercials, into the future.

GETTING RELIGION IN PRIME TIME

The hovering power of punishment in American cop shows suggests the Christian roots of the genre as a whole, a characteristic that has been noted by cultural critic Elijah Siegler. Siegler claims that religion is "at the heart" of *NYPD Blue,* something that might come as a surprise to Don Wildmon, the leader of the right-wing Christian American Family Association, which protested the show because of its explicit violence and lewd language. Cop shows exhibit an eclectic version of Christianity that includes, at different times and in different shows, the confessional associated with Catholicism, the evangelical Protestant idea of personal redemption, the social gospel understanding of crime as linked to poverty, and the belief in eternally punishable guilt.[25] The idea that Christianity is punitive and that it is this characteristic—more than forgiveness and love —that marks this dominant genre of American television, is not likely to be a popular idea among Christians who prefer their religion in its more kindly forms. It might also come as an unpleasant surprise to non-Christian fans of cop shows.

Some critics have suggested that television, as a ritual medium with qualities akin to religious practices, has a substantial effect on society. "Contemporary cultures examine themselves through their arts, much as traditional societies do via the experience of ritual," write Horace Newcomb and Paul M. Hirsch. "Ritual and the arts offer a metalanguage, a way of understanding who and what we are, how values and attitudes are adjusted, how meaning shifts." The adjusting of values and the shift of meaning suggest that the place of ritual is also a location of social change. "The skewed demography of the world of television is not quite so bizarre and repressive once we admit that it is the realm in which we allow our monsters to come out and play," they write, including in their categories of plot structures and characters that differ from everyday reality television's emphasis on "cowboys, detectives, bionic men, and great green hulks; fatherly physicians, and glamorous female detectives," terming these "part of the dramatic logic of public thought."[26]

Television critics often describe such genres as the police show, the Western, and the romantic comedy in ways that suggest ritual. The 1998 textbook *Reaching a Critical Mass: A Critical Analysis of Television Entertainment* by Robert Abelman, for instance, lays out the basic plot of a television drama as involving five stages that could easily describe other cleansing rituals, such as Christian baptism or "being saved": status quo, pollution, guilt, redemption, and purification. As strange as such a religious-appearing structure might seem in our cop shows, it is easy to find when one starts looking. The pollution and purification ritual provides form for the standard crime-and-punishment television show. For example, one 2004 *CSI: NY* segment begins in Central Park. When a kid harasses a man, mounted police officers respond to cries from onlookers. A gunshot rings. An officer falls. His horse runs wildly into the street, crashes into a taxi, then drops onto the concrete. This is the moment of pollution. It affects not just those in the park but the entire metropolis. "No one sleeps in New York City until the shooter's caught," says Detective Mac Taylor, head of the New York crime lab and the show's star. Even the animal community is polluted, as the horse, which survives its traffic accident, bears a bullet that will reveal the killer. But removing the bullet, the veterinarians say, will kill the horse.[27]

When the officers determine that there's guilt, the pollution broadens to the entire country. The sniper is a Gulf War veteran who was dishonorably discharged. The episode, broadcast during the Iraq War, raises the question of what American foreign violence does to its domestic order. Once the officers finger the guilty sniper, redemption of the city, the animal world, and the country is possible. And once he is punished, the various communities undergo purification. At the end of the episode, even the horse, once destined for sacrifice on the altar of the police investigation, has survived.

Partly because they are societal rituals, intuitively perceived as magical and dangerous, television cop shows have served as magnets for societal anxieties in the United States. They have provoked congressional investigations, been isolated to late evening viewing when children are supposedly not watching, blamed for surges in adolescent violence, and curbed in their language and images.[28]

Ritual also explains why, in spite of prevalent anxieties and diatribes against cop shows, the genre has persisted. In late twentieth- and early twenty-first-century America, the public seemed to need crime-and-punishment shows. Early efforts to put them down met with limited success, as Senator Thomas J. Dodd's investigations of violence in television during the early 1960s suggest. The networks responded to the Senate hearings with a new squeamishness toward violence that led to the rise of the situation comedy and prompted one onlooker to describe Dodd's hearings as "the death knell of action programming." But within a few years, action programming, like the return of the repressed, was back, and so were images of violent cops. They have been with us since.

TORTURE AND 24

In the week that marked the one-year anniversary of the Abu Ghraib revelations, an episode of the Fox show 24 opened with a scene of the Counter Terrorist Unit medical clinic. Lying in a hospital bed, attended by physicians, was the terrorism suspect who, in the last seconds of the previous episode, had screamed in pain as the show's hero, Jack Bauer, broke the bones in his hand. As Fox pumped out advertisements for 24's season finale, the newspapers boiled over with revelations of real torture by U.S. officers. Then the finale came, and Jack and company saved Los Angeles from a nuclear bomb thanks to a wild series of strategies that included brutal torture.

In the days that followed, Amnesty International issued what amounted to an all-points bulletin for Bush administration officials: "The officials implicated in these crimes are . . . subject to investigation and possible arrest by other nations while traveling abroad." Like Jack Bauer, the 24 star who in the final scene of the last episode flees to Mexico, Donald Rumsfeld and George W. Bush were wanted men, accused of breaking international law. Rarely has fictional television seemed so entwined with our national political life.

In 24, the would-be crimes are so huge and imminent that the antiterrorism team believes it does not have the luxury of playing by the rules.

Anxiety—which the show manipulates with exaggerated plot twists— explains some of 24's appeal. The shadow of 9/11 hangs over the show. And torture itself has a unique power to horrify.

Kiefer Sutherland, an executive producer on the show as well as the star who plays Jack Bauer, seems driven to address the places where his show intersects with American guilt. He talks like a liberal. "Do I personally believe that the police or any of these other legal agencies that are working for this government should be entitled to interrogate people and do the things that I do on the show? No, I do not," he said in an interview with Charlie Rose.[29]

Joel Surnow, also an executive producer, has connected 24's realism with an appearance of conservatism. "Doing something with any sense of reality to it seems conservative," he told the right-wing paper the *Washington Times*, which praised the show. Surnow informed the paper that 24's writers are both liberal and conservative, that 24 doesn't "try to push an agenda" but is "committed to being non-PC." He also offered a defense of torture under extreme circumstances, the sort that characterize the world of 24. "If there's a bomb about to hit a major U.S. city and you have a person with information . . . if you don't torture that person, that would be one of the most immoral acts you could imagine." Surnow didn't admit this, but the continual regurgitation of situations involving imminent bombings and torture separates 24 from reality and renders it a fantasy show. Impending disaster has rarely, if ever, accompanied the real tortures that appear in our newspapers.[30]

Torture on 24 is as contradictory as the statements of its producers. In the 2005 season, 24 depicted torture and terrorism as married. The show's logic ran like this: a nuclear bomb launched from Iowa was in the air on its way to . . . no one knew where. The target was almost certainly a large coastal city. The hardworking counterterrorism employees who never ate, used the toilet, or slept, whose cell phone batteries never died, needed to stop the explosion from killing millions of innocent people. They had no information on the bomb. They did, however, have a suspect in custody.

It's an unfair competition. If you place torture of a few people, innocent or not, next to an imminent nuclear holocaust, torture seems necessary. But 24's torture voyeurism is uncomfortable. The program differs from many cop shows; it does not mince around pain. Physical hurt is audible and visible on 24, and often difficult to watch. The pain contrasts harshly with the "happy violence" critics of television have complained about for decades. That 24 insists on rendering pain with such clarity is disturbing in light of the fact that the show's torturers sometimes cause extreme hurt to the wrong people. The possibility of torturing an innocent is a hovering concern of 24, which can't help but speak to what happened at Abu Ghraib prison in Iraq.

The use of physical pain enables Jack and his fellow terrorism fighters to get to the source of a terrorist plot; it is a route to higher truth. Physical pain has become a means of finding the guilty and purifying the community. Los Angeles and Washington D.C., may not be gathering around a pond to witness a ducking, but pain is a redemptive force in the television world of 24.

CONFOUNDING REALITY

If you love reality TV, you can blame one still-young network and two shows: Fox television and its long-fledged fledglings, *America's Most Wanted* and *COPS*. These shows aren't just reality programs. They started the genre or at least (if one allows for the prior existence of *Candid Camera*) its dramatic version.[31]

Fox first began broadcasting in 1986. In 1988, it launched *America's Most Wanted*, which became the first Fox series to attain first-place ranking for its time slot. In 1989, the network followed *America's Most Wanted* with *Cops*, the first dramatic reality show.[32]

In its most lasting manifestation, reality TV is preoccupied with crime and punishment. *Cops* and *America's Most Wanted* both appear on Saturday evenings, in the hours following local news broadcasts. Unlike most television police dramas, the two reality shows air during what the other networks traditionally set aside as family viewing time. *America's Most Wanted* and *Cops* each follow their own characteristic formula.

Cops offers a brief, subtitled introduction, providing the place and time, the name of the featured officer, and the type of call, for instance, "suspicious vehicle." Other than that, the voice of the show is almost entirely that of the police officer, who describes what is happening and offers interpretations of, or moral commentary pertinent to, events. Criminals do speak on the show, though they rarely have names and do not get the last word. The show features low-level crimes such as drunkenness, public disturbances, and theft.

John Walsh, whose son was abducted from a shopping mall and later beheaded, hosts *America's Most Wanted*.[33] Walsh, whose authority derives from his strong voice and demeanor in addition to his experience as a victim, presents information on people wanted by the FBI through dramatized stories and reenactments. He frames each story with calls for public action. In contrast to *Cops*, this show emphasizes extreme and violent crimes and murders. Although such crimes are statistically rare, Walsh makes them seem pervasive, probable, personal. In December 2003, for instance, he described a group of men who dress as utility workers and then stalk, rob, and sometimes attack their victims. "Look, this pack of jackals has got to be stopped before they attack you or your family," he said.

Cops and *America's Most Wanted* are linked to each other by their airing time, their network, their sentiments toward the alleged criminals, and sometimes their subject matter. On January 19, 2005, for instance, both shows featured segments on Las Vegas, a popular tourist location with a reputation for gambling, quick marriages and divorces, and topless dancers. The shows linked this low-level immorality to crime.

In its Las Vegas broadcast, *Cops* depicts drunk young women from Minnesota urinating in the street, then, in an emphasis on violent crime unusual for the show, embarks on a murder investigation. "This is probably the killer right here," says an officer of a man who is sitting outside an apartment building. After the officer takes the suspect to a hospital before booking him, *Cops* returns to the Las Vegas strip and to a man who is insisting, "I am the loneliest man in the world. No one wants me." The man, whom the officers say they have picked up before, has stowed numerous cans of beer in his pants and underwear. He has also, he says, stolen women's garments because he likes to wear them.

The show then turns back to the murder. A search of one suspect's room turns up a bloody tank top and a red T-shirt. The officer informs the television audience that witnesses put one murderer at the scene in a red T-shirt and that the other suspect has admitted to wearing a tank top on the night in question. The officer also discovers the victim's Social Security card in a backpack belonging to one of the two suspects. The officer says she is pleased; the investigation has turned out well. This episode of *Cops* includes an epilogue. The two accused murderers plead not guilty to charges of conspiracy to commit robbery, kidnapping, and murder. The last words of the show appear in print: "Prosecutors have asked for the death penalty for Kevin and Randy."

A few minutes later, *America's Most Wanted* opens with the announcement, "To date we have captured 848 fugitives. Now you can join the hunt." Video game footage appears on the screen, as if all audience members are engaged in an electronic quest—as, in fact, we are.

That night, after chasing murderers in two other towns, *America's Most Wanted* travels to Las Vegas, which, the host intones, "took her money, then it took her life." The bright lights on this side of town, Walsh indicates, belong to squad cars. "Welcome to the dark side of Las Vegas," he says. In a hotel, a maid finds a woman strangled with curtain strings. The once-wealthy victim is a gambling addict who long ago "gambled herself into poverty." The alleged murderer turns out to be "the most helpful guy" at the local mission.

As is true of police dramas, the goal of both these reality shows is punishment, most of which happens outside of and after what we see on screen. The alleged criminals leave the screen, setting off to the punishment that the shows suggest they deserve and will get. The proximity of the low-level crime of *Cops* and the terrifying strange murders of *America's Most Wanted* implies continuity and a link between the two.

REALITY VS. REALITY PROGRAMMING

Just how real is the reality in *Cops* and *America's Most Wanted*? If there is any connection between our media culture and the ways that we punish, the question is critical. Studies of television viewers indicate that people watch nonfiction television differently than they watch fictional programming. They tend to interpret nonfiction shows, such as the news and documentaries, as accessing reality and the violence these shows depict as more upsetting than that in comedies and dramas.[34]

Cops and *America's Most Wanted* infiltrate our social and cultural realities in numerous ways. A few things can be said about the ever-increasing number of captures recorded by *America's Most Wanted*. For one thing, most of the viewers haven't actually "captured" any "fugitives." Those accomplishments belong predominantly to law enforcement. Nonetheless, the television audience receives frequent invitations to join a vigilante movement of the airwaves, an invocation that includes an implicit call to action by asking viewers to phone in tips to—not the police—but the show itself. *America's Most Wanted* also includes praise for viewers who have reported sightings of the suspect. The show often features a map of the United States, indicating where the suspect might be based on clusters of viewer tips. The word "fugitive" implies the phrase "fugitive from justice." The implication is that those people numbered in *America's Most Wanted* statistics have evaded justice. The show rarely mentions the possibility that the "fugitive" might turn out to be a case of mistaken identity.

Although the shows are careful to skirt slander, they often imply that the individuals they discuss are guilty. "Here's a couple of slime balls whom the U.S. Marshals say still need mopping up," said host John Walsh on May 31, 2005. *Cops* admonishes that "all suspects are innocent until proven guilty in a court of law," but the featured officers often tell the audience otherwise. "He'll be going to jail," says an officer about a man who allegedly pushes his girlfriend out of a moving car (she is not, at least in the show, seriously injured). "Another bad guy off the streets."

Research on *Cops* indicates that many viewers believe the show presents reality. In 1995, Mary-Beth Oliver and Blake Armstrong published a survey of *Cops* audiences in Virginia and Wisconsin. The audiences reported that they understood the reality show as much more realistic than television crime dramas. Other studies suggest that viewers distinguish between reality TV, which they view as a source of information, and television that is just entertainment. Viewers indicate that reality programs about crime resemble the news.[35]

Cops realism, though, is more extreme than that of any newscast. Television news sifts and winnows reality, presenting "the most important stories of the day," filtered via a news anchor and reporters. *Cops* claims to present unmediated experience.

The producers of *Cops* present the show as real life on screen. "It's unpredictable, it's immediate, it's raw, it's real," producer John Langley, who first brought *Cops* to television, told the *Palm Beach Post* in 2002. "You can't fake that. To this day, there's no other show on television that has no host, no narrator, no script and no actors."[36] The supposed access to "raw" reality is a theme Langley sounds again and again in interviews. "It's television in its purest form," Langley told the *Norfolk Virginian-Pilot* also in 2002. "We open a window into a universe that most people seldom see."[37]

But Langley makes other statements that reveal his awareness of the many ways *Cops* diverges from lived police work. You can't make good television from a dull shift when the officers sit in their squad cars filling out paperwork. "With the crime numbers falling, it means we have to keep our six crews on the streets longer and longer," Langley told the *Virginian-Pilot*. "We stick around waiting for something to happen."[38] That little admission suggests a big contradiction between what *Cops* claims to do and what it does: the "raw" reality of *Cops* is edited, shaped, censored.

In 1998, the *Virginian-Pilot* was explicit about what "television in its purest form" would not show. In the city of Chesapeake, reported the paper, "one of their finest accidentally shot a *Cops* cameraman" while cameras recorded the incident, which did not seriously injure him. Despite the exciting footage and sound effects that probably resulted, the first shooting injury of a *Cops* employee would not make prime time: "Producer [Murray] Jordan said he has no plans to broadcast footage of the accident. And besides, each police department previews rough drafts of proposed shows, and can veto embarrassing scenes." Despite the show's vaunted rawness, Jordan's comments make clear that *Cops* is not journalism. "We are not the media," Jordan told the paper. "We are in the entertainment business."[39]

The *Virginian-Pilot* did comment, however, that it was surprising how many instances of "excessive force, constitutionally illegal searches and smart-mouthed officers antagonizing suspects" did make the cut. Media scholars have noted the same phenomenon. "Enough rough handling is left in to raise the suspicion that producers are not worried about offending audience members with such material; on the contrary, the calculation is that imperfections—errors on the side of repression rather than leniency—only serve to add more personalism and hypercompetence of the cops in action."[40]

Cops sends many signals, all designed to persuade audiences to buy what the show is selling: pretend reality. These include handheld video recorders, subtitles listing the time and place of the action, and camera position. In December 2003, the filming, which began at "1:42 a.m." in the French Quarter of New Orleans, took place from the back seat of the squad car. Other camera angles include a front seat side view of the officer. The effect: audience members are accompanying the officers on a ridealong. Some media scholars claim that the reality signals so dominant in *Cops* are an inheritance of crime dramas. Numerous fictional police shows, including *Hill Street Blues, Homicide: Life on the Streets, NYPD Blue, Dragnet, Law and Order,* and *CSI,* have used case files, unsteady cameras, forensic science, or echoes of real news reports to lend realism to their fictions.

These enhanced reality shows affect real-life policing. For instance, fans of *Cops* sometimes mistake the reenactment for the real thing. "In several instances, viewers have turned in the actor who played the fugitive in a dramatization," notes one *Cops* scholar.[41]

Officials in charge of finding violent crooks have sometimes turned to *America's Most Wanted* for help, a role reversal that makes the television show seem more in touch with crime and criminals than the police are. *America's Most Wanted* has been so effective in building its reputation for finding perpetrators that, in the aftermath to the two biggest acts of terrorism on U.S. soil—the Oklahoma bombing and the attack on the World Trade Center—the show's host, John Walsh, received calls from the U.S. government, including (after September 11, 2001) the White House. Local governments also acknowledge the show's importance. The Web site of the Outagamie County Sheriff's Department, a jurisdiction that includes Appleton and Kaukauna, Wisconsin, maintains a list of important links to such sites as the state's sex offender registry, the FBI's Most Wanted List, animal control information, the Wisconsin Department of Justice, and the jail visitor's guide. Topping the list, for alphabetical reasons, is *America's Most Wanted.*[42]

Cops has affected cultural understandings of crime fighting. In one ethnographic study, the police officers of St. Louis Park, Minnesota, perceive television police, including those of *Cops,* as competitors. "On TV, they get credit for everything," an officer said. "Here, we only get credit for something that can go into the crime statistics."[43]

The study also implies that the police of St. Louis Park see crime shows as altering the public's behavior. When a real-life wanted man opens the door in response to an officer's knock, the officer asks, "Buddy, why did you let us in? You could have just shut up and not answered the door." The arrested man answers, "I thought I had to let the cops in." After booking the man, the arresting officer comments, "Thank God they [the public] watch too many *Cops* shows—they [TV cops] never walk away from a door."[44]

The influence of *Cops* can take more ostentatious forms. In 2003, the *Worcester (MA) Telegram and Gazette*, in an article on the local vice squad, described the arrest of a man charged with selling crack cocaine. To celebrate the arrest, the squad played a recording of the popular reggae song "Bad Boys," the theme song to *Cops*. "It's a ritual marking busts considered significant by team members, and is performed correctly only if the tape player volume is set a notch or two above blaring," reported the paper. " 'Song still chokes me up,' one of the veteran detectives said with a hint of a smile and a tug on imaginary heart strings."[45]

A similar occurrence took place in Shirley, Long Island, in 1994. At 3:00 a.m., as police rounded up inhabitants of an alleged crack house, a crowd equipped with a video camera gathered on the sidewalk to taunt the suspects with the popular reggae song by Ian Lewis: "Bad boys, bad boys, whatcha gonna do? Whatcha gonna do when they come for you?"[46] These quirky happenings are the light side of a darker question: could these shows influence our crime and punishment reality in more extensive, less innocuous, ways?

Much of what *Cops* depicts is not reality. As several studies have shown, reality crime programs exaggerate arrest rates (one study found a televised arrest rate of 60 percent for all crimes committed as compared to an actual rate of 18 percent on American streets), the numbers of white police (while underrepresenting the number of black officers), and the rate of violent crimes in comparison with nonviolent offenses. In the shows Mary Beth Oliver analyzed, 87 percent of the suspects were connected with violent crimes. The FBI's numbers, by contrast, identify only 13 percent of all crimes committed as violent ones.[47]

In another study, published in 1998, researchers found that "reality-based programs appear to embody many characteristics that point to the likelihood of several harmful influences." The researchers noted, "These shows portray a world that is much more crime infested than is actually the case, they cast people of color in the role of the villain, and they are perceived as realistic by many of their viewers." This inclination, though pronounced in connection with the reality TV audience, was much less strong among viewers of fictional crime dramas. The study did not measure whether the reality shows produced this effect in their viewers or whether the viewers chose to watch the shows because they already had a tendency to overestimate crime rates. The researchers suggest that the relation between attitude and reality show viewing may be a circular one.[48]

At the least, this study suggests that those concerned about the effect of television on real lives, public fears, and social policy should consider giving extra attention to reality TV. If these shows are changing our public, our culture, and our national policy, that influence is likely to tend in the direction of harsher punishment.

STORY AT TEN: LOCAL NEWS AND OTHER CRIME DRAMAS

In the late 1970s, some local evening news programs began to entertain. Like the fictional dramas they imitated, the news shows featured quantities of crime and punishment. By the late 1990s, local news programs almost without exception operated by a similar formula. They began with serious crimes, a strategy often called "the murder of the day." The opening murders in *CSI* and those in today's newscasts serve similar purposes: to hook frightened, curious, titillated viewers. Local news programs emphasize that ribbons of fear bind together our diverse, contradictory populace. When a local news station emphasizes fear, it redefines not only the "news" but also democracy.

Citizens trust television news. Surveys indicate that Americans trust local news more than other news media. "In 1985, a third of the public (34 percent) said they could believe 'all or most' of what they saw on local television news," reported the Project for Excellence in Journalism in 2003, citing statistics from the Pew Research Center. "In 2002, that had declined to one-fourth of the public (26 percent)." Yet the popularity of television news remains strong. Americans turn to local news for information more than they do any other source.[49]

American newscasts are similar, no matter where you watch them. The Project for Excellence in Journalism conducted a five-year study of local news and found a common formula: the "hook and hold" strategy. "The approach begins with a natural desire to hook viewers at the start," according to a 2005 report. "That is done by putting stories that are supposedly 'live,' eye-catching and alarming at the top of the newscast."[50]

This "surprisingly static, formulaic structure" leads to disproportionate treatment of some subjects over others. In its five-year study, the project found that news about "public safety" made up 36 percent of all stories but accounted for almost two-thirds (61 percent) of stories leading broadcasts. "Indeed, 13 percent of all newscasts began with three crime stories in a row, back to back to back."[51]

In 1993, the *Washington Post* looked at news broadcasts in five large cities and cited teasers, including these:

"Tonight, an exclusive interview with a man who is accused of stalking and beating his wife" (from a Chicago station)
"Vicious criminals are on the loose in San Diego. A 10 News extra"
"Imagine the horror of pulling into your own driveway, only to be confronted by a gun-waving carjacker" (from a Los Angeles station)
"Two different children, two different vicious attacks. First a little boy mauled by a Rottweiler. . . . It's a Night Team exclusive." (from a Miami station)[52]

Media critic Steven Stark, who in *Glued to the Set* cites both the Project for Excellence in Journalism and the *Washington Post* surveys, titled his chapter on the local news "Television's Biggest Scandal."[53] As Stark's history makes clear, local news was not always so alarming. It changed, as did so much else linked to crime and punishment in America, in the 1970s. "Until about 1970, local news—with its mix of local stories, weather, and sports delivered in a low-key broadcast—was an insignificant part of the television day," writes Stark. That changed when stations realized they could make money off the inexpensive-to-produce broadcasts because, unlike syndicated shows, local news allowed the station to keep any profits.[54]

In the 1970s, "the locals frequently turned to such sensationalist topics as crime." The stations also began to rely on a "small group of media consultants," who gave similar advice no matter the market. "That explains the subsequent uniformity."[55] In changing their identities, the local stations took their cues not from other nonfiction programming but from police dramas. "Crime shows like *Kojak* attracted the largest audience," writes Stark. The news became an entertainment genre.[56]

By taking its formal cues from dramas, local television news foundered into some troubling ethical realms. Between 1993 and 1996, as the country's murder rate slipped by 20 percent, the number of murder stories reported on ABC, NBC, and CBS network broadcasts rose by 721 percent. "Since 1993 crime has been the most heavily covered topic on the network evening news with 7448 stories, or 1 out of every 7 stories on all topics," observed the Center for Media and Public Affairs in a 1997 report that uncovered these statistics.[57] "Humankind may have had more blood-thirsty eras, but none as filled with images of crime and violence as the present," wrote media critic George Gerbner.[58]

As the crime rate fell, numerous polls indicated that Americans be-lieved the opposite was happening. "How did it come about that by mid-decade [of the 1990s] 62 percent of us described ourselves as 'truly des-perate' about crime—almost twice as many as in the late 1980s, when crime rates were higher?" asks Barry Glassner in *The Culture of Fear*. One of Glassner's insights is that an emphasis on crime and disaster masks more pressing concerns that are harder to report, require more analysis, can be controversial, and do not make for good visuals.[59]

In this way, violence, rather than economic or other concerns, be-came a threat around which the American democracy could coalesce. "Fear is one of the few things that Americans share," writes social scien-tist David Altheide in *Creating Fear: News and the Construction of Crisis*. Altheide argues that a rising "discourse of fear" led Americans to define their society as constantly under threat.[60]

Altheide didn't look at the local news. He examined large city news-papers and national television news broadcasts. He found striking in-creases in the word "fear" in both. For instance, from 1985 through 1994, use of the word "fear" in the *Los Angeles Times* increased by 64 percent. From 1990 to 1994, use of the word in ABC evening news broadcasts jumped by 173 percent. "The use of *fear* in headlines and text increased from 30 to 150 percent for most newspapers analyzed over a seven- to ten-year period, with 1994 the peak year," Altheide writes. Although "fear" appeared in connection with many subjects, "many of these increases were associated with more emphases on crime reporting."[61]

The word "crime" was coming to incorporate its frequent companion "fear," so that saying one would signal the other. Between 1987 and 1996, "the association of *fear* with *violence* and *crime* had increased sixfold." Altheide also argues that "fear" expanded in meaning and was increas-ingly used as a substitute for less charged words "such as *concern, rele-vance, trouble, query, issue, item,* and many others."[62] Altheide noticed a similar increase in use of "victim," which, he argues, became a status identity in American culture.[63]

FEAR AND AMERICAN LIVES

Studies suggest that nonfiction programming can have real-life effects, and many of those derive from that new democratic American value: fear. The most famous argument along these lines comes from George Gerbner, who coined the phrase "mean world syndrome." Gerbner argued that the more one is exposed to televised depictions of violence, the more one believes life to be dangerous. Such viewers "may accept and even welcome," Gerbner reports, "repressive measures such as more jails, capital punishment, harsher sentences."[64]

A summary description from a study of audiences for police reality TV showed the programs "were most enjoyed by viewers who evidenced higher levels of authoritarianism, reported greater punitiveness about crime, and reported higher levels of racial prejudice."[65] But cause and effect are a question in Gerbner's and other research on this topic. Do people become frightened or punitive because of what they watch on television, or do they watch television because they are frightened or punitive? Is there a mutual, reinforcing relation between fear of crime and television representations of it? The research is not clear-cut. But a few things are crystalline. The media emphasize fear, which they attach to crime. Implicit in the crime news and crime shows is punishment.

What punishment has done to television—and what television has done to punishment—is important because television is an agent of cultural change. The United States after three decades of punishment TV, punishment religion, and punishment politics is a more punitive country than it was. Many of us, a much larger spectrum than those we house in our Big Houses, may live to regret the new America we helped invent.

CHAPTER 10

Stunning Technology

IN THE 1990S A COMPANY called Stun Tech invented the REACT (Remote Electronically Activated Control Technology) belt. An electronic shocking device secured to a person's waist, the belt was the hot new item in corrections gear. The device appealed to guards because they could apply punishment without having to go near the prisoner wearing the belt. They could set off the eight-second, 50,000-volt stun from as far away as three hundred feet.[1]

Stun Tech claimed the device was "100 percent non-lethal." Sales boomed in 1994 when the federal Bureau of Prisons decided to use the belt in medium- and high-security lockups. By 1996, the U.S. Marshals Service, more than one hundred county agencies, and sixteen state correctional agencies employed the belt for prisoner transport, courtroom appearances, and medical appointments. By 2002, the manufacturer, now known as Electronic Defense Technology (EDT), claimed it had sold 1,900 belts, which had been worn more than 65,000 times by prisoners across the country.[2]

Human rights groups were aghast. "The stun belt looks to be a weapon which will almost certainly result in cruel, inhuman, or degrading treatment," a violation of international law, said Brian Wood of Amnesty International in 1996. The use of the stun belt in U.S. prisons "will inevitably encourage prison authorities—including those in torturing [nation] states—

to do likewise," said Wood, who believed the chances were very high that the belt would eventually be used for torture.[3]

Stun Tech's promotional materials recommended the belt as a psychological tool, an effective deterrent for potentially unruly inmates, and a humane alternative to guns or nightsticks. In its mid-1990s version, the REACT belt was available as a one-size-fits-all minimal-security belt (a slim version designed for low visibility in courts) or as a high-security transport belt, complete with wrist restraints. Both came attached to a nine-volt battery. In the late 1990s, EDT added to its product line a "Band-It" that fastens around the ankle or wrist. "Where the Belt could only be worn around the waist, the Band-It can be worn on 8 different parts of the body," according to the company Web site. "Even 2 systems can be used at the same time."[4] This last sentence appears to imply that in the case of some particularly wayward prisoners, guards may subdue the disobedient with simultaneous shocks.

Early advertising for Stun Tech displayed bravado. When activated, the stun belt shocks its wearer for eight seconds, with three to four milliamps, and 50,000 volts of "continuous stun power," noted the company. The painful blast, which company representatives advertised as "devastating," knocks most of its victims to the floor, where they may shake uncontrollably and remain incapacitated for as long as fifteen minutes. Two metal prongs, positioned just above the left kidney, leave welts that can take up to six months to heal.

According to two physicians and a 1990 study by the British Forensic Science Service, electronic devices similar to the belt may cause heart attack, ventricular fibrillation, or arrhythmia, and may set off an adverse reaction in people with epilepsy or on psychotropic medications. Stun Tech denied that its belt could cause fatalities. But a death involving a stun device manufactured by the company, soon raised serious questions about the belt's safety.

In 1995, a Texas corrections officer suffered a heart attack shortly after receiving a shock from an electric shield similar in design to the stun belt. Like many other Texas corrections workers, Harry Landis was in training to use the electric riot shield. Like the stun belt, the taser, and the stun gun, the shield is an electronic shocking device. Guards frequently use the shield when removing prisoners from their cells. But on December 1, 1995, something went terribly wrong. As part of the training, Landis was required to endure two 45,000-volt shocks. Shortly after the second shock, Landis collapsed and died.[5]

The Texas Department of Criminal Justice, which had used the shields to subdue prisoners since September 1995, immediately suspended their use. The maker of the shield denied that it had killed Landis: "We're very sorry this happened," said John McDermit, president of Nova Products, Inc., "but there certainly was no connection between his training and his death."[6]

Jimmy Wood, the Coryell County justice of the peace who conducted an inquiry into Landis's death, told a different story. "Landis was in fairly decent shape as far as physical appearance is concerned," he said. "He did have a history of heart problems. But was he going to die this day if he didn't experience an electric shock? No, he wasn't." According to Jimmy Wood, Landis's autopsy showed that he died as a result of cardiac dirhythmia due to coronary blockage following electric shock by an electronic stun shield. "The electric shock threw his heart into a different rhythmic beat, causing him to pass away."[7]

"The shield worked as it was intended to," said Mark Goodson, an engineer who conducted tests on the shield following Landis's death. "Now comes the problem. The manufacturer puts in its literature that the shield will not hurt anyone, including people with a heart condition. But they have not done studies on people with heart conditions. They haven't done studies on people at all. They conducted their tests on animals—anesthetized animals. Do you see the danger here? In one word: adrenaline."[8] Goodson explained that this is a problem with all pulsed electrical stun technology. "No one can even define a safe voltage. . . . We don't even have an idea if it is safe or not for the general population."

McDermit continued to believe that Landis's death was mere coincidence. "We think that just happened to be a timing problem," he said.[9]

STORY: A LESS-LETHAL CONFERENCE

The stun belt and its relatives are supposed to be nonlethal or, at the very least, less-lethal. At the 1996 Law Enforcement and Corrections Technology Conference in Los Angeles, I talked to less-lethal weapons manufacturers, representatives of the National Institute of Justice, officials of the Rome and Phillips laboratories, and executives of correctional facilities. They were all proud of the newest "less-lethal" technologies. They told me about products already on the market: mace, pepper spray, beanbag bullets, rubber bullets, plastic bullets, and the stun belt. They also let me in on some new ideas: a cannon-like instrument that shoots a sticky net, disorienting lights, sounds that cause nausea, sticky foam, aqueous foam "doped with pepper spray," and a gun that heats its victim's body up to 107 degrees Fahrenheit. Many of these devices inflict significant pain. Some are potentially deadly (sticky foam, for instance, can seal a person's lungs; the sticky net, shot at close range, has knocked the head off of many a dummy).

Michael Keith, president of MK Ballistic Systems, maker of the beanbag bullet (coarse material stuffed with lead shot), explained how such products develop: "All technology starts low-tech." His own beanbag bullet had to go through some adjustments when corrections officials discovered that at close range it punctured bodies. So corrections personnel shot from farther away. The stun belt, Keith added, is "just a modified dog collar."

Although his work is in beanbag bullets, not stun technology, Keith had many ideas for improving the belt. He would install a tracking device and a timer, and make the belt impossible for the wearer to remove. An inmate who escaped would get a jolt every thirty seconds or so until he was "in need of serious medical attention," Keith said. "The guy would be frog-jumping in the backseat. I wouldn't say it should kill him. That wouldn't go over in our society."

The sponsor of the Los Angeles conference was the American Defense Preparedness Association. The organization (which has since merged with the National Defense Industrial Association) publishes *National Defense* magazine and organizes many other conferences with such titles as "Enhancing the Individual Warrior," "Undersea Warfare," and "Bomb and Warhead."

Conference participants thrilled to the idea of combating "internal enemies." "I don't think our defense against an internal enemy is any different from a defense against an external enemy that might be threatening our borders," said Sherman Block, then-sheriff of Los Angeles County.

During conference breakout sessions, we watched film clips from *Star Trek, RoboCop, Star Wars, Gunsmoke,* and Clint Eastwood Westerns. "The police firearm is more reminiscent of Wyatt Earp than it is of *Star Trek's* Captain Kirk. We do indeed have a technology gap," said Alan Bersin, the conference chairman. To justify closing the gap, the industry was stressing the importance of manipulating the American public's fear of crime. "Think about the public's concern about crime and translate that concern into a national agenda—into new solutions, new technologies," said Jeremy Travis, director of the National Institute of Justice. "How can we build a public demand, and marry that demand to production?"

THE COURTS GET WIRED

Stun Tech's advertising material asserts that "merely wearing the belt is not a violation of civil rights. As long as it is not used for officer gratification or punishment, liability is non-existent." Leaving aside the issue of "officer gratification," the belt seems popular precisely for its punishment potential. And it is being used even before defendants are proven guilty.

In December 1994, Bruce Sons was on trial for the murder of a California highway patrol officer. Sons was forced to wear a stun belt. The belt went off accidentally, shocking Sons. His attorney, Troy Childers, requested that the belt be removed. The judge denied Childers's request, demanding that Sons wear the belt until he testified.[10]

In April 1995, James Oswald stood trial for robbery and the murder of a Wisconsin police officer. The Waukesha, Wisconsin, court system required Oswald to wear the stun belt. Oswald's attorney, Alan Eisenberg, objected. "I was worried that they would accidentally stun him into the middle of next week—which proved to be a true prediction," said Eisenberg in a 1996 interview. "I argued that it was a Nazi torture device." The car carrying Oswald crashed during a police chase on the day of the crime. Oswald, who was hospitalized and placed in a body cast, appeared in court in a wheelchair throughout his trial. According to Eisenberg, Oswald was unable to walk and unable to run. The court, not convinced that Oswald's disabilities were real, required both shackles and the stun belt.[11]

Authorities acknowledged that the belt was accidentally set off once, shocking Oswald. Oswald claimed he was stunned twice and was being tortured. Eisenberg believed that the court's insistence that Oswald wear the belt "was part of a multiphase effort to torture this guy. Many of the people who had responsibility for him were friends of the deceased. It was like a chicken in a fox coop."[12]

Once the REACT belt goes off, there is no stopping it. Although a blast of between one and three seconds is enough to paralyze almost anyone temporarily, the manufacturer set the timer at eight seconds in order to account for differences in bodily resistance to the belt, explained

Jim Kroncke, a Stun Tech trainer. Even if, as often happens, the belt knocks its wearer to the floor after a half-second, the wearer must endure the entire eight-second stun. The REACT belt is not equipped with a switch that would allow a guard to end an unintentional activation.[13]

In June 1998, Ronnie Hawkins, a petty thief, served as his own attorney during a California sentencing trial. Under California's three-strikes law, he was subject to a life term. Hawkins had, as his third offense, stolen a bottle of aspirin. The Long Beach Superior Court required Hawkins to wear the stun belt. Hawkins, who was HIV positive, had, as the court papers record it, threatened to "spit on deputies to give them AIDS."

Hawkins was obnoxious during the hearing, loudly interrupting the judge. After one disruption, Judge Joan Comparet-Cassani warned Hawkins, "You are wearing a very bad instrument, and if you want to feel it, you can. But stop interrupting." Hawkins interrupted the judge three more times. Comparet-Cassani ordered Hawkins's guard to shock him.[14]

Hawkins's words after the eight-second jolt suggest that the experience undermined his ability to represent himself. "I would like for the record to reflect that at this point I am afraid to say anything. I am going to get electrocuted, shock treatments for talking. . . . I haven't displayed any violence, any disruptive [behavior]."[15]

Hawkins sued Los Angeles County, claiming the shock had interfered with his right to a fair trial. The county settled the case for $250,000. The Commission on Judicial Performance privately disciplined Judge Comparet-Cassani.[16]

In 2002, the California Supreme Court ruled that use of the stun belt in courtrooms interfered with the right of defendants to represent themselves. It ruled that California courts should use traditional restraint methods, such as handcuffs or shackles, instead.[17]

Amnesty International recorded other questionable uses of the stun belt. The state of Louisiana, it reported in 1999, regularly dresses minimum-security prisoners who are HIV positive in the belt solely because of their medical condition. The group also claimed that at Red Onion State Prison in Virginia, white guards shocked black prisoners while using racist slurs.[18]

When I asked Stun Tech president Dennis Kaufman to send me a copy of the company's promotional video for the REACT belt, he warned me that many viewers find the footage graphic. "There are about thirty people jumping around like Mexican jumping beans," he said.

Kaufman was right: the video is graphic. But it shows only law-enforcement and corrections officers wearing the belt. All have been warned and given time to prepare themselves psychologically for the shock. During the eight-second blast, all are clearly in pain. The officers in the video fall onto gym mats or onto grass. One guard, panicked by the shock, dives headlong into a portable movie screen and a metal cart. "Watch his head," yells an off-camera voice.

I called Kaufman several days later to check some facts. He asked me if I had received the video. "It makes great party viewing," he said.

Advertising brochures for the REACT belt in the 1990s were accompanied by an affidavit signed by a single medical doctor, Robert Stratbucker of the University of Nebraska Medical Center. Stratbucker conducted a series of safety tests using the Stun Tech Ultron II device. Stratbucker did his tests on anesthetized swine.

An anesthetized pig is very different from a human being who dreads electrocution. In their own way, the company representatives acknowledged this. Kroncke, the trainer for the company, called the belt's effect on prisoners "very psychological," adding that, "at trials, people notice that the defendant will be watching whoever has the monitor." He pointed out that the belt has never caused anyone to defecate or killed anyone. "If it ever kills anyone," said Kroncke, "I think it's going to be from fright."[19]

Kaufman also blamed fear for any potential physical danger. "We don't recommend that it be placed on anyone who has a heart condition. The reason is that, if they have to wear it for eight hours, there's a tremendous amount of anxiety. The fear will elevate blood pressure as much as the shock will." But, he added, "the technology we are using is not capable of causing a heart attack."[20]

A 1990 study by the British Forensic Science Service, a British government agency, came to some rather different conclusions. The British scientists found that high-voltage, high-peak, short-duration pulses, such as those the stun belt inflicts, are dangerous. The study describes stun devices as "capable of causing temporary incapacitation of the whole body: a body-widespread immobilizing effect." A one-to-two-second shock, noted the scientists, would probably cause the victim to collapse. A three-to-four-second shock would have an incapacitating effect on the entire body for up to fifteen minutes. Since the shock is distributed via electric currents throughout the entire body, including the brain, the chest region, and the central nervous system, the researchers concluded that "anyone in contact with the victim's body at the time of shocking was also likely to receive a shock," and that they "could not discount the possibility of ventricular fibrillation." This is to say that a stun device could potentially kill someone.[21]

Although EDT advised guards not to use the belt on inmates with a known heart condition, this precaution hardly eliminates all potential dangers. For one thing, some at-risk hearts appear healthy. "You shock someone with 50,000 volts of electricity and that person has some unrecognized congenital problem or conduction mechanism in their heart, and you put them at great risk for arrhythmia," said Armond Start, a medical doctor and former head of the National Center for Correctional Healthcare Studies. "You can't predict this. You can't determine the conduction mechanism in a heart. Arrhythmia mostly happens in healthy hearts."[22]

Start questioned Electronic Defense Technology's claims that the belt is medically safe. When he served as medical director of the Texas state prison system, stun guns, closely related to the belts, were being employed. The state eventually stopped using them. "Having dealt with the stun gun, I know that that was implemented without a good medical evaluation. If corrections is true to form, they have implemented this [the stun belt] the same way. Show me a refereed study on this thing." Kaufman responded that an independent, refereed medical study had never been conducted on the REACT belt.[23]

Some correctional officers wonder about the belt's real purpose. Chase Riveland, former assistant secretary of the Wisconsin Department of Corrections and former secretary of the Washington State Department of Corrections, criticized the stun-belted work crews as a "symbolic statement," designed to give the public an illusion of increased safety. "The thing that concerns me most is the public image that is left out there that says this is going to fix something, stop crime and violence. I guess I don't believe that. The question becomes, how far do we go in brutalization?"[24]

In June 1996, Amnesty International asked the U.S. Bureau of Prisons to suspend use of the electroshock belt, citing the possibility of physical danger to inmates and the potential for misuse. The agency has not complied. In 2000, the United Nations Committee against Torture asked the United States to ban the belt. The United States has not done so.[25]

STORY: "PLEASE STUN YOURSELF WITH THIS"

At nine on one early spring evening in 1996, I arrived at the Outagamie County Jail in Appleton, Wisconsin, and pressed the rear-door buzzer. A voice came over the loudspeaker, requesting my name. The door unlatched. I entered the bright hallway. No one appeared to greet me. I was slightly disoriented but had little choice in direction—there were no turnoffs or stray passages. I rounded a corner and came face-to-face with a large elevator door, which opened immediately.

Upstairs, I met Kroncke, the Stun Tech trainer. He led me into a large, glassed-in office, where several stun devices lay carefully arranged on a table. I asked if one of them was a stun gun.

"I don't call this a stun gun," said Kroncke. "I call it an electric restraining device. If someone calls it a stun gun, I hand it over to the officer and say, 'Please stun yourself with this.'" He held the stun device up in the air and pressed a button. The device crackled, and a miniature bolt of lightning leapt between the two metal prongs at its tip. The muscles in my stomach clenched.

One requirement of the eight-hour course for officers who carry stun devices, explained Kroncke, is that "you have to stun yourself." Officers in his training courses generally stunned themselves in the large thigh muscle—not the place, it occurred to me, where an officer was likely to shock a disobedient inmate. Because of the body's reflex reaction to electrical shock, a self-stun generally lasts less than half a second, that is, less than the average shock needed to "take someone down" and much less than the stun belt's eight-second discharge. An eight-second stun is not required for officers undergoing the six-hour training for the stun belt. But many officers, Kroncke assured me, elected to try it.

I asked if the shock from the stun belt hurt. Yes, he said, "It does a number on you. It feels like two needles. And it will leave some pretty severe marks." He described the time when he allowed himself to be shocked with the belt. He had built up a tolerance by taking "hits" with the electronic restraining device. He prepared himself psychologically to withstand the belt. "I had it all planned out. I was going to count 'one thousand one, one thousand two.' I never heard the beep. I was down on my back, spinning around. It was devastating. It hurt tremendously." He told me the welts on his back took two months to heal.

Despite the pain, some officers seemed to take pleasure in attempting to defy the belt. Kroncke described officers at the Appleton facility who bet each other Mountain Dews, claiming that they would be able to remain standing the entire eight seconds of the shock—a rare feat. For those who did undergo the belt, Kroncke offered pocket calculators and T-shirts. He told me the other officers had nicknamed him "Fifty," for 50,000 volts.

When I asked Kroncke if he would allow me to try the stun belt, he turned grave. "You would not want to wear this belt," he said. "I would not recommend it." So I asked if I could shock myself with the stun gun. Kroncke had me sit in a chair, press the prongs against my leg, look up at him, and pull the trigger. I felt a powerful smack and was immediately fatigued. My arm and leg jumped apart in reflex. Kroncke informed me that I had shocked myself for "much less than half a second."

ELECTROSHOCK ABROAD

In a 1997 report on the spread of electroshock torture, Amnesty International listed the United States along with Algeria and China in a section titled "Recent Cases of the Use of Electroshock Weapons for Torture or Ill-Treatment."[26] A decade earlier, the United States seldom appeared as a culprit in Amnesty reports. But by 1997, the United States had become a leading manufacturer and exporter of push-button electroshock devices, which Amnesty claimed were unsafe and were ending up in the hands of torturers. Of the one hundred companies listed in the report, forty-two were based in the United States. According to Amnesty International, countries that had received stun weapons exported from the United States between 1987 and 1997 included Yemen, Panama, Saudi Arabia, Mexico, Argentina, the Philippines, the United Arab Emirates, Ecuador, Cyprus, and Thailand.[27]

Among the many U.S. manufacturers and traders of electroshock weapons mentioned in the report was Nova Products, Inc., of Cookeville, Tennessee, maker of tasers and other electronic devices.[28] As John McDermit, head of Nova Products admitted, "It's possible to use anything for torture, but it's a little easier to use our devices."[29]

Stun Tech of Cleveland, Ohio, was also listed in Amnesty's report.[30] In 1996, Stun Tech's Kaufman told me he was eager to begin marketing the belt to other countries. "Many nations have shown interest," said Kaufman. At the time, Stun Tech was already selling its device, Ultron II, abroad.[31]

Would Stun Tech willingly market the stun belt to prison facilities in China, Mexico, or Saudi Arabia, three countries known for their human rights abuses? Yes, said Kaufman, "We can deal with certain countries under the Free Trade Agreement without a problem." I asked if Stun Tech conducted research on the prison systems of the countries with which it trades. Kaufman told me it did not.

ELECTROSHOCK AT HOME

A few years after the great migration of stun weaponry from the United States overseas, a similar instance of punishment creep happened at home. High-powered tasers, higher in wattage than conventional stun weapons, became weapons of choice for police officers. The proliferation of tasers in police departments across the country led to unconventional uses. Among those hit by tasers have been elderly people, children as young as one year old, people apparently suffering diabetic shock and epileptic seizures, people already bound in restraints, and mental hospital patients. Police used tasers against protesters at the 2003 Miami Free Trade Area of the Americas demonstration and against rowdy fans at the 2005 Fiesta Bowl. School systems employ the weapons, with some officers carrying tasers in elementary schools.[32]

Early tasers, those used from the 1970s until the early 1990s, were lower-wattage devices. "The original taser operated on only five watts and was followed by Air Taser on seven watts," notes a November 2004 Amnesty International report. Taser International introduced its Air Taser in 1994. Then, in 1998, according to its advertising, "the company began Project Stealth: the development of the higher-power weapons to stop extremely combative, violent individuals who were impervious to non-lethal weapons." Project Stealth led to the M26, a taser with twenty-six watts of power. In 2003, Taser International started selling an additional version of the twenty-six-watt taser, the X26, which is light enough for police officers to carry at all times.[33] William Bozeman, a medical doctor in the Wake Forest University Department of Emergency Medicine, investigated the safety of tasers for the Justice Department. "They've increased the amount of wattage that's delivered." Above fourteen watts, he says, you get "electro-muscular disruption." According to Taser International, that's the point. The "uncontrollable contraction of the muscle tissue" allows the taser "to physically debilitate a target regardless of pain tolerance or mental focus," according to the company Web site. The tasers "directly tell the muscles what to do: contract until the target is in the fetal position on the ground."[34]

Doctors, reporters, and human rights groups have raised questions about the safety of these devices, which shoot two barbs designed to pierce the skin. The barbs are at the end of electrical wires carrying 50,000 volts. In summer 2004, the *New York Times* reported that at least 50 people had died shortly after being hit with a taser. By November 2005, when Amnesty International released its report, that number had risen to more than 70. In March 2006, Amnesty issued a second report, noting that the number of deaths occurring after taser use was quickly mounting. The human rights organization cited 156 deaths in the United States over the previous five years.[35]

In Portland, Oregon, police used a taser to shock a seventy-one-year-old blind woman four times on her back and once on the right breast. They also pepper-sprayed her and beat her.[36]

On June 9, 2003, Eunice Crowder was at home when a city official came to clean up overgrown plants and debris in her yard. When Crowder objected, the official called the police, who soon arrived on the scene. The *Portland Oregonian* reported that Crowder, who claimed to be hard of hearing, ignored police commands and tried to climb into a city truck to retrieve her possessions, which had been removed from the yard. According to the police, when they tried to stop Crowder, she kicked at them. At that point they used pepper-spray and a taser to subdue her. They then handcuffed Crowder and yelled at her to stand up. "And she says, 'I bet you wouldn't yell at your mom like that,'" her lawyer, Ernest Warren Jr., told a radio station. One of the officers responded, "My mom is seventy-four." She said, "Well, I'm seventy-one."[37]

In 2004, Crowder agreed to a $145,000 settlement from the city of Portland. The police department admitted no wrongdoing. Less than a month after the settlement, the Portland Police Bureau announced it would limit acceptable uses of the taser. The new policy prohibited shocks to people's faces and heads and advised police to think about other options before using the weapon against the elderly, pregnant women, and children. The policy also required officers to seek permission from a commander before stunning crowds during demonstrations.[38]

Crowder isn't the oldest person hit by a taser. In October 2007, Chicago police used a taser on a woman who was eighty-two.[39] Seventy-five-year-old Margaret Kimbrell of Rock Hill, South Carolina, was subjected to a taser when she refused to leave a nursing home and, the police claimed, tried to hit an officer. She describes the electricity from the taser as traveling "all over your chest like a big snake or something worming to try to get out." Kimbrell says, "I prayed, 'Lord, Jesus, make it quicker.' I was waiting to die so the pain would go away."[40]

Some of Taser International's own materials suggest that shocking senior citizens may pose a danger. In a November 2004 report, Amnesty International cites a "certified lesson plan" from the company that warns it is "not advisable" to use its high-power devices on someone who is pregnant or elderly.[41] A study of available medical literature commissioned by Taser International notes that older people may have particular vulnerabilities. "Elderly subjects and those with preexisting heart disease are perhaps at an increased risk of cardiac complications and death following exposure to large quantities of electrical energy," wrote Anthony Bleetman of the University of Birmingham.[42]

In February 2005, Chicago police used the device against a fourteen-year-old boy, who went into cardiac arrest but survived, and a fifty-four-year-old man, who died. The Cook County medical examiner determined that the shock from the taser caused the man's death. Taser International disputes the finding, as does Daniel Dugan of the Chicago Police Department, who points out that the man had a lethal amount of metamphetamine in his system.[43]

For years, Taser International insisted that its products were safe. "The ADVANCED TASER has a lower injury rate than other nonlethal weapons and has had no reported long-term, adverse aftereffects," noted the company Web site in 2005.[44] But by 2006, the company was making more modest claims: "While there are certain risks and dangers faced by officers and individuals in the situations where TASER devices can be used, TASER devices are a safer use-of-force alternative that are more effective than other types of force."[45]

Police like tasers, sometimes for good reason. Greg Pashley, officer and spokesperson for the Portland Police Department, says the taser "is effective in ending what could otherwise be a violent conflict without injuries. We're finding that time and again."[46] Many other officers add praise of their own. "It's increasingly a less lethal weapon of choice," says

Scott Folsom, police chief at the University of Utah. "It doesn't have residual effects. It's proven to be a relatively safe and effective tool."[47]

Many police departments report that the use of tasers has reduced injuries and fatalities. The city of Phoenix saw a 54 percent drop in police shootings the year it began to use tasers. In 2003, Seattle, which also uses tasers, for the first time in fifteen years had no shootings involving officers. That correlation has made tasers popular.[48] "As of October 2004, over 6,000 police departments in the United States and abroad had purchased TASER products," according to the company Web site in early 2005. "Over 200 police departments—including Phoenix, San Diego, Sacramento, Albuquerque, and Reno—have purchased TASER products for every patrol officer."[49]

But Amnesty International says the tasers are making it too easy for the police to use excessive force. "While police shootings in Phoenix fell from twenty-eight to thirteen in 2003, tasers were used that year in 354 use-of-force incidents, far more than would be needed to avoid a resort to lethal force," reported the organization.[50] A number of stories in the Amnesty report involve police use of tasers on people already restrained, including two strapped to gurneys. In Pueblo, Colorado, "a police officer applied a taser to the man while he was restrained on a hospital bed, screaming for his wife."[51]

"That was a case where a rookie officer did not understand appropriate use of a taser," says Pueblo police chief Jim Billings. Although the incident involved a misunderstanding of policy, rather than maliciousness, the officer received "a pretty heavy suspension."[52]

Amnesty International wants the devices temporarily banned "pending a rigorous, independent, and impartial inquiry into their use and effects."[53] In response to the Amnesty report, Taser International issued a press release accusing the human rights organization of being "out of step with law enforcement worldwide."

Police have also used electroshock devices on children. On December 10, 2004, police in Pembroke Pines, Florida, used a taser on a twelve-year-old boy who tried to stab another child with a pencil while on a school bus and then became combative with police. Commander Ken Hall, public information officer for the Pembroke Pines police, says the case "was looked at very closely, obviously because of the controversial nature" and found to be "within the parameters of our policy."[54] In November of that same year, a Miami-Dade officer shocked a twelve-year-old Florida girl who was playing hooky. At the moment he shocked her, she was running from him.[55]

In May 2004, a nine-year-old runaway girl, handcuffed and sitting in a Tucson police vehicle, was shocked with a taser when she began to kick at the car and bang her head. The Pima County attorney general's office conducted an investigation of the incident and decided not to bring criminal charges against the officer who used the taser. "In all likelihood, the use of the taser prevented" the girl "from injuring herself any further," wrote David L. Berkman, the chief criminal deputy.[56]

According to records Taser International supplied to the Associated Press, even one-year-olds have been shocked. Additionally, the company told the *San Jose Mercury News* that its taser is safe for toddlers.[57]

In October 2004, police officers in Miami were dispatched to an elementary school where they encountered "a mentally disturbed student bleeding and holding a piece of glass." According to the police report, "Upon their arrival, the officers were confronted by a highly agitated and disturbed male bleeding and smearing blood on his face while clutching a piece of glass in his left hand." The officers tried to talk the boy into giving up the glass and tossing it into a wastebasket. The boy refused and "attempted to cut his leg with the shard of glass," after which officers shocked the boy to keep him from hurting himself more extensively. The boy, who was six years old, "dropped the glass and was subdued without further incident."[58]

The officers who shot the boy acted "for his own safety and to stop him from hurting himself," says Juan DelCastillo, spokesman for the Miami-Dade police. As for the appropriateness of shocking a six-year-old, DelCastillo's response is, "Our understanding is that there has been research" and that the taser causes "no aftereffects." There is "no reason that would cause harm to someone younger than an adult."[59]

"We have no evidence in terms of human testing to indicate that there is a dangerous outcome for any certain category of groups" exposed to tasers, says Steve Tuttle, vice president of communication for Taser International. Tuttle says the company has done studies on bodies affected by alcohol, stress, and acidosis. Taser International has not been able to test on children or people affected by cocaine, however, says Tuttle, and "won't be able to specifically target" the elderly. Care must be taken because "these are people in extenuating circumstances," says Tuttle. "I'm not going to use a taser on my mother. She was born in 1934." But when force is necessary, he says, the taser "is the safer" method, safer than guns and nightsticks.[60]

Electricity near the heart can be dangerous, explains John Webster, professor emeritus of biomedical engineering at the University of Wisconsin, "because it might cause ventricular fibrillation." Webster and a team of University of Wisconsin researchers investigated the taser's effects on the heart for the U.S. Department of Justice.[61]

Webster was using pigs for his study because their hearts were nearly identical to those of humans. In spring 2006, Webster reported that tasers could cause ventricular fibrillation in pigs; that is, the device can stop a pig heart.[62]

A scientist who tested some of the early tasers for the Canadian government recommended that the government ban the devices. Andrew Podgorski says his tests showed the devices could cause death. He says that children could be especially vulnerable.[63]

Rudolph Crew, superintendent of Miami-Dade schools, disturbed by the use of a taser on a six-year-old, put his concerns in writing. In a November 16, 2004, letter to the police department, he wrote, "While I acknowledge the need of law enforcement officers on occasion to subdue and to restrain members of the public, I believe that certain tactics should never be used in dealing with young children—particularly within a school."[64] In early January 2005, the Miami-Dade police revised their guidelines. The new policy "requires officers to consider factors such as age, size, and weight," in addition to other considerations, reported the Associated Press.[65]

Tony Hill, the Democratic whip in the Florida State Senate, was so concerned that he sponsored a bill to prohibit schools from using tasers on schoolchildren. "Every day here in Florida," says Hill, there are reports of "use of a taser on someone." But it was a group of tasings at schools near Palatka, Florida, that first made him wonder about the appropriateness of the weapon. "They all were African American kids. That raised a red flag."[66] Crew and Hill are bucking a trend: the increasingly common use of tasers against students. According to Taser International, 32 percent of the police departments it interviewed include tasers in local school systems.[67]

Perhaps because stun devices, despite causing pain, usually leave no visible marks, those who carry them sometimes use them in situations that in previous years might have been solved with words. "A police officer has been charged with using a Taser on his partner during an argument over whether they should stop for a soft drink," reported the Associated Press on December 8, 2005. The officer was fired.[68]

Taser International, which features the slogan "Saving Lives Every Day" on its Web site, is also hawking tasers directly to consumers.[69] "Choose your citizen taser device," exhorts the company. There are three consumer models to choose from, including one with a fifteen-foot range. The police version, the M-26, has a range of up to twenty-one feet. Presumably, in a taser duel between a police officer and a consumer, the officer would win.[70]

The standard consumer models sell for $399.95, $599.95, or $999.00. In 2007, Taser introduced the C-2, a cheaper consumer model. The new taser, which remains locked until buyers go through a background check, sells for $299.99. It is "available in four designer colors: Black Pearl, Titanium Silver, Electric Blue, and Metallic Pink," according to the press release.[71]

The man on the street could shoot to hurt. On January 26, 2005, Jim Weiers, house speaker in the Arizona legislature, announced that he would propose a bill that would allow the state's "police officers and ordinary citizens the use of lethal force in confronting people who threaten them with remote stun guns such as tasers," reported the Associated Press.[72]

On June 7, 2008, a federal jury decided that Taser International was responsible for the death of Robert Heston, Jr., who was shocked in 2005 by Salinas, California, police. The court awarded Heston's family $6 million. It was the first such decision against the company. "We've filed a motion to appeal for a new trial," says Tuttle of Taser International. "We are disappointed in the decision. We don't think it's supported by the facts."[73]

ELECTROSHOCK CREEP

Consumer, crowd-control, and school use of a high-powered police weapon like the Taser illustrates that punishment creep is anything but nineteenth century. But pain in contemporary corrections and policing is almost never called "corporal" and almost never called "punishment."

Guards don't claim to beat the Devil out of recalcitrant inmates. The linguistic choices of the moment, instead, are "humane," "restraint," "control," and "nonlethal."

In its return to corporal punishment under the guise of restraint and control, the American prison system resembles American popular culture. Corrections cannot acknowledge the religious meanings that underscore current punishment practices. It is a secular institution. Yet, influenced by a culture that, in the 1970s began to posit evilness as inhabiting children and criminals, our prison system has adopted discipline methods that can cause pain and that echo the old religious punishments.

CHAPTER 11

The Return to Restraint

THE DEVIL'S CHAIR

IN THE EARLY 1990S, Benjamin Rush's tranquilizing chair returned to American prisons and jails. The late twentieth-century version was built of plastic and metal, instead of wood, and it lacked the box that had once encased people's heads. It had a new name: the restraint chair. But like its predecessor, the chair immobilized prisoners and mental patients.[1] Belts and cuffs of this "chair" prevent the prisoner's legs, arms, and torso from moving. To jail and prison employees it is known as the "strap-o-lounger," the "barcalounger," the "we care chair," and the "be sweet chair." Inmates and their lawyers have other names for the device: "torture chair," "slave chair," and "Devil's chair."[2] This restraining device has led to many serious abuses, including torture and death.

The restraint chair was designed for violent prisoners who pose an immediate threat to themselves or others. But according to interviews with prisoners, lawyers, and restraint chair manufacturers, as well as a review of court cases, jail videotapes, coroners' reports, and scattered news stories, it is clear that as the millennium drew to a close, the restraint chair was being used in an improper—and sometimes sadistic—manner:

- Restraint chairs have been used for punishment of nonthreatening behavior.

- Children have been strapped into the chairs for nonviolent behaviors.
- Inmates and detainees have been strapped nude into restraint chairs.
- Prisoners have been left in restraint chairs for as long as eight days. In some cases, the jail staff failed to manipulate the prisoners' limbs to protect against blood clots.
- Prisoners have been required to testify while in restraint chairs.
- Prisoners have been interrogated while in restraint chairs.
- Prisoners have been injured while in restraint chairs.
- Prisoners have been tortured by being hooded, pepper-gassed, beaten, or threatened with electrocution while in the chairs.
- At least fifteen people have died under questionable circumstances after being strapped into a restraint chair.

Use of the restraint chair is widespread: jails, state and federal prisons, the Immigration and Naturalization Service, the U.S. Marshals Service, state mental hospitals, juvenile detention centers, and foreign governments are all equipped with the chair.[3] In 2000, Amnesty International called for a federal investigation into the use of the restraint chair. The device "is an issue of great concern to us," said Angela Wright, a researcher at Amnesty's headquarters in London. "It appears to be used in some jurisdictions as a front-line or even routine form of control, including as a punishment for disruptive or annoying behavior."[4]

On December 20, 1994, Shedrick Brown struggled with guards while being forced into a restraint chair in the Hillsborough County Jail in Tampa, Florida. After more than four hours in the chair, he was found unresponsive, having suffered a stroke. He died an hour later. In March 1995, the Hillsborough County Medical Examiner's Office ruled his death a homicide.[5]

In another incident, on April 17, 1995, Carmelo Marrero died in the Sacramento County Jail while strapped in a restraint chair. The county coroner's office ruled his death an accident. Officially, it resulted from "probable acute cardiac arrhythmia, due to probable hypoxemia, due to combined restraint asphyxia, and severe physical exertion, due to apparent manic psychotic episode." As Supervising Deputy Coroner Phil Ehlert explained to the *Sacramento Bee,* restraint asphyxia is "a lack of oxygen caused by a highly agitated state exacerbated by the imposed restraint." A class-action lawsuit against the jail, which was collectively settled for

$755,000, claimed that the device had repeatedly been used for torture at the jail and that Marrero's death was a direct result of his time in the restraint chair.[6]

Scott Norberg died in June 1996 in Arizona of what the Maricopa County medical examiner labeled accidental "positional asphyxia" after he was pushed into a restraint chair with his head forced to his chest, gagged, and shocked with a stun gun. Maricopa County and its insurance carrier settled a wrongful death lawsuit with Norberg's family for $8.25 million in 1998.[7] The Sheriff's Department has a policy of not commenting on any litigation, but says its jail is "humane" and "constitutionally run."

On December 3, 1996, twenty-two-year-old Anderson Tate was arrested after a routine traffic stop and taken to the St. Lucie County Jail in Florida. He swallowed cocaine. "I don't want to die. I'm burning up," he said, according to jail footage. "I'm 300 degrees. I have too much cocaine in my system." As Tate was dying, "he was in the chair for three hours, moaning and chanting prayers, while jailers taunted him and ignored his pleas for help. Two deputies were dismissed after an administrative investigation by the Sheriff's Department, but no criminal charges were filed."[8]

Michael Valent, a mentally ill prisoner, died after spending sixteen hours nude in a restraint chair in a Utah prison in March 1997. The deputy chief medical examiner, Edward Leis, confirmed that Valent's prolonged restraint "is the main precipitating factor leading to blood clots and his death." A lawsuit brought by Valent's mother ended in a $200,000 settlement with the state of Utah. The state stopped using the restraint chair.[9]

Also in March 1997, Daniel Sagers died in an Osceola County, Florida, jail after guards placed him in a restraint chair and beat him, using a towel to force his head back so violently that they damaged his brain stem. Sagers, who was mentally ill, was being held at the jail for firing a shotgun on a golf range. His family eventually won a $2.2 million civil lawsuit. In December 1998, a former corrections officer was convicted of manslaughter in Sagers's death. Two other guards pleaded no contest to charges of battery and were placed on probation.[10]

Demetrius Brown, a twenty-year-old mentally ill man, died in Jacksonville, Florida, on October 31, 1999, after a guard used a choke hold while others attempted to strap him into a restraining chair. "The manner of death," concluded the medical examiner's report, "is homicidal."[11]

On February 23, 2000, Hazel Virginia Beyer, who had been brought to the Johnson City Jail in Tennessee on charges of public drunkenness, was placed in the chair because jail staff considered her a suicide risk. About an hour and a half later, a crisis response worker found Beyer unconscious; she had slipped down in the chair so that the straps were choking her. Beyer remained in a coma until her death, which an autopsy attributed to a lack of oxygen supply to the brain. The autopsy determined that her placement in the restraint chair was a proximate cause of death. Judge Dennis Inman dismissed a $5 million wrongful death suit against the jail, ruling that the death was accidental and that staff had used the chair "solely for Beyer's protection."[12]

On June 26, 2001, at Florida's Columbia County Detention Center, Albert Lee Cothran, a homeless man arrested for loitering and suspicious behavior, was placed in the restraint chair for the second time in twenty-four hours due to combativeness. He died of a heart attack while in the chair. He had been left unsupervised for nearly an hour. Amnesty International termed the lapse in supervision, "a clear breach of national and international standards on the use of restraints."[13]

On July 6, 2001, Kevin Coleman, a prisoner at the David Wade Correctional Center in Louisiana, died after being held in a restraint chair for three days with periodic breaks to eat, use the toilet, and take showers. Coleman, who earned his stay in the chair by resisting attempts to get him to leave his cell for a court appearance, was doused with pepper spray and shocked with a stun shield before being restrained in the chair.[14]

Charles Agster was placed in the chair on August 6, 2001, while in the Madison Street Jail in Phoenix, Arizona. Agster was thirty-three years old but had a mental age of about twelve years. Police arrested him following complaints about his "disturbed" behavior while in a store. At the jail and hog-tied, Agster started to crawl under a bench. Guards punched and kicked him, then put him into a restraint chair with a spit mask hooding his face. A few minutes later, a staff member noticed that Agster was not breathing. An autopsy said cause of death was "positional asphyxia due to restraint."[15]

This list is but a sampling of people who died while in custody. If you happen to live near where one of these deaths occurred, you might have read about the restraint chair, but it is unlikely that you would have a full picture of the varieties of death and mistreatment that have happened in connection with the device.

On the night of July 6, 1999, James Livingston was having a psychotic episode. He believed his brother-in-law was trying to kill him. Livingston, a thirty-year-old man with schizophrenia from Tarrant County, Texas, ran to the police for protection. Eight hours later, Livingston was dead. He had spent much of that time in and out of a restraint chair.[16]

The Tarrant County Medical Examiner's Office determined that Livingston's death was caused by bronchial pneumonia. But that's not the whole truth, says Richard Haskell, a lawyer who represented Livingston's mother, Maxine Jackson, in a suit against the Tarrant County Sheriff's Department, which the department settled for $100,000. According to Haskell, Livingston's last stint in the chair killed him. "So far as we know, he was pepper-sprayed in the face and then placed in a restraint chair." Pepper spray "inflames the mucous membranes, causing closing of the eyes, coughing, gagging, shortness of breath," notes a 1998 Amnesty International report on human rights abuses in the United States. "There is considerable concern about its health risks." Livingston was not allowed to wash the pepper spray from his eyes and face in apparent violation of Tarrant County Sheriff's Department procedures, says Haskell. "He was not decontaminated, and he was left alone in a room. Within twenty minutes he was dead."[17]

The Tarrant County Sheriff's Department declined to comment, both in 2000 because of pending litigation, and in 2008 because the current administration was not involved in Livingston's death.

Deputy Mark Lane Smith was the first person to perform artificial respiration on Livingston in an unsuccessful attempt to revive him. When another deputy took over, wrote Smith in a Detention Bureau Report, "I then removed myself from the area and walked into the sally port, where I threw up from inhaling pepper gas residue from inmate Livingston." It's hard to imagine the terror felt by someone who is buckled into a restraint chair after being pepper-sprayed, says Haskell. "You wouldn't do that to a dog."[18]

The chair that held James Arthur Livingston for more than four hours on that night was manufactured by KLK, Inc., of Phoenix, Arizona. The KLK chair sells for $2,290, plus a $190 crating charge. This "Violent Person Restraint Chair" (the company's name for the device) "has been in use by the sixth largest sheriff's office jail system in the nation for four (4) years, with a ninety (90 *percent*) percent reduction in injuries compared to the previous four (4) years," brags the company advertising. "Special sizes or colors upon request."[19]

I telephone KLK and reach Teresa Dominguez, a production coordinator with the company. She tells me the chair is sold mainly to prisons and mental hospitals but says she can give me no other information. On her advice, I fax a list of questions for the company's officers. After more than a week without a response, I call back. "They basically said they can't answer the questions," says Dominguez. "The owner . . . saw the fax and said, 'No, we won't answer these.'" The company also declined to answer questions about the death of James Arthur Livingston. But Dominguez says the chair isn't to blame. "How they use the chair, I imagine, would be the question."[20]

Another manufacturer is more forthcoming. Dan Corcoran is president of AEDEC International, Inc., of Beaverton, Oregon, which manufactures the popular Prostraint Violent Prisoner Chair. Corcoran says his chair is "humane" and was designed to be so. "You know, when you take a little bird and it's lost and confused, and at first its heart is beating?" he asks. But if you fully cup that bird in your hands and immobilize it, the bird, he says, "calms down." So, too, says Corcoran, with human beings. The chair "makes a real nice sit for them."

What about allegations that the restraint chair has been linked to several deaths and that it is easily misused? "The people who want to do good start gainsaying it, calling it a medieval instrument of torture," says Corcoran, who "has no patience" with this stance. "It's a way of getting attention."

When I ask Corcoran for a press packet, he tells me he doesn't have one "because every lawyer who doesn't have a job" will want to get hold of the press packet and take his words out of context. He will, however, tell me the chair's cost: "900 bucks. If you get the accessories, $1,300." He will also tell me who his customers are: "mostly county jails," but also state prison systems, the U.S. Bureau of Prisons, the U.S. Immigration and Naturalization Service, the U.S. Marshals Service, and the Forest Service. "Park Service, too," he says. "Every state, every province has it." Corcoran says he has sold "thousands" of the chairs. But as to the exact number, "We don't tell anybody that, in court or otherwise."

Corcoran also exports his restraint chairs, but "only [to] the countries that really believe in human rights," he says. "A lot of countries are looking into them right now. We're kind of ticklish about selling them to third world countries that don't have human rights because then there really is

a possibility that they might be abused." But, he adds, you can use anything for torture.[21]

One country that has gotten Corcoran's OK and now owns AEDEC
restraint chairs is the United Arab Emirates. According to Amnesty International's 2002 report on the United Arab Emirates, "flogging was imposed as a judicial punishment. . . . Reports of death in custody, forcible
return, torture and ill-treatment were received." "Cruel, inhuman, or degrading punishments, including flogging and amputation, were repeatedly imposed" in 1999.[22]

A flier for the chair recommends its use for "Interrogating Prisoners"
and for detaining people in "Holding Tanks in Mass Entertainment Facilities (Concert Halls, Collisiems [sic], etc.)."[23] It appears to be used primarily in the intake and booking sections of local jails. Many of those who
end up in the chair have not been convicted of a crime and have landed in
jail for minor offenses, such as public drunkenness.

SACRAMENTO'S LACK OF RESTRAINT

In February 1999, the Sacramento Sheriff's Department settled a class-
action lawsuit alleging that deputies were torturing people, many of them
women and minorities, with a restraint chair. The settlement, $755,000,
was the largest ever for alleged officer misconduct in the department's
history. The Sacramento case alleged numerous and repeated forms of
torture, including mock executions, where guards strapped inmates into a
Prostraint chair and told them they were about to be electrocuted.[24]

Katherine Martin, a 106-pound woman with a heart condition, claimed
she spent eight-and-a-half hours in the chair after she was wrongly accused
of touching a guard. She alleged that the straps had been pulled so tight that
they had sliced skin from her back and shoulders and cut off circulation to
her extremities and that she suffered permanent nerve damage. She also
claimed that she was given no liquids, that she was taunted and mocked, that
her requests to use the bathroom were denied, and that she ended up
urinating on herself. Martin was originally brought into the jail on suspicion
of public drunkenness. This charge was later dismissed.[25]

Videotapes from the Sacramento jail played an important role in the
case. In one tape, Ronald Motz calls through the window of his cell, asking
for his lawyer. "Motz, this is the last time we're going to tell you, sit down,"
says a police officer. "Your attorney's not here, and the phone doesn't work."

Motz continues to call out. After a break in the tape, guards wrap a spit mask around his face and restrain him in a chair. "I just want to call my attorney," says Motz. "You don't get to call an attorney," says the officer. "Why?" asks Motz. The officer tells him that he can't make the call because he was "drunk in public."

A few seconds later, the guard says, "You were going to be released in about five hours. Now you're not."

"What did I do wrong—ask for my attorney?" asks Motz.

"You weren't following directions," says the guard.

The videotapes also show a woman named Gena Domogio being put into the chair naked. She yells at the guards who are kneeling on her back and spits blood on the floor, apparently because her mouth has been injured. The guards respond by wrapping her face in a towel. They keep the towel on her face and at one point appear to hold it against her mouth as they force her into the chair, although she repeatedly says that she has a thyroid problem and that she can't breathe.

Kimberly Byrd was reportedly taken to the hospital after she passed out in the chair where she had been hooded and tightly bound, according to a letter Amnesty International wrote to the Sacramento County Sheriff's Department in March 1999. In the videotape of her restraint, she is obviously terrified. "I'm going to die. Please don't let me die," she says over and over again.

The Sacramento case, *Geovanny D. Lobdell vs. County of Sacramento et al.*, listed AEDEC International, Inc., as a defendant. Dan Corcoran of AEDEC gave a deposition on June 8, 1998, to attorney Stewart Katz. Many of Katz's questions referred to a "manufacturer's warning" sheet Corcoran distributes to his clients: "The purpose of the Prostraint Violent Prisoner Chair is to provide law enforcement and correctional officers with the safest, most humane, and least psychologically traumatizing system for restraining violent, out-of-control prisoners," reads the statement of purpose included on the warning. "The chair is not meant to be an instrument of punishment and should not be used as such."

Here are selections from Corcoran's deposition:

Q. What testing did you do?

A. I put various friends in there. I yanked on [the straps] as hard as I could, and I'm physically apt. I could cause no pain to them whatsoever. . . .

Q. Are there any physical conditions that you believe should lead to a person not being restrained in the chair?

A. No arms, no legs.

Q. All right. So you don't believe the chair should properly be used on amputees or people born without fully developed limbs.

A. The chair wouldn't be functional unless they had appendages. . . .

Q. Is it a fair statement that it's your opinion that the chair is less psychologically traumatizing than the alternatives you mentioned [these included, in Corcoran's words, "four-pointing, chained to a bench, strapped to a bed"]?

A. Yes.

Q. Is that opinion based upon any medical or psychological expert work in the field?

A. No. . . .

Q. Now [your statement of purpose says]: "It is an especially useful tool for restraining drug- or alcohol-affected prisoners," period.

   My question, sir, what is your evidence for believing that it is especially useful for people who are on drugs?

A. Because medical restraints at that time are very dangerous.

Q. And what is the basis for saying the medical restraint at that point is dangerous?

A. Because they have not diagnosed what is in their bloodstream already, and whatever is put in there is compounded.

Q. Was there any scientific literature you relied on to come to this conclusion?

A. That's common sense. . . .

Q. Did you do any testing on people who were under the influence of drugs or narcotics?

A. No.

Q. Did you do any testing for people who are under the influence or feeling the effects of alcohol?

A. No. . . .

Q. All right. Now, the last sentence under your "statement of purpose": "The chair is not meant to be an instrument of punishment and should not be used as such." Why did you include that sentence?

A. Because Mexico asked to purchase 200 of them, and I wouldn't sell them to Mexico.

Q. And why wouldn't you sell them to Mexico?

A. As any instrument, car, toilet plunger, they can all be abused. There was too high a potential without—we have a high, much higher standard in this country than other countries do. That's why the chair does work here and people will buy it. . . .

Q. People go to the bathroom while they are seated in the chair. Are there provisions in the design of the chair to evacuate those excretions?

A. Yes.

Q. What are those?

A. Not to evacuate but contain.

Q. What are those?

A. The thing is cupped. Blood-borne pathogens and bodily fluids are contained in the person's clothes. I felt that was a better choice than let the pathogens go into the cell and infect other people. . . .

Q. . . . Have you looked at any of the literature regarding how long a person can safely be restrained in a Prostraint Chair?

A. There is no literature that I know of. . . .

Q. . . . Have you done any studies, research, as to the maximum amount of time an individual can be restrained in your restraining chair without causing a physical injury?

A. No. . . .

Q. Now, if you thought the chair wasn't punishing, why wouldn't you sell those chairs to Mexico?

A. Because I have seen enough movies, and I may be stereotyping, but there could be interrogations. I didn't want that to happen. . . .

Q. Is it a correct statement that you marketed the Prostraint restraining chair for use which includes interrogating prisoners?

A. Yes. . . .

Q. Do you know if any customers purchased ten restraint Prostraint chairs?

A. Yes.

Q. And has anyone purchased ten?

A. Yes, or more than ten.

Q. What entity would that have been?

A. I think both the states of Florida and the state of Georgia for the juvenile division. They require it.

RESTRAINT ACROSS THE NATION

The use of the restraining chair in jails and prisons across the country has provoked some lawsuits. In August 1999, a Knox County, Tennessee, judge ruled that the confession of robbery suspect E. B. "Boyd" Collier was involuntary and illegal because it came while he was confined in a restraint chair during his five-hour interrogation. "While such a chair may be useful, it can easily cross the line as a coercive force," wrote Criminal Court Judge Mary Beth Leibowitz.[26]

A March 1996 Department of Justice investigation of the Maricopa County jails in Arizona found that the Sheriff's Office used stun guns on prisoners while they were confined in restraint chairs, including one case where jail staff used a stun gun against a prisoner's testicles. According to Amnesty International, one inmate, Richard Post, was forced into a restraint chair in a manner that "reportedly damaged his spinal cord, resulting in significant loss of upper body mobility." In August 1999, Maricopa County agreed to pay Post $800,000 to settle his claims that jail guards had used excessive force against him.[27]

In 1997, jail officials in Maricopa County told Amnesty International that the jail system owned sixteen chairs and had used them about six hundred times in the previous six months. Because of a settlement agreement responding to a Department of Justice lawsuit, the Maricopa County Jails restricted use of restraint chairs and stun guns, beginning in 1998.[28]

In August 2006, the Maricopa County Jails, in a further step, announced that it would stop using the thirty-five restraint chairs it then had and would replace them with four-point restraints.[29]

Alleged misuse of the restraint chair led the U.S. Department of Justice to file a 1996 lawsuit against Iberia Parish Jail in Louisiana, claiming that the jail deputies, as a matter of course, subjected inmates to "cruel and unusual punishment and physical and mental torture" by confining them to restraint chairs for hours and forcing them to sit in their own excrement. One inmate was allegedly held in the chair for eight days, another for forty-three hours. In a pretrial settlement, the jail authorities agreed to stop using the restraint chair.[30]

In Ventura County, California, a class-action lawsuit led a federal judge to issue a preliminary injunction banning the chair on November 15, 1999. The county no longer uses restraint chairs.[31]

The lawsuit alleged that during one eighteen-month period, 377 people had been strapped into the chair at the Ventura County Jail and that one inmate had been left in the chair for thirty-two hours. "Data . . . show that the Sheriff Department's misuse of that chair flows from a practice of restraining nonviolent arrestees for extended periods of time in violation of the arrestees' Fourteenth Amendment rights," wrote U.S. District Judge Lourdes Baird in her fifty-page decision. "The policy allows deputies to require restrained arrestees to either urinate or defecate on themselves and be forced to sit in their own feces or 'hold it.' "[32]

A BIG HOUSE IN THE COUNTRY

In the same years that saw the return of the tranquilizing chair, U.S. prisons also revisited isolation. Although most prisons have isolation cells, long-term solitary confinement of the kind practiced at the Eastern State Penitentiary was by the twentieth century generally thought cruel and outmoded.

But in the early 1990s solitary again seemed like a solution. Inmates at supermaximum security prisons live in isolation cells for about twenty-three hours a day. Unlike the penitentiary, the supermax has nothing to do with religious conversion. The difference between isolation in the penitentiary and in the supermax lies in purpose, argues law and social policy expert Jonathan Simon. "The supermax prison uses its architectural and technological capacities not to transform the individual but to contain his toxic behavioral properties at reasonable fiscal, political, and legal costs."[33]

A lingo of containment accompanies the supermaxes, sometimes called "secure housing units," or "management control" facilities. "Pelican Bay State Prison is designed to house the state's most serious criminal offenders in a secure, safe and disciplined institutional setting," notes the Web site of the California supermax.

As for those restrained, secured, managed, and controlled, the adjectives applied to them emphasize the thing being contained. "This is for the toughest of the tough, the real bad actors," said Governor Tommy Thompson of Wisconsin when he signed a bill into law to create the state's supermax.[34]

Accusations that extensive solitary confinement leads to mental illness have returned. The rumors have medical studies to back them.

"There are few if any forms of imprisonment that appear to produce so much psychological trauma and in which so many symptoms of psychopathology are manifested," wrote Craig Haney, a professor of psychology at the University of California–Santa Cruz, in 2003. "The findings are robust."[35]

The "Level One Handbook" is the rule guide for the most punitive sector of the Supermax Correctional Institution (SMCI) in Boscobel, Wisconsin. "All visits at SMCI will take place via video visitation," it stipulates. "There will be no face-to-face visits."

"Because of the sensory deprivation, things take on a new meaning. Just to see people was a big bonus even if they were just guards," wrote one inmate of the supermax in Boscobel. "To hear people talk about real events, since there were no newspapers, TV news or radio to keep you informed, I know why so many guys go completely insane within this kind of environment. It's because that's what it's designed to do—drive you crazy."[36]

In 2001, a group of inmates sued the Boscobel supermax, claiming the facility was an "incubator of psychosis." "Prisoners at SMCI are locked alone in their windowless cells all but four hours per week," wrote Terry Kupers, a psychiatrist and professor at University of California–Berkeley. "Under these extreme conditions, symptoms begin to emerge."[37]

Kupers documented the decline:

Prisoner 8, who has not been diagnosed with a mental illness, reports "I walk around for hours in my cell talking to myself. . . . I wake up crying and afraid. . . . I see someone standing in the corner of my cell, I saw the Devil come up out of the toilet, I couldn't sleep all night." . . .

Prisoner 18, a thirty-five-year-old African American man who seems very paranoid to me on mental status examination, shows me a copy of a letter he wrote to the Bureau of Health Services about the way the officers poison his food, poison the water, poison the air, and poison his clothing. He tells me "the poison attacks your brain like tiny bombs."

Prisoner 19, a seventeen-year-old African American youth who has been at SMCI since July, 2000, tells me he smells strong scents (olfactory hallucinations), he hears cars all the time, he hears voices of people talking about him, he is always anxious, he has a strong startle reaction especially when he hears a door open, he feels like he is in a daydream most of the time, and he believes the officers are not real—they are corpses that are already dead.[38]

In 2001, the class-action lawsuit filed by inmates of the supermax prison at Boscobel alleged that mental illness was "endemic" at the prison. A judge ordered the removal of all mentally ill inmates, which Ed Garvey, a court-appointed attorney in the case, says amounted to "about one-third of the prisoners." Some of the inmates at the Boscobel prison, including those who had the most severe reactions to their isolation, were juveniles.[39]

Supermaxes do not necessarily house the worst of the worst. Some of the prisoners are dangerous and unrepentant, but many others are simply difficult inmates—not necessarily violent ones. Around 21 percent of the inmates at the Boscobel prison were "transferred to Supermax [in order] to free space in segregation units at other prisons," reported the *Milwaukee Journal Sentinel* in 2001.[40]

In none of these cases of excessive restraint involving either the restraint chair or long-term isolation did a guard literally bring the wrath of God down on an inmate. But our culture associates criminals with evil. We prefer our evils securely restrained.

CHAPTER 12

Abu Ghraib, USA

TOLERATING TORTURE

ON SEPTEMBER 11, 2001, a horrific murder of thousands took place. The atrocity quickly became a cultural touchstone; a hideous, galvanizing event that many citizens witnessed in televised real time; a moment when it became apparent that a determined "they" wanted to hurt "us"; a nightmare that played again and again on televisions and in people's minds. The allegations of torture that would follow a few years later are almost as famous. The names "Abu Ghraib" and "Guantánamo Bay" seem to contain the misdirection of American revenge.

The tortures had linguistic precursors. For many pundits and writers, after September 11 torture seemed useful. One of the first to speak the formerly forbidden word was Jonathan Alter of *Newsweek*. Less than two months after the attack, Alter wrote, "In this autumn of anger, even a liberal can find his thoughts turning to . . . torture." Although Alter explained that he was not talking about "cattle prods or rubber hoses," he expressed frustration with the slow pace of the investigation into the attacks. "Couldn't we at least subject them to psychological torture?" he wrote. "Or deportation to Saudi Arabia, land of beheadings?"[1]

Alter walks a line—he considers torture but declines to advocate it overtly. Some of his fans were less persnickety. In a *New York Times* interview with reporter Jim Rutenberg that appeared a week later, Alter said that he had met left-leaning people who confided that they agreed with him. Those readers understood his column as favoring physical torture.[2]

The same New York Times article found serious discussions of torture in other media, including the Wall Street Journal and the online magazine Slate. The article also cited the Fox News channel, where an anchor asked, "Should law enforcement be allowed to do anything, even terrible things, to make suspects spill the beans?" On the CNN program Crossfire, Tucker Carlson observed that torture was a "bad" thing, but "some things are worse. And under certain circumstances, it may be the lesser of two evils. Because some evils are pretty evil."[3]

The journalists interviewed by Rutenberg said they felt obligated to raise the subject of torturing suspects given the possibility that some of those who were not talking during interrogations might know of an up-coming attack. They also observed that the American public was already conversing about torture as a real possibility "in bars, on commuter trains, and at dinner tables."[4]

The media-torture dalliance lasted months. In February 2002, on the MSNBC show Alan Keyes Is Making Sense, Keyes opened by acknowledg-ing the U.S. history of opposing torture and then announced, "We now face in the context of this terrible terrorist threat the possibility that we, ourselves, may be forced by circumstances to resort to the very abuse that we have opposed." Keyes entertained the Harvard criminologist Alan Dershowitz as his guest that day. Dershowitz made clear that he favored legalizing torture because "you'd better have accountability."[5]

ILL-TREATMENT ON OUR SHORES

There were signs that U.S. democracy was shaking. In the months after the terrorist attack, the Bush administration arrested many Arab and Muslim immigrants. These people became known as the "September 11 detainees."

Many of those rounded up on orders of Attorney General John Ash-croft claim they were beaten; locked in solitary confinement; injected with substances against their will; or denied blankets, food, and toilet paper. In November 2001, Amnesty International sent Ashcroft a memorandum in which it expressed concern "that many of those detained during the 11 September sweeps are held in harsh conditions, some of which may violate international standards for humane treatment." The memorandum cited "allegations of physical and verbal abuse of detainees by guards, and failure to protect detainees from abuses by other inmates."[6]

In a 2002 interview, Traci Billingsley, a spokesperson for the United States Bureau of Prisons, denied that any prisoner in a federal institution had been mistreated. "All inmates are treated in a fair, impartial manner and are treated in a humane way," she said.[7] County jails also disputed the complaints against them. For months, the Bush administration blocked the requests of Human Rights Watch and Amnesty International to visit and interview government detainees.

Most of the September 11 detainees were eventually deported for visa violations. Their claims of abuse lingered. In a June 2003 report, the Office of the Inspector General of the Department of Justice determined, "the evidence indicates a pattern of abuse by some correctional officers against some September 11 detainees, particularly during the first months after the attacks" at Brooklyn's Metropolitan Detention Center (MDC). "Most detainees we interviewed at the MDC alleged that MDC staff physically abused them."[8]

Michael J. Wildes was once a federal prosecutor. In autumn 2001, he came to represent five Israeli detainees who were stopped near the George Washington Bridge on September 11. According to Wildes, they were "caught horsing around with the backdrop of the World Trade Center behind them." Apparently, the Israelis, who had accents, were viewed as Arabs.[9]

One of the five, Oded Ellner, alleged that he was injected with "a series of shots" at the MDC in Brooklyn. "He thought it was under the guise of stopping sexually transmitted diseases," said Wildes. "He didn't know what substance was being injected into him."

Ellner now lives in Israel. When contacted, he declined to talk in detail about his allegations. "I can't do an interview on what happened to me in the jail because I don't want to remember what happened to me in the jail," he said by phone. "All I want now is a peaceful life."[10]

Steven Gordon, a New York–based attorney, also represented the five Israelis. Gordon said that the men "were in solitary for two months." Two of them suffered beatings at the hands of guards. One was Omer Marmari. "Guards took him out of the cell he was in and put him in one that didn't have the video camera," Gordon said. Then they "moved his body across the box springs, and his legs got all cut up." Another detainee, Sivan Kurzberg, was also beaten, according to Gordon. Guards hit Kurzberg "about the head and body and pushed his face up against the wall for no apparent reason." All five were deported and returned to Israel.[11]

There are plenty of other cases. Shakir Baloch, a medical doctor and a Canadian citizen originally from Pakistan, was held for two months in solitary confinement in a high security unit at the MDC, according to his lawyer, Joel Kupferman, of the National Lawyers Guild, and MacDonald Scott, the membership coordinator for the organization. For two weeks, both advocates claimed, he was denied toilet paper. Baloch also said that he was not served halal food. Scott, who is also an activist with the Coalition for the Human Rights of Immigrants, said that when Baloch first entered the center, guards pushed him, "were throwing him back and forth from wall to wall."[12]

Some of the detainees claimed that other inmates beat them up. They also raised questions about the complicity of the guards charged with their care.

Uzi Bohadana found trouble waiting for him at the Madison County Jail in Canton, Mississippi. Bohadana, a twenty-four-year-old Israeli citizen who before the attacks had lived in Hollywood, Florida, was arrested on September 14, said his attorney, L. Patricia Ice. "INS alleged he was working for wages without authorization."[13]

Bohadana said he was driving a truck at the time. The FBI picked him up at a Canton storage facility "on an allegation that I'm a suspect of the bombing." The bureau then transferred Bohadana to the Madison County Jail for the weekend.[14]

At the jail, Bohadana was put in a cell with inmates who were there on criminal charges. "After two days, [the other inmates] decide I'm a terrorist, for some reason," said Bohadana. He ended up with a broken jaw and seven stitches on the right eye. "I was hospitalized for two days to make the surgery." Ice said Bohadana had to have his jaw wired.

Bohadana believes he may have been set up for the beating. "I don't know who told them because no one knew that except the guards. Figure it out by yourself," he said. Before the attack, a guard had been constantly on duty outside the cell, said Ice. "The guard disappeared for an hour during the attack," she said. "It was one hour before [another] guard found him." The Madison County Jail referred my request for comment to a lawyer, who did not return repeated calls.

The mistreatment was not only on the domestic front. A little over a year after the attacks, the *Washington Post* revealed that U.S. government forces in Afghanistan were making use of techniques of torture. Then there is Guantánamo Bay and the disturbing revelations that some of the "enemy combatants" we were supposed to fear were children as young as thirteen. Finally, there is Abu Ghraib.[15]

ABU GHRAIB, USA

One of the most famous proper nouns to come to prominence in the last several years is in itself a container of pain: Abu Ghraib. In May 2004, Seymour M. Hersh published in the *New Yorker* an account of torture and severe ill treatment at Abu Ghraib prison, an American military jail in Iraq. A week earlier, *Sixty Minutes 2* had aired the same allegations, along with graphic photographs.[16]

When the Abu Ghraib story broke, I had been reporting on abuse and mistreatment in our nation's jails and prisons for eight years. My response was recognition. When I first saw the photo, taken at the Abu Ghraib prison, of a hooded and robed figure strung with electrical wiring, I thought of the Sacramento, California, city jail. When I heard that dogs had been used to intimidate and bite at least one detainee at Abu Ghraib, I thought of the training video shown at the Brazoria County Detention Center in Texas. When I learned that the male inmates at Abu Ghraib were forced to wear women's underwear, I thought of the Maricopa County jails in Phoenix, Arizona. And when I saw the photos of the naked bodies restrained in grotesque and uncomfortable positions, I thought of the Utah prison system.

When Donald Rumsfeld visited Abu Ghraib on May 13, 2004, he said of the abuse, "It doesn't represent American values."[17] But the images from Iraq looked all too American to me. In the weeks after the Abu Ghraib story broke, reporters and commentators kept asking, how could this happen? My question was, why were we surprised when many of these same practices were already occurring at home?

In February 1999, the Sacramento Sheriff's Department settled a class-action lawsuit alleging numerous acts of torture, including mock executions where guards strapped inmates into a restraint chair, covered their faces with masks, and told the inmates they were about to be electrocuted.[18] When I read a report in the *Guardian* of London of May 14 that it had "learned of ordinary soldiers who . . . were taught to perform mock executions," I couldn't help but remember the California jail.[19]

The jail system in Maricopa County is well known for its practice of requiring inmates to wear pink underwear, and it is notorious for using stun guns and restraint chairs.[20] Then there's the training video used at the Brazoria County Detention Center in Texas. In addition to footage of beatings and stun gun use, the videotape included scenes of guards encouraging dogs to bite inmates.[21]

According to the Red Cross, inmates at the Abu Ghraib jail suffered "prolonged exposure while hooded to the sun over several hours, including during the hottest time of the day when temperatures could reach 50 degrees Celsius (122 degrees Fahrenheit) or higher." Many of the Maricopa County Jail system inmates live outdoors in tent cities, even on days that reach 120 degrees in the shade. During the 2003 heat wave, the Associated Press reported that temperatures inside the jail tents reached 138 degrees.[22]

Two leaders of the guards at Abu Ghraib, Ivan L. (Chip) Frederick II and Charles Graner, had careers back home as corrections officers. Graner, whom the *New York Times* described as one of "the most feared and loathed of the American guards" at Abu Ghraib, worked at Greene County Prison in Pennsylvania. According to a 1998 article in the *Pittsburgh Post-Gazette*, guards at the Greene facility behaved in ways that eerily anticipate the allegations from Abu Ghraib.[23]

The *Post-Gazette* reported that guards at the Greene County prison beat inmates, sexually mistreated inmates with nightsticks, and conducted "nude searches in which every body orifice is examined in full view of other guards and prisoners." An inmate claimed that guards had used his blood to write "KKK" on the floor.[24] Although twelve guards eventually lost their jobs, Graner was, according to the *New York Times*, "not involved in that scandal." A lawsuit by another inmate held at Greene accused Graner of beatings and other mistreatment, though the lawsuit ended up being dismissed.[25]

According to the investigation carried out by Major General Antonio M. Taguba on behalf of the U.S. Army, there was "credible" evidence that one Abu Ghraib inmate suffered forced sodomy "with a chemical light and perhaps a broom handle." The Taguba report notes that U.S. soldiers were involved in "forcibly arranging detainees in various sexually explicit positions for photographing" and "forcing groups of male detainees to masturbate themselves while being photographed and videotaped." Guards beat inmates and wrote insulting epithets on their bodies.[26]

Guy Womack, attorney for Graner, says the treatment at Abu Ghraib "went against his training and experience as a corrections officer." Graner "protested" and "reported the matter to his superiors," but was told "he must follow" orders from Military Intelligence. As a result, says Womack, "Graner complied with all such orders."[27]

At the very least, Graner moved from one prison where abuse was commonplace to another. Abu Ghraib was a familiar environment.

In a Utah prison, Michael Valent, a mentally ill prisoner, died in March 1997 after spending fourteen of his last sixteen hours nude in a restraint chair. As it turns out, Valent's death has a connection to Abu Ghraib. Lane McCotter was serving as the director of the Utah State Department of Corrections on the day that Valent was put in the restraint chair. He was one of the officials in the Utah system who advocated frequent use of restraint chairs and restraint boards on inmates. After Valent died, McCotter resigned. Six years later, McCotter was in charge of reconstructing Abu Ghraib, though he has denied involvement in the abuses.[28]

My point is not whether McCotter or Graner are personally responsible for Abu Ghraib. Whatever their personal responsibility, they are part of a well-established system and an American culture.

In another incident that happened during McCotter's watch, an inmate at the Utah State Prison "was shackled to a steel board on a cell floor in four-point metal restraints for twelve weeks in 1995. He was removed from the board on average four times a week to shower. At other times he was left to defecate while on the board. He was released from the board only following a court order."[29]

The practice of forcing prisoners to soil themselves allegedly occurred in Iraq as well. On May 6, 2004, the *Washington Post* published a description of the abuses Hasham Mohsen Lazim said he had endured at Abu Ghraib. After guards beat, hooded, and stripped him, "Graner handcuffed him to the corner of his bed," where he remained for days. "We couldn't sleep or stand," Lazim told the paper. "Even to urinate, we had to do so where we sat."[30]

Although most of the allegations from Abu Ghraib describe the torture and mistreatment of men, Iraqi women have also been subjected to rape behind bars. "Several women held in Abu Ghraib jail were sexually abused, including one who was raped by an American military policeman and became pregnant," according to a source who had spoken with one of the female Abu Ghraib detainees, the *Guardian* reported in May 2004.[31]

Here, too, there is a resemblance between the reports from Iraq and incidents at prisons and jails in the United States. In 1999 Amnesty International reported, "Many women in prisons and jails in the USA are victims of sexual abuse by staff, including sexually offensive language; male staff touching inmates' breasts and genitals when conducting searches; male staff watching inmates while they are naked; and rape."[32] "That was not part of my sentence, to . . . perform oral sex with the officers," Tanya Ross, who was jailed in Florida, told *Dateline NBC* in 1998.[33]

Amnesty International has reports of "prolonged forced standing and kneeling" in Iraqi military prisons, as well as allegations of "the excessive and cruel use of shackles and handcuffs" at Guantánamo. Again, the Iraqi allegations seem almost to be extracted from earlier Amnesty International writings on human rights abuses in the United States.[34]

In a 1998 report on the treatment of women in U.S. prisons, Amnesty International noted, "International standards restrict the use of restraints to situations where they are necessary to prevent escape or to prevent prisoners from injuring themselves or others or from damaging property. In the USA, restraints are used as a matter of course. A woman who is in labor or seriously ill, even dying, may be taken to a hospital in handcuffs and chained by her leg to the bed."[35]

In an earlier report on the United States, Amnesty observed, "In Alabama, prisoners have sometimes been tied to a restraint pole (known as the 'hitching rail') as punishment, sometimes for hours in the sweltering heat or freezing conditions. At Julia Tutwiler Prison for Women in Alabama, inmates have been handcuffed to the rail for up to a day."[36] The state of Alabama says it stopped using the hitching post in the late 1990s. In a deposition from the case *Rivera vs. Sheahan, et al.*, Chicago's Cook County Jail acknowledged that it would shackle a hospitalized inmate in a coma.[37]

The Red Cross mentioned deaths in prison in Iraq. The U.S. government has also investigated some of the deaths. Out of the 65,000 prisoners held by the United States in the Iraq and Afghanistan wars, "At least 108 people have died in American custody in Iraq and Afghanistan, most of them violently, according to government data," reported the Associated Press on March 15, 2005. "Roughly a quarter of those deaths have been investigated as possible abuse by U.S. personnel."[38]

Inmates have died in U.S. prisons and jails under suspicious circumstances as well. The Bureau of Justice Statistics compiles information on the cause of death in custody in U.S. prisons and jails. Prisons and jails around the country self-report the data as part of the bureau's Death in Custody Data Collection Program. In U.S. prisons in 2001 through 2002, there were eight homicides against inmates in custody that were not committed by other inmates. In U.S. jails from 2000 through 2002, the number was thirty. The homicide numbers do not include deaths that result from such factors as poor medical treatment.[39]

How could such things happen in the United States?

Particularly in the last couple of decades, with the rise of ever-harsher criminal justice laws, Americans have become hardened to the people we put in detention or behind bars. We have acquired a set of unexamined beliefs: (1) people who land in jail deserve to be there; (2) criminals are bad people—almost subhuman—who can't be rehabilitated; (3) therefore, punishment can be as harsh as possible; and (4) we don't need or want to know the details. These beliefs are constantly reaffirmed—by pundits in our news media, in our television shows and movies, even in video games. They may help to explain why revelations of prison and jail abuse in the United States, which have been numerous in the past two decades, can fall on deaf ears in this country even as they prompt protest from other countries. The revelations at Abu Ghraib shock us because our soldiers abroad seem to have acted out behaviors that we condone, yet don't face up to, at home.

When we tolerate abuse in U.S. prisons and jails, it should not surprise us to find U.S. soldiers using similar methods in Iraq. George Bush said he was exporting democracy to Iraq, but he seems to have exported a much uglier aspect of American public policy—some of the most sadistic practices employed in the U.S. prison system.

Epilogue

A LITTLE GOOD NEWS

IN HIS 1787 ESSAY "An Enquiry into the Effects of Public Punishments upon Criminals, and upon Society," Benjamin Rush worried that punishments in the town square would cause "the principle of sympathy" to "cease to act altogether."[1] Rush warned that public punishments harm other forms of social cohesion, including familial love. Once "the principle of sympathy" ends, he wrote, "misery of every kind will then be contemplated without emotion or sympathy—the widow and the orphan —the naked—the sick, and the prisoner, will have no avenue to our services or our charity."[2] His is a warning suitable for his contemporaries, who listened to him, and for our own age, which has not.

Beliefs about community purification through pain and retribution did not disappear—even when most of the country thought them outmoded, archaic, extinct. However embarrassing or cruel those ideas came to seem, they lingered in a kind of cultural underlayer. And when they returned to dominate our culture, they did so energetically. David Garland's description of the new retribution suggests Freud's "return of the repressed." In his attempt to understand our jagged break with the past, Garland suggests that pervasive American thinking about social order may have changed profoundly.[3]

The new punishment may even be undoing the nation's ability to hold a democratic vote. Some critics argue that the numbers of disenfranchised voters with criminal records are now so vast that they could tip national elections, including (because of Florida's tough felon disenfranchisement law) possibly the presidential election of 2000.[4]

In 1974 Robert Martinson asked "what works?" in prison rehabilitation. His devastating conclusion was that little could help offenders reintegrate into society without reoffending.[5] In short, he was wrong. Researchers continue to undo Martinson's overbroad claims. They find that certain carefully administered styles of rehabilitation do work.

It is important to note here that many studies of rehabilitative programs are suspect. David Farabee, a University of California–Los Angeles psychologist who wrote *Rethinking Rehabilitation: Why Can't We Reform Our Criminals?* criticized such research to the *Chicago Tribune* in 2005. "The majority [of programs] are never evaluated. . . . Of those that are evaluated, the strongest support for those programs comes from the lowest quality studies."[6]

Given the flawed research on both sides of the rehabilitation question, I will mention just one study by Joan Petersilia, a respected criminology professor at the University of California–Irvine. I chose it both because of Petersilia's reputation and because the study, which looked at programs touted as alternatives to prison, was highly critical of them. It found that offenders in alternative intensive supervision programs "by and large were not prison-bound but rather were high-risk probationers."[7] Nor did intensive supervision programs shrink overall costs. People in boot camps, under electronic monitoring, and in drug testing had close supervision that probably uncovered more violations that got them sent to prison. In such cases, governments ended up paying for both the prison sentence and the alternative program.

Nonetheless, Petersilia's study included "an important and tantalizing finding." Among participants in alternatives that combined surveillance with drug treatment, employment, and community service, recidivism dropped by as much as 10 to 20 percent below programs that did not have such components. This is to say that programs that attempted to address the needs of convicts in numerous ways managed to change people.[8]

People make the cultures they inhabit. In that hope there is bad news and also a bit of good. The United States will eventually learn whether its Enlightenment heritage has in it the cultural persistence retribution has shown. Much more than individual pain is at stake. Humaneness, empathetic comprehension of an individual's suffering, belief in a person's ability to change (a belief system that includes the American tradition of class mobility), elections where racial minorities have a voice equivalent to their numbers, communal generosity to the vulnerable, and, finally, democracy—an Enlightenment creation if there ever was one—are all at risk.

Part of the trouble is that revenge can be a vote-getter. Some campaigning politicians suggest new uses for execution. Tom Coburn, a medical doctor, former state representative, and current U.S. senator, told an Associated Press reporter during his 2004 campaign, "I favor the death penalty for abortionists and other people who take life." Coburn won 53 percent of the vote, handily defeating his Democratic opponent, who garnered only 41 percent.[9]

Other politicians advocate that punitive physical disfigurements be broadcast on television. In late 2005, on a television show called *Nevada Newsmakers,* Las Vegas mayor Oscar Goodman waxed creative. "In the old days in France, they had beheadings of people who committed heinous crimes," he said, and then explained that although Las Vegas had a lovely highway system, "these punks come along and deface it. I'm saying maybe you put them on TV and cut off a thumb. That may be the right thing to do."[10] A year later, Goodman took back his thumb-severing comment, saying he had simply wanted to start discussion. He suggested, instead, that the city lock graffiti artists into stocks and let passersby paint their faces.[11]

Even if such statements are jokes, the country maintains real laws and practices that verge on promoting vigilantism. Florida's 2005 gun law, in popular parlance called "stand your ground" and also "shoot first," is one example. The law, a legislative echo of *Death Wish,* had ninety sponsors and enormous support in the state legislature as well as the backing of the National Rifle Association. It enlarged the legal meaning of shooting in self-defense. Killing in response to fear no longer has to come as a last resort in Florida. Instead, a person who meets up with someone she or he believes to be threatening "has no duty to retreat and has the right to stand his or her ground and meet force with force, including deadly force."[12]

In June 2006, the *Orlando Sentinel* looked at thirteen cases in which people felt threatened and, protected by the "stand your ground law," chose force. "They killed six men and wounded four more," reported the paper. "All but one of the people shot were unarmed."[13] Within a year, the law inspired similar legislative measures in fourteen states.[14]

A threat of extreme physical hurt to criminals is the bright voice of the moment. It echoes in the cells and booking rooms where some of our inmates suffer, and even in Abu Ghraib. But it coexists with a language of humaneness that is our Enlightenment inheritance.

Many Christians still care about prisons and inmate physical treatment. Sister Helen Prejean stirred debate with her 1993 book *Dead Man Walking* and counseled Pope John Paul II on American capital punishment. Prejean has also spoken against torture, while at the same time acknowledging the agony that victims of crime can feel.[15]

In 1999, Pope John Paul II visited St. Louis, Missouri, and before an audience of 20,000 denounced the death penalty as "cruel and unnecessary."[16] The Catholic Church's official stance against capital punishment is a significant countertrend to those described in this book.

And there are others. Today, some of the most outspoken defenders of inmate physical safety are members of the Christian Right. When I began writing this book, I called numerous Christian Right groups, including Dobson's Focus on the Family, Jerry Falwell Ministries, the Family Research Counsel, Don Wildmon's American Family Association, and the Christian Coalition to ask if these groups published materials on criminals and punishment and whether their organizations took a stance on the issue. The groups were disinclined to speak about the subject, which intrigued me as I had already looked at some of the punitive statements Christian Right leaders had made about crime and criminals in the 1980s. But in 2004, almost to an organization, they referred me to a group called Prison Fellowship.

Former Nixon special counsel Chuck Colson, the founder of Prison Fellowship, was once a prisoner. His group holds that inmates can change their lives. The metamorphoses Prison Fellowship seeks is primarily spiritual. "The best way to transform our communities is to transform the people within those communities—and truly restorative change comes only through a relationship with Jesus Christ," is the message found at the Prison Fellowship Web site. Colson's group echoes the philosophy of Benjamin Rush and the liberal Christians, Quakers, and Unitarians in the years after the Revolutionary War.

Justice Fellowship, a sister organization to Prison Fellowship, fights physical mistreatment. Justice Fellowship president Pat Nolan, a leader of the Republican Party who went to prison in 1994, served on the Commission on Safety and Abuse in America's Prisons, which issued a devastating 2006 report to Congress on abuse in corrections facilities.[17]

The influential work of Prison Fellowship and of Sister Helen Prejean suggests that humane ideas on prisons are emerging once again from religious groups. The Quakers have never lost their interest in the physical treatment of prisoners. Beginning in 2005, the Unitarians again took up the issue of prison reform.[18] Religious groups are hardly the only organizations working against prisoner abuse. An assortment of minority voices, many on the left, in the academy, and in the older generation of corrections officers, insist on the importance of humane prisons. Those voices, along with the bits of evidence that rehabilitation does turn some criminals into law-abiding people, are the small hope of this book.

In late summer 2007, movie critics began to wonder why the revenge thriller had returned to theaters. The independent film *Descent*, in which a woman avenges her date rape, was released on August 10. The film's producer described *Descent* as "equally shocking, controversial, and graphic." Although *Descent* had a narrow distribution, *Death Sentence*, on cinema screens across the country, featured Kevin Bacon as a father exacting revenge on the gangs that killed his sons and wife. September 14 saw the nationwide release of *The Brave One*, starring Jodie Foster as a woman who seeks out potential muggers with murderous vengeance after the murder of her fiancé.

Accompanying these filmic returns to revenge was a remake of the thriller *The Star Chamber*. In the 1983 original, Michael Douglas is a judge frustrated when a man he considers guilty gets off on a technicality. A fellow judge then informs Douglas's character that a secret circle of justices hires a hit man to kill criminals who go free.[19] But for a copyright tangle, *Death Wish* would be on its way to remake, reported *New York Times* critic David M. Halbfinger.[20]

The fistful of revenge thrillers caused a surge of social analysis among critics. Why, during a time of low crime rates, should the revenge genre, whose heyday was the 1970s and 1980s, return?[21] In his article, Halbfinger asks the moviemakers what they were thinking. *The Brave One*, for instance, acknowledges public feeling that the big cities are safer. Foster's character Erica and her fiancé walk comfortably through Central Park seconds before the attack blackens their world. Summarizing the words of the film's director, Halbfinger writes, "The brutal attack she barely survives . . . is a reminder that in this age even a pristine city can be just one senseless act away from utter chaos." He adds, in his own pained observation, "Plummeting crime rates provide little comfort to those who become the statistical anomalies."[22]

Erica's response resembles that of Paul, the protagonist of *Death Wish*. She kills low-level crooks. Some reviewers found Erica's selection of victims to be a little much. "At first accidentally and then deliberately, Erica becomes a vigilante, shooting down a murderous husband who is also a convenience-store robber, a pair of iPod thieves who are also potential rapists and a few other bad guys whose badness is similarly overdetermined," writes *New York Times* critic A. O. Scott.[23]

Reviews of *The Brave One* make reference to *Death Wish*, but in the Bronson film vigilantism appears—to raucous public celebration—in the context of what the main character calls high "crime rate statistics." In *The Brave One*, what reviewer Halbfinger called the "statistical anomalies" of an otherwise safe city reveal something central to vigilantism; revenge has little to do with crime stats.

The Brave One echoes our national ethos. The crime rate may be low, but the rate of imprisonment is, compared to the historical record, extraordinarily high, as are public expenditures for crime control and punishment. The United States also has the highest imprisonment rate and the longest sentences in the world, frequently imprisoning those who would go free in other countries. If the United States is less crime ridden, its official behaviors are no less punitive.[24]

In the first pages of this book, I quoted Samuel Walker's argument that American justice is and always has been "popular justice." Via "delegated vigilantism," the public can condone physical abuse of suspects and convicts without ever meeting a criminal. One means of interpreting the emotional argument of *The Brave One* is to understand it as one more avenue for "delegated vigilantism." Scott, the *Times* critic, suggests as much, calling *The Brave One* "a pro-lynching movie that even liberals can love."

The Brave One spent a week as box office number one and a month in the top ten. The film grossed $13 million in its first week and nearly $30 million by week three. Bloggers, attendees, and reviewers reported audiences that applauded and cheered at the moment when the film's main character, Erica, first takes hold of a gun. The official Web site of the movie bore the words "How Many Wrongs to Make It Right?"[25]

NOTES

INTRODUCTION: AMERICAN LIVING IN A TIME OF PUNISHMENT

1. Daniel Lazare, "Stars and Bars," http://www.thenation.com/doc/20070827/ lazare, posted August 9, 2007 (accessed August 20, 2007); Marie Gottschalk, *The Prison and the Gallows: The Politics of Mass Incarceration in America* (New York: Cambridge University Press, 2006), 1; Michael Tonry, "Symbol, Substance, and Severity in Western Penal Practices," *Punishment and Society* 3, no. 43 (October 2001): 517–536. Cited in Gottschalk, *Prison and the Gallows*, 1; U.S. Department of Justice, Bureau of Justice Statistics, http://www.ojp.usdoj .gov/bjs/correct.htm (accessed June 13, 2008); Darryl Fears, "New Criminal Record: 7.2 Million," *Washington Post*, June 12, 2008; Jennifer Warren, principal author, *One in 100: Behind Bars in America 2008*, report (Washington, DC: Pew Center on the States, 2008), 5.

2. Michael Tonry, *Thinking about Crime: Sense and Sensibility in American Penal Culture* (New York: Oxford University Press, 2004), vii, 97–139; Lazare, "Stars and Bars."

3. Fox Butterfield, "Asylums Behind Bars: Prisons Replace Hospitals for the Nation's Mentally Ill," *New York Times*, March 5, 1998; *Jones 'El v. Berge*, Judgment in a Civil Case, Case no. 00-C-0421-C (W.D. Wisconsin, June 24, 2002) (unpub.).

4. Scott Shane, David Johnston, and James Risen, "Secret U.S. Endorsement of Severe Interrogation," *New York Times*, October 4, 2007.

5. The sociologist David Garland describes this same disparity in *The Culture of Control: Crime and Social Order in Contemporary Society* (Chicago: University of Chicago Press, 2001), 4–5.

6. See Alice Morse Earle, *Curious Punishments of Bygone Days* (Chicago: Herbert S. Stone, 1896), 148.

7. Philip Jenkins, *Decade of Nightmares: The End of the Sixties and the Making of Eighties America* (New York: Oxford, 2006), 5–6, 140–143; Garland, *Culture of Control*, 2, 8–20, 26, 76, 98–102. Jonathan Simon, *Governing through Crime: How the War on Crime Transformed American Democracy and Created a Culture of Fear* (Oxford: Oxford University Press, 2007), 4–6. Lisa McGirr, *Suburban Warriors: The Origins of the New American Right* (Princeton: Princeton University Press, 2001), 4–5, 225–226.

8. See Pieter Spierenburg, ed., *Emergence of Carceral Institutions: Prisons, Galleys and Lunatic Asylums, 1550–1900* (Rotterdam: Erasmus Universiteit, 1984); Pieter Spierenburg, *The Prison Experience: Disciplinary Institutions and Their Inmates in Early Modern Europe* (New Brunswick: Rutgers University Press, 1991); Michel Foucault, *Discipline and Punish: The Birth of the Prison*, trans. Alan Sheridan (New York: Pantheon, 1977), 16. Regarding the 1970s shift, see, e.g., Garland, *Culture of Control*, 53–73; Tonry, *Thinking about Crime*, 209–210.

9. See, e.g., Michael Kerrigan, *The Instruments of Torture* (Guilford, CT: Lyons Press, 2001); David Garland, *Punishment and Modern Society: A Study in Social Theory* (Chicago: University of Chicago Press, 1990), 235; Garland, *Culture of Control*, 104, 133.

10. Thomas G. Blomberg and Karol Lucken, *American Penology: A History of Control* (Hawthorne, NY: Aldine de Gruyter, 2000), 23, 33.

11. Jenkins, *Decade of Nightmares*, 140–143, 227–229; other scholars who have made similar arguments include Garland, *Culture of Control*, 185, and Joanna Bourke, *Fear* (Emeryville, CA: Shoemaker and Hoard, 2006), 329.

12. Samuel Walker, *Popular Justice: A History of American Criminal Justice* (New York: Oxford University Press, 1980), 3–4.

13. Ibid., 4.

14. Ibid.

15. A. J. Frutkin, "Crime-Time TV Expands," *MediaWeek* 13, no. 18 (May 5, 2003): 6. See also Maureen Ryan, "Shooting for Ratings, Cop Shows Persist Formula Works, So Look for More Crime Dramas on Summer, Fall Schedules," *Chicago Tribune*, April 24, 2005; and A. J. Frutkin, "New Crime Hours Break In," *MediaWeek* 15, no. 2 (January 10, 2005): 6.

16. See the Nielsen ratings for February 23–29, 2004; David Carr, "Saying Goodbye to a True 'NYPD Blue' Detective," *New York Times*, March 1, 2005; Kevin D. Thompson, "Arresting Television," *Palm Beach Post*, February 9, 2002.

17. Jerrold K. Footlick with Mary Lord, "The Criminal Mind," *Newsweek*, February 27, 1978, p. 91.

18. Jenkins, *Decade of Nightmares*, 18, 194.

19. Bourke, *Fear*, 24–25, 92; Henry Addington Bruce, *Your Growing Child: A Book of Talks to Parents on Life's Needs* (New York: Funk and Wagnalls, 1927), 78; quoted in Bourke.

20. Editorial, "Making Sure the Protectors Protect," *New York Times*, July 16, 2007.

21. Robert L. Jamieson Jr., "Schools in Kent Fail Decency Test," *Seattle Post-Intelligencer*, August 16, 2004.

22. Steven Macpherson Watt, Deborah Labelle, Ann Beeson, Kary Moss, Human Rights Working Group, American Civil Liberties Union of Michigan, American Civil Liberties Union, "Petition Alleging Violations of the Human Rights of Juveniles Sentenced to Life without Parole in the United States of America," petition submitted to Inter-American Commission on Human Rights, February 21, 2006, p. 3.

23. Peter Applebome, "How We Took the Child Out of Childhood," *New York Times*, January 8, 2006. See also William Strauss and Neil Howe, *Generations: The History of America's Future, 1584–2069* (New York: Harper Perennial, 1992), 337.

24. See, e.g., Blomberg and Lucken, *American Penology*, 30.

25. Benedict Carey, "For the Worst of Us, the Diagnosis May Be 'Evil,'" *New York Times*, February 8, 2005.

26. The most prominent of these considerations is Michel Foucault's *Discipline and Punish*; Stuart Banner, *The Death Penalty: An American History*, 2d ed. (Cambridge: Harvard University Press, 2003), 99–100.

27. Elaine Scarry, *The Body in Pain: The Making and Unmaking of the World* (New York: Oxford University Press, 1987), 4, 3–5, 60–61.

28. Sasha Abramsky, *Conned: How Millions Went to Prison, Lost the Vote, and Helped Send George W. Bush to the White House* (New York: New Press, 2006); www.demos.org.

29. See also Simon, *Governing through Crime*, 201.

CHAPTER 1. WHEN PUNISHMENT IS THE SUBJECT,
RELIGION IS THE PREDICATE

1. Benson John Lossing, *The American Historical Record*, vol. 1 (n.p.: Chase and Town, 1872), 205–206. Part of this letter is cited in Earle, *Curious Punishments*, 19–20.

2. See, e.g., Blomberg and Lucken, *American Penology*, 25–26; D. S. Bailey, *Homosexuality and the Western Christian Tradition* (Hamden, CT: Archon, 1975), 100, 119, 123, 126–127, 170; and Wayne C. Bartee and Alice Fleetwood Bartee, *Litigating Morality: American Legal Thought and Its English Roots* (Westport, CT: Praeger/Greenwood), 1992. Louis P. Masur, *Rites of Execution: Capital Punishment and the Transformation of American Culture, 1776–1865* (New York: Oxford University Press, 1989), also discusses both the roots and the development of American punishment in the context of Christianity. My interests parallel Masur's in some respects, and his history has influenced this book. But Masur's preoccupation is with execution rather than corporal punishment. He also tends to see a single transformation, post–American Revolution, rather than what appears from my vantage point as a

circular movement, or at the least a two-hundred-plus-year battle over the meaning and practice of American punishment.

3. For a statement on the importance of colonial community religious expiation of crimes, see Blomberg and Lucken, *American Penology,* 33.

4. Council of Trent (1551. XIV, can. v).

5. *The American Heritage Dictionary of the English Language,* 4th ed. (New York: Houghton Mifflin, 2000).

6. Banner, *Death Penalty,* 32–36; Foucault, *Discipline and Punish,* 59–69, 73.

7. Daniel A. Cohen, *Pillars of Salt, Monuments of Grace: New England Crime Literature and the Origins of American Popular Culture, 1674–1860* (Amherst: University of Massachusetts Press, 2006), ix, x.

8. Banner, *Death Penalty,* 44–48, 170; V. A. C. Gatrell, *Hanging Tree* (Oxford: Oxford University Press, 1994), vii, 7.

9. Banner, *Death Penalty,* 70–71.

10. Most of these punishments make an appearance in Earle, *Curious Punishments,* 1–10, 138, 140, 144, 148, 96, 101–105. Thomas Jefferson recommended, "Whoever shall be guilty of Rape, Polygamy, or sodomy with man or woman, shall be punished, if a man, by castration, if a woman, by cutting through the cartilage of her nose a hole of one half inch in diameter at the least." Thomas Jefferson, *The Writings of Thomas Jefferson,* ed. Albert Ellery Bergh, vol. 1 (Washington, DC: Thomas Jefferson Memorial Association, 1905), 226–227. Cited in Friedman, *Crime and Punishment in American History,* 73.

11. Blomberg and Lucken, *American Penology,* 23, 25–26; Bailey, *Homosexuality and the Western Christian Tradition,* 100, 119, 123, 126–127, 170, and Bartee and Bartee, *Litigating Morality.* Masur, in *Rites,* also discusses both the roots and the development of American punishment in the context of Christianity.

12. See Ernst H. Kantorowicz, *The King's Two Bodies* (Princeton: Princeton University Press, 1957, 1997), 506.

13. See, e.g., Mark D. Cahn, "Punishment, Discretion, and the Codification of Prescribed Penalties in Colonial Massachusetts," *American Journal of Legal History* 33, no. 2 (April 1989): 107, 135; David D. Hall, *Puritanism in Seventeenth-Century Massachusetts* (New York: Holt, Rinehart, and Winston, 1968), 64; Earle, *Curious Punishments,* 141.

14. Mary Beth Norton, *Founding Mothers and Fathers: Gendered Power and the Forming of American Society* (New York: Vintage, 1997), 350–351.

15. D. S. Bailey, *Homosexuality and the Western Christian Tradition,* 100, 119, 123, 126–127, 170. Bartee and Bartee, *Litigating Morality,* 34.

16. Bartee and Bartee, *Litigating Morality,* 34.

17. W. R. Staples, ed., *Proceedings of the First General Assembly of the Incorporation of Providence Plantation and the Code of Laws Adopted in 1647* (Providence: Charles Bunett, 1847), 31–32. Quoted In Bartee and Bartee, *Litigating Morality,* 37.

18. M. Watt Espy and John Ortiz Smylka, "Executions in the United States,

1608–2002: The Espy File," 4th ed. (Ann Arbor: Inter-university Consortium for Political and Social Research, 2004) (hereafter Espy file), www.icpsr .umich.edu/NACJD.

19. Ibid.

20. Norton, *Founding Mothers*, 349.

21. Ibid., 349, 470.

22. Ibid., 349–350.

23. Ibid., 356–357, 471.

24. Ibid., 356–357; Espy file.

25. David D. Hall, ed., *Puritans in the New World: A Critical Anthology* (Princeton: Princeton University Press, 2004), 141; Kenneth Silverman, *The Life and Times of Cotton Mather* (New York: Harper and Row, 1984), 89.

26. Paul Boyer and Stephen Nissenbaum, eds., *The Salem Witchcraft Papers: Verbatim Transcripts of the Legal Documents of the Salem Witchcraft Outbreak of 1692*, vol. 1 (New York: Da Capo, 1977), 26–27, 241; Espy file.

27. Espy file; Boyer and Nissenbaum, *Salem Witchcraft Papers*, 89; John Winthrop and Thomas Weld, "A Short History of the Rise, Reign, and Ruin of the Antinomians," in Hall, *Puritans*, 213.

28. Kai T. Erikson, *Wayward Puritans: A Study in the Sociology of Deviance* (New York: John Wiley and Sons, 1966), 67.

29. Erikson, *Wayward Puritans*, 4. Emile Durkheim, *The Division of Labor in Society*, trans. George Simpson (Glencoe, IL: Free Press, 1960).

30. Erikson, *Wayward Puritans*, 67.

31. Ibid., 67, 138–139.

32. See Garland, *Punishment and Modern Society*, and *Culture of Control*, 3, 101. See also Tonry, *Thinking about Crime*, 99, 108, 157, 161.

33. Silverman, *Life and Times*, 87. Hale quoted in Silverman.

34. Boyer and Nissenbaum, *Salem Witchcraft Papers*, 4–5. Lori Lee Wilson, *The Salem Witch Trials* (Minneapolis: Twenty-first Century, 1997), 23.

35. Cotton Mather, *Memorable Providences, Relating to Witchcrafts and Possessions* (Boston: Richard Pierce, 1689), "Witchcrafts and Possessions, the First Exemple," sect. 3.

36. Ibid., sect. 4.

37. Ibid., sect. 5.

38. Ibid., sect. 20.

39. Boyer and Nissenbaum, *Salem Witchcraft Papers*, 7, 9–10, 25.

40. Allan I. Macinnes and Arthur H. Williamson, *Shaping the Stuart World, 1603–1714: The Atlantic Connection* (Leiden: Brill, 2006), 20; Paul Samuel Reinsch, "English Common Law in the Early American Colonies" (Ph.D. diss., University of Wisconsin, 1899), 45; John Alfred Poor, *The First Colonization of New England* (New York: Anson D. F. Randolph, 1862), 42–43.

41. John D. Cushing, ed., *Colony Laws of Virginia, 1619–1660* (Wilmington, DE: Michael Glazier, 1978), 1:96; David H. Flaherty, ed., William Strachey, comp., *For the Colony of Virginea Brittania: Lawes, Divine, Morall and Martiall* (Char-

lottesville: University Press of Virginia, 1969), 10–11; Ronald J. Pestritto, *Founding the Criminal Law: Punishment and Political Thought in the Origins of America* (Dekalb: Northern Illinois University Press, 2000), 46.

42. Pestritto, *Founding*, 47; "Articles, Lawes, and Orders, Divine, Politique, and Martiall for the Colony in Virginea: first established by Sir Thomas Gates Knight, Lieutenant Generall, the 24th of May 1610," in Peter Force, *Tracts* (Gloucester, MA: Peter Smith, 1963), 10, 11, 12–13. See also Peter George Mode, *Source Book and Bibliographical Guide for American Church History* (Menasha, WI: Collegiate Press, 1921), 10–11; and John Andrew Doyle, *English Colonies in America* (New York: Holt, 1889), 138–139.

43. Pestritto, *Founding*, 46–47. He is summarizing Flaherty, *Laws Divine, Morall and Martiall*.

44. Pestritto, *Founding*, 46, 48.

45. Espy file.

46. See Espy file as well as Negley Teeters, *Scaffold and Chair: A Compilation of Their Use in Pennsylvania, 1682–1962* (Philadelphia: Pennsylvania Prison Society, 1963), 41.

47. Peter Linebaugh, *The London Hanged* (New York: Verso, 2003), xxii; Christopher Hill, *Puritanism and Revolution: Studies in Interpretation of the English Revolution of the Seventeenth Century* (Basingstoke, U.K.: Palgrave MacMillan, 1997), 198.

48. Sir Leon Radzinowicz, *A History of English Criminal Law and Its Administration from 1750*, 4 vols., vol. 1, 1848–68 (New York: Macmillan, 1948), 4; Douglas Hay, "Property, Authority, and the Criminal Law," in *Albion's Fatal Tree: Crime and Society in Eighteenth-Century England*, ed. Douglas Hay, Peter Linebaugh, John G. Rule, E. P. Thompson, and Cal Winslow (New York: Pantheon, 1975), 20.

49. Hay, "Property, Authority," 17.

50. Ibid., 29.

51. See Banner, *Death Penalty*, 7–8; Blomberg and Lucken, *American Penology*, 35.

CHAPTER 2. "A HEART IS NOT WHOLLY CORRUPTED"

1. Benjamin Rush, *Letters of Benjamin Rush*, ed. L. H. Butterfield (Princeton: Princeton University Press, 1951), vol. 1, 330–331.

2. Ibid., 372.

3. Ibid., 371–372.

4. Nine Reid-Maroney, *Philadelphia's Enlightenment, 1740–1800: Kingdom of Christ, Empire of Reason* (Westport, CT: Greenwood, 2001), xii–xiii.

5. Rush, *Letters*, vol. 1, 437.

6. Ibid.

7. Ibid.

8. Randolph Shipley Klein, *Science and Society in Early America: Essays in Honor of Whitfield J. Bell Jr.* (Philadelphia: American Philosophical Society, 1986), 228.

9. Pestritto, *Founding*, 14. Although I depend on Pestritto's work for information in this and the next chapter, Pestritto was more interested in the effect of new political perspective on punishment reforms than on the religious aspect of the revolution in punishment. Pestritto does not comment on the religious overtones of the Rush letter, but he does note the coincidence between the young U.S. government and Rush's conviction that a criminal who could love a dog could change for the better.

10. Rush, *Letters*, vol. 1, 388, 260.

11. Rush, "Thoughts upon Female Education, Accommodated to the Present State of Society, Manners, and Government, in the United States of America," *Essays, Literary, Moral, and Philosophical*, 2d ed. (Philadelphia: Thomas and William Bradford, 1806), 79.

12. Ibid., 75.

13. Ibid., 87.

14. Ibid., 87.

15. Rush, "Thoughts upon the Amusements and Punishments, Which Are Proper for Schools," *Essays*, 57 74, 65.

16. Ibid., 66.

17. Ibid.

18. Ibid., 68.

19. Rush *Letters*, vol. 2, 820–821, quoted in Masur, *Rites*, 66.

20. See, e.g., James Parton, *Life of Thomas Jefferson, Third President of the United States* (New York: Houghton Mifflin, 1883), 574; and Charles B. Sanford, *The Religious Life of Thomas Jefferson* (Charlottesville: University of Virginia Press, 1984), 101.

21. Benjamin Rush, *Considerations on the Injustice and Impolicy of Punishing Murder by Death* (Philadelphia: Matthew Carey, 1792), 19.

22. Benjamin Rush, "An Enquiry into the Effects of Public Punishments upon Criminals and upon Society," *Essays*, 138, 143, 147.

23. Gatrell, *Hanging Tree*, 269–270. On the issue of middle- and upper-class anxiety toward executions, see also P. Spierenburg, *Spectacle of Suffering*. Banner also addresses the "opposition to capital punishment" as part of "a larger change in sensibility," *Death Penalty*, 108. See also Masur, *Rites*, 4–5.

24. Benjamin Rush, "An Enquiry into the Consistency of the Punishment of Murder by Death, with Reason and Revelation," *Essays*, 164, 165–166; Benjamin Rush, *An Enquiry into the Effects of Public Punishments upon Criminals and upon Society* (Philadelphia: Joseph James, 1787), 5, 7.

25. Rush, "Public Punishments," *Essays*, 150.

26. Masur, *Rites*, 42–43.

27. Cohen, *Pillars of Salt*, x.

28. Masur, *Rites*, 45; Nathan Strong, "A Sermon Preached in Hartford, June 10, 1797, at the Execution of Richard Doane" (Hartford: Elisha Babcock, 1797), 13.

29. Strong, "Sermon," 12.

30. Ibid., 3.

31. Ibid.

32. Foucault, *Discipline and Punish*, 7–8, 47–54.

33. Masur, *Rites*, 7, 66–68.

34. Bernard Wishy, *The Child and the Republic: The Dawn of Modern American Child Nurture* (Philadelphia: University of Pennsylvania Press, 1968), vii, 11–19, 32–33.

35. For a discussion of Penn's contributions to American law, see O. F. Lewis, *The Development of American Prisons and Prison Customs, 1776–1845: With Special Reference to Early Institutions in the State of New York* (Montclair, NJ: Patterson Smith, 1967), 10–12.

36. Staughton George, Benjamin N. Nead, and Thomas McCamant, eds., *Charter to William Penn and Laws of the Province of Pennsylvania, 1682–1700* (Harrisburg, PA: Lane S. Hart, State Printer, 1879), 14–15, 24–27; Pestritto, *Founding*, 15–16; Harry Elmer Barnes, *The Evolution of Penology in Pennsylvania* (Indianapolis: Bobbs-Merrill, 1927), 29.

37. Barnes, *Evolution of Penology in Pennsylvania*, 30. See Pestritto, *Founding*, 15–17.

38. Pestritto, *Founding*, 15, 17.

39. George, Nead, and McCamant, *Charter to William Penn*, 100; Pestritto, *Founding*, 17.

40. George, Nead, and McCamant, *Charter to William Penn*, 107–113; Pestritto, *Founding*, 18.

41. Pestritto, *Founding*, 18–19.

42. William Bradford, *An Enquiry How Far the Punishment of Death Is Necessary in Pennsylvania* (Philadelphia: Dobson, 1793), 18, 19.

43. Lawrence H. Gipson, "The Criminal Codes of Pennsylvania," *Journal of Criminal Law* 7 (1915): 331. Pestritto, *Founding*, 19–20.

44. Spierenburg, *Emergence of Carceral Institutions;* Spierenburg, *Prison Experience;* see Linebaugh, *London Hanged*, 14, 23–41.

45. Edward L. Ayers, *Vengeance and Justice: Crime and Punishment in the Nineteenth-Century American South* (New York: Oxford University Press, 1984), 36.

46. See Simon, *Governing through Crime*, 146, and Ayers, *Vengeance*, 40.

47. See Masur, *Rites*, 82–83; Michael Meranze, *Laboratories of Virtue: Punishment, Revolution, and Authority in Philadelphia, 1760–1835* (Chapel Hill: University of North Carolina Press, 1996), 183.

48. Masur, *Rites*, 4–5.

49. Ibid., 54–57.

50. See Cesare Beccaria, *An Essay on Crimes and Punishments*, trans. from the Italian; with a commentary, attributed to Mons. de Voltaire; trans. from the French, 2d ed. (London, Printed for F. Newbery at corner of St. Paul's Church-yard, 1769); John Locke, *Two Treatises of Government* (London: C. and J. Rivington, 1824), 141. Regarding restriction on capital punishment in other countries before the Revolutionary War, see Gatrell, *Hanging Tree*, 8–9.

51. Thomas Jefferson, *Autobiography* (New York: G. P. Putnam's Sons, 1914), 71. Rush, "A Plan for Establishing Public Schools in Pennsylvania and for Conducting Education Agreeably to a Republican Form of Government," *Essays*, 2.

52. Jefferson, *Autobiography*, 71.

53. Benjamin Rush, *Letters*, vol. 1, 436–437, 372; Jefferson, *Writings*, 301; Jefferson, *Autobiography*, 73–74.

54. Jefferson, *Autobiography*, 118.

55. This is not to argue that trial by jury and habeas corpus are peculiarly American or revolutionary ideas as both have European antecedents. My point is Jefferson's insistence that they accompany freedoms intrinsic to American governance.

56. Jefferson, *Autobiography*, 72–73.

57. Ibid., 74; *American Heritage Dictionary*, 4th ed.

58. As quoted in John Hampden Hazelton, *The Declaration of Independence: Its History* (New York: Dodd, Mead, 1906), 494.

59. Foucault, *Discipline and Punish*, 141–169, 195–228.

60. Benjamin Rush, *Letters*, vol. 2, 1052. Also see interview with Pennsylvania Hospital archivist Stacey Peeples, *All Things Considered*, NPR, May 10, 2001.

61. Blomberg and Lucken, *American Penology*, 54; Negley K. Teeters, "The Early Days of the Eastern State Penitentiary at Philadelphia," *Pennsylvania History* 16, no. 4 (October 1949): 295, 297.

62. Teeters, "Early Days of the Eastern State Penitentiary," 295.

63. Elizabeth Olson, "U.S. Prisoner Restraints Amount to Torture, Geneva Panel Says," *New York Times*, May 18, 2000.

CHAPTER 3. REFORMING THE REFORMS

1. Eastern State Penitentiary, Philadelphia, "Six-Page History," Web site of the Eastern State Penitentiary, http://www.easternstate.org/history/sixpage.html (accessed September 27, 2007); George Washington Smith, "A View and Description of the Eastern Penitentiary of Pennsylvania" (Philadelphia: Philadelphia Society for Alleviating the Miseries of Public Prisons, 1830), 3.

2. Smith, "Eastern Penitentiary," 2–3.

3. Eastern State Penitentiary, "Six-Page History." See also Blomberg and Lucken, *American Penology*, 53.

4. Smith, "Eastern Penitentiary," 2.

5. Ibid., 3.

6. Ibid., 5–6.

7. Rush, "Public Punishments," *Essays*, 150. *American Heritage Dictionary*, 4th ed., s.v. "penitentiary."

8. Jeremy Bentham, *The Panopticon Writings*, ed. Miran Bozovic (London: Verso, 1995), 29–95.

9. Foucault, *Discipline and Punish*, 141–169, 195–228.

10. Boston Prison Discipline Society, "Thoughts on Prison Discipline" (Boston: James Munroe, 1839), 15.

11. Teeters, "Early Days of the Eastern State Penitentiary," 295.

12. Boston Prison Discipline Society, "Thoughts," 15.

13. Francis Lieber, "Prison Discipline," *North American Review* 104 (July 1839): 36–37.

14. Masur, *Rites*, 86–87.

15. Eileen McHugh, brochure for "Both Sides of the Wall," exhibit on the Auburn Prison, Cayuga Museum, April 12–August 31, 2003 (Auburn, NY: Cayuga Museum, 2003), 1–2.

16. Ibid., 3–4.

17. Boston Prison Discipline Society, "Thoughts," 15.

18. J. Harrie Banka, *An Illustrated History and Description of State Prison Life by One Who Has Been There* (Toledo, OH: Globe Publishing, 1871), 96 (hereafter *Description of State Prison Life*).

19. D. L. Dix, *Remarks on Prisons and Prison Discipline in the United States* (Boston: Munroe and Francis, 1845), 17–18.

20. Ibid., 13–14.

21. Ibid., 14.

22. Ibid., 24, 18.

23. McHugh, "Both Sides," 3–4.

24. Ibid., 3.

25. Ibid., 3–4.

26. Andrew Shuman, "The Management and Discipline of Our Prisons," *Western Monthly* 1 (January–June, 1869).

27. Foucault, *Discipline and Punish*, 8–10; Gatrell, *Hanging Tree*, 269–270. On the issue of middle- and upper-class anxiety toward executions, see also Spierenburg, *Spectacle of Suffering*. See also Masur, *Rites*, 6. Banner also addresses the "opposition to capital punishment" as part of "a larger change in sensibility," *Death Penalty*, 108.

28. Charles Spear, *Essays on the Punishment of Death* (Boston: Published by the author, 1844; London: John Green, 1844), 52, 73–74.

29. Masur, *Rites*, 6.

30. Philadelphia Society for Alleviating the Miseries of Public Prisons, *Sketch of the Principal Transactions of the "Philadelphia Society for Alleviating the Miseries of Public Prisons," from Its Origin to the Present Times* (Philadelphia: Merrihew and Thompson, Printers, 1859), inside front cover.

31. Ibid., inside front cover.

32. Ibid., 6–8.

33. Ibid., 19.

34. Garland, *Culture of Control*, 26–28.

35. Timothy Alden Taylor, *The Bible View of the Death Penalty: Also, a Summary of the Webster Case* (Worcester, MA: S. A. Howland, 1850), 18.

36. Ibid., 19–20.

37. Ayers, *Vengeance*, 34.

38. Ibid., 19.

39. Ibid., 24.
40. Ibid., 13.
41. Ibid., 25.
42. Representative Louis Reneau of Servier County in *Nashville Whig*, December 2, 1826. Quoted in Ayers, *Vengeance*, 46.
43. *Greensborough Patriot*, February 21, 1846; *Southern Recorder*, December 14, 1858. Quoted in Ayers, *Vengeance*, 69.
44. For analysis of the repressed presence of retributive ideas into the twentieth century and their return in the late years of that century, see Garland, *Culture of Control*, 41.
45. Dix, *Remarks*, 22.
46. Boston Prison Discipline Society, "Series of Numbers on Prison Discipline from One to Ten," *Reports of the Prison Discipline Society, Boston* (Boston: Press of T. R. Marvin, 1855), 88.
47. Ibid., 81.
48. Ibid., 81–82.
49. Ibid., 89.
50. Ibid., 91.
51. Ibid., 92.
52. Philadelphia Society for the Alleviation of the Miseries of Public Prisons, "The Pennsylvania System of Prison Discipline Triumphant in France" (published by the Philadelphia Society for the Alleviation of the Miseries of Public Prisons, Philadelphia: printed by I. Ashmead, 1847), 12.
53. Ibid.
54. Ibid., 16.
55. Ibid., 9.
56. Stuart Grassian, M.D., "Testimony on Impact of Isolation," Commission on Safety and Abuse in United States Prisons (July 19, 2005), 2. Available on the Web site of the Commission on Safety and Abuse in America's Prisons, www.prisoncommission.org/statements/grassian_stuart.pdf (accessed June 10, 2008).
57. Peter Scharff Smith, "From the Modern Penitentiary to Supermax Prisons," Danish Institute of Human Rights. Available at: http://humanrights.palermo.magenta-aps.dk/news/featureuk/isolation_pss_eng/ (accessed January 18, 2008).
58. U.S. Supreme Court *In re Medley*, 134 U.S. 160 (1890).
59. Smith, "From the Modern Penitentiary to Supermax Prisons."
60. Banka, *Description of State Prison Life*.
61. Ibid., 257.
62. Ibid.
63. Ibid., 40–41.
64. Ibid., 96.
65. Ibid., 99.
66. Ibid., 109–110.

67. Ibid., 110.
68. Ibid.
69. Ibid., 111.
70. Philadelphia Society, *Eastern Penitentiary*, 5.
71. Banka, *Description of State Prison Life*, 135–136.
72. Ibid., 136.
73. Ibid., 189.
74. Ibid., 189–190.
75. Ibid., 190.
76. Ibid., 196.
77. Ibid., 197–198.
78. Ibid., 221, 225.
79. Ibid., 254.
80. Ibid., 525–526.
81. Ava Arndt, "Touching London: Contact, Sensibility and the City," in *The City and the Senses: Urban Culture since 1500*, ed. Alexander Cowan and Jill Seward (Aldershot: Ashgate, 2007), 97–98. Also see G. J. Barker-Benfield, *The Culture of Sensibility: Sex and Society in Eighteenth-Century Britain* (Chicago: University of Chicago Press, 1992), 9.
82. Elizabeth B. Clark, " 'The Sacred Rights of the Weak': Pain, Sympathy, and the Culture of Individual Rights in Antebellum America," *Journal of American History* 82, no. 2 (September 1995): 463, 464–465, 470–471.
83. Ibid., 488, 492.
84. Jennifer Mason, *Civilized Creatures: Urban Animals, Sentimental Culture, and American Literature, 1850–1900* (Baltimore: Johns Hopkins University Press, 2005), 16, 27.
85. Ibid., 153, 24.
86. Ibid., 122, 123.
87. Banka, *Description of State Prison Life*, 525–526, inside front cover.

CHAPTER 4. PUNISHMENT CREEP

1. Bartee and Bartee, *Litigating Morality*, 13, 34.
2. Warren Burton, *The District School as It Was, by One Who Went to It*, ed. Clifton Johnson (Boston: Lee and Shepard, 1897), 44; Earle, *Curious Punishments*, 101–105.
3. Masur, *Rites*, 6.
4. Espy file.
5. Described in William W. Brown, *The Narrative of William W. Brown, an American Slave. Written by Himself*, electronic ed. (Chapel Hill: University of North Carolina, 1996), 151. Available at http://docsouth.unc.edu/fpn/brownw/menu.html.
6. Ayers, *Vengeance*, 61.
7. Mississippi, chap. 92, sec. 110, Digest of Stat., p. 770; Mississippi Act of June 18, 1822, sec. 32. Other colonies and states had similar laws. See, e.g.,

Thomas D. Morris, *Southern Slavery and the Law, 1619–1860* (Chapel Hill: University of North Carolina Press, 1999), 211. Judge George McDowell Stroud, *A Sketch of the Laws Relating to Slavery in the Several States of the United States of America* (New York: Negro Universities Press, 1856), e.g., 64–65, 68, 71.

8. Josiah Henson, *The Life of Josiah Henson, Formerly a Slave, Now an Inhabitant of Canada, as Narrated by Himself,* electronic ed. (Chapel Hill: University of North Carolina, 2001), 1.

9. Frederick Douglass, *Narrative of the Life of Frederick Douglass, an American Slave; Written by Himself,* ed. Houston A. Baker, Jr. (New York: Penguin, 1982), 97–98.

10. Ibid., 97.

11. Ibid., 98–99.

12. Ibid., 118–119.

13. See Ellwood P. Cubberley, *Public Education in the United States: A Study and Interpretation of American Educational History,* 2d ed. (Boston: Houghton Mifflin, 1934), 57.

14. Small, *American Education,* 390; Alice Morse Earle, *Child Life in Colonial Days* (New York: MacMillan, 1899), 197.

15. Clifton Johnson, *Old-Time Schools and School Books* (New York: Macmillan, 1925), 122, 43; Earle, *Child Life,* 198.

16. See, e.g., Blomberg and Lucken, *American Penology,* 43–44; see also Harry Elmer Barnes, *The Story of Punishment* (Boston: Stratford, 1930).

17. Charles L. Coon, *North Carolina Schools and Academies, 1790–1840: A Documentary History* (Raleigh: Edwards and Broughton, 1915), 763–764.

18. Burton, *District School,* 42–43. "Half the time was spent in calling up scholars for little misdemeanors" cited in Small, *American Education,* 394.

19. Burton, *District School,* 43. "Stooping posture" cited in Small, *American Education,* 394.

20. Small, *American Education,* 391; Burton, *District School,* 43.

21. Lyman Cobb, *The Evil Tendencies of Corporal Punishment as a Means of Moral Discipline In Families and Schools* (New York: Mark H. Newman, 1847).

22. Earle, *Curious Punishments,* 132.

23. Ibid., 132–133.

24. Ibid., 124–127.

25. Ibid., 128–131; Francis Grose, *A Classical Dictionary of the Vulgar Tongue: A Dictionary of Buckish Slang, University Wit, and Pickpocket Eloquence,* 2d ed. (London: S. Hooper, 1788), s.v. "wooden horse," pages not numbered. Earle, *Curious Punishments,* quotes this passage from a later edition of the book, 129.

26. This story appears in numerous histories of Paul Revere. See, e.g., Elbridge Henry Gross, *The Life of Colonel Paul Revere* (Boston: Joseph Cupples, 1891). Quoted in Earle, *Curious Punishments,* 131.

27. Louis Clinton Hatch, *Administration of the American Revolutionary Army* (New York: Longmans, Green, 1904), 14–15.

28. Earle, *Curious Punishments*, 131.

29. John M. Copley, *A Sketch of the Battle of Franklin, Tenn.; with Reminiscences of Camp Douglas*, electronic ed. (Chapel Hill: University of North Carolina, 1998), 92.

30. Ibid., 94, 131.

31. Ibid., 133–134.

32. See, e.g., Wishy, *Child and the Republic*, vii, 32–33; Mason, *Civilized Creatures*, 16, 27; and Clark, " 'Sacred Rights of the Weak,' " 463, 464–465, 470–471, 488, 492.

33. Douglass, *Narrative of the Life*, 55–56.

34. Coon, *North Carolina Schools and Academies*, 441.

35. See, e.g., Samuel Chester Parker, *The History of Modern Elementary Education* (Boston: Ginn, 1912), 242–244; Joseph Lancaster, *Improvements in Education, as It Respects the Industrious Classes of the Community*, 3d ed. (New York: Collins and Perkins, 1807).

36. Lancaster, *Improvements*, 85.

37. Ibid., 86.

38. Ibid.

39. Ibid., 86–87.

40. Ibid., 87.

41. Ibid., 87–88, 95.

42. Ibid., 88.

43. *Commercial Directory: A Topographical Description, Extent, and Production of Different Sections of the Union* (Philadelphia: J. C. Kayser, 1823), 22, 24, 132, 213, 217, 225.

44. Small, *American Education*, 398.

45. Massachusetts Education Committee, *Reports on the Abolition of Corporal Punishment in the Public Schools*, House Document 335 (Boston: Wright and Potter, 1868), 45; Albert Smith and John Hopkins Morrison, *History of the Town of Peterborough, Hillsborough County, New Hampshire* (Peterborough, NH: G. H. Elis, 1876), 107. Both of these quoted in Donald R. Raichle, "The Abolition of Corporal Punishment in New Jersey Schools," in *Corporal Punishment in American Education*, ed. Irwin Hyman (Philadelphia: Temple University Press, 1979), 62.

46. Wishy, *Child and the Republic*, 28.

47. Ibid., vii, 32–33.

48. Harriet Martineau, "Herod in the Nineteenth Century," *Once a Week* 1 (September 3, 1859): 195–198; George Ackerly, *On the Management of Children* (New York, 1836), 61. On play as "Christian liberty," see Horace Bushnell, *Views of Christian Nurture* (Hartford: Hunt, 1847), 339–340. All quoted in Wishy, *Child and the Republic*, 43.

49. Wishy, *Child and the Republic*, 44; Edgar W. Knight, ed., *A Documentary His-*

tory of Education in the South before 1860, vol. 5 (Chapel Hill: University of North Carolina Press, 1953), 241–242. Mentioned in Wishy.

50. Catharine Maria Sedgwick, *Home*, electronic resource (Charlottesville: University of Virginia, 2000), 16. Transcribed from Catharine Maria Sedgwick, *Home* (Boston: James Munroe, 1835), 16. Wishy also discusses this scene, *Child and the Republic*, 46–48.

51. Sedgwick, *Home*, 16–17.

52. Ibid., 19.

53. Ibid., 22.

54. Ibid., 22, 25, summarized in Wishy, *Child and the Republic*, 47.

55. Wishy, *Child and the Republic*, 49–51, 99–110.

56. Barbara A. Bardes and Suzanne Gossett, "Catharine Maria Sedgwick, 1789–1867," in *The Heath Anthology of American Literature*, 5th ed., vol. 2, ed. Paul Lauter (New York: Houghton Mifflin, 2005).

57. Cobb, *Evil Tendencies*, 7.

58. Ibid., 14, 8–9.

59. Ibid., 79.

60. Ibid., 76.

61. Jacob Abbott, in *Gentle Measures in the Management and Training of the Young*, quoted in Wishy, *Child and the Republic*, 101.

62. Ibid., 108–109.

63. Ibid., 109.

64. Henry Teonge, *The Diary of Henry Teonge, Chaplain on Board HM's Ships* (New York: Routledge, 2004), 262.

65. Geoffrey Abbott, *Execution* (New York: Macmillan, 2006), 201–202.

66. Cobb, *Evil Tendencies*, 83.

67. Richard Henry Dana Jr., *Two Years Before the Mast* (Cambridge:: Houghton Mifflin, 1895), 104.

68. Herman Melville, *White Jacket* (Oxford: Oxford University Press, 1849, 1990), 143, 146, 148.

CHAPTER 5. VIGILANTISM AND PROGRESSIVISM

1. See David J. Rothman, *Conscience and Convenience: The Asylum and Its Alternatives in Progressive America* (Boston: Little, Brown, 1980), 3–5, 17, 44–46; Alex Lichtenstein, *Twice the Work of Free Labor: The Political Economy of Convict Labor in the New South* (London: Verso, 1996), 16; Jacquelyn Dowd Hall, "'The Mind That Burns in Each Body': Women, Rape, and Racial Violence," in *Powers of Desire: The Politics of Sexuality*, ed. Ann Snitow, Christine Stansell, and Sharon Thompson (New York: Monthly Review Press, 1983), 328; Roberta Smith, "An Ugly Legacy Lives On, Its Glare Unsoftened by Age," *New York Times*, January 13, 2000.

2. Banner, *Death Penalty*, 169.

3. Anita Weier, "McCaffrey Took 18 Minutes to Die; 1851 Execution Was Last

Ordered by State," *Capital Times*, March 1, 2003; Mike Miller, "State's Only Execution So Ghastly It Led to Reform: Capital Punishment Outlawed 2 Years Later," *Capital Times*, June 11, 2001.

4. D. J. Tice, "A Century of Stories. In 1905 and 1906, St. Paul Officials Bungled the Hangings of Two Murderers: Gruesome Publicity Inspired Censorship of Local Newspapers but Helped Lead to the Abolition of Minnesota's Death Penalty," Associated Press, July 6, 1997.

5. Llewellyn Hughes, article in *Humanity and Its Problems*, April 1924. Quoted in Barnes, *Story of Punishment*, 233–234.

6. See, e.g., Edward Mornin and Lorna Mornin, *Saints* (Grand Rapids: Eerdmans, 2006), 136; Geoffrey Abbott, *Execution* (New York: Macmillan), 2006; Martin Luther, *A Commentary on St. Paul's Epistle to the Galatians* (Philadelphia: Smith and English, 1860), 106–107. James Gardner, *Faiths of the World* (Whitefish, Mont.: Kessinger, 2003), 138–139; Barnes, *Story of Punishment*, 233.

7. Smith, "Ugly Legacy." Marcus K. Garner, "U.S. Senate Apologizes for Not Enacting Anti-Lynching Legislation," *Chicago Daily Southtown*, June 14, 2005.

8. Bill Arp, *From the Uncivil War to Date, 1861–1903*, p. 55, electronic ed. Retrieved from http://docsouth.unc.edu/fpn/arp/menu.html.

9. W. E. B. Du Bois, "Religion in the South," in Booker T. Washington, W. E. B. Du Bois, *The Negro in the South* (Philadelphia: George W. Jacobs, 1907), 180.

10. Smith, "Ugly Legacy."

11. Stewart E. Tolnay and E. M. Beck, *Festival of Violence: An Analysis of Southern Lynchings* (Champaign: University of Illinois Press, 1995), 26. *Intelligencer*, quoted in Tolnay and Beck.

12. Ayers, *Vengeance*, 238.

13. Ibid., 238–240.

14. Ibid., 240. Ayers draws on Kai T. Erikson, *Wayward Puritans: A Study in the Sociology of Deviance* (New York: John Wiley and Sons, 1966), and John Demos, *Entertaining Satan: Witchcraft and the Study of Early New England* (New York: Oxford University Press, 1982).

15. See, e.g., Paul S. Boyer and Stephen Nisserbaum, *Salem Possessed: The Social Origins of Witchcraft* (Cambridge: Harvard University Press, 1974), 101–102; Ayers, *Vengeance*, 241.

16. Ayers, *Vengeance*, 243.

17. See, e.g., Phyllis Whitman Hunter, *Purchasing Identity in the Atlantic World: Massachusetts Merchants, 1670–1780* (Ithaca: Cornell University Press, 2001), 69.

18. Ayers, *Vengeance*, 262, 255.

19. Rothman, *Conscience*, 18–19; "Investigation of the Lansing, Kansas, Penitentiary," January 7, 1909, manuscript in Oklahoma State Archives, Oklahoma City, 40, 60, quoted in Rothman, 20–21. To an extent, my own understanding of Progressive prison reform derives from Rothman's. But writing more

than thirty-five years after Rothman, my understanding of the possibilities of science-supported rehabilitation in punishment is more optimistic than his.

20. Rothman, *Conscience*, 3–5, 17, 44–46. See also Blomberg and Lucken, *American Penology*, 63, 74.

21. Blomberg and Lucken, *American Penology*, 63.

22. Jonathan Simon, *Poor Discipline: Parole and the Social Control of the Underclass, 1890–1900* (Chicago: University of Chicago Press, 1993), 4. David Garland (*Punishment in Modern Society*) and David Rothman (*Conscience*) also make this argument.

23. Blomberg and Lucken, *American Penology*, 63.

24. Rothman, *Conscience*, 5. Blomberg and Lucken, *American Penology*, 68–70.

25. Rothman, *Conscience*, 44–45, 69–72.

26. L. Frank Baum, *The Patchwork Girl of Oz* (New York: Harper Collins, 1995), 195.

27. Ibid., 196–197.

28. Ibid., 197.

29. Ibid., 197, 200.

30. Ibid., 200.

31. Ibid.

32. Ibid.

33. Ibid.

34. The reformatories often housed men ages sixteen to twenty-six and called themselves "colleges." See Blomberg and Lucken, *American Penology*, 71.

35. Linda Wheeler, "Some Want to See Parts of Closing Prison Preserved as Historic Site," Associated Press, October 20, 1999.

36. William H. Taft, first annual message, December 7, 1909, electronic copy, American Presidency Project, University of California, Santa Barbara, http://www.presidency.ucsb.edu/ws/index.php?pid=29550 (accessed September 28, 2007).

37. Wheeler, "Some Want to See Parts of Closing Prison Preserved as Historic Site"; see the Fairfax County Web document on the prison, http://www.fairfaxcounty.gov/dpz/laurelhill/history/prison.pdf (accessed January 18, 2008).

38. Rothman, *Conscience*, 46.

39. See Garland, *Culture of Control*, 55–57. Edgardo Rotman, "The Failure of Reform: United States, 1865–1965," in *The Oxford History of the Prison: The Practice of Punishment in Western Society*, ed. Norval Morris and David J. Rothman (New York: Oxford University Press); Yale Kamisar, "Hard Time," *New York Times*, February 11, 1996.

40. Garland, *Culture of Control*, 8, 15.

41. Leon D. Whipple, *Story of Civil Liberty in the United States* (New York: Vanguard, 1927), 236. Quoted in Walter Wilson, *Forced Labor in the United States* (New York: International, 1933), 59–60.

42. Mabel A. Elliott, *Coercion in Penal Treatment: Past and Present*, ser. 2, no. 5 (Ithaca: Pacifist Research Bureau, 1947), 38, 41.

43. Wilson, *Forced Labor,* 73–74.
44. Ibid., 68–69.
45. Elliott, *Coercion,* 41.
46. Lichtenstein, *Twice the Work,* 16.
47. Ibid., xvi, 16.
48. Wilson, *Forced Labor,* 34–35.
49. See Lichtenstein, *Twice the Work,* 18, 35.
50. Ibid., 26.
51. Ibid., 51.
52. Georgia General Assembly, *Proceedings of the Joint Committee Appointed to Investigate the Condition of the Georgia Penitentiary* (1870; repr. New York: Arno, 1974), 141–142. Lichtenstein, *Twice the Work,* 53–54.
53. Wilson, *Forced Labor,* 71. See also Lichtenstein, *Twice the Work,* 182–183.
54. Wilson, *Forced Labor,* 71.
55. Lichtenstein, *Twice the Work,* 182–183.
56. Wilson, *Forced Labor,* 55–56.
57. John L. Spivak, *Georgia Nigger* (Georgia: Patterson Smith, 1969; orig. pub. New York: Brewer, Warren and Putnam, 1932), 201.
58. Ibid., 237.
59. Ibid., 209.

CHAPTER 6. THE DEVILISH GENERATION

1. William Peter Blatty, *The Exorcist* (New York: Harper and Row, 1971), 338.
2. Ibid., 1.
3. Ibid., 194.
4. Jenkins, *Decade of Nightmares,* 4.
5. Ibid., 10–12. See also Piele, "Neither Corporal Punishment Cruel nor Due Process Due."
6. Jenkins, *Decade of Nightmares,* 6, 11, 18–19, 194.
7. "The Graduate 1968: Can You Trust Anyone under 30?" "The Cynical Idealists of '68," *Time,* June 7, 1968, p. 78, quoted in *The Disobedient Generation: Social Theorists in the Sixties,* ed. Alan Sica and Stephen Turner (Chicago: University of Chicago Press, 2005), 4.
8. "The Youth Crime Plague," *Time,* July 11, 1977, p. 25.
9. Jerrold K. Footlick with Mary Lord, "The Criminal Mind," *Newsweek,* February 27, 1978, p. 91.
10. Jenkins, *Decade of Nightmares,* 18, 194.
11. Nicholas Cavendish, *The Powers of Evil* (New York: G. P. Putnam's Sons, 1975), viii, 12, 3–4, 41.
12. See Jenkins, *Decade of Nightmares,* 83–84.
13. Ibid. See also Piele, "Neither Corporal Punishment Cruel nor Due Process Due," and Bourke, *Fear,* 329.
14. Jenkins, *Decade of Nightmares,* 146–147.
15. Ira Levin, *Rosemary's Baby* (New York: Signet, 1997; orig. pub. 1967), 44–45.

16. Ibid., 45.
17. Ibid., 76, 81.
18. Ibid., 297.
19. Blatty, *Exorcist*, 99.
20. Ibid., 199.
21. Peter Traverse and Stephanie Reiff, *The Story Behind The Exorcist* (New York: Crown, 1974), 167; Jon Landau, "The Devil in Mr. Friedkin," *Rolling Stone*, February 1974, p. 64, quoted in Traverse and Reiff, *Story Behind The Exorcist*, 158.
22. Colin L. Westerbeck Jr., "The Banality of Good," *Commonweal*, 1974, quoted in Traverse and Reiff, *Story Behind The Exorcist*, 161.
23. Traverse and Reiff, *Story Behind The Exorcist*, 171.
24. Stephen King, *Carrie* (New York: Pocket/Simon and Schuster, 1974), 102.
25. Ibid., 13.
26. Ibid., 58.
27. Ibid., 212, 214.
28. Arthur Lyons, *The Second Coming* (New York: Dodd, Mead, 1970), 114.
29. Ibid., 113.
30. Ibid., 12.
31. Pope Paul VI, "Confronting the Devil's Power," public address, November 15, 1972.
32. Ibid.
33. Jenkins associates this book with the 1970s rise in interest in evil and the supernatural, *Decade of Nightmares*, 84.
34. Billy Graham, *Angels: God's Secret Agents* (New York: Doubleday, 1975), 5.
35. Ibid., 5–6.
36. Ibid., 7–8.
37. Jenkins, *Decade of Nightmares*, 138–140, 236–242.
38. Ibid., 18–19.
39. McGirr, *Suburban Warriors*, 4.
40. Ibid., 4, 225–226.
41. Ibid., 241.
42. Ibid., 240–241.
43. Ibid., 243–245, 246.
44. Ibid., 247, 257.
45. Norman Mailer, *The Executioner's Song* (Boston: Little, Brown, 1979), 106.
46. Ibid., 305.
47. Ibid., 473. Cited in Jenkins, *Decade of Nightmares*, 140.
48. Ibid., 613.
49. Ibid., 494.
50. Ibid., 304.
51. "The American Underclass," *Time*, August 29, 1977, pp. 14, 15, quoted in *The "Underclass" Debate: Views from History*, ed. Michael B. Katz (Princeton: Princeton University Press, 1993).

52. "The Youth Crime Plague," *Time*, July 11, 1977, p. 25.

53. See "The American Underclass," *Time*, August 29, 1977, pp. 14, 15; Katz, *"Underclass" Debate*, 4–21, 5.

54. William Julius Wilson, *The Declining Significance of Race: Blacks and Changing American Institutions* (Chicago: University of Chicago Press, 1978), 1–2.

55. Ibid., 89, 92.

56. Ibid., 92.

57. William Julius Wilson, *The Truly Disadvantaged: The Inner City, the Underclass, and Public Policy* (Chicago: University of Chicago Press, 1987), 46.

58. Thomas J. Sugrue, *The Origins of the Urban Crisis* (Princeton: Princeton University Press, 1996), 5.

59. Ibid., 8.

60. Sugrue, *Origins*, 261; "Mayor's Committee—Community Action for Detroit Youth Report," chap. 2: "Target Area Youth: Their Life Style," in Detroit NAACP, 1963, pt. 1, box 23.

61. "Plight of Black Men," *The NewsHour with Jim Lehrer*, March 29, 2006, electronic version, http://www.pbs.org/newshour/bb/economy/jan-june06/blackmen_3-29.html (accessed September 21, 2007).

62. Bruce Western, *Punishment and Inequality in America* (New York: Russell Sage Foundation Publications, 2006).

63. Kevin M. Kruse and Thomas J. Sugrue, "Introduction: The New Suburban History," in *The New Suburban History*, ed. Kevin M. Kruse and Thomas J. Sugrue (Chicago: University of Chicago Press, 2006), 1.

64. Ibid., 1–2.

65. Kruse and Sugrue, *New Suburban History*, 6. David M. P. Freund, "Marketing the Free Market: State Intervention and the Politics of Prosperity in Metropolitan America," in Kruse and Sugrue, *New Suburban History*, 12.

66. Michael B. Katz, "The Urban Underclass as Metaphor of Social Transformation," in *The "Underclass" Debate: Views from History*, ed. Michael B. Katz (Princeton: Princeton University Press, 1993), 6–7.

67. Michael B. Katz, *Poverty and Policy in American History* (New York: Academic Press, 1983), 134.

68. Ibid., 134–135.

69. Ibid., 155–156.

70. Tara-Jen Ambrosio and Vincent Schiraldi, "From Classrooms to Cell Blocks: A National Perspective," report, Justice Policy Institute, Washington, DC, February 1997. See also Roberto Suro, "More Is Spent on New Prisons Than Colleges," *Washington Post*, February 24, 1997, p. A12.

71. Jenkins, *Decade of Nightmares*, 11, 236–242.

72. Mike Gray, *Drug Crazy* (New York: Random House, 1998), 94.

73. Richard M. Nixon, message to Congress, June 17, 1971. Gray, *Drug Crazy*, 95.

74. Gray, *Drug Crazy*, 56.

75. David F. Musto, *The American Disease: Origins of Narcotic Control*, 3d ed. (Oxford: Oxford University Press, 1999), 148. Quoted in Gray, *Drug Crazy*, 56–58.

76. Gray, *Drug Crazy,* 58, 57, 60.

77. George H. W. Bush, address before a joint session of Congress, February 9, 1989.

78. Marc Mauer and Ryan S. King, *A Twenty-five-Year Quagmire: The War on Drugs and Its Impact on American Society* (Washington, DC: Sentencing Project, 2007), 3.

79. Max Weber, *The Protestant Ethic and the Spirit of Capitalism* (New York: Routledge, 1995), 163.

80. Anthony Giddens, introduction to Weber, *Protestant Ethic,* xxvi.

CHAPTER 7. FLOGGING FOR JESUS

1. Edwards phrase quoted in Arthur W. Calhoun, *A Social History of the American Family,* vol. 1 (Cleveland: Arthur C. Clarke, 1917), 108.

2. Jonathan Edwards, "Thoughts on the Revival of Religion in New England, 1740," in *Works,* 4 vols. (New York: Robert Carter and Brothers, 1881), 3:340.

3. See, e.g., Newton Edwards and Herman G. Richey, *The School in the American Social Order,* 2d ed. (Boston: Houghton Mifflin, 1963), 56–57.

4. Massachusetts Public Law of 1647. Nathaniel Shurtleff, *Records of the Governor and Company of the Massachusetts Bay* (Boston: W. White, 1853), vol. 2, p. 203.

5. Quoted in Calhoun, *Social History,* 112.

6. George M. Marsden, *Jonathan Edwards: A Life* (New Haven: Yale University Press, 2003), 26.

7. Ibid., 5.

8. Ibid., 20.

9. Philip Greven, *Spare the Child: The Religious Roots of Punishment and the Psychological Impact of Abuse* (New York: Alfred A. Knopf, 1991), 20–21; Philip Greven, *Child-Rearing Concepts* (Itasca, IL: F. E. Peacock, 1973), 77–78.

10. Carol F. Karlsen and Laurie Crumpacker, eds. *The Journal of Esther Burr, 1754–1757* (New Haven: Yale University Press, 1984), 95. Quoted in Greven, *Spare the Child,* 21–22. Also see Philip Greven, *The Protestant Temperament: Patterns of Child-Rearing, Religious Experience, and the Self in Early America* (New York: Alfred A. Knopf, 1977), 35–36.

11. Greven, *Spare the Child,* 21.

12. Dorchester Town Records, January 14, 1645, quoted in *Fourth Report of the Record Commissioners of the City of Boston* (1883), vol. 41, p. 56. Cited in Piele, "Neither Corporal Punishment Cruel," 95.

13. Edwards and Richey, *School,* 67.

14. Quoted in Walter Herbert Small, *American Education: Its Men, Ideas, and Institutions* (New York: Arno, 1969), 384.

15. Ibid., 385–386.

16. Ibid., 385.

17. Dale Roylance, "Of Sin and Salvation: Early American Children's Books at Princeton," *Princeton University Library Chronicle* 59, no. 2 (Winter 1998): 211. Benjamin Keach, "War with the Devil," quoted in Roylance, 213.

18. James Janeway and Cotton Mather, *A Token for Children* (Orlando: Soli Deo Gloria, 1994); James Janeway, *A Token for Children*, quoted in Sanford Fleming, *Children and Puritanism* (New Haven: Yale University Press, 1933), 66.

19. See the Soli Deo Gloria version of this book published in 1994; http://www .graceandtruthbooks.com/listdetails .asp?ID=1056andRP=/puritans/ (accessed September 27, 2007).

20. Jessica McBride, "Mother Defends 'Shaming' at Church: DA's Office Reviewing Case of Girl Disciplined by Parents Who Struck Her," *Milwaukee Journal Sentinel*, July 15, 1998.

21. Jesse Garza, "DA's Office Looking into Whether Discipline of Girl at Church Went Too Far," *Milwaukee Journal Sentinel*, July 14, 1998.

22. Greven, *Spare the Child;* Bruce A. Ray, *Withhold Not Correction* (Phillipsburg, NJ: P and R Publishing, 1978), 15.

23. See http://www.family.org/docstudy/aboutdrdobson.cfm for information on Dobson's books. The Pearls' first book, *To Train Up a Child*, is cited as a best seller in the *Charlotte News Observer*, March 16, 2006. The Christian Web site "Homeschool Information," http://homeschoolinformation.com/child-training.htm, mentions that Fugate's book is a "Christian best seller," having sold more than 200,000 copies. The Barna Group, "Half of All Americans Read Christian Books and One-third Buy Them" (Ventura, CA: Barna Group, January 27, 2003).

24. Francine Vida, "Support for Spanking: Most Americans Think Corporal Punishment Is OK," analysis by Julie Crandall, ABCNEWS.com, November 8, 2002 (accessed October 4, 2007). At this writing, corporal punishment of schoolchildren remains legal in some states. "Corporal Punishment in U.S. Public Schools, 1999–2000 School Year: Data Released February 2003," Center for Effective Discipline, available at http://www.stophitting.com/dis atschool/facts.php#Punishment%20in%20U.S.%20Public (accessed September 30, 2007). Murray A. Straus and Anita K. Mathur, "Social Change and Trends in Approval of Corporal Punishment by Parents from 1968 to 1994," in *Violence against Children*, ed. D. Frehsee, W. Horn, and K. Bussman (New York: Walter de Gruyter, 1996), 91–105.

25. Benjamin Spock, *The Commonsense Book of Baby and Care* (New York: Duell, Sloan, and Pearce, 1946), 271.

26. Benjamin Spock and Michael B. Rothenberg, *Baby and Child Care* (New York: Pocket Books, 1985), 408.

27. "Remembering Dr. Spock," *The NewsHour with Jim Lehrer*, March 16, 1998.

28. See, e.g., Don Boys, *Is God a Right-Winger?* (Indianapolis: Goodhope, 1984), 30n23.

29. www.focusonthefamily.com/aboutus/A000000531.cfm; http://www.focu sonthefamily.com/press/focusvoices/; http://www.focusonthefamily.com/ press/focusvoices/ (accessed September 6, 2007).

30. James Dobson, *The New Dare to Discipline* (Wheaton IL: Tyndale House,

1992), 20–21, 63, 65. James Dobson, *The New Hide or Seek* (Grand Rapids: Fleming H. Revell, 1974, 1979, 2001), 47.

31. Lisa Whelchel, *Creative Correction: Extraordinary Ideas for Everyday Discipline* (Wheaton, IL: Tyndale House, 2000), 21.

32. Ibid., xiv.

33. Ted Tripp, *Shepherding a Child's Heart* (Wapwallopen, PA: Shepherd, 1995), 106.

34. Ray, *Withhold Not Correction*, 81.

35. Phillip Lancaster, "The Loving Art of Spanking," *Home School Digest: The Quarterly Journal for Family Discipleship* 14, no. 3 (2003): 64.

36. Ibid., 63.

37. Michael and Debi Pearl, *No Greater Joy*, vol. 2 (Pleasantville, TN: No Greater Joy Ministries, 1999), 52.

38. Tripp, *Shepherding*, 156.

39. J. Richard Fugate, *What the Bible Says about Child Training* (Tempe, AZ: Aletheia, 1980), 144. Quoted in Greven, *Spare the Child*, 79.

40. Jonathan Lindvall, "Chastening Children," *Home School Digest: The Quarterly Journal for Family Discipleship* 9, no. 1 (1999): 32.

41. James Dobson, *The Strong-Willed Child* (Wheaton, IL: Tyndale House, 1978, 1984), 17; Roy Lessin, *Spanking: A Loving Discipline* (Minneapolis: Bethany House, 1975, 2002), 47; Lancaster, "Loving Art of Spanking," 62.

42. Whelchel, *Creative Correction*, 163; Pearl and Pearl, *No Greater Joy*, 32.

43. Dobson, *Strong-Willed Child*, 12–14.

44. Dobson, *Dare to Discipline*.

45. Interview with Joey Salvati, 2006.

46. Ibid.

47. Ibid.

48. Ibid.

49. Ibid.

50. Michael Aubele, "Paddle-maker Sees Himself on Mission," *Pittsburgh Tribune-Review*, December 16, 2002. Interview with Sue Lawrence, 2006.

51. Greven, *Spare the Child*, 79–81.

52. Mandy Locke, "Dead Child's Mom Sought Discipline Tips; Lynn Paddock Ordered Books by a Minister and His Wife That Recommended Using Pipe to Spank Kids," *Charlotte News Observer*, March 16, 2006.

53. Claire Osborn, "Hurt Boy Recounts His Brutal Lashing; Boy Said Pastor Struck Him 100 Times, Told His Stepdad to Finish Job," *Austin American-Statesman*, December 4, 2003; cross examination in the case.

54. Claire Osborn, "Fate of Pastor, Twin Is Uncertain; Jury Retires for the Night without Setting Sentences after Teen Says That He, Too, Had Been Mistreated," *Austin American-Statesman*, December 12, 2003.

55. *CNN Connie Chung Tonight*, CNN, July 10, 2002.

56. Affidavit for Warrant of Arrest and Detention of Joshua William Thompson,

Municipal Court Austin, Texas, July 8, 2002; "Good Book Lesson Gone Bad," CBS, July 10, 2002.

57. Affidavit for Warrant of Arrest and Detention of Joshua William Thompson.

58. *State of Texas vs. Joshua William Thompson and Caleb Thompson*, No. 9-03-4175 and 9-03-4174, 403rd District Court of Travis County, Texas, State's Notice of Intent to Introduce Outcry Statement, September 19, 2003; Osborn, "Fate of Pastor, Twin Is Uncertain."

59. Jim Vertuno, "Pastor Says He Hit Boy, Denies It Was 100 Times," Associated Press State and Local Wire, December 9, 2003; Osborn, "Hurt Boy Recounts His Brutal Lashing."

60. *State of Texas vs. Joshua William Thompson*, Trial Court Cause No. 9-03-4175, 403rd District Court of Travis County, Texas, Reporter's Record, vol. 9, cross examination, December 9, 2003, 119–129.

61. Jim Vertuno, "Pastor, Twin Get 26 Years in Beating Case," Associated Press, December 12, 2003.

62. "Central Texas Church Settles Lawsuit over Boy's Beating," Associated Press State and Local Wire, May 6, 2004.

63. Josh Mankiewicz, "Spare the Rod: Welfare Services Investigate the House of Prayer Church in Georgia for Corporal Punishment," *Dateline NBC*, December 14, 2001.

64. Barnini Chakraborty, "Trial for Alleged Church Beatings," Associated Press, October 8, 2002; Steve Visser and Jill Young Miller, "Child Discipline at Root of Church Trial," *Atlanta Journal-Constitution*, October 9, 2002.

65. *State of Georgia vs. Arthur Allen Jr. et al.*, Criminal Action File No. 2002SC00433, Charge: Cruelty to Children, in the Superior Court of Fulton County, State of Georgia, partial transcript of jury trial proceedings before the Honorable T. Jackson Bedford Jr., Judge, Atlanta Judicial Circuit, October 8, 2002, 6.

66. Ibid., 10–11.

67. *State of Georgia vs. Arthur Allen Jr. et al.*, Charge: Cruelty to Children, in the Superior Court of Fulton County, State of Georgia, Clerk's No. 2002SC00433, indictment, January 18, 2002.

68. "House of Prayer Pastor Expected to Appear in Court," Associated Press State and Local Wire, August 25, 2003.

69. Mankiewicz, "Spare the Rod"; Daniel Yee, "Jury Receives House of Prayer Church Beating Case," Associated Press State and Local Wire, October 14, 2002.

70. Tony Rizzo, "Trial Ordered in Death of Boy, 9; Parents, Baby Sitter Face Murder Charges," *Kansas City Star*, April 18, 2003.

71. "Church Members Support Parents Charged in Child's Death," Associated Press State and Local Wire, January 2, 2003.

72. Ibid.

73. Tony Rizzo, "Father Says Women Disciplined Children," *Kansas City Star*,

September 25, 2003; "Judge Rules Donna Walker Can Be Extradited to Indiana," Associated Press State and Local Wire, September 24, 2003.

74. *State of Kansas vs. Christy Edgar, in the District Court of Johnson County, Kansas,* Criminal Department, No. 03CR0128, State's Response to Defendant's Motion for Severance, April 29, 2003, 1.

75. "Father, Baby Sitter Sentenced in Death of 9-Year-Old," Associated Press State and Local Wire, November 19, 2003; *State of Kansas vs. Christy Edgar, in the District Court of Johnson County, Kansas,* Criminal Department, No. 03CR0128, Kansas Sentencing Guidelines Journal Entry of Judgment.

76. "Father, Baby Sitter Sentenced in Death of 9-Year-Old," Associated Press.

77. "Church Member Sentenced to Probation in Abuse Case," Associated Press, February 7, 2004.

78. Murray A. Straus, *Beating the Devil Out of Them: Corporal Punishment in American Families* (New York: Lexington, 1994), 112.

79. Dobson, *Strong-Willed Child,* 171.

80. Ibid., 31, 34–35.

81. Fugate, *What the Bible Says,* 127, 121.

82. Ray, *Withhold Not Correction,* 24.

83. Beverly LaHaye, *How to Develop Your Child's Temperament* (Eugene, OR: Harvest House, 1977), 2.

84. Fugate, *What the Bible Says,* 149–150.

85. Ray, *Withhold Not Correction,* foreword.

86. *Presidential Biblical Scorecard* (Costa Mesa, CA: Biblical News Service, 1984), 14–15.

87. Ibid., 28.

88. Harold G. Grasmick, John K. Cochran, Robert Bursick Jr., M'Lou Kimpel, "Religion, Punitive Justice, and Support for the Death Penalty," *Justice Quarterly* 10, no. 2 (1993): 289.

89. Jerry Falwell, *Listen America!* (New York: Bantam, 1981), 6, 60; Jerry Falwell, "Where the Battle Rages," sermon, November 17, 1996.

90. Jerry Falwell, "The Spiritual Renaissance in America," sermon, 1986.

91. Fugate, *What the Bible Says,* back cover.

92. Falwell, *Listen America!* 91.

93. Jerry Falwell, "The Battle for the Bible," sermon, 1996. Available on the Web site of Thomas Road Baptist Church, http://trbc.org/new/sermons.php?url=961124.html (accessed January 18, 2008).

94. "Robertson Advocates Stoning," *Freedom Writer,* Institute for First Amendment Studies, July–August 1997, 15.

95. Ad for Boys, *Is God a Right-Winger? Trumpet,* newsletter of the American Coalition of Unregistered Churches.

96. Boys, *Is God a Right-Winger?* 34.

97. Ibid., 25–26, 62–63.

98. Ibid., 42.

99. Ibid., 62.

100. Ibid., 5.

101. Alice Miller, *For Your Own Good: Hidden Cruelty in Child-Rearing and the Roots of Violence*, trans. Hidegarde and Hunter Hannum (New York: Farrar, Straus, and Giroux, 1983). Greven (in *Spare the Child*) and Milburn and Conrad also discuss Miller's work.

102. Miller, *For Your Own Good*, 43, 63–83.

103. Michael A. Milburn and Sheree D. Conrad, *The Politics of Denial* (Cambridge: MIT Press, 1996), 54.

104. Ibid., 62.

105. Ibid., 119–120.

106. Harold G. Grasmick, Carolyn Stout Morgan, and Mary Baldwin Kennedy, "Support for Corporal Punishment in Schools: A Comparison of the Effects of Socioeconomic Status and Religion," *Social Science Quarterly* 73, no. 1 (March 1992): 185.

107. Harold G. Grasmick, Elizabeth Davenport, Mitchell B. Chamlin, and Robert J. Bursick, Jr., "Protestant Fundamentalism and the Retributive Doctrine of Punishment," *Criminology* 30, no. 1 (1992): 38–39, 40.

108. Larry B. Stammer, "The Rev. Rousas John Rushdoony; Advocated Rule by Biblical Law," *Los Angeles Times*, March 3, 2001; Peter J. Leithart, "Old Geneva and the New World: The Reverend Rousas J. Rushdoony, 1916–2001," *Weekly Standard*, March 26, 2001.

109. Gary North, "R. J. Rushdoony, R.I.P.," February 10, 2001, available at LewRockwell.com.

110. Rousas John Rushdoony, *Institutes of Biblical Law* (Philipsburg, NJ: P and R Publishing, 1973), 1.

111. Ibid., 4.

112. Jeff Ziegler, "Puritan Storm Rising," *Puritan Storm*, vol. 1, no. 1, available at http://forerunner.com/puritan/puritan.html.

113. Quoted in Frederick Clarkson, "Christian Reconstructionism: Theocratic Dominionism Gains Influence," *Public Eye*, March–June 1994. Available at http://www.publiceye.org/magazine/v08n1/chrisre2.html (accessed January 18, 2008).

114. Jay Rogers, "An Interview with George Grant." Available at http://forerunner.com/revolution/grant.html (accessed January 18, 2008).

115. Walter Olson, "Invitation to a Stoning: Getting Cozy with Theocrats," *Reason*, November 1998. Available at http://www.reason.com/news/show/30789.html (accessed October 5, 2007).

116. William Einwechter, "Stoning Disobedient Children?" *Christian Statesman*, electronic edition, January–February 2003 (originally appeared in the January 1999 edition of the *Chalcedon Report*).

117. Gary DeMar and Skipp Porteous, interview on *Sound Off*, Superstation WSB, Atlanta, printed in *The Best of the Freedom Writer*, Institute for First Amendment Studies, November 1995, 8–10.

118. Rushdoony, *Institutes*, 450–511.

119. Greg L. Bahnsen, *By This Standard: The Authority of God's Law Today* (Tyler, TX: Institute for Christian Economics, 1985), 276.

120. Frederick Clarkson, *Eternal Hostility: The Struggle between Theocracy and Democracy* (Monroe, ME: Common Courage, 1997), 62.

121. Eric Holmberg, "An Interview with Andrew Sandlin," transcribed and edited by Jay Rogers, available at http://forerunner.com/revolution/as.html (accessed January 18, 2008).

122. Lynn Smith, "Bowed, but Unbroken?" *Los Angeles Times*, March 22, 1993.

123. Quoted in Clarkson, *Eternal Hostility*, 82.

124. Stephen J. Hedges, David Bowermaster, and Susan Headden, "Abortion: Who's Behind the Violence?" *U.S. News and World Report*, November 14, 1994.

125. Hedges et al., "Abortion."

126. Joe Frolik, "Doctor's Death Hurts Anti-Abortion Groups," *Cleveland Plain Dealer*, March 13, 1993.

127. By Dan Barry, "Icon for Abortion Protesters Is Looking for a Second Act," *New York Times*, July 20, 2001.

128. Gary North, *Lonegunners for Jesus: Letters to Paul Hill* (Tyler, TX: Institute for Christian Economics), 4.

129. "The Winner's Circle: Tom Coburn, a Radical Republican Who Favors the Death Penalty for Abortionists Pulls Off a Surprise Win in Oklahoma," *People*, November 15, 2004, p. 56; Ron Jenkins, "Coburn Different Kind of Political Cat," Associated Press, July 9, 2004.

CHAPTER 8. PAIN BECOMES VALUABLE AGAIN

1. Jenkins, *Decade of Nightmares*, 138.

2. Robert E. Burns, *I Am a Fugitive from a Georgia Chain Gang* (Athens, GA: University of Georgia, 1997), xvii.

3. Howard G. Green, *I Am a Fugitive from a Chain Gang*, ed. John E. O'Connor (Madison: University of Wisconsin Press, 1981), 14.

4. Robert E. Burns, *I Am a Fugitive from a Georgia Chain Gang* (New York: Vanguard, 1932), 56, 57.

5. John E. O'Connor, "Introduction," in Green, *Fugitive*, ed. O'Connor.

6. Book cited and summarized in Garland, *Culture of Control*, 55–57.

7. Ibid., 69–71.

8. *Struggle for Justice: A Report on Crime and Punishment in America Prepared for the American Friends Service Committee* (New York: Hill and Wang, 1971), vi.

9. Ibid., v, vii. Garland also discusses this document in *Culture of Control*.

10. Ibid., 33, 85.

11. Ibid., 23.

12. Jessica Mitford, *Kind and Unusual Punishment: The Prison Business* (New York: Vintage, 1974; orig. pub. New York: Alfred A. Knopf, 1973), 7, 298.

13. Robert Martinson, "What Works—Questions and Answers about Prison Reform," *Public Interest* 35 (Spring 1974): 25.

14. Robert Martinson, "New Findings, New Views: A Note of Caution Regarding Sentencing Reform," *Hofstra Law Review* 7 (Winter 1979): 244, 252.

15. Garland, *Culture of Control*, 8–9, 59–61; James Q. Wilson, *Thinking about Crime* (New York: Basic Books, 1975), 209. Cited in Jenkins, *Decade of Nightmares*, 134.

16. Ronald Reagan, quoted in K. Beckett, *Making Crime Pay* (New York: Oxford University Press, 1997), 47. Cited in Garland, *Culture of Control*, 136. Garland notes the description's kinship to horror movie images.

17. James Q. Wilson, "Crime and Public Policy," in *Crime*, ed. James Q. Wilson and J. Petersilia (San Francisco: Institute of Contemporary Studies, 1995), 492. Cited in Garland, *Culture of Control*, 256.

18. "Now for the Bad News: A Teenage Time Bomb," *Time*, January 15, 1996. Cited in Robin Templeton, "Superscapegoating Teen 'Superpredators' Hype Set Stage for Draconian Legislation," *Extra!* January/February 1998.

19. Peter Annin, " 'Superpredators' Arrive," *Newsweek*, January 22, 1996, p. 57.

20. L. Dorfman, K. Woodruff, V. Chavez, and L. Wallack, "Youth and Violence on Local Television News in California," *American Journal of Public Health* 87, no. 8 (August 1997):1311–1316. Cited in Templeton, "Superscapegoating."

21. Vincent Schiraldi and Mark Kappelhoff, "Where Have the 'Superpredators' Gone?" Salon.com, May 13, 1997.

22. Garland, *Culture of Control*, 136.

23. U.S. Department of Justice, Bureau of Justice Statistics, "1994: U.S. Department of Justice, the Nation's Prison Population Grew Almost 9 Percent Last Year," Wednesday, August 9, 1995.

24. U.S. Department of Justice, Bureau of Justice Statistics Web page: http://www.ojp.usdoj.gov/bjs/prisons.htm; Tonry, *Thinking about Crime*, 3.

25. Tonry, *Thinking about Crime*, 22.

26. Ibid., 3–4.

27. Ibid., 5.

28. Ilyana Kuziemko and Steven D. Levitt, "An Empirical Analysis of Imprisoning Drug Offenders," National Bureau of Economic Research Working Paper No. 8489, September 2001, 1; Tonry, *Thinking about Crime*, 15, 81, 134.

29. Gottschalk, *Prison and the Gallows*, 6.

30. Ibid., 7.

31. Ibid., 8.

32. Ibid., 11.

33. Ibid., 133.

34. Ibid., 152.

35. Lazare, "Stars and Bars."

36. Garland, *Culture of Control*, 22–26.

37. Ibid., 48.

38. Ibid., 101.

39. Ibid., 101–102.

40. Simon, *Governing through Crime*, 4–6.

41. Ibid., 4, 5.

42. Ibid., 173, 207.

43. Ibid., 6, 7, 8–9.

44. Ibid., 9–10.

45. Ibid., 6.

46. Ibid., 6, 4.

47. Graeme Newman, "Book Review of *Conscience and Convenience: The Asylum and Its Alternatives in Progressive America,* David J. Rothman," *Crime and Delinquency* 27 (July 1981): 426.

48. Graeme Newman, *Just and Painful* (New York: Free Press, 1985; electronic version, Guilderland, NY: Harrow and Heston, 1995), available at http://www.albany.edu/grn92/jp00.html (accessed September 28, 2007).

49. See Garland, *Punishment and Modern Society,* 207.

CHAPTER 9. POP CULTURE AND THE CRIMINAL ELEMENT

1. Cotton Mather, *Diary of Cotton Mather, 1681–1708* (Boston: Plimpton Press, 1911), 276, 278–279.

2. Mather, *Diary,* 279, quoted in Vernon L. Parrington, *Main Currents in American Thought, 1620–1800* (New York: Harcourt Brace, 1927), 110. "Climbing over Pues and Heads" mentioned in Cohen, *Pillars of Salt,* 3.

3. Parrington, *Main Currents,* 110.

4. Mather, *Diary,* 279–280; quoted in Parrington, *Main Currents,* 110.

5. Cohen, *Pillars of Salt,* x.

6. Ibid., ix.

7. Ibid., 252.

8. Foucault, *Discipline and Punish,* 10.

9. Tom Gunning, "The Cinema of Attractions: Early Film, Its Spectator, and the Avant-Garde," *Wide Angle* 3 (1986): 56–62. Cited in Henry Jenkins, *The Wow Climax: Tracing the Emotional Impact of Popular Culture* (New York: New York University Press, 2007), 7.

10. "Top 10 Broadcast TV Programs for the Week of July 16, 2007," Nielsen Media Research, http://www.nielsenmedia.com (accessed July 27, 2007).

11. Jenkins, *Wow Climax,* 4.

12. "Astronaut's Attorney: She Did NOT Wear Diapers," Associated Press, June 29, 2007.

13. Sergei Eisenstein, "Montage of Attractions," in *The Eisenstein Reader,* ed. Richard Taylor (London: British Film Institute, 1998), 30. Jenkins, *Wow Climax,* 6.

14. Mark Seltzer, *True Crime: Observations on Violence and Modernity* (New York: Routledge, 2007), 2.

15. Ibid., 10.

16. Cohen, *Pillars of Salt,* x.

17. Steven D. Stark, *Glued to the Set* (New York: Free Press, 1997), 33, 245. *Entertaining Crime: Television Reality Programs,* ed. Mark Fishman and Gray Caven-

der (New York: Aldine de Gruyter, 1998), 9. The *Dragnet* radio program is available online at http://www.archive.org/details/Dragnet_OTR (accessed June 18, 2008).

18. Stark, *Glued to the Set*, 34–35.

19. "Jack, Be Nimble!" *Time*, March 15, 1954, online edition (accessed June 9, 2008). Cited in Stark, *Glued to the Set*, 34.

20. Ibid., 32.

21. William Boddy, "Senator Dodd Goes to Hollywood: Investigative Video Violence," 162–184, in *The Revolution Wasn't Televised: Sixties Television and Social Conflict*, ed. Lynn Spiegel and Michael Curtin (New York: Routledge, 1997), 162, 176.

22. See Stark, *Glued to the Set*, 35–36, 237–242.

23. Dan Weikel, "The Times Poll: More in O.C. Now Rate Crime as No. 1 Concern," *Los Angeles Times*, August 28, 1994.

24. Quoted in Frutkin, "New Crime Hours Break In," 6.

25. Elijah Siegler, "God in the Box," 199–216, in *God in the Details: American Religion in Popular Culture*, ed. Eric Mazur (New York: Routledge, 2000), 205; Frank Rich, "The Greatest Dirty Joke Ever Told," *New York Times*, March 13, 2005.

26. Horace Newcomb and Paul M. Hirsch, "Television as Cultural Forum," 564, in *Television: The Critical View*, ed. Horace Newcomb (Oxford: Oxford University Press, 2006), 561–573.

27. Robert Abelman, *Reaching a Critical Mass: A Critical Analysis of Television Entertainment* (Mahwah, NJ: Lawrence Erlbaum Associates, 1998), 406.

28. Victor Witter Turner, *The Ritual Process: Structure and Anti-Structure* (New York: Aldine Transaction, 1995), 108–109.

29. "Interview with Cast and Creators of Hit Show '24,'" *Charlie Rose Show*, May 20, 2005.

30. Christian Toto, "'24': An Hour of Realism," *Washington Times*, April 29, 2005.

31. Abelman, *Critical Mass*, 419.

32. Ibid.

33. Karen Brandon, "After Hundreds of Arrests, John Walsh Still Feels Wanted," *Chicago Tribune*, December 31, 2001.

34. See W. J. Potter, "Perceived Reality in Television Effects Research," *Journal of Broadcasting and Electronic Media* 32, no. 1 (Winter 1988): 23–41.

35. Mary Beth Oliver and G. Blake Armstrong, "Predictors of Viewing and Enjoyment of Reality-Based and Fictional Crime Shows," *J and MC Quarterly* 72, no. 3 (1995): 559–570.

36. Kevin D. Thompson, "Arresting Television," *Palm Beach Post*, February 9, 2002, p. 1D.

37. Larry Bonko, "'Cops' Brings Viewers Something That's 'Real, Raw and Unvarnished,'" *Virginian-Pilot*, April 26, 2002.

38. Ibid.

39. Mike Mather, "Cops in Hampton Roads: Popular TV Show Is Hitting the Streets with Area Police, Capturing the Good, the Bad and the Ugly on Tape," *Virginian-Pilot*, July 25, 1998.

40. Pamela Donovan, "Armed with the Power of Television: Reality Crime Programming and the Reconstruction of Law and Order in the United States," in *Entertaining Crime*, ed. Mark Fishman and Gray Cavender (New York: Walter de Gruyter, 1998), 132.

41. Ibid., 87.

42. Brandon, "John Walsh." The Web site of the Outagamie County Sheriff's Department is available at http://www.co.outagamie.wi.us/sheriff/index.htm (accessed June 15, 2008).

43. David D. Perlmutter, *Policing the Media: Street Cops and Public Perceptions of Law Enforcement* (Thousand Oaks, CA: Sage, 2000), 115.

44. Ibid., 81.

45. Jay Whearley and Mark Melady, "The Drug Toll: WPD Vice Squad Has Been on a Roll," *Worcester (MA) Telegram and Gazette*, March 2, 2003.

46. Donovan, "Armed," 117.

47. Mary Beth Oliver, "Portrayals of Crime, Race, and Aggression in 'Reality-Based' Police Shows: A Content Analysis," *Journal of Broadcasting and Electronic Media* 38, no. 2 (Spring 1994).

48. Mary Beth Oliver and Blake Armstrong, "The Color of Crime: Perceptions of Caucasians' and African Americans' Involvement in Crime," in *Entertaining Crime*, ed. Fishman and Cavender, 30.

49. "Online Papers Modestly Boost Newspaper Readership," survey, the Pew Research Center for the People and the Press, July 30, 2006. Available at http://people-press.org/reports/display.php3?ReportID=282. Also see the center's study of the 2004 election: "Cable and Internet Loom Large in Fragmented Political News Universe," survey, the Pew Research Center for the People and the Press, January 11, 2004. Available at http://people-press.org/reports/display.php3?ReportID=200.

50. Project for Excellence in Journalism, "The State of the News Media: An Annual Report on American Journalism: Local TV Content Analysis, The Hook and Hold Approach," March 15, 2005. Online version available at http://www.journalism.org/node/732 (accessed June 8, 2008).

51. Ibid.

52. Howard Kurtz, "Murder! Mayhem! Ratings! Tabloid Sensationalism Is Thriving on TV News," *Washington Post*, July 4, 1993; cited in Stark, *Glued to the Set*, 177–178.

53. Stark, *Glued to the Set*, 177.

54. Ibid., 178.

55. Ibid.

56. Ibid., 179.

57. Center for Media and Public Affairs, report, *In the 1990s TV News Turns to Violence and Show Biz* (Washington, DC: Center for Media and Public Affairs,

1997), 1. Quoted in Rick Ruddell, *America Behind Bars* (El Paso, TX: LFB Scholarly Publications, 2004), 34.

58. George Gerbner, foreword to Mike Budd, Steve Craig, and Clay Steinman, *Consuming Environments: Television and Commercial Culture* (New Brunswick: Rutgers University Press, 1999), xiv.

59. Barry Glassner, *The Culture of Fear* (New York: Basic Books, 1999), xi, 23–49.

60. David Altheide, *Creating Fear: News and the Construction of Crisis* (Hawthorne, NY: Aldine de Gruyter, 2002), 38.

61. Ibid., 38, 65.

62. Ibid., 74.

63. Ibid., 89.

64. George Gerbner, "Global Media Mayhem," *Global Media Journal* 1, no. 1 (Fall 2002) (Purdue University Calumet), online edition, http://lass.calumet.purdue.edu/cca/gmj/fa02/gmj-fa02-gerbner.htm (accessed September 29, 2007).

65. Mary Beth Oliver and G. Blake Armstrong, "Predictors of Viewing and Enjoyment of Reality-Based and Fictional Crime Shows," *Journalism and Mass Communication Quarterly* 72, no. 3 (1995): 565.

CHAPTER 10. STUNNING TECHNOLOGY

1. Interview with Dennis Kaufman, president, Stun Tech, 1996. In 2004, the company became a subsidiary of Stinger Systems, which manufactures the Band-It Prisoner Transport of Courtroom Control System, an electronic restraint device that fastens around the leg or arm and can be set off from 175 feet away. "Report of Independent Registered Public Accounting Firm, S-1/A Sec Filing, Filed by Stinger Systems, Inc on 11/14/2005," http://sec.edgar-online.com/2005/11/14/0000950144-05-011816/section42.asp (accessed June 15, 2008); http://www.stingersystems.com/band-it.aspx (accessed June 15, 2008).

2. Interview with Dennis Kaufman, 1996; Arthur Santana, " 'Murder Inc.' Defendants Wore Stun Belts; Judge Permitted Marshals to Use Shock Devices for Additional Security at Trial," *Washington Post*, March 24, 2003.

3. Interview with Brian Wood, Amnesty International, 1996.

4. Electronic Defense Technology Web site, http://www.media22.com/site/products/react/index.htm (accessed September 29, 2007).

5. "Riot Shield's Use Halted after Death," *Austin American-Statesman*, December 3, 1995.

6. Interview with John McDermit, 1996.

7. Interview with Jimmy Wood, 1996.

8. Interview with Mark Goodson, 1996.

9. Interview with John McDermit, 1996.

10. Amnesty International, *United States of America—Use of Electro-Shock Stun Belts*, June 12, 1996.

11. Ibid.; interview with Alan Eisenberg, 1996; "Murder Trial," *Wisconsin State Journal,* June 11, 1994.

12. "Oswald Zapped," *Wisconsin State Journal,* May 9, 1995; interview with Alan Eisenberg, 1996.

13. Interviews with Dennis Kaufman and Jim Kroncke, 1996.

14. Laura Loh, "Appeals Court Upholds Ban on Using Stun Belts against Courtroom Defendants," City News Service, May 30, 2001.

15. Ibid.

16. Kenneth Ofgang, "Justices Strictly Limit Use of Stun Belts to Restrain Defendants," *Los Angeles Metropolitan News-Enterprise,* August 23, 2002.

17. Ibid.

18. Amnesty International, "United States of America—Cruelty in Control? The Stun Belt and Other Electro-Shock Equipment in Law Enforcement," June 8, 1999.

19. Interview with Jim Kroncke, 1996.

20. Interview with Dennis Kaufman, 1996.

21. M. N. Robinson, C. G. Brooks, and G. D. Renshaw, "Electric Shock Devices and Their Effects on the Human Body," *Medical Science and Law* 30, no. 4 (1990).

22. Interview with Dennis Kaufman, 1996; interview with Armond Start, 1996.

23. Interview with Armond Start, 1996; interview with Dennis Kaufman, 1996.

24. Interview with Chase Riveland, 1996.

25. Sabrina Eaton, "Rights Group Seeks Stun Belt Ban," *Plain Dealer,* June 13, 1996; Bradley S. Klapper, "U.S. Must Do More to Combat Sexual Violence in Its Prisons, U.N. Report Says," Associated Press, May 20, 2006.

26. Amnesty International, *Arming the Torturers: Electro-Shock Torture and the Spread of Stun Technology,* March 4, 1997, available at http://web.amnesty.org/library/Index/ENGACT400011997.

27. Ibid.

28. Ibid.

29. Interview with John McDermit, 1997.

30. Amnesty International, *Arming the Torturers.*

31. Interview with Dennis Kaufman, 1996.

32. Regarding the popularity of tasers, see, e.g., Alex Berenson, "As Police Use of Tasers Soars, Questions over Safety Emerge," *New York Times,* July 18, 2004; regarding use on elderly people, see, e.g., "Chicago Police Tasered 82-Year-Old Woman," Associated Press, November 6, 2007; regarding use on children as young as age one, see "Taser Use on 9-Year-Old Raises Questions," Associated Press, May 26, 2004, and "Taser Use on Teens," *San Jose Mercury News,* September 16, 2004; regarding use on epileptics, see, e.g., "Lakewood Settles Lawsuit over Taser Use on Epileptic for $90,000," Associated Press, January 21, 2008, and Jay Bookman, "Taser Death Review Was Long Overdue," *Atlanta Journal-Constitution,* August 4, 2005; regarding use on people

in diabetic shock, see, e.g., Kristen Kridel, "Sheriff Changes Stun Gun Rules," *Sarasota Herald-Tribune,* July 28, 2005; regarding use on FTAA protestors, see Gwen Shaffer, "Force Multiplier," *New Republic,* August 2, 2004; regarding use at the Fiesta Bowl, see Matthew D. Laplante, "Ute Fans Zapped by Tasers at Game," *Salt Lake Tribune,* January 5, 2005; regarding use in hospitals and psychiatric hospitals, see, e.g., John Curran, "Spate of Taser Incidents Renews Debate over Whether Police Are Too Reliant on the Devices," Associated Press, August 23, 2007; regarding use in schools, see Gigi Douban and Carol Robinson, "City Police May Wield Stun Guns in Schools," *Birmingham (AL) News,* September 30, 2004, and "Stun Guns Option for Birmingham Schools," Associated Press, September 30, 2004.

33. Amnesty International, *United States of America—Excessive and Lethal Force? Amnesty International's Concerns about Deaths and Ill-Treatment Involving Police Use of Tasers,* November 30, 2004, http://www2.taser.com/company/pages/factsheet.aspx (accessed October 7, 2007). www.taser.com (accessed February 2005). On tasers and Taser International, see also Anne-Marie Cusac, "The Trouble with Tasers," *Progressive,* April 2005. See http://www.taser.com/products/law/Pages/TASERX26.aspx; http://www2.taser.com/company/pages/factsheet.aspx (accessed October 7, 2007).

34. Interview with William Bozeman, 2005; www.taser.com (accessed February 2005).

35. Berenson, "Questions over Safety Emerge"; Amnesty International, *Excessive and Lethal Force?;* "Amnesty International: Taser Deaths on the Rise Report Cites 156 Fatalities from Police Stun Guns over the Past Five Years," Associated Press, March 27, 2006.

36. Steve Duin, "Even Blind Old Ladies Terrify the Cops," *Portland Oregonian,* April 25, 2004.

37. Ibid.; Alex Jones, GCN Radio Network, http://Prisonplanet.Tv/Audio/042704warren.htm (accessed October 7, 2007).

38. Maxine Bernstein, "Portland Police Issue Draft of Stun Gun Policy," *Portland Oregonian,* May 18, 2004; "Portland Police Settle in Excessive Force Suit," Associated Press State and Local Wire, April 23, 2004; Robert Anglen, "Police Expand Use of Taser: Safety Questions Create Call for Restrictions on Stun Gun," *Arizona Republic,* November 7, 2004.

39. "Chicago Police Tasered 82-Year-Old Woman," Associated Press, November 6, 2007.

40. Interview with Margaret Kimbrell, 2005; "Brief," *Myrtle Beach Sun-News,* December 30, 2004.

41. Amnesty International, *Excessive and Lethal Force?*

42. Anthony Bleetman and Richard Steyn, *The Advanced Taser: A Medical Review,* April 23, 2003, http://www.taser.com/documents.UK_Review%20_Bleetman.pdf (accessed February 2004).

43. Leah Hope, "Pathologist Says Taser Used by Chicago Police Killed Man," ABC Chicago Channel 7, July 29, 2005. Interview with Daniel Dugan, 2008.

44. www.taser.com (accessed February 2005).

45. www.taser.com (accessed June 2006).

46. Interview with Greg Pashley, 2005.

47. Interview with Scott Folsom, 2005.

48. "Police-Involved Shootings Lowest in 14 Years," Phoenix Police Department press release. Available at http://www2.Taser.Com/Research/Statistics/Pages/Fielduseandstatistics.Aspx (accessed October 7, 2007). For Seattle information, see "Injury Reduction Stats Public," available at www.taser.com (accessed October 7, 2007).

49. www.taser.com (accessed February 2005).

50. Amnesty International, *Excessive and Lethal Force?*

51. Ibid.

52. Interview with Jim Billings, 2005.

53. Amnesty International, *Excessive and Lethal Force?*

54. "Fla. Police Officer Uses Stun Gun on 12-Year-Old," Associated Press, December 20, 2004; interview with Ken Hall, 2005.

55. Susannah A. Nesmith, "Miami Schools Chief Speaks Out against Taser Use," *Miami Herald*, November 20, 2004; "Stun Gun Controversy Safe against Children?" *Good Morning America*, ABC, November 15, 2004.

56. "Sergeant Who Used Taser on Girl Cleared of Criminal Wrongdoing," Associated Press, June 19, 2004; press release, Office of the Attorney General, http://www.pcao.pima.gov/press.htm (accessed February 2005).

57. "Taser Use on 9-Year-Old Raises Questions"; "Taser Use on Teens."

58. Offense Incident Report, Miami Police Department, October 20, 2004.

59. Interview with Juan DelCastillo, 2005.

60. Interview with Steve Tuttle, 2008.

61. Interview with John Webster, 2005.

62. Alex Berenson, "The Safety of Tasers Is Questioned Again," *New York Times*, May 25, 2006.

63. Berenson, "Questions over Safety Emerge"; interview with Andrew Podgorski.

64. Letter from Rudolph Crew, superintendent of Miami-Dade Public Schools to the Miami-Dade Police Department, released November 19, 2004.

65. Lisa Orkin Emmanuel, "Miami-Dade Police Given Revised Guidelines on Stun Gun Use," Associated Press, January 13, 2005.

66. Interview with Tony Hill, 2005.

67. Douban and Robinson, "City Police May Wield Stun Guns in Schools"; see also "Stun Guns Option for Birmingham Schools."

68. "Mich. Officer Accused of Using Taser on Partner during Fight about Soda," Associated Press, December 8, 2005.

69. http://www2.taser.com/company/pages/building.aspx (accessed October 7, 2007).

70. www.taser.com (accessed February 2005).

71. www.taser.com (accessed September 18, 2007). "TASER International Begins Shipments of Highly Anticipated TASER C2 Personal Protector," Taser International press release, July 19, 2007.

72. Jacques Billeaud, "Proposal Would Allow Lethal Force on Suspects with Stun Guns," Associated Press State and Local Wire, January 26, 2005.

73. Jim Johnson, "Taser Held Responsible in Salinas Death," *Monterey County Herald*, June 7, 2008; "Jury Finds Extended TASER Device Application 15 Percent Responsible for Arrest Related Death of Robert C. Heston," Taser International press release, June 7, 2008; interview with Steve Tuttle, 2008.

CHAPTER 11. THE RETURN TO RESTRAINT

1. Amnesty International, "USA: Rights for All," October 1, 1999, includes a similar description of the chair.

2. Anne-Marie Cusac, "The Devil's Chair," *Progressive*, April 1, 2000; http://www.blacksteel.com/hcs/index.cgi?section=Collection&mode=1&start=8 (accessed October 7, 2007); *Guerra v. Drake*, 371 F.3d 404 (8th Cir. 2004); Greg Burton, " 'Devil's Chair' Remains in Use at County Jails; Inmate's Death Led to Moratorium on Device at Utah State Prison; Restraint Chair Still Used by County Jails," *Salt Lake Tribune*, November 22, 1998.

3. Interview with Dan Corcoran, president, AEDEC International, 2000.

4. Interview with Angela Wright, researcher, Amnesty International, 2000.

5. Vickie Chahere, "Attorney Raises Questions about Death of Inmate," *Tampa Tribune*, March 28, 1997.

6. Brian Maffly, "Maker: Chair Not Used as Intended; But Mother Still Sues Company over Her Son's 'Torture' Death; Chair Maker Named in Lawsuit," *Salt Lake Tribune*, May 22, 1997; Dave Marash, "The Chair: Electric Stun Guns and Restraint Chairs Are Often Misused in Prisons," *ABC News Nightline*, July 20, 2000; Amnesty International, "USA: Rights for All." See also the series of articles on the restraint chair by the *Sacramento Bee*, including: Ramon Coronado and Andy Furillo, "Inmate Death Prompts FBI Investigation," *Sacramento Bee*, June 7, 1995; Andy Furillo, "Coroner Rules Jail Inmate's Death Accidental," *Sacramento Bee*, July 1, 1995; Andy Furillo, "Abuse of Inmates Punished: Two Sheriff's Deputies Get 15-Day Suspensions," *Sacramento Bee*, October 23, 1996; Andy Furillo, "Lawyer's Release of Jail Videos Blasted," *Sacramento Bee*, October 23, 1997; Andy Furillo, "Lawyer Hired for Officers in Jail-Death Probe," *Sacramento Bee*, June 14, 1995; Denny Walsh, "Woman's Suit Claims Deputies Mistreated Her," *Sacramento Bee*, September 7, 1996; Ramon Coronado, "Family Files Claim in Inmate's Death, *Sacramento Bee*, September 13, 1996; Denny Walsh, "2 File Lawsuits over Jail's Use of Inmate-Restraining Chair," *Sacramento Bee*, December 13, 1996; Denny Walsh, "5th Claim of Torture in Chair," *Sacramento Bee*, February 1, 1997; Denny Walsh, "2 More Lawsuits Slam Sheriff over Jail's 'Pro-Straint Chair,' " *Sacramento Bee*, March 27, 1997; Denny Walsh, "Suit in Inmate's Death Calls Sheriff's Agency Callous," *Sacramento Bee*, April 4, 1997; Steve

Wiegand, "Scheming Cops Keeping Jobs?" *Sacramento Bee,* April 30, 1997; Andy Furillo, "FBI Is Probing Mock Executions by Jail Deputies," *Sacramento Bee,* September 5, 1996; Andy Furillo, "Craig Disputes 'Mock Executions,' " *Sacramento Bee,* September 7, 1996; Andy Furillo, "Videotapes Surface in Suit over Jail 'Prostraint' Chair," *Sacramento Bee,* October 22, 1997; Andy Furillo, "No Charges over 'Mock Executions,' " *Sacramento Bee,* March 20, 1998; Andy Furillo, "County Pays $755,000 to Settle Jail-Chair Suits," *Sacramento Bee,* February 23, 1999; Denny Walsh, "Lawsuit Filed over Use of Jail Restraint Chair," *Sacramento Bee,* December 29, 2007.

7. "Family of Ex-BYU. Football Player to Get $8.25 Million," Associated Press, January 12, 1999; Tony Ortega, "Sanitized for Joe's Protection: Sheriff's Summary of Probe into Inmate's Death Omits Alarming Details," *Phoenix New Times,* October 24, 1996.

8. "Jail Tapes Show Man's Pleas Ignored as He Died after Swallowing Cocaine," Associated Press, February 8, 1997. Amnesty International, "USA: Rights for All."

9. Sheila R. McCann, "Experts Rip Prison for Chair Death; They Claim Staff Violated Standards," *Salt Lake Tribune,* February 12, 1998; Jane Wells, "Mentally Ill Prisoner Michael Valent's Death Due to Being Placed in a Restraint Chair for 16 Hours Has Forced Changes at the Utah State Prison," *CNBC News,* August 26, 1998.

10. "Former Corrections Officer Found Guilty in Death of Inmate," Associated Press State and Local Wire, December 22, 1998; "Former Corrections Officer Testifies about Death of Inmate," Associated Press, December 15, 1998; "Family Questions Death of Jail Inmate," United Press International, March 17, 1997; *Tampa Tribune,* May 20, 1998, Florida/Metro edition.

11. "Autopsy: Inmate's Heart and Lungs Stopped Because of Neck Restraint," Associated Press State and Local Wire, December 3, 1999; Duval County Medical Examiner's Office report on the death of Demetrius Brown.

12. "Court Decides Not to Hear Death Involving Chair Restraint," Associated Press State and Local Wire, March 6, 2003; Amnesty International, "Unnecessary Death, Injury and Pain Caused by the Use of Restraint Chairs," press release, March 5, 2002; "Johnson City Sued for Using Restraint Chair on Prisoner Who Died," Associated Press State and Local Wire, State and Regional, April 16, 2001.

13. Amnesty International, "United States of America—The Restraint Chair: How Many More Deaths?" February 25, 2002.

14. Ibid.

15. Ibid.

16. "Inmate Was Restrained for 4 Hours; 31-Year-Old Died in Custody," Associated Press State and Local Wire, July 22, 1999.

17. Amnesty International, "USA: Rights for All"; interview with Richard Haskell, 2000.

18. Detention Bureau Report of Deputy Mark Lane Smith, Tarrant County Sheriff's Department; interview with Richard Haskell, 2000.

19. Information on the chair that held Livingston came from documents received in response to a public records request to the Sheriff's Department, Tarrant County, Texas.

20. Interview with Teresa Dominguez, 2000.

21. Interview with Dan Corcoran, 2000.

22. Amnesty International, *Annual Report, 2002*, entry for United Arab Emirates.

23. AEDEC advertising materials.

24. See, e.g., "Controversial Devices Used to Restrain Violent Prisoners," *ABC News Nightline;* "The Chair," *ABC News Nightline;* Amnesty International, "A Briefing for the UN Committee against Torture"; Amnesty International, "USA: Rights for All." See also the excellent *Sacramento Bee* reporting on the restraint chair.

25. Walsh, "2 File Lawsuits over Jail's Use of Inmate-Restraining Chair."

26. "Police Use of Restraining Chair Voids Suspect's Confession," Associated Press State and Local Wire, August 13, 1999.

27. Amnesty International, "USA: Rights for All"; Amy Silverman, "Simply Stunning Federal Probe Finds Excessive Force, Poor Medical Care at County Jails; Stun Gun Used on Inmate's Testicles," *Phoenix New Times,* July 11, 1996; on Post, see also Tony Ortega, "Jailers Show a Paraplegic Who's Boss; Richard Post Was Taken to Jail in His Wheelchair for Mouthing Off in a Bar. Joe Arpaio's Detention Officers Saw Him as Such a Threat, They Strapped Him into a Medieval Restraint Chair—and Broke His Neck," *Phoenix New Times,* January 23, 1997.

28. Amnesty International, "USA: Rights for All"; "Justice Department Report Criticizes Arizona Sheriff," Associated Press, January 10, 1998; Tony Ortega, "The Justice Department Investigates the County Sheriff's Office Again," *Phoenix New Times,* December 10, 1998.

29. "MCSO Will No Longer Use Controversial Restraint Chairs in Jails," Associated Press State and Local Wire, August 22, 2006.

30. Amnesty International, "USA: Rights for All."

31. Megan K. Stack, "Question of Restraint: Corpus Christi Jailhouse Deaths Focus Attention on Chairs," Associated Press State and Local Wire, September 26, 2000; interview with Ventura County Chief Deputy Mark Ball, 2008.

32. "Federal Judge Bans Use of Restraint Chair in Ventura County Jail," Associated Press State and Local Wire, November 22, 1999; U.S. District Judge Lourdes Baird, preliminary injunction against the Ventura, California, County Jail, November 15, 1999.

33. Simon, *Governing through Crime,* 153.

34. Richard P. Jones, "Not All at Supermax Are 'Real Bad Actors,'" *Milwaukee Journal Sentinel,* October 21, 2001.

35. Craig Haney, "Mental Health Issues in Long-Term Solitary and 'Supermax' Confinement," *Crime and Delinquency* 49, no. 1 (January 2003): 124–156.

36. "Coming to the Boscobel Supermax, by an Inmate in WI," *FFUP Newsletter,*

Autumn 2005, http://www.geocities.com/forumforunderstandingprisons/comingtoboscobel.html (accessed September 29, 2007).

37. David Callender, "Suit Calls Supermax Incubator of Psychosis," *Capital Times*, June 30, 2001; Terry A. Kupers, "Report on Mental Health Issues at SMCI," Human Rights Watch, October 22, 2001. Available at hrw.org/reports/2003/usa1003/ Wisconsin_Expert_Kupers_El_Jones.pdf. Lawyers for detainees held in extensive isolation at U.S. prison camps have made similar claims. In May 2008, the *New York Times* reported, "Detainees' lawyers argue that the effects of intense isolation have gradually turned the prison camp [at Guantanamo Bay] into something of a highly fortified mental ward." William Glaberson, "Detainees' Mental Health Is Latest Legal Battle," *New York Times*, April 26, 2008.

38. Kupers, "Report on Mental Health Issues"; David Callender, "Out of Supermax, Teen Revives," *Capital Times*, December 15, 2001.

39. Callender, "Suit Calls Supermax Incubator of Psychosis"; *Jones 'El v. Berge*, Judgment in a Civil Case, Case no. 00-C-0421-C (W.D. Wisconsin, June 24, 2002) (unpub.); interview with Ed Garvey, 2004.

40. Richard P. Jones, "Not All at Supermax Are 'Real Bad Actors' "; "Court Ruling on Isolation Conditions at Supermax Prisons," National Public Radio, March 14, 2002; "Supermax Not for Kids," *Capital Times*, June 13, 2001; "Settlement Calls for Major Changes to Supermax; Tentative Deal Would Change Name of Prison, Alter Rules on Cell Conditions, Inmate Treatment," *Milwaukee Journal Sentinel*, January 4, 2002.

CHAPTER 12. ABU GHRAIB, USA

1. Jonathan Alter, "Time to Think about Torture," *Newsweek*, November 5, 2001.

2. Jim Rutenberg, "Torture Seeps into Discussion," *New York Times*, November 5, 2001.

3. Ibid.

4. Ibid.

5. Alan Keyes, "Making Sense of Torture," *Alan Keyes Is Making Sense*, MSNBC, February 4, 2002.

6. Amnesty International, "United States of America—Amnesty International's Concerns Regarding Post September 11 Detentions in the USA," March 14, 2002.

7. Interview with Traci Billingsley, 2002.

8. *The September 11 Detainees: A Review of the Treatment of Aliens Held on Immigration Charges in Connection with the Investigation of the September 11 Attacks*, Office of the Inspector General of the U.S. Department of Justice, June 2003.

9. Interview with Michael Wildes, 2002.

10. Interview with Oded Ellner, 2002.

11. Interview with Steven Gordon, 2002.

12. Interview with MacDonald Scott and Joel Kupferman, 2002.

13. Interview with Patricia Ice, 2002.

14. Interview with Uzi Bohadana, 2002.

15. Alan Cooperman, "CIA Interrogation under Fire; Human Rights Groups Say Techniques Could Be Torture," *Washington Post*, December 28, 2002; Dana Priest and Barton Gellman, "U.S. Decries Abuse but Defends Interrogations; 'Stress and Duress' Tactics Used on Terrorism Suspects Held in Secret Overseas Facilities," *Washington Post*, December 26, 2002.

16. Seymour M. Hersh, "Torture at Abu Ghraib," *New Yorker*, May 10, 2004; "Abuse of Iraqi POWs by GIs Probed," *Sixty Minutes 2*, April 28, 2004.

17. Josh White, "Rumsfeld Visits Prison in Iraq," *Washington Post*, May 14, 2004.

18. See, e.g., "Controversial Devices Used to Restrain Violent Prisoners," *ABC News Nightline*, July 21, 2000; "The Chair; Electric Stun Guns and Restraint Chairs Are Often Misused in Prisons," *ABC News Nightline*, July 20, 2000; Cusac, "Devil's Chair"; Amnesty International, "A Briefing for the UN Committee against Torture," May 4, 2000; Amnesty International, "USA: Rights for All"; Amnesty International, "Not Part of My Sentence," March 1999; and Amnesty International, *Betraying the Young*, November 1998. See also the excellent *Sacramento Bee* reporting on the restraint chair.

19. Suzanne Goldenberg, "Iraq Crisis: Interrogation: US Forces Were Taught Torture Techniques: Soldiers Accounts Reveal Widespread Use of Sleep Deprivation and Mock Executions," *Guardian*, May 14, 2004.

20. Anne-Marie Cusac, "Abu Ghraib, USA," *Progressive* 68, no. 7 (July 1, 2004): 19; Barry Graham, "Star of Justice," *Harper's Magazine* 302, no. 1811 (April 1, 2001): 59.

21. "Former Brazoria Jailer Convicted of Civil Rights Violation," Associated Press, November 2, 1999.

22. *Report of the International Committee of the Red Cross (ICRC) on the Treatment by the Coalition Forces of Prisoners of War and Other Protected Persons by the Geneva Conventions in Iraq during Arrest, Internment and Interrogation*, February 2004; Ananda Shorey, "Phoenix Sizzling through Hottest July on Record," Associated Press, July 25, 2003.

23. Hersh, "Torture at Abu Ghraib"; Mike Bucsko and Robert Dvorchak, "Guard Left Troubled Life for Duty in Iraq," *New York Times*, May 14, 2004; Paul Von Zielbauer and James Dao, "Lawsuits Describe Racist Prison Rife with Brutality," *Pittsburgh Post-Gazette*, April 26, 1998.

24. Von Zielbauer and Dao, "Lawsuits Describe Racist Prison."

25. Bucsko and Dvorchak, "Guard Left Troubled Life."

26. "The 'Taguba Report' on Treatment of *Abu Ghraib* Prisoners in Iraq," Article 15–6 Investigation of the 800th Military Police Brigade.

27. Interview with Guy Womack, 2008.

28. Cusac, "Devil's Chair"; Burton, " 'Devil's Chair' Remains in Use at County Jails"; Greg Burton, "Utahns Who Rebuilt Prison Are in Hot Seat; Critics Wonder Why Contractors with Questionable Rights Records at Home Were Chosen to Play a Major Role in Iraq; Utahns Who Rebuilt Prison Are Criticized," *Salt*

Lake Tribune, May 16, 2004; "The Wardens Neglect, Brutality, Prisoner Deaths," *World News Tonight with Peter Jennings*, ABC, May 20, 2004.

29. Amnesty International, "USA: Rights for All."

30. Scott Wilson, "Ex-Detainee Tells of Anguishing Treatment at Iraq Prison," *Washington Post*, May 6, 2004.

31. Luke Harding, "Focus Shifts to Jail Abuse of Women," *Guardian* (London), May 12, 2004.

32. Amnesty International, "Not Part of My Sentence."

33. Robert Bazell, "Honor Guard? Women Who Suffer Sexual Abuse at the Hands of Guards While in Prison," *Dateline NBC*, November 1, 1998. See also Amnesty International, "Not Part of My Sentence."

34. Irene Kahn, "An Open Letter to President Bush on the Question of Torture and Cruel, Inhuman, or Degrading Treatment," Amnesty International, May 7, 2004.

35. Amnesty International, "Not Part of My Sentence."

36. Amnesty International, "USA: Rights for All."

37 *Alicia Rivera v. Sheahan et al.* (N.D. Ill.) 97 C 2735.

38. "Scores Died in U.S. Custody in War Zones, Military Officials Report," Associated Press, March 16, 2005.

39. U.S. Department of Justice, Bureau of Justice Statistics Data, 2004.

EPILOGUE: A LITTLE GOOD NEWS

1. Rush, *Public Punishments*, 1787 ed., 1, 5.

2. Ibid., 5, 7–9.

3. Garland, *Culture of Control*, 3, 5–6, 193–205.

4. Abramsky, *Conned*, 1–3, 12; www.demos.org.

5. Robert Martinson, "What Works—Questions and Answers about Prison Reform," *Public Interest* 35 (Spring 1974): 22–54. Garland, *Culture of Control*, 64.

6. Rex W. Huppke, "Record Numbers of Ex-Cons Return to Illinois Streets: More People Ask How to Help Them Adjust," *Chicago Tribune*, June 19, 2005.

7. "A Decade of Experimenting with Intermediate Sanctions: What Have We Learned?" Paper presented by Joan Petersilia, April 1, 1998, Washington, DC, at Perspectives on Crime and Justice: 1997–1998 Lecture Series. Series: Research Forum U.S. Department of Justice, Office of Justice Programs, National Institute of Justice.

8. Ibid.

9. Ron Jenkins, "Coburn Different Kind of Political Cat," Associated Press, July 9, 2004; David Averill, "GOP Takeover of Oklahoma Almost Complete," *Tulsa World*, November 7, 2004, p. G6.

10. "Off with Their Thumbs!" World's Editorial Writers, *Tulsa World*, November 7, 2005. "Mayor: Sever Thumbs of Graffiti Artists," Associated Press, November 4, 2005.

11. "An 'Outrageous' Statement?" *Las Vegas Review-Journal*, July 25, 2006.

12. Adam Liptak, "15 States Expand Right to Shoot in Self-Defense," *New York Times*, August 7, 2006; Fred Grimm, "New Law Gives Too Many People a License to Kill," *Miami Herald*, August 24, 2006.

13. Henry Pierson Curtis, "Gun Law Triggers at Least 13 Shootings," *Orlando Sentinel*, June 11, 2006.

14. Grimm, "New Law Gives Too Many People a License to Kill."

15. Sister Helen Prejean, *Death of Innocents* (New York: Random House, 2004), 113–118, 129–130; http://www.prejean.org/NewsFrom.html.

16. John Bookser Feister, "The Pope Visits St. Louis," *St. Anthony Messenger*, April 1999, online edition, www.americancatholic.org/Messenger/Apr1999/feature1.asp#F6 (accessed September 14, 2007).

17. See www.pfm.org.

18. Unitarian Universalist Association, "Criminal Justice and Prison Reform: 2005 Statement of Conscience," available at http://www.uua.org/actions/criminal-justice/05reform.html.

19. David M. Halbfinger, "Unease in the Air and Revenge on the Screen," *New York Times*, August 26, 2007, online version (accessed September 13, 2007).

20. Ibid.

21. Ibid.

22. Ibid.

23. A. O. Scott, "Packing Heat after a Cold-Hearted Crime," *New York Times*, September 14, 2007, online version (accessed June 8, 2008).

24. Adam Liptak, "Inmate Count in U.S. Dwarfs Other Nations'," *New York Times*, April 23, 2008, online version (accessed June 8, 2008).

25. http://www.rottentomatoes.com/m/brave_one/numbers.php (accessed October 4, 2007); see, among many other examples, the responses to the blog. http://popwatch.ew.com/popwatch/2007/09/jodie-foster-vi.html (accessed October 4, 2007); http://thebraveone.warnerbros.com/ (accessed October 4, 2007).

INDEX